The Mormon Quest for Glory

The Mormon Quest for Glory

*The Religious World of the
Latter-day Saints*

MELVYN HAMMARBERG

OXFORD
UNIVERSITY PRESS

OXFORD
UNIVERSITY PRESS

Oxford University Press is a department of the University of Oxford.
It furthers the University's objective of excellence in research, scholarship,
and education by publishing worldwide.

Oxford   New York
Auckland   Cape Town   Dar es Salaam   Hong Kong   Karachi
Kuala Lumpur   Madrid   Melbourne   Mexico City   Nairobi
New Delhi   Shanghai   Taipei   Toronto

With offices in
Argentina   Austria   Brazil   Chile   Czech Republic   France   Greece
Guatemala   Hungary   Italy   Japan   Poland   Portugal   Singapore
South Korea   Switzerland   Thailand   Turkey   Ukraine   Vietnam

Oxford is a registered trademark of Oxford University Press
in the UK and certain other countries.

Published in the United States of America by
Oxford University Press
198 Madison Avenue, New York, NY 10016

Library of Congress Cataloging-in-Publication Data
Hammarberg, Melvyn, author.
The Mormon quest for glory : the religious world of the Latter-day
Saints / Melvyn Hammarberg.
pages cm
Includes bibliographical references.
ISBN 978-0-19-973762-8
1. Church of Jesus Christ of Latter-day Saints.   2. Mormon Church.
3. Mormons—Religious life.   I. Title.
BX8635.3.H36 2013
289.3'32—dc23
2012042887

1 3 5 7 9 8 6 4 2
Printed in the United States of America
on acid-free paper

This book is dedicated to my wife and friend, Yuehong Wang ("Hong") Hammarberg, and to my mentor and friend, Murray G. Murphey. Without either of them, this undertaking would not have reached its conclusion.

Contents

Preface   *ix*

Acknowledgments   *xiii*

1. The Religious Culture of the Latter-day Saints   1

2. The Life Plan of the Latter-day Saints   25

3. Becoming a Latter-day Saint   53

4. I Am a Child of God   76

5. Choose the Right   96

6. We Thank Thee, O God, for a Prophet   119

7. For the Strength of Youth   137

8. Endowed from on High   171

9. Preach My Gospel   197

10. Becoming a Convert   225

11. Celestial Marriage: A New and Everlasting Covenant   253

12. Disciplinary Councils   268

13. Lives of Service   287

14. 'Til We Meet Again   317

References   331

Scriptural References   345

Index   347

Preface

The title of this book is meant to suggest the goal-directed understanding of those who claim identity as members of the Church of Jesus Christ of Latter-day Saints (LDS) (also known as Mormons), while the subtitle acknowledges their commitment to a religious worldview. These two themes reflect the work of anthropologist Wendell H. Oswalt (1986), who suggested that all societies encode and express life-cycle patterns from birth to death and also exhibit common themes, such as communication, technology, social-economic systems, political life and law, population dynamics, and expressive arts. I call this combination of lifecycles and lifeways a cultural model or "life plan."

The life plan of the Latter-day Saints is just such a cultural model, a variant on the program outlined by Erik H. Erikson in his study of identity and the life cycle (1994 [1959]) . This life plan informs the self-understanding and self-awareness of members of the LDS Church today. It elaborates schemas (or scripts) that guide Mormons in acquiring cultural knowledge so that they may make informed decisions, allowing them to reach their cultural goals. The highest of these goals are embedded in temple ordinances of exaltation, which lift the nuclear family and its kinship connections up to the status of eternal bonds.

The structure of the Mormon life plan involves three overarching life worlds, beginning with pre-mortal existence, unfolding through mortal existence and culminating in post-mortal existence, viewed together as "one eternal round." The self has experience through all three life worlds. The key feature of the self is that it possesses "agency," and the notion of personhood involves the immortal spirit as wrapped in a mortal body. The central stages of the life plan consist of birth, infancy, early and later childhood when the basic framework of the life plan is taught and learned, including the chief virtue of obedience. This stage is followed by young adulthood, marked by distinctive gender roles for young men in the Aaronic priesthood (in roles as deacons, teachers, and priests) and young women acquiring virtue (through group activities in Beehive, MIA, and Laurel groups) and anticipating motherhood. The chief virtue for both young men and young women is chastity.

Adulthood is marked by the ordinance of endowment in the temple, with worthiness as the necessary condition for temple participation. Ideally, for young men, marriage may be delayed so that they may undertake a two-year mission on behalf of the church where such missions offer a main gateway for the entrance of converts to the church's organizational structure and belief system. The strongest expectation of young adulthood is that both young men and young women will marry (although some young women choose first to undertake missions of 18 months). Temple marriage itself is given a distinctive church marking as a sealing "for time and eternity" under Melchizedek priesthood authority, in contrast to civil marriage, which is for "time only." The church opposes same-gender marriage while also seeking to affirm Heavenly Father's love for all people. Raising a family is the highest form of service as members seek to exemplify the Christ-like life. In many other ways, members are called to serve their fellow members and the worldwide community as well. Some returned missionaries may draw aid from the perpetual education fund (later to be repaid). Humanitarian service has increasingly seen the LDS members acting to meet natural disasters in all parts of the globe.

Full adulthood is reached when a person may look to their partner in marriage for loving support, to their parents and grandparents for guidance, and to their children and children's children for the hope of the world to come. Death, in LDS understanding, is the death of the body as the spirit lives on, and even so the body will be transformed to immortal perfection by the resurrection on the image of Jesus as the Christ, while the earth will become the kingdom of God in its celestial glory.

The epic journey of the Saints from Nauvoo, Illinois, to the Great Basin was part of a westward movement culminating in what is now a global reach. This movement was led by the church's second president and prophet, Brigham Young. He continued to guide the revitalization movement that Joseph Smith had begun. Now, Thomas S. Monson is the church's 16th president as the living prophet, seer, and revelator.

The ethos of the life of the Latter-day Saints is expressed through the demands of the human journey, memorialized in William Clayton's anthem, in which the first verse conveys the challenges to be faced with hard work and the promise of God's grace:

Come, Come, Ye Saints/no toil nor labor fear/But with joy wend your way/ Though hard to you this journey may appear/Grace shall be as your day/'Tis better far for us to strive/Our useless cares from us to drive/Do this, and joy your hearts will swell/All is well! All is well! (Lyrics by William Clayton 1846).

***

The interviews that form the basis for this book were conducted over the course of many years. Every reasonable effort has been made to track down the subjects of those interviews and obtain their permission to use the material I collected from them. In many cases, I have been unable to do so, and have employed pseudonyms for those whom I have not been able to locate. If any interview subjects come forward post-publication, appropriate adjustments will be made in future printings, as needed.

Acknowledgments

Thank you to the following institutions and individuals:

University of Pennsylvania Research Funds
Penn Museum of Archaeology and Anthropology
American Philosophical Society

Ben Pykles
Beverly Smaby
Bob Fairbanks
Christine Tate
Claude Welch (deceased)
Damon Smith
Dean May (deceased)
Ennis Anderson (deceased)
Jeff Iorio
John Caughey
Kathy Fairbanks
Kim Smith (deceased)
Kristen Goodman
Larry Logue
Lavina Fielding Anderson
Lynn Payne
Mary McConaghy
Maxine Stone Davidson
Perry Cunningham
Rex Cooper
Sasha Grossman
Steven Olsen
Theo Calderara
Vera Welch

The Mormon Quest for Glory

I

The Religious Culture of the Latter-day Saints

MEMBERS OF THE Church of Jesus Christ of Latter-day Saints see themselves actively transforming the world and its people into the kingdom of God on earth, anticipating the millennial reign of Jesus Christ prior to the final judgment. In the process, they also believe they are achieving personal standing among the community of all spirit persons—whether previously born into this mortal life, living now, or yet unborn—who will be organized as immortal celestial families for eternity. This vision of the past, present, and future is cosmic in scope, yet grounded in an American restoration of all things that Latter-day Saints (LDS) believe are ancient, sacred, and eternal.

In the 1990 *Melchizedek Priesthood Leadership Handbook* (Corporation of the President 1990:3), the church succinctly stated its purpose in a mission statement, identifying the processes by which that purpose would be achieved:

> The Lord declared that it is his work and glory "to bring to pass the immortality and eternal life of man" (Moses 1:39). He has established His Church to help with this great work. Accordingly, the Church's mission is to "invite all to come unto Christ" (D&C 20:59) "and be perfected in him" (Moroni 10:32). This mission has three dimensions, and priesthood leaders have a particular responsibility for them:
>
> 1. Proclaim the gospel of Jesus Christ to every nation, kindred, tongue, and people.
> 2. Perfect the Saints by preparing them to receive the ordinances of the gospel and by caring for the poor and needy.
> 3. Redeem the dead by performing vicarious ordinances of the gospel for them.

I call this effort by the members of the church to build the kingdom of God on earth their "quest for glory." They refer to it as "this great work," which indeed it is—awesome in its magnitude and power and detail. And while they see themselves as instruments of this work—"to bring to pass the immortality and eternal life of man"—its final completion and glory is ascribed to the Lord. It is his kingdom on earth that they see themselves building by proclaiming the gospel, perfecting the Saints, and redeeming the dead.

An Ethnographic Approach

My approach in this study of the LDS is ethnographic in the anthropological sense (van der Elst 2003; Agar 1996; Crane and Angrosino 1984; Spradley 1979). By observing members of the church in their many roles, participating with them in the rounds of their activities, and interviewing and discussing with them what I learned, my aim was to understand and represent the culture of the church. This meant describing and analyzing aspects and features of the LDS Church's history, rituals, social organization, kinship structures, gender roles, basis for authority, artistic traditions, use of the media, recruitment of new members, and other component parts that comprise this culture, organized as a theory of the life plan of its members. All of these components enter into the church's culture and are expressions of it, and so are the subject matter and evidence for what I present (Oswalt 1986; Erikson 1980 [1959]; Linde 1993). Anthropologists seek what they term an "emic" (or insider's) view of what members learn and share in an effort to construct a more general, theoretical (or "etic") model of how the cultural system works using the study of language as an approach (Pike 1954:8–9).

The church's culture in this dual emic/etic sense is constituted most centrally by the beliefs, values, and knowledge of the LDS through which they interpret the world and on the basis of which they act in and toward it. That world is what they experience as a conceptual, cognitive, attitudinal, behavioral, and physical reality. The church's culture, then, is to be understood primarily as a set of structures of knowledge and standards for behavior that are learned and used to interpret the social actions of self and others.

In the words of anthropologist Ward Goodenough, a society's culture consists "of what one has to know, or profess to believe, in order to operate in a manner acceptable to its members in every role that they accept for any one of themselves" (Goodenough 1981:109). This definition equates culture with learned and shared knowledge and views this knowledge as distributed among roles, and role and status relationships, very much in keeping with the formulations of Robert K. Merton (1968). Thus, the content of culture involves the systems of standards, or norms, by which members come to know one another according to learned and shared understandings within recognized social boundaries. My anthropological account of the Mormon "life plan" is a cultural model that serves to shape and direct acculturation within the church. This model was initially described in an *Expedition* magazine article (Hammarberg 2002a:7–15) and is realized socially as the organization of diversity in this study of Mormonism, as presented in chapter two.

Among the LDS, their cultural world includes their relationships to God, whom they refer to as Heavenly Father (and occasionally refer to Heavenly Mother as well); Jesus Christ and other persons and aspects of a divine order; their sense of themselves as people bearing an LDS identity; the time and space dimensions that give structure to their world as involving both mortal and immortal aspects; the norms and values that help them establish claims as a people of God; the temples, meetinghouses, and other forms of material culture that express their identity and mark their world; and the goals or motives that drive their actions in that world. Thus, what the LDS call their "spiritual understanding" of life in the world is my concern. It is what anthropologists like Robert Redfield (1960), A. Irving Hallowell (1967 [1955]:75–110), and Michael Kearney (1984) have called a people's "worldview."

In this study I write as a social scientist with the aim of seeking to understand the LDS on their own terms, not to set them against other religious understandings. In the words of anthropologist Jack David Eller, "anthropology does not approach religion to falsify it nor to verify it nor even to judge it. Anthropology is not the seminary, intending to indoctrinate the student into any one particular religion. It is not apologetics, attempting to prove or justify some religion; neither is it an exercise in debunking any or all religions.... Anthropology can best be thought of as the science of the diversity of humans, in [their culture,] their bodies and their behavior. Thus, the anthropology of religion will be the scientific investigation of the diversity of human religions" (Eller 2007:2).

I affirm these comments because the LDS often wish to assess the biases of those who write about them, as to whether the writer is friend or foe, and often believe those biases are revealed by an author's religious persuasion or more general philosophical outlook. Thus, I wish to acknowledge at the outset that I am not a believer, but I am interested in belief systems and ritual practices such as those of the LDS, grounded in historical events and constructed with a vision of the future, that provide leaders and participants with a sense of personal identity and social understandings of what they believe life is all about. Although there are numerous other groups descended from the message of Joseph Smith the Prophet, this study is restricted to the culture of only one, the Church of Jesus Christ of LDS—the large and expanding Salt Lake City, Utah-based group.

The Background of the Present Study

Surprisingly perhaps, my decision to study the LDS arose in an academic rather than a personal context in the early 1970s—as a faculty member in the department of American civilization at the University of Pennsylvania. I initially referred to and thought of the LDS as "the Mormons," or followers of the Book of Mormon. The term "Mormon" is, of course, the name of a central figure portrayed as a prophet-historian in the Book of Mormon, but was then accepted by followers as a general term for all those who traced their heritage to the 19th-century vision experiences of Joseph Smith Jr. (see figures 1.1 and 1.2) and his organization of the "restored" Church of Jesus Christ as he understood it. The most complete biography of Smith as the prophet-founder is Richard Bushman's *Joseph Smith: Rough Stone Rolling* (2005), but many others have been written about his life, including John Henry Evans (1966 [1933]); Robert D. Anderson (1999); David Persuitte (2000); and Dan Vogel (2004); with a classic personality study offered by Fawn M. Brodie in *No Man Knows My History: The Life of Joseph Smith* (1971 [1945]). The earliest study of Joseph Smith, begun after his death in 1844, was by his mother, Lucy Mack Smith, recently issued in a critical variorum edition edited by Lavina Fielding Anderson (2001).

In the early 1970s, under the leadership of Murray G. Murphey (1967), the faculty of the department of American civilization at the University of Pennsylvania decided to study the complex culture of American society using a pluralistic model that focused on diverse American subcultures and their relations over time in the construction of an understanding of the overall culture of the society as a whole. We thought of this approach as employing an ethnographic model for the study of American society, treating subgroups and bounded culture areas in approximate two-generation (50-year) spans of time as units of analysis for purposes of comparison and generalization.

Thus, each faculty member chose a different ethnographic unit for research and teaching; these were rotated as course offerings in the graduate program. Anthony N. B. Garvan, a founding member of the Penn department, selected the Massachusetts Bay colony in its first 50 years and also chose Philadelphia in the two generations leading to the Revolutionary War as his interests (see Murphey 1992). Murray G. Murphey, and later Drew Gilpin Faust (now president of Harvard University), chose South Carolina during the 50 years before the Civil War, Gordon Kelly (now at the University of Maryland) selected Chicago from 1880 to 1930 as that city became the preeminent Midwestern metropolis. John Caughey (also now at Maryland) developed an ethnography of the Old Order Mennonites, and Patrick Malone (now at Brown University) focused on industrialization in

FIGURE 1.1 Joseph Smith is shown here in his role as lieutenant general and commanding officer of the Nauvoo Legion, the militia of the city of Nauvoo. This is one of very few portraits done of the prophet during his lifetime. Although the artist was not highly accomplished, the profile likeness is considered to be quite accurate. This image is similar to the one described in the history of the church, June 25, 1842: "Sat for a drawing of my profile to be placed on lithograph of a map of the City of Nauvoo." Sutcliffe Maudsley (1809–1881), *Lieutenant General Joseph Smith.* Richard G. Oman and Robert O. Davis, *Images of Faith: Art of the Latter-Day Saints* (Deseret Book Co.: 1995). Reproduced by permission of the Intellectual Property Division of the Church of Jesus Christ of Latter-day Saints.

FIGURE 1.2 In the companion print, Emma Hale Smith is shown in a formal dress holding an ivory-handled riding crop. She owned this pair of portraits following the martyrdom of the Prophet Joseph and his brother Hyrum, and the pictures were later passed on to her son Alexander Hale Smith and his descendants. The artist joined the church in England in 1840. His trade involved making patterns to reproduce pictures and designs for textiles; this aided him in making profile portraits of his clients. Immigrating to Nauvoo in 1842, Maudsley was engaged to create portraits of church leaders and their wives. Several dozen images of Joseph Smith are extant, most of them copies done by the artist from two or three of his original portraits. Sutcliffe Maudsley (1809–1881), *Emma Hale Smith*. Richard G. Oman and Robert O. Davis, *Images of Faith: Art of the Latter-Day Saints* (Deseret Book Co.: 1995). Reproduced by permission of the Intellectual Property Division of the Church of Jesus Christ of Latter-day Saints.

Pawtucket, Rhode Island. There were yet other selections that were used in building a graduate curriculum based upon comparative research.[1] This approach clearly conceived of American culture as reflecting a complex and diverse society from its colonial beginnings to the present, a changing constellation that linked social groups and subcultures over the course of time (Murphey 1979).

I noticed that my colleagues were geographically focused on groups and culture areas east of the Mississippi River. Having grown up in St. Paul/Minneapolis, Minnesota, in a family that generally traveled westward, I decided that my ethnography would be a western one. And as I thought about distinctive groups in the American West, my mind came to rest upon the LDS, or "the Mormons," as I then understood them. I had done an undergraduate paper on the life of Joseph Smith Jr., whose vision experiences in the 1820s provided the basis for founding the church and for his claims as its prophet, seer, and revelator (see figure 1.3). After Smith's murder in June 1844, most members followed the new Mormon leader, Brigham Young, and made their way westward across the Rocky mountains to the shores of Salt Lake in the great basin (see figure 1.4).

It seemed to me, then, that the Mormons offered a special challenge as a distinctively American religious group that had colonized Utah and other parts of the western culture area, represented most fully in Thomas F. O'Dea's classic study *The Mormons* (1957). Thus, the initial impetus for my interest in the Mormons was part of a general plan for the graduate program in American civilization at Penn, which had a variety of ethnographies as its empirical base, in relation to the anthropological concept of culture and a wide range of social science and humanistic theories and methods (Murphey 1994).

I made my first research trip to Utah in the summer of 1972 under a grant from the American Philosophical Society. The timing was propitious because the eminent economic historian Leonard J. Arrington had only recently been named church historian (Arrington 1998:78–79). I wrote to him explaining my interest and in response, he provided an introduction to one of the general authorities in the church, Apostle Mark E. Petersen, who met with me after my arrival in Salt Lake City. I remember Apostle Petersen as a tall, dignified,

---

1. A number of additional faculty members participated in framing this comparative ethnographic approach, each with a specialty of their own, including David Orr (material culture), Janet Tighe (history and sociology of science), Karin Calvert (social history), Janice Radway (popular culture), Robert Schuyler (historical archaeology), and Antoine Joseph (economics).

FIGURE 1.3 This group portrait depicts Joseph Smith together with several members of the first presidency and the quorum of the twelve. They are, from left to right, Hyrum Smith, Willard Richards, Joseph Smith, Orson Pratt, Parley P. Pratt, Orson Hyde, Heber C. Kimball, and Brigham Young. The artist, William Major, joined the church in England. He arrived in Nauvoo in 1844 and began the portrait during this time, but he may have added images of the Pratt brothers later. Known as the first professional artist in the Salt Lake Valley, Major actively painted portraits and landscapes until his untimely death in England while serving at a mission. William W. Major (1804–1854), *Joseph Smith and Friends*. Richard G. Oman and Robert O. Davis, *Images of Faith: Art of the Latter-Day Saints* (Deseret Book Co.: 1995). Reproduced by permission of the Intellectual Property Division of the Church of Jesus Christ of Latter-day Saints.

and gracious man. To Arrington, it was important to gain the support of the general authorities for opening the church's historical archives to new scholarly use, and to maintain lines of communication with the more conservative church leaders like Apostle Petersen and Ezra Taft Benson (see Arrington 1998:58, 144–146, 215).

Arrington had surrounded himself with a team of rigorously trained academic historians and social scientists, including James B. Allen, Davis Bitton, Glen Leonard, and Dean Jessee, who were then beginning to mine one of the "richest" collections of records in the world (Arrington 1998:81–87). And, with a grant from the American Philosophical Society to gather primary source material, I was equally excited to be able to acquire photographic and microfilm copies

FIGURE I.4 This painting depicts several of Brigham Young's closest friends, advisors, and colleagues in the mid-1860s. From left to right, they are John V. Long, husband of the artist and Brigham's clerk; John Lyon, a writer and librarian; John Young, the apostle son of Brigham; Edwin Woolley, a successful Salt Lake businessman and bishop who lived across the street from Brigham; George A. Smith, an apostle and the church historian, who worked next door to Brigham's office; Lorenzo Snow, an apostle and brother-in-law of Brigham; Heber C. Kimball, a close friend from Brigham's upstate New York days and Brigham's counselor in the first presidency; Brigham Young himself; and Daniel Wells, another neighbor and counselor. Behind the group are images of deceased members of the first presidency, from left to right, Jedediah M. Grant, Joseph and Hyrum Smith, and a bust of Willard Richards. The artist, a native of Kent, England, immigrated to Utah in 1854 and began teaching art classes in Salt Lake City. She was the first woman artist in Utah. Sarah Ann Burbage Long (1826–1878), *Brigham Young and His Friends*. Richard G. Oman and Robert O. Davis, *Images of Faith: Art of the Latter-Day Saints* (Deseret Book Co.: 1995). Reproduced by permission of the Intellectual Property Division of the Church of Jesus Christ of Latter-day Saints.

of many important documents to take back to Penn for research and teaching, materials that were at that time available in few places other than Utah.

Thus, my initial graduate seminars on the LDS, beginning in 1973, concerned the settlement of Utah in the period from 1847, when the first pioneer companies arrived in the valley, until the first decade of the 20th century, when the ending of the plural marriage system was bringing to a close the first Utah "pioneer" phase of the church's history (Arrington 1958; Quinn 1985; Lyman 1986). I taught that seminar every other year into the mid-1980s, intending to write a study of the pioneer period. That period has now been admirably described in David L. Bigler's *Forgotten Kingdom* (1998). A further analysis that focuses on changing Mormon racial and ethnic beliefs and practices is Armand L. Mauss's *All Abraham's Children* (2003).

Of course, many other eager minds were at work on these newly available materials, resulting in what may fairly be called a scholarly explosion of published work on the 19th and 20th century history of the LDS that is perhaps as extensive and insightful as work on the Puritans of New England or the Virginia colonies, and compares favorably to scholarly work on any other American subgroup, religion, or region. The bibliographic resources today are voluminous and well-documented (Whittaker 1995; Allen, Walker, and Whittaker 2000; Flake and Draper 2004). However, I put off my own Mormon work in order to publish *The Indiana Voter* (1977), to represent the United States Information Agency in Iran as a visiting scholar for a year, and to follow interests in psychology that carried me into research on post-traumatic stress disorder among Vietnam combat veterans (Hammarberg 1989; 1992; with Silver 1994). Still, the Mormons were never far from my mind or interest, and I returned to Utah on several research visits in the 1980s, slowly shifting from a historical to a contemporary perspective on the culture of the LDS Church. With a full year's sabbatical in 1994–1995, I decided to do ethnographic fieldwork within the church in Utah, the West, and elsewhere, employing firsthand ethnographic fieldwork as a basis for a contemporary study of the church.

Today, at the beginning of the 21st century, members of the church acquire a set of beliefs that are often summarized in brief, personal testimonies about their spiritual knowledge—a practice deeply rooted in LDS Church history. At their core, in Carolyn Gilkey's (1994) words, these testimonies of belief are statements such as "the Church is true," "Heavenly Father (God) lives," "the (current) President of the Church is a living prophet today," "the gospel is true," "Jesus Christ is the savior," "Joseph Smith was a prophet" in this dispensation, "the LDS Church is the only true Church," and "the Book of Mormon is the true word of God" (Gilkey 1994, appendix C:259–262). Gilkey has analyzed these testimonies, and their companion prayer forms, from public expressions in LDS worship services and the children's primary teaching program. They are summaries of the truth claims of the church and its members, offered as a foundational basis on which worthy members, and others, may live their lives.

Ethnographic Fieldwork Research Methods

This study is grounded in participant-observation-interview field research methods, also known as "ethnographic" or "qualitative" research methods (Michael H. Agar 1996; Paul Kutsche 1998; James P. Spradley 1979; Paul Bohannan and Dirk van der Elst 1998; Glynis M. Breakwell 1990; and Stanton Wortham 2001). For some aspects of quantitative data analysis, I relied on H. Russell Bernard's *Research Methods in Anthropology* (2002). I undertook my first nine months of fieldwork in the Crystal Heights second ward in Highland stake beginning at the end of June 1994, with additional research in two other local wards, Alderwood second ward in Lynnwood Washington stake, Washington, and Country Club ward in Phoenix East stake, Arizona. A "ward" (or a new "branch") is a congregation of the LDS Church numbering about 400 to 700 members; a "stake" is a combination generally of five to eight wards. Claudia Bushman reported that living in an LDS ward is much like living in a large family (Bushman 2006:31). To these experiences, I added periodic research in the Pennsylvania Philadelphia Mission (April 1995 through April 2008), and another sustained five months of follow-up residency for research and writing in Salt Lake City during the summer of 1997 (May through July), and again in the Salt Lake City area in fall 2007 and spring 2008. I made a number of further brief visits after the turn of the century, including a period of observation during the 2002 Olympics (Hammarberg 2002). I was present at several general conferences in the first decade of the 21st century, including the funeral of President Gordon B. Hinckley on February 2nd, 2008.

Thus, this study covers the entire presidency of Gordon B. Hinckley, during which I participated widely in the life of the church at local levels, seeking to inform my understanding through direct observation. I also conducted more than 80 tape-recorded personal interviews generally lasting an hour to an hour and half each and held several focus group discussions with local members in these periods and settings. This direct field experience among members within local wards and stakes of the church was augmented by attendance at semiannual general conferences (both in person and via satellite broadcasts), stake conferences and fireside gatherings, and by interviews at several levels of the church priesthood hierarchy, but mostly by participation in a variety of activities common to Salt Lake City as the central place of the church.

While observing local missionary activity in several areas of the church, my focus was on the personal side of participation, missionary work, and convert experiences, rather than the international aspects of Mormonism. Still, I interviewed missionaries active in the Pennsylvania Philadelphia Mission and returned missionaries from foreign as well as stateside missions in several Salt

Lake City wards, and for interpretive purposes, I have used the written journals and diaries of several missionaries similar to those published by Gordon
Shepherd and Gary Shepherd as *Mormon Passage: A Missionary Chronicle* (1998).
Several returned missionaries, who were participants in Penn's Wharton School
of Business and Lauder Institute M.B.A. degree programs, wrote papers concerning aspects of their mission experience (David C. Salisbury 2000; Andrew
Jensen 2004; Ryan Michael Faerber 2006). Needless to say, the missionary
enterprise of the church has been a massive undertaking, currently involving more than 50 thousand single young adults (from 19 to 25 years of age),
for commitments lasting from 18 months (for women) to two years (for men).
These numbers mean that about 20 to 30 thousand new recruits are trained at
17 training centers each year to take up the work, at their own time and expense,
in more than 160 countries on every inhabited continent.

Three other forms of data were integrated with this fieldwork: my qualitative analyses of church curriculum materials for primary (age 18 months to 11
years), Sunday school (age 12 to adulthood), and relief society materials (for
adult women age 18 and older), as well as published material for the (male)
Aaronic and Melchizedek priesthoods (age 12 to 17, and 18 and older, respec-
tively); qualitative analyses of visual materials (film and video) employed by
the church in its presentation of its beliefs to members and nonmembers,
where the message units are not so much words and phrases as images; and
the results of a quantitative questionnaire survey of the Crystal Heights neighborhood, including both LDS members and nonmembers.

The church also publishes three monthly magazines for its members—
Ensign (for adults), *New Era* (for adolescents), and *Friend* (for the youngest age
groups)—plus *Liahona* (in multiple languages for its international members)
and a weekly *Church News* supplement to the *Deseret News*. I have been a sub-
scriber and regular reader of many of these publications for the better part of
several decades. Because they feature writings (or discourses) by the general
authorities, I have accessed this material as the authoritative public voice of
the church in a universal sense.

More specifically, the general authorities conduct the semiannual general conferences of the church, and their discourses are both recorded and
published in *Ensign* as the official proceedings of those meetings. These discourses are, in effect, a form of current scripture, and commentaries on the
meanings of past scriptures contained in the Bible, the Book of Mormon, the
Doctrine and Covenants, and the Pearl of Great Price. This scriptural "canon"
among the LDS, then, is an open one, with recent additions being made to
the Doctrine and Covenants and the Pearl of Great Price. Members of the
church recognize that I am not a member, even as I have sought to give voice

and representation to those who are. I do not provide extensive survey data gathered or compiled by other researchers (Corcoran 1994; Cornwall, Heaton, and Young 1994; Heaton, Bahr, and Jacobson 2004; Jacobson, Hoffmann, and Heaton 2008). Nonetheless, I have sought to provide a qualitative picture of the church in the contemporary present.

I do, however, bring to this project some 25 years of background research, grounded in the graduate-level American civilization seminar that I taught periodically at the University of Pennsylvania beginning in the early 1970s about the Mormon settlement of Utah. During the past ten years, I have taught graduate-level fieldwork-oriented ethnography as a member of Penn's anthropology department.

I think of the audience for this book as the educated lay public, as well as scholars and other students of the LDS. In the scholarly community, I hope it will interest anthropologists, religious studies specialists, Americanists, psychologists, sociologists, historians, and students within other disciplines and interdisciplinary fields. The lay public includes all members of the church, as well as those who have a special interest in the LDS (e.g., those who came to Utah for the 2002 Winter Olympics and those concerned with the former presidential aspirations of Mitt Romney and the political offices held by many other members).

A Solemn Assembly: Sustaining a New Prophet

With the death of President Ezra Taft Benson on May 30, 1994, and the dissolution of the three-member first presidency, the highest quorum in the church, the responsibility of priesthood leadership passed to the senior living apostle, Howard W. Hunter, who was then serving as president of the second highest quorum, the quorum of the twelve Apostles. Funeral services were held on June 4th for President Benson. Then on Sunday morning, June 5th, the quorum of the twelve apostles met in the temple at Salt Lake City, Utah, and ordained and set apart Howard W. Hunter, age 86, as the 14th president of the Church of Jesus Christ of LDS, and as its prophet, seer, and revelator. Called to serve with him were Gordon B. Hinckley, age 83, as first counselor, and Thomas S. Monson, age 67, as second counselor. Set apart by President Hunter, these two men along with Hunter himself, constituted the new first presidency, the pinnacle of power in the church that was established on April 6, 1830, by Joseph Smith Jr., the first prophet, seer, and revelator. Howard W. Hunter would be sustained as the new president during the next general conference, scheduled for October 1–2, 1994, in Salt Lake City; this gathering would also be known as a "solemn assembly."

I arrived at Temple Square about 8:45 a.m. for the 10:00 a.m. meeting on October 1st. Already lines of people waiting for seats stretched outside the gates and around the block. I secured press credentials from Don Lefevre, head of church media relations, and a photographer's badge that would allow me to move about inside the turtleback-roofed tabernacle. After my name was checked on the press list, I was ushered to the first row of the balcony just above the speaker's stand on the south side, mixing with the TV crews, national media photographers, and local reporters. Someone from media relations passed out advance copies of the morning talks.

At about 9:55 a.m., President Howard W. Hunter, the new prophet and president of the church arrived on the north side of the stand. Because of Hunter's infirmities, aides helped him ascend the stairs to the speaker's platform directly across from me. Slowly, using a walker, he moved across the stand to one of the three centrally positioned chairs reserved for members of the first presidency. With a momentary pause, a turn of his head, and broad smile, Hunter acknowledged the choir, members of the Twelve Apostles, and the assembled congregation. And as he proceeded, the congregation began spontaneously singing in hushed tones:

> We thank thee, O God, for a prophet
> To guide us in these latter days.
> We thank thee for sending the gospel
> To lighten our minds with its rays.
> We thank thee for every blessing
> Bestowed by thy bounteous hand.
> We feel it a pleasure to serve thee,
> And love to obey thy command.
>
> Hymn 19; Hymns of the Church of Jesus Christ of
> Latter-day Saints (1985)
> Text: William Fowler

A few moments later, the other two members of the first presidency moved to their chairs—Gordon B. Hinckley, the first counselor (on the president's right), and Thomas S. Monson, the second counselor (on the president's left). The members of the quorum of the twelve took their places in the first row across the front of the stand, and in front of them descending toward the congregation in rows of red upholstered chairs were the presidency of the seventy, the first and second quorums of the seventy, the three members of the presiding bishopric, and the nine women who comprised the presidencies of the relief society, young women, and primary. Having arrived in Salt Lake City in June, I was more than four months into my research at the time of the general conference.

Although the general conference has convened on the first weekend in every October and April for more than a century and a half, this session was special—designated as a solemn assembly—because a new prophet would be sustained in his calling as the president of the church. The Mormon Youth Chorus opened the meeting with an anthem, followed by the invocation. President Hinckley, who was conducting the session as first counselor, moved to the podium and announced the first order of business, the sustaining of church leaders. He announced that Howard W. Hunter had been called, ordained, and set apart as president of the LDS Church, and as its living prophet, seer, and revelator—and that all those present (including those participating by satellite television hookups in nearly 2,000 stake centers and other church buildings around the world, and by about 1,100 cable television systems in the United States) would now have the opportunity of sustaining him as president, as their priesthood quorums were called out, by raising their right hands up to the square. The first presidency was called. They stood, and Hunter with his two counselors signified their assent with raised right hands. Next the twelve apostles were called, rose, and gave their assent with the same sign. Then members of the seventy followed, then the presiding bishopric. Then the men assembled in the tabernacle and those in the stake centers rose as members of the Melchizedek priesthood were called, followed by the young men ages 12 through 17 as members of the Aaronic priesthood. And then, in a final call, all other members of the church, including women, girls, and boys under age 12, were asked to sustain their prophet by standing as a body with upraised right hands. I scanned the audience in the tabernacle. Although an opposing vote was called for, I saw only affirmation. The decisions were unanimous.

The same procedure was followed for Hunter's two counselors, then the twelve, the seventy, the presiding bishopric, and the presidencies of the relief society, Sunday school, young women, and primary, until all of the general authorities of the church and the leaders of the auxiliaries had been sustained.

President Hunter was next called to the podium to address the faithful. A hush fell over the already reverent congregation. He thanked the members for their sustaining vote and acknowledged his sadness on the passing of his predecessor, Ezra Taft Benson. He spoke of his many prayers to be equal to this high and holy calling in relation to the 13 other men who had preceded him in this calling in this dispensation. He said he felt the weight of responsibility and his deep dependence on the Lord beyond the veil in accepting this sacred calling (Hunter 1994:7–9).

Referring to both his travels around the world and his disability, President Hunter recounted trips among the Saints in North and South America, Europe and Eastern Europe, Asia, Australia, Africa, and the Pacific Islands. Many times he had been to the Holy Land, he said, and had walked where Jesus walked, knowing that his walk may be slower now but his mind was nonetheless clear, and that his spirit is young.

He affirmed that each man who is ordained an apostle and set apart as a member of the quorum of the twelve is also sustained as a prophet, seer, and revelator. The first presidency and the quorum of the twelve apostles are called and ordained to hold the keys of the priesthood, and also have the authority and responsibility to govern the church, to administer its ordinances, to teach its doctrine, and to establish and maintain its practices.

Hunter was taking office amid controversy over the excommunication of six influential intellectuals in the church, who were raising serious questions about life in the church. He indicated that he would act in concert with his counselors and the twelve, and that no decision emanates from the first presidency and the quorum of the twelve unless there is total unanimity among all concerned. He quoted former President Joseph F. Smith to the same effect. And then, reflecting his statement to the press at the time of his ordination four months earlier, he said that he invited all members of the church to live with continuous attention to the life and example of Jesus Christ, especially with the love, hope, and compassion that he displayed. It was his prayer that we will treat each other with more kindness, courtesy, patience, and forgiveness.

He invited to return to the church those who had transgressed or been offended, acknowledging that the path of repentance, though sometimes hard, nonetheless lifts one ever upward and leads to a perfect forgiveness.

President Hunter offered to stand with those who are hurt or are struggling and afraid, to help dry their tears. He asked all members to look to the temple as the great symbol of their membership so that they may be known as a temple-attending people (Hunter 1994:7–9).

He advised members to keep a picture of the temple in their home so that their children may see it. Teach them, he said, about the purposes of the house of the Lord. Have them plan in their earliest years to go there and to remain worthy of that blessing. In the ordinances of the temple, he said, the foundations of the eternal family are sealed in place.

Before the gathered members, the president testified that the impressions of the Spirit have weighed heavily upon him in considering these matters. God our Eternal Father lives, he said. And Jesus Christ, our Savior and Redeemer, guides his church today through his prophets. It was his prayer that all members will have ears to hear and hearts to feel, and the courage to follow the apostles in the name of Jesus Christ (Hunter 1994:7–9).

The Death of Howard W. Hunter and, Once Again, a New Prophet

President Hunter's genuine humility touched many people as he sought reconciliation during his brief presidency. Everyone knew that his health was not good. And after nine months in office, he died at age 87 on March 3, 1995. Once again, in accordance with a tradition dating to 1844–1846 and the ascendance of Brigham Young, the senior member of the quorum of the twelve, now Gordon B. Hinckley, age 84, succeeded to the presidency on March 12, 1995, following the funeral of Howard W. Hunter.

Like Hunter, Gordon B. Hinckley was ordained as president and set apart by his brethren in the quorum of the twelve. He was then sustained in office as the 15th president of the LDS Church in a solemn assembly at the next general conference of the church on April 1, 1995, in a manner similar to President Hunter, except for the first time the relief society voted as a group and also the young women (between the deacons and the whole membership). In his sermon on Sunday morning, April 2, President Hinckley encouraged the members to stand a little taller, to lift their eyes and stretch their minds to greater comprehension and understanding of the grand millennial mission of this church. This is a season to be strong, he said. It is a time to move forward without hesitation, knowing well the meaning, the breadth, and the importance of the church's mission (Hinckley 1995:71). Gordon Bitner Hinckley now stood in the train of men who traced their role and standing to Joseph Smith Jr., the 19th-century prophet whose visions and revelations were to his followers nothing less than the restoration of the one true church as the kingdom of God on earth.

Gordon B. Hinckley was called and ordained an apostle by David O. McKay on September 30, 1961. Like all of the apostles, he was designated as a prophet, seer, and revelator. But now, at age 84, as the 15th president of the church, he was the man who would guide it into the 21st century. Hinckley was particularly well prepared for that task. As his biographer, Sheri Dew, wrote:

> By the time he became president of the church, he had labored nearly 60 years at church headquarters, the first 23 of them in relative anonymity. But now, after 38 years of service as a general authority, and 15 of those in the first presidency, his influence in such vital areas as missionary work, temple building and temple work, church finance, and public affairs [was] well documented (Dew 1996:x).

As the successive deaths of Presidents Ezra Taft Benson and Howard W. Hunter suggest, no one can predict the length, duration, or accomplishments of any particular presidency, though all have come to this position after long careers as church leaders and have often reached advanced years of age. Earlier in the 20th century, David O. McKay served for 19 years as president of the church, still the longest tenure, and died in 1970 at age 96; Joseph Fielding Smith became president of the church at age 93 and served two and a half years and died at age 95; Harold B. Lee became president of the church at age 73 and served only 18 months; Spencer W. Kimball overcame severe health problems and became president of the church at age 78 and died after 12 years at age 90; Ezra Taft Benson served as president for eight years and died at age 94; and Howard W. Hunter served only nine months and died at age 87.

These transitions of leadership manifested what social theorist Max Weber has called "the institutionalization of charisma" or the "charisma of office" (Weber 1968:57–61). The church was now led by 15 men, three in the first presidency and 12 in the quorum of the twelve. Their rise to leadership was entirely from within, providing sustained conservation of the church's value orientations and doctrinal standards. Aside from the possible infirmities of age, the transition in leadership has been relatively smooth and without contention. Everyone knows his or her part in the culture of the LDS Church, including the limits and boundaries of their access to revelation. Each individual person is entitled to seek revelation for their own personal needs and the needs of certain others: parents for their family; the priesthood according to their office and role; a bishop for his ward; a stake president for his stake; general authorities for their institutional and area responsibilities; the apostles and first presidency for the well-being of the church; with the president (in consultation with his counselors and the apostles) as the recipients of revelation for the well-being of the entire church in the world.

The Anthropology of Religion as the Framework for this Study

Culture is the single most important concept in the anthropology of religion and the most important feature that distinguishes human beings from all other living creatures; it makes us who we are and gives us the capacity to innovate and expand what we can do, but it also provides the power for great evil. As Dirk van der Elst has noted, "Culture is not a biological function; it is a body of knowledge and operations outside yourself. But to be useful, it also has to be inside your mind. Getting it from out there into your head is called learning. The more culture you learn, the better armed you are in the struggle to survive, and the fuller a life you can lead" (van der Elst 2003:30).

This view of culture as knowledge may be contrasted with several other orientations to culture, including material artifacts, thought-based behavior, and distinctive value orientations. In their textbook *Anthropology: The Cultural Perspective* (second edition), James P. Spradley and David W. McCurdy labeled Sir Edward Tylor's 1871 definition of culture as an omnibus definition: "Culture...is that complex whole which includes knowledge, belief, art, law, morals, custom, and any other capabilities and habits acquired by man as a member of society" (Spradley and McCurdy 1975:4; originally published in Tylor, *Primitive Culture*, 1871). These authors then wrote: "Whatever definition of culture one adopts, it is important to recognize that all definitions imply a theory with implicit assumptions about human beings." Their own definition "emphasizes the cognitive dimension of experience: Culture is the acquired knowledge that people use to interpret experience and to generate behavior" (Spradley and McCurdy 1975:4–5), thus linking culture with its universal uses through experience, knowledge, artifacts, and behavior.

Our interest here is with culture and religion. Again, there are many definitions of religion, including E. B. Tyler's "minimal," compact definition of religion as "the belief in spiritual beings" (quoted in Jack David Eller, *Introducing Anthropology of Religion: Culture to the Ultimate*, 2007:7), which still leaves open the further definition of "spiritual being." Eller lists six more definitions of religion according to different authors:

1. James Frazer: "a propitiation or conciliation of powers superior to man which are believed to direct and control the course of nature and human life" (1958:58–59).
2. William James: "the feelings, acts, and experiences of individual men in their solitude, so far as they apprehend themselves to stand in relation to whatever they may consider the divine" (1958:34).
3. Emile Durkheim: "a unified system of beliefs and practices relative to sacred things, that is to say, things set aside and forbidden—beliefs and practices which unite into one single moral community called a Church, all those who adhere to them" (1965:62).
4. Paul Radin: "[religion] consists of two parts: the first an easily definable, if not precisely specific feeling; and the second certain acts, customs, beliefs, and conceptions associated with this feeling. The belief most inextricably connected with the specific feeling is a belief in spirits outside of man, conceived as more powerful than man and as controlling all those elements in life upon which he lay most stress" (1966:107).

5. Anthony Wallace: "a set of rituals, rationalized by myth, which mobi-
   lizes supernatural powers for the purpose of achieving or preventing
   transformations of state in man and nature" (1966:107).
6. Sherry Ortner: "a metasystem that solves problems of meaning (or
   Problems of Meaning) generated in large part (though not entirely)
   by the social order, by grounding that order within a theoretically
   ultimate reality within which those problems will 'make sense'"
   (1978:152).
7. And Clifford Geertz provided a seventh and perhaps the most commonly quoted contemporary definition of religion as "(1) a system of
   symbols which act to (2) establish powerful, pervasive, and long-lasting
   moods and motivations in men by (3) formulating conceptions of a
   general order of existence and (4) clothing these conceptions with
   such an aura of factuality that (5) the moods and motivations seem
   uniquely realistic" (1973:90). (See Eller 2007:7–8.)

Eller goes on to list several further orientations among scholars, culminating
with Robin Horton's notion that "religion can be looked upon as an extension of
the field of people's social relationships beyond the confines of purely human
society [in which the] human beings involved see themselves in a dependent
position vis-à-vis their nonhuman alters" (1960:211). Eller concludes that "religion is an extrapolation of culture... "to the ultimate. In other words, religion
is the discourse, the language and practice, or the means by which human
society and culture is extended to include the nonhuman" (Eller 2007:9).

Beginning in the next chapter, I develop what Eller (2007:25) calls a "modular" or "building block" approach to the religion of the LDS, focused on their
"life plan" as a model of human development and its consummation in the
kingdom of God. This approach takes seriously Wallace's (1966:52) view that
religion begins from the "supernatural premise" that "souls, supernatural
beings, and supernatural forces exist." He then elaborates this premise in
terms of 13 basic units or "minimal" religious acts that can be fitted to the life
course as ritual complexes rationalized according to the dynamic LDS system
of values and beliefs.

My use of the modular approach will proceed at two linguistic levels: the
higher, more abstract and conceptual level that is concerned with worldview;
and the lower, more immediate, concrete, and vivid language that is used as
a "script" in everyday understandings. Figure 1.5 provides a structural image
of worldview orientations as proposed by A. Irving Hallowell (1967), in which
the axis of worldview is the orientation of the self. The notion of the self is
itself highly variable from one cultural system to another, and so is subject

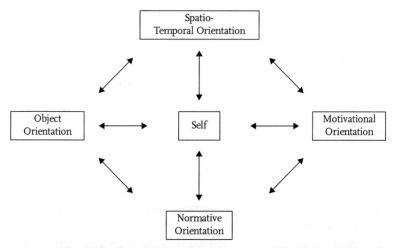

FIGURE 1.5 The Self and Its Behavioral Environment. This representation shows the five worldview orientations that were the basis for A. Irving Hallowell's discussion of self-awareness as a generic human trait. Accordingly, all cultures share certain functional orientations as presented in this figure.

to redefinition as it is applied in a particular study. At a later point, I develop the notion of self as understood by the LDS, using an approach suggested by philosopher-psychologist William James (1890:1:291–323). Hallowell, however, suggests that how self is conceived depends on its relationship to the four other conceptual frames, which he denominates as the spatial-temporal orientation; the object orientation having to do with things other than the self (but including living entities as objects); motivational orientations that have to do with wishes, dreams, and goals; and normative orientations dealing with values, standards, and the desirable. Each of these orientations bears a relationship not only to the self-orientation, but also to each of the other four orientations.

In contrast to these worldview orientations are the everyday items that mark and express these orientations, such as automobiles, horses, and rockets as objects within varying transportation systems; watches, clocks, and psychological memories as expressing differing temporal frames; championships, blue ribbons, moon flights as invoking goals; and love, competition, and discipline as differing value orientations. Clearly, these examples are more concrete aspects of our everyday experience and affect the ways in which the self may be conceptually manifested and put to daily use. Thus, the modular or scripted approach may be conceived at two or more levels in relation to everyday thought and action and in relation to more abstract worldview concepts.

Stability and Change in the LDS Church

One hundred and fifty years after the death of the prophet Joseph Smith, I had come west to Salt Lake City in June 1994 in order to experience Mormonism firsthand in this central place of the LDS Church and had already twice witnessed the quiet and dignified transition in leadership at the highest levels, first with the passing of Howard W. Hunter, and then again in 2008 after the death of Hunter's successor, President Gordon B Hinckley.

What I did not know then, but know now, was that President Hinckley would serve nearly 13 years as president of the church and its leading prophet, seer, and revelator, the first among a select group of equals. He would lead the church during its most brilliant period of expansion, growing from about nine million members to more than 13 million, with more than half residing outside the United States. Under his leadership, the church received new expression in the mass media, undertook a massive program of temple construction, instituted the Perpetual Education Fund (Carnack 2004) to assist returned missionaries from third-world countries in obtaining needed skills, and dramatically expanded the church's humanitarian aid around the world in the face of any number of natural disasters.

And then, at age 97, as the oldest living prophet and after a brief illness, he died, instigating a ritual drama of leadership transition similar to those for the men who had gone before him (Hammarberg 2008b:42–43). This study then became an ethnographic account of the people and religious culture of the Church of Jesus Christ of LDS during the presidency of Gordon B. Hinckley as prophet, seer, and revelator.

In achieving the purposes of the church, no person is more important than the living prophet. He is the church's direct and primary link with God as Heavenly Father, and by revelation, speaks for God and Jesus Christ to the church and all its members, providing encouragement in keeping their covenants and offering direction for their lives. The concept and implementation of continuing revelation through the living prophet provides a way for the church to adapt to its changing environment while also maintaining continuity with its own past and is a central feature of the belief system. Over longer or shorter periods of time, the church as a cultural system provides considerable stability as part of most members' ordinary everyday lives, characterized by minor programmatic and individual adjustments. Still, change is always present, and the doctrine of continuing revelation invites consideration of change in the LDS Church.

The paradigm for cultural change in the LDS Church depends on revelation and tradition, and has been of two sorts—evolutionary change and quasi-revolutionary change. Most notable change by way of revelation has tended to be evolutionary in the limited sense of a further working-out, or puzzle-solving, in terms of well-established beliefs, doctrines, and practices, similar to what Thomas S. Kuhn has described as "normal science" (Kuhn 1970:35–42). Change in how the word of wisdom has been understood among the LDS has been of this limited scope—modifications to a health code now encourage exercise and a well-rounded diet and restrict the use of tobacco, alcohol, coffee, and illegal drugs. Many 19th-century leaders drank wine, for instance, but none do so today. In the past, exercise was often overlooked, but it is now encouraged (though not required). Minor modifications of temple ordinances, including practices like the use of a filmed ritual, modifications in temple clothing, and the use of symbolic gestures for earlier, more replete washings and anointings, would fit into this category of normal evolutionary religious change.

A second category of religious change may be characterized as quasi-revolutionary. When President Wilford Woodruff announced the manifesto in 1890, withdrawing official support for new plural marriages, the change carried in its wake a wide range of ramifications for understanding celestial glory and the exercise of authority through the Melchizedek priesthood, as well as the practical aspects of maintaining already existing plural families (Embry 1987). Historian D. Michael Quinn (1985) has shown in detail that this "working-out" carried forward for 15 years and beyond, and involved internal disputes, challenges to the seating of Reed Smoot as a U.S. senator, considerable duplicity among church officials, and an extensive reworking of doctrine. A second quasi-revolutionary change, in the lifetime of many currently living members, was the 1978 revelation on priesthood authority that opened the priesthood to all worthy men; priesthood had formerly been denied to men of black African ancestry, but was now bestowed without regard to race or ethnicity (Mauss and Bush 1984). Just as the 1890 manifesto accommodated the wider monogamous American culture of that time, so the 1978 revelation on priesthood accommodated the church's global missionary outreach (Mauss 2003; Embry 1994).

A third kind of religious change might be envisioned and designated as revolutionary in the sense proposed by anthropologist Anthony F. C. Wallace's (1956) account of "revitalization movements," which today would require something on the order of disengaging the LDS Church from its singular Christian orbit and re-engaging with other non-Christian world religions, such as Buddhism (Conze 1959; Borg 1997), Hinduism (Knott 1998), or Islam (Ruthven 2006); this would challenge and change Christianity as the central feature of Joseph Smith's restoration and the continuing revelations of his successors, even as the rise of the church in the 1820s through the 1840s may be viewed as a revitalization movement in its own period of gestation. This revitalization-movements model is again being examined in respect to native North American peoples, as well as peoples in the South Pacific (Harkin 2007). There are no signs of a revolutionary change of this magnitude within mainline Mormonism today, but it may be seen, perhaps, in the political throes of such change going on in Tibetan Buddhism as it faces off against Chinese nationalism (Goldstein and Kapstein 1998). In the sense of the need to respond to culture change, the LDS Church led by a living prophet has been highly adaptive and has served its people very well without resorting to a fuller, revolutionary religious transformation.[2]

Continuing revelation through a living prophet underlies one of the most prominent values among the LDS—obedience. Because the living prophet is believed to speak for Heavenly Father (God) and Jesus Christ, the prophet's words and directives have an authority that is binding upon all members of the church. The doctrines of continuing revelation through a living prophet, obedience through the authority of the Melchizedek priesthood, and the building up of the kingdom of God on earth by all members as a foretaste of the celestial kingdom are complementary. The church is not a democracy, but rather a theocracy in which the living prophet holds the keys of celestial glory and is believed to speak with the savior's voice. Therefore, among the LDS, the quest for glory is the effort to realize the kingdom of God through the righteousness of Christ. In the words of a contemporary hymn:

We listen to a prophet's voice and hear the Savior too
With love he bids us do the work the Lord would have us do.
The Savior calls his chosen seer to preach the word of God,
That men might learn to find the path marked by the iron rod.

(Hymns 1985:22)[3]

---

2. Gordon Shepherd and Gary Shepherd have published an important new study of the role of revelation in religion titled *Talking with the Children of God: Prophecy and Transformation in a Radical Religious Group* (Urbana, IL: University of Illinois Press, 2010).

3. "We Listen to a Prophet's Voice." Text: Marylou Cunningham Leavitt, b. 1928. Music: Darwin Wolford, b. 1936. ©1979 Sonos Music Resources, a division of Jackman Music Corporation. Used by permission.

2

The Life Plan of the Latter-day Saints

ONE OF MY first interviews in the Crystal Heights second ward was with Ennis Anderson, the high priests' group leader. The high priests are generally older men in the Melchizedek priesthood who have held positions as bishops and counselors, served on stake high councils, or in stake presidencies, or as general authorities, or in other ways held positions of responsibility at the ward, stake, and general church levels. They are organized as a quorum at the stake level, which holds meetings and has responsibilities as a group in each ward and are led by a group leader with one or two assistants. A primary responsibility is to make monthly "home teaching" visits to families and households in the ward, usually in companion with Aaronic priesthood teachers and priests or Melchizedek priesthood elders. They also receive service project assignments of various kinds. High priests like Ennis filled their identities as Mormons by bearing this role as full adult male members of the church's priesthood (Anderson 1994).

The Ennis Anderson Family

In his occupational life, Ennis Anderson worked as the senior supervisor of mechanical services (heating, air conditioning, fountain pumps, and water towers) for 25 buildings on Temple Square, including the two tabernacles, two visitor's centers, several other church buildings and parking facilities, and the church headquarters building. He introduced me to the organizational side of life in the church's wards and stakes and to the personal side of life in the church.

Ennis, age 56, was the youngest of three siblings in his family of origin and was married to his wife Priscilla, age 52, who was also the youngest of three siblings. Their parents on both sides were deceased, but all had been active

Mormons. In turn, Ennis and Priscilla were the parents of four children. The two oldest, Gaylan and Lisa, were married and beginning their own families, while the two youngest, Chad and Joy, were still at home. Chad had recently returned from a two-year mission in Harrisburg, Pennsylvania.

The church leaders place a very high premium on family bonds and treat the nuclear family as the basic social unit in the church, connected as part of an extended kin network going from one generation to the next. It is within the family context that church teaching and learning receives its first expressions and where genealogical work is done that allows for temple ordinances connecting the living and the dead (see table 2.1).

One of our early interviews focused on genealogy and temple work. Both Ennis and Priscilla were "born in the covenant," which means that their parents had been "sealed" in a temple marriage; because Ennis and Priscilla had also been sealed in a temple marriage, their four children were also born in the covenant. Furthermore, Ennis explained that he and his wife often joined other couples in the Crystal Heights second ward in doing temple

Table 2.1. Religious Groups by Gender for the Crystal Heights Second Neighborhood, 1995

Religious Groupings		N	Male	Female	Total
LDS	(72.1%)	331	48.0%	52.0 %	100%
Non-LDS	(22.0%)	101	46.5%	53.5%	100%
No Religious Affiliation	(5.9%)	27	59.3%	40.7%	100%
Total Neighborhood	100.0%	459	48.4%	51.6%	100%

Notes: In demographic terms, the Crystal Heights second neighborhood involves three basic variables: religious group identity, gender identity, and age group identity. As shown in table 2.1, religious group identity partitions the neighborhood between LDS (72. 1%), persons of non-LDS religious affiliation (22.0%), and those with no religious affiliation (5.9%). While more than 20 different religious groups are represented in this neighborhood, virtually all of them are versions of Christianity, and no one of them alone is large enough to challenge the predominance of the LDS.

The gender division of the neighborhood departs from a 50/50 division in a series of steps— first among the LDS at a 48% male and 52% female division, then among the non-LDS religious in a 46.5% male and 53.5% female division, and last among those without a religious affiliation at a 59.3% male and 40.7% female division.

The weight of the LDS demographic dominance involving two-thirds of the community provides a normative balance in terms of male/female gender relations. Source: Crystal Heights Survey, 1995.

work for their deceased ancestors and others (Anderson 1994). Rhetorically, he asked,

> Wouldn't it be nice if [the church] had this genealogy temple work implemented so that you could go to the temple and ask to have a number come up that represents your family line, and the names would appear on the computer of all the people that are on that line. And some day that will be possible. We're close to that now. For example, you could submit names that are ready now and have them approved and go "do" them. We've come that far.

What Ennis meant by being able to "do" them was a reference to temple ordinance work for the dead. In doing their own ancestral family work, Ennis and Priscilla discovered that someone had already cleared a whole family line back to Norway so that when going to the temple, they could ask to perform the ordinance work for those names. He was suggesting that I might have a similar experience or become interested in genealogy myself.

This conversation made clear that being a Mormon involved formally describing oneself as a Latter-day Saint (LDS), which carried with it a host of beliefs, values, and actions that defined the members of this couple as male and female descendants in a line of ancestors who were also identified as Mormons. They thought of themselves as the parents of four children who would also be Mormons in the next generation, and each of these parents bore further identities as respective members of the relief society and the Melchizedek priesthood.

Identity and Enculturation as a Latter-day Saint

As the interview with Ennis Anderson made clear, giving expression to identity as an LDS involves much more than temple work. Ennis was born in the covenant, was baptized, became a member of the church priesthoods, married, entered into temple work, raised a family, traced his genealogy, performed work for the dead, and was in other ways living life as an LDS while holding down a full-time job. The concept of identity pertains to all of these activities as parts of the church's life plan for its members.

The Concept of Identity

Anthropologist Anthony F. C. Wallace offered a cognitive view of identity that linked together social role, verbal expression, emotional display, motivation,

social action, values, and other manifestations of cultural knowledge as features of an *identity image*. Wallace (1967, 65) wrote:

> By *identity* I mean any image, or set of images, either conscious or
> unconscious, which an individual has of himself [or herself]. An image,
> in this sense, may be recognized introspectively as an internal visual or
> verbal representation; it can often be observed directly in others as an
> explicit claim by word, deed, paralanguage, or gesture; and also it can be
> inferred, more or less systematically, from behavior which is not primar-
> ily intended as an identity assertion. The full set of images of self (or total
> identity) refers to many aspects of the person, on a number of levels of
> generality: his [or her] appetites,...strengths and capabilities,...vulner-
> abilities and weaknesses,...past experiences,...moral qualities,...social
> status and role,...physical appearance, and so on. There is no require-
> ment that the several images which compose total identity be either
> mutually relevant, or available to simultaneous awareness, or noncon-
> tradictory [and may therefore] be variously compartmentalized....

Following sociologist Irving Goffman (1959) and anthropologist Ward
Goodenough (1967), we may also say that an individual's *persona* in any given
interaction is some composite selection of these images, employed by the individual in relation to others in a particular context for the "presentation of self."
Further, anthropologist John L. Caughey (2006; 1980) has suggested that both
personal identity and social identity enter into this presentation of self, as was
the case with Ennis Anderson, who presented himself as a baptized and confirmed temple-worthy member of the LDS Church, holding the Melchizedek
priesthood designation.

Content and Value Dimensions

Furthermore, any assertion of identity in any of its aspects is open to threats
that may challenge or undercut identity claims or expression, as has been proposed by social psychologist Glynis M. Breakwell (1986). Breakwell's theory
of coping with threatened identity proposes that the development of an individual's identity structure occupies the entire lifespan in its biological grounding, while developing according to individual experience over biographical
time, and is comprised of both content and value dimensions. The content
of the individual's identity structure "comprises the characteristics which the
individual considers to actually describe himself or herself and which, taken
together as a syndrome, mark him or her as a unique person different in psychological profile from all others" (12).

Social identity, on the one hand, is that part of the self derived from group memberships, interpersonal relationships, social position, and status. On the other hand, personal identity, following Caughey's (1980:173–174) view, consists of the "systems of classification with which the people of a particular society [or group] sort themselves [by means of evaluative judgments] into *kinds of persons*."

> Labels for social identities, such as "lawyer," "professor," or "uncle" refer to social positions (e.g., occupational, age/sex, and kinship categories) which carry rights and duties vis-à-vis the occupants of matching social positions (Goodenough 1965:3–4). Social identities are based on rules of conduct which specify what someone in one social capacity (e.g., "customer") owes to and can demand from someone in another social capacity (e.g., "waitress," "valet," "owner") (Goodenough 1965:8; cf. Spradley and Mann 1975). On the other hand, [evaluative] labels for personal identity, such as "jealous," "shy," or "aggressive," are understood to refer not to social roles but to what someone is like "as a person." Taken as "personal and independent of one's social or occupational station in life" (Goodenough 1963:178; cf. Goodenough 1965:4), they are considered to refer to an individual's "personality," "temperament," or "character."

In addition to the content aspect of the structure of identity, Breakwell (1986:19) proposes a value aspect within which "each element of the content dimension will have a value attached to it, positive or negative, attributed on the basis of social beliefs and values in interaction with previously established personal [and group] value codes." Wallace (1967:65) elaborated more fully on this value aspect of identity contents (or states):

> Thus, one can rank the states (or contents) themselves on a scale of value, from least desirable to most desirable. The state in which the individual truly believes himself [or herself] to be, within any one identity aspect at a given point in time, may be called his *real* identity; the most desirable state and the least desirable state may be called *ideal* and *feared* identities respectively; and in many cases it may be convenient to specify one of the intermediate states as the *indifferent* identity because it is at the zero point between positive and negative value.

For example, the occupational identity of an LDS is largely a matter of indifference with respect to church membership, though some occupations (say, as a bartender) would be subject to considerable negative identity evaluation and probable exclusion from church membership or expressed as strong advice to "get a new job."

Enculturation

Culture, then, is a social product, arising from the history of interpersonal and intergroup relations construed as learned and shared knowledge. This knowledge predates any individual's apprehension of any portion of it and so constitutes what Dirk van der Elst (2003) has termed "culture as given." In the process of acquiring this cultural knowledge, or any portion of it, we (human beings) lay the groundwork for what van der Elst also called "culture as choice."

In the remainder of this chapter, I present the age-structured, gender-salient cultural model of the church's life plan that has guided my research. This life plan model shapes individual LDS perceptions and integrates cognition, feeling, and action in support of interpretable everyday experience. According to cognitive anthropologist Roy D'Andrade (1995), such a model is built up from concepts and categories that serve as the foundational content for more elaborate scripts and schemas as part of a taken-for-granted reality.

A life plan as a cultural model is an elaborated set of schemas (or scripts) that serve to guide individual members of a group or society in making decisions and acquiring that cultural knowledge (or "capital") that will enable them to achieve their goals. Life plans tend to exhibit stability and predictability so that members of the society can anticipate what comes next as life unfolds. These plans are the basis on which an older generation advises and guides a younger generation in order to meet culture-specific contingencies. At the same time, life plans as cultural models are always undergoing revision in response to changes in the wider environment and within the society itself. In van der Elst's terms, learning and sharing "culture as given" leads to acting on "culture as choice." The life plan allows one generation to teach and train the next generation, while making those modifications and changes that aim to maintain the relevance of the cultural life plan.

The Plan of Salvation

In the small church book *True to the Faith* (2004), the LDS refer to their version of a cultural life plan as "the plan of salvation" (Alma 24:14; Moses 6:62), "the great plan of happiness" (Alma 42:8), "the plan of redemption" (Jacob 6:8; Alma 12:30), and "the plan of mercy" (Alma 42:15), told as mythic stories (115):

> The plan of salvation is the fullness of the gospel. It includes the Creation, the Fall, the Atonement of Jesus Christ, and all the laws, ordinances, and doctrines of the gospel. Moral agency, the ability to choose and act for ourselves, is also essential in Heavenly Father's

plan. Because of this plan, we can be perfected through the Atonement, receive a fullness of joy, and live forever in the presence of God. Our family relationships can last throughout the eternities (*True to the Faith*, 2004:115).

Three Main Life-Worlds

According to the LDS view, every person's life involves three main life-worlds—the pre-mortal life (or the preexistence), mortal life, and life after death (or post-mortal life). "As you come to understand the plan, you find answers to questions asked by so many: Where did we come from? Why are we here? Where do we go after this life?" (115). Figure 2.1 provides a chart that summarizes the plan of salvation by distinguishing the pre-earth life, the life of mortality, and the spirit world life, the latter of which results in worlds or kingdoms of glory—the telestial, terrestrial, or celestial—each of which may be further refined and distinguished from "outer darkness." The implication is that Satan and his spirit followers were cast out from pre-earth life, and some small remnant will remain in outer darkness after the millennial consummation, judgment, and resurrection.

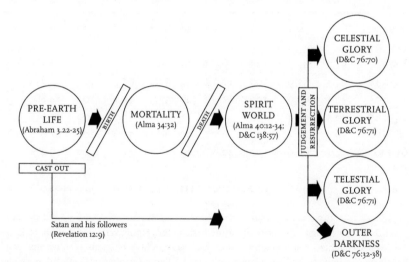

FIGURE 2.1 The Plan of Salvation.
This diagram is intended to answer three universal questions: Where did we come from? Why are we here? Where are we going after this life? In terms of the diagram, our earth life (or mortality) is only part of our eternal existence. The whole universe is subject to transformations of state. The diagram is part of Lesson 1, "A Loving Father—An Eternal Plan," *Preparing for Exaltation: Teacher's Manual* (Salt Lake City, Utah: Intellectual Reserve, 1998), 3.

Therefore, spiritual self-awareness is conceived as beginning in the pre-existence, when the spirit self, as a member of the hosts of heaven partici-pated in what LDS call "the council in heaven," posited to have occurred before the creation of the earth and to have included all of Heavenly Father's spirit children. In this council, Heavenly Father presented his plan of salva-tion and chose Jesus Christ, his eldest son, to work out its conditions as the redeemer of humankind. Another spirit son, Lucifer, also sought the son's role as redeemer, promising to "redeem all mankind that one soul shall not be lost" (Moses 4:1–4), but at the cost of agency. (See table 2.2.) The handbook *True to the Faith* offers this summary of the preexistence:

Table 2.2. **Age and Gender by Religious Affiliation in the Crystal Heights Neighborhood, 1995**

| Age Cohorts | LDS Church Affiliation | | | | | Non-LDS Church Affiliation | | | | |
| | Gender Percent | | | | | Gender Percent | | | | |
	Male	Female	Total	Age%	N	Male	Female	Total	Age%	N
Youngest to 7	63.8	36.2	100	17.5%	58	64.3	35.7	100	10.9%	14
8 to 11	52.2	47.8	100	6.9%	23	50.0	50.0	100	3.1%	4
12 to 18	44.1	55.9	100	10.3%	34	37.5	62.5	100	6.2%	8
19 to 25	39.1	60.9	100	13.9%	46	57.9	42.1	100	14.8%	19
26 to 45	46.5	53.5	100	21.5%	71	41.9	58.1	100	33.6%	43
46 to 60	56.7	43.3	100	9.1%	30	46.4	53.6	100	21.9%	28
61 and Over	39.1	60.9	100	20.8%	69	58.3	41.7	100	9.4%	12
Total	48.0	52.0	100	100.0%	331	49.2	50.8	100	100.0%	128

Notes: Table 2.2 brings into focus the three basic demographic variables that characterize the Crystal Heights second neighborhood: LDS vs. non-LDS religious identity, male and female gender identity, and age identity cohorts. A balanced gender ratio of 48% male and 52% female among LDS members overall is matched in the neighborhood among the non-LDS with a gender ratio of 49% male and 51% female. This balanced proportion, however, covers a modest underlying variation by gender among the religious identity categories (see table 2.1) with males predominating among those aged seven and under on both sides of the neighborhood religious divisions, while older LDS women reach 60.9% of the age group 61 and over. Again, the LDS dominance in the local demographic divisions is on the order of 3:1 (331:128), with modest age identity cohort variation.

Throughout your pre-mortal life, you developed your identity and increased your spiritual capabilities. Blessed with the gift of agency, you made important decisions, such as the decision to follow Heavenly Father's plan. These decisions affected your life then and now. You grew in intelligence and learned to love the truth, and you prepared to come to the earth, where you could continue to progress (*True*, 2004:116).

Agency

The central issues in this story are "agency," "obedience," and "eternal progression," resulting in the freedom of all spirits to choose the good, right, and beneficial order of life as proposed by Jesus Christ, or be coerced to salvation as proposed by Lucifer. In what is referred to as the "war in heaven," one-third of the hosts of heaven chose Lucifer's plan and were then cast down to earth as the devil (or Satan) and his angels (Abr. 3:25–28; D&C 29:36–40). Mortal life on earth is therefore viewed as a time of testing in the face of dissent and opposition, of learning how to use one's agency properly within the church as the kingdom of God on earth, and as preparation for a post-mortal existence that offers immortality and eternal life in the presence of Heavenly Father in the celestial kingdom.

Mortal existence therefore is the second phase of life in which the church as the kingdom of God on earth plays the central role. This story of mortal life may be told in several ways—as a journey, a series of spiritual stages, or a process of learning. President Spencer W. Kimball employed the image of a journey in his book *The Miracle of Forgiveness* (1969:1). He said that it is the goal and purpose of the spirits of men to come to this earth and travel a path of individual experience that is sometimes dangerous, other times safe, sometimes sad, and sometimes happy. The road is marked by divine purpose.

A popular view of the human lifecycle is Erik H. Erikson's (1980, 1959) epigenetic stage theory of life course development from infancy to old age. As shown in Figure 2.2, each biologically grounded stage in Erikson's view involves a tension between ongoing growth and some form of moratorium or strain. The lifecycle is therefore marked by psychosocial crises. Erikson's model rested on, but modified, Sigmund Freud's notion of psychosexual stages, in part by adding and elaborating several stages of adulthood concerned with intimacy, generativity, and integrity. Adolescence was the central period of identity consolidation versus identity confusion, which followed on childhood issues of "trust," "autonomy," and "initiative" (129).

Erikson's model may be considered a universal theory that would apply to all human persons, whereas the life plan concept suggests a high degree of

	1	2	3	4	5	6	7	8
I INFANCY	Trust vs. Mistrust				Unipolarity vs. Premature Self-differentiation			
II EARLY CHILDHOOD		Autonomy vs. Shame, Doubt			Bipolarity vs. Autism			
III PLAY AGE			Initiative vs. Guilt		Play Identification vs. (Oedipal) Fantasy Identities			
IV SCHOOL AGE				Industry vs. Inferiority	Work Identification vs. Identity Foreclosure			
V ADOLESCENCE	Time Perspective vs. Time Diffusion	Self-certainly vs Identity Consciousness	Role Experimentation vs. Negative Identity	Anticipation of Achievement vs. Work Paralysis	Identity vs. Identity Diffusion	Sexual Identity vs. Bisexual Diffusion	Leadership Polarization vs. Authority Diffusion	Ideological Polarization vs. Diffusion of Ideals
VI YOUNG ADULT				Solidarity vs. Social Isolation		Intimacy vs. Isolation		
VII ADULTHOOD							Generativity vs. Self-absorption	
VIII MATURE AGE								Integrity vs. Disgust, Despair

FIGURE 2.2 From *Identity and the Life Cycle* by Erik H. Erikson.
Copyright©1980 by W. W. Norton & Company, Inc. Copyright©1959 by International Universities Press, Inc. Used by permission of W. W. Norton & Company, Inc.

cultural relativity with different cultures constructing particular life plan models. The Mormon life plan arrangement may be shown in some detail using the ideas of LDS President Spencer W. Kimball.

In Kimball's (1969:2) view, some persons lose their way completely in their life journey, while others in large measure "achieve their goals and reach their happy destinations." In following their spiritual mentor (Jesus), they are cooperating with the Creator in his stated purpose of realizing the fullness of life: "For behold, this is my work and my glory—to bring to pass the immortality and eternal life of man" (Moses 1:39). Mortal life in Kimball's LDS view, then, is the time when a person's eternal spirit (immortal) acquires a physical body (in mortality) providing new opportunities to learn and grow, to choose to "come unto Christ," and through eternal progression to become worthy of eternal life.

The third stage in the LDS life plan is life after death. When the body dies, the spirit self enters the spirit world to anticipate the resurrection; then (in the words of *True*, 2004:116–117) "your spirit and body will be reunited, and you will be judged and received into a kingdom of glory." This post-mortal stage involves both the resurrection of all people by virtue of Christ's atonement and a judgment of personal worthiness in relation to the covenants that members have made with the Lord, resulting in each person being "assigned to an eternal dwelling in a specific kingdom of glory," either the celestial, the terrestrial, or the telestial kingdom. "The glory you inherit will depend on the depth of your conversion, expressed by your obedience to the Lord's commandments" (*True*, 2004:92). For most members most of the time, the three stages reduce to two, the contrast between this world and the spirit world.

Born in the Covenant

If a person's first status is as a preexistent spirit, the first major transition (or transformation) in the LDS cultural life plan is human gestation and birth. During birth the spirit self acquires a human body and passes through a veil between the preexistence and mortal existence during which memories of the preexistence are clouded over and largely forgotten. Shortly after birth, an ordinance called the blessing of children (D&C 20:70) is performed during the regular monthly fast and testimony meeting held in the local ward meetinghouse.

As Susan Buhler Taber (1993:9–20) has shown, the content of the fast and testimony meeting varies from month to month and individual by individual, but routinely includes ordinances like the naming and blessing of children and the confirmation of newly baptized members. Ordinances, in LDS understanding, are rituals that enhance the physical, emotional, and spiritual welfare of recipients; they must be done in mortality under the authority of the church's Melchizedek priesthood. This priesthood is bestowed on all worthy men age 18 years of age and older and is construed as possessing the power to act in God's name.

The naming and blessing ordinance formally and officially bestows a name upon the child so that the appropriate church records can be created. The Melchizedek priesthood holder performing this ordinance, usually the child's father or grandfather, then continues to pronounce an individualized blessing upon the child, his or her parents, and the siblings (if any), and sometimes the extended family as well. These blessings encapsulate the hopes and desires of the officiator and the community for the child.

This ritual of blessing and naming inaugurates infancy and early childhood. Children whose parents have been sealed in a temple marriage are referred to as having been born in the covenant of their parents' marriage, and all children who are so blessed become "children of record." In President Kimball's (1969:1) image of life as a journey, he wrote that the journey leads through infancy characterized by carefree activities but rapid learning and through childhood with its disappointments and stubbed toes. Childhood sometimes includes injured feelings, but it also has keen excitements. Then follows youth with its exuberance, likes and dislikes, fears and hopes, and intensities; then comes a period of young married relationships with responsibilities, competitions, ambitions, family-rearing, accumulation of household goods; and finally older age with achievements, culminations, goal-reaching, relaxation, and retirement (Kimball, 1969:1).

Early Childhood

The LDS view a child during the first seven years of life as morally innocent, though acquiring an initial spiritual awareness. In the earliest stage, children under 18 months remain in their parents' care during church services. Then, between 18 months and age three, the ward (congregation) offers a nursery class with a lesson and activities. When children turn three, they become members of primary, the teaching program of the church for its children, including junior primary for children ages three through seven and senior primary for those ages eight through 11.

The first seven years are important years of learning about Heavenly Father and the order of heaven, while children are gaining a foothold in their own mortal life and its moral meanings. After age seven, LDS view a child as accountable not only to Heavenly Father but also to other people. They must be appropriately prepared and taught to take on this increased responsibility. Personal agency or choice, therefore, is to be exercised through obedience to God's laws and commandments.

The Age of Accountability

One of the most important early choices a child makes concerns whether to be baptized into the church, and junior primary keeps this choice before the children. Although this decision cannot be carried out before age eight (and, as a practical matter, the decision is largely made by parents), it depends spiritually and conceptually on the development of an initial testimony of the truth of the gospel. In her dissertation, Carolyn Flatley Gilkey (1994:79–80) compared children's testimonies to those of adults in a local ward. She said none were given by children younger than seven, and when teenagers were asked, "they recalled that they were eight or nine when they first stood up." But in some wards very young children (sometimes three- and four-year-olds) were coached by siblings to give brief recitations with some of the content of prayers, such as this one: "I'm thankful for my mom and dad and grandma and grandpa/and what they taught me/and I know this church is true/in the name of Jesus Christ, amen."

Adult testimonies had opening and closing formulas, and included core affirmations of personal knowledge that Heavenly Father lives, the church is directed by a prophet, the gospel is true, Jesus is the divine savior, Joseph Smith was a prophet, the Book of Mormon is true, plus a number of other structural elements (Gilkey 1994:83–86). The elaboration of core content through the quiet influence of the Holy Ghost is also noted in the review essay *True to the Faith* by Lavina Fielding Anderson (2006:72).

Further, the Holy Ghost, the comforter, is viewed as confirming the truth of the gospel by manifesting itself in warm and peaceful feelings, and some-times as warnings. The ordinance of baptism (D&C 20:68–74; 2 Ne. 9:23–24), then, marks a second point of transition, which, when coupled with the ordi-nance of confirmation to receive the gift (or power) of the Holy Ghost (D&C 20:38–43; 33:15), bestows membership in the church and inaugurates the sec-ond stage of childhood. From this point forward, members, while remaining worthy, are considered to have the Holy Ghost as a constant companion upon whom they may readily call.

Later Childhood

Later childhood from ages eight through 11 is a period of learning more about the gospel while broadening the members' spiritual awareness and experi-ence, and thus increasing and strengthening their testimony. The curriculum of senior primary for these boys and girls focuses on the living prophet (the president of the church) and the scriptures (the LDS standard works of the Old and New Testaments, the Book of Mormon, the Doctrine and Covenants, the Pearl of Great Price, and LDS Church history). Acquiring a testimony, then, is a form of learning confirmed by the Holy Ghost, a spirit being who is viewed as a manifestation of Heavenly Father's presence and guidance through warm and peaceful feelings.

In addition to the Sunday primary classes, children ages eight through 11 are encouraged to participate in several further programs, including the gospel in action that encourages setting and achieving self-directed goals under the supervision of his or her primary teacher, and the twice-monthly midweek achievement days program for girls and the authorized weekly cub scout program for boys under designated group leaders. The aim of these programs is to "provide opportunities for the children to live the gospel, increase bonds of friendship, learn skills, and give service" (*Primary Handbook* 1998:236).

Young Adulthood

These activities for boys and girls, and the increasing strength of their testimony, serve as partial preparation for the next stage in the cultural life plan, which begins at age 12. At this age, boys are ordained to the Aaronic priesthood and participate in the young men social, scouting, and recreational programs, while girls enter the young women achievement program. These programs implement a gender distinction and partial social separation by gender that continues through the remainder of the life plan. The previous 1985 curriculum separated the ten-year-olds as Merrie Misses (girls) and Blazers (boys) for one year prior to meeting together again in their 11-year-old classes, a kind of anticipatory socialization for highlighting the subsequent distinctions of gender (see the *Primary Handbook* 1985:4–5). Young men are called, set apart, and ordained into the Aaronic priesthood by a special ordinance. The complementary status for young women is preparation for motherhood, with its powers, duties, rights, and responsibilities, but there is no separate and special ordinance that confers it; and even though young men are also instructed in the powers, duties, rights, and responsibilities of potential fatherhood, traditionally, the paired roles are priesthood and motherhood, not fatherhood and motherhood.

From age 12, then, young men and young women follow separate but parallel paths while also sharing many joint social and service activities. The young men move through their priesthood callings as deacons (ages 12 and 13), teachers (ages 14 and 15), and priests (ages 16 and 17), involving age-graded powers and responsibilities. For instance, Susan Buhler Taber (1993:90) indicates that a deacon's "most visible duty is passing the sacrament to the congregation," while teachers assist in home teaching, and priests "offer the sacramental prayers and may baptize." She also indicates that the young women have parallel groups called Beehives, MIA Maids, and Laurels, led by young women leaders "who teach the girls on Sunday mornings during the last hour of meetings at the same time as priesthood meetings and relief society [and] help the girls plan and carry out Wednesday night activities" (148). (See figure 2.3.)

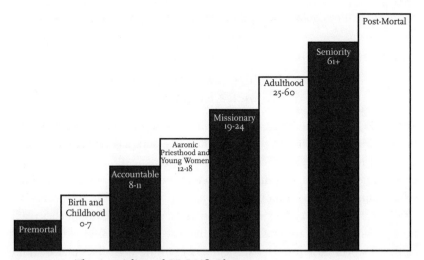

FIGURE 2.3 The Age-Adjusted LDS Life Plan.
The diagram presents the main changes in the Mormon life plan for mortality between the pre-mortal and the post-mortal stages. The inspiration for this step sequence might be Erik H. Erikson's stage model of socio-cultural changes with respect to individual development. While Erikson emphasized universal epigenetic developmental changes, an ethnographic approach depends much more on the particular content of Mormon stages that are wedded to Mormon cultural experience.

During their teen years, the young people learn church standards of worthiness that are common to all church members—the word of wisdom, chastity, obedience, and tithing—and usually participate in a study program called "seminary" for high-school age students. Seminary comprises an hour of scriptural instruction each weekday during the school year and is conducted as a coed program. Beginning at age 12, both young men and young women may participate in vicarious baptisms for the dead as their first experience with temple ordinances. Many of them also test the limits of these standards, and some drop out in order to explore the wider world beyond the church.

At a time when many people are looking toward retirement, Mormons face an increasingly active adulthood and old age. I recall my first visit to Salt Lake City with my family when we boarded a shuttle bus at Temple Square for a short ride to Welfare Square. An elderly couple served as hosts (or tour guides) for those of us wishing to learn more about the church welfare program. Engaging in conversation informally, we asked about their role and whether this was a church assignment. The response was that they were volunteers, and that retirement for them meant they could now fully enjoy their life because they could commit themselves fully to the real work they always wanted to do.

The Melchizedek Priesthood and the Women's Relief Society

At age 18, young men are eligible to advance from the Aaronic priesthood to the Melchizedek priesthood and to be ordained elders, a prerequisite for being endowed in the temple which, in turn, is a prerequisite for departing on a proselytizing mission. Beginning at age 12, teenagers of both sexes are interviewed annually by the bishop or one of his counselors for their "worthiness," which carries with it a new kind of seriousness, probing the candidate's readiness to assume adult responsibilities within the church as God's kingdom on earth. In worthiness interviews, members examine their lives and commitment to the gospel in consultation with their ward bishop and stake president, who have a scripted list of questions that are employed for self-examination (e.g., keeping the word of wisdom, sustaining the living prophet, paying a full tithe, behaving honestly, eschewing sexual misconduct, having a testimony, and giving service). If candidates and their ecclesiastical leaders find that they meet worthiness standards according to the church's norms in these matters, then they receive a "recommend" signed by the two leaders (and the candidates themselves) that will admit them to the temple to participate in temple ordinances. The physical "recommend" is a plastic bill-fold-size identification card much like a driver's license.

Baptism for the dead is the first temple ordinance and the earliest ordinance in which young people may participate, beginning at age 12. The temple ordinances known as the "ordinances of exaltation" include washings and anointings preparatory to the endowment, and then the endowment itself, which may be followed by marriage and adoption sealings for time and eternity, which are the central temple ordinances. These ordinances are always performed first for oneself and subsequently as vicarious ordinances for those who have died without having done this temple work on earth. The endowment itself symbolizes and enacts central elements in the creation story and plan of salvation, and includes covenants of fealty to Heavenly Father and the church. A sealing in marriage for time and eternity may follow upon the endowment, as the basis for an eternal family. These temple ordinances are central symbols of adult participation in the life of the church. No one may go on a mission or be sealed in a temple (celestial) marriage without first taking out (or receiving) his or her endowments (*True to the Faith*, 2004:170–172).

Going on a Mission

An early image of missionary work in the church was painted by the Danish artist C. C. A. Christiansen, who depicted the prophet Joseph Smith preaching to Native Americans in a frontier setting (Jensen and Oman 1984:102, plate 90). Smith was dressed formally in a coat, his own special costume in contrast to those of his Native American auditors. From the beginning, members of the LDS Church have sought converts as a way of expanding the society of those who would understand themselves as LDS. And in the second half of the 20th century, church growth came to depend on the conversion of investigators even more than natural fertility. The mission program of the church encompassed both young men and, beginning shortly before World War I, young women. Thus, undertaking a voluntary mission became part of the identity fabric of the church in response to the call of church presidents.

Though not all young men (and now young women) will meet the ideal for a missionary voiced by former president of the church Ezra Taft Benson (1990), many do meet this missionary standard and Benson's clarion call. His ideals were clear; he wanted young people who were morally clean and faithful in church attendance. He held up an image of young men who magnified the priesthood and earned a scout "duty to God" award. He believed that the seminary program was helpful in developing a "burning testimony" of the Book of Mormon as an LDS scripture. This ideal youth would then be well prepared to undertake a mission and to carry those good habits through his lifetime (Benson 1990:8).

Today, more than 50,000 young men and women are serving 18-month to two-year missions on all continents around the world. Seventeen missionary training centers prepare them for this voluntary undertaking. According to church standards, young men have a duty to serve a mission, if possible, while young women, now constituting 10 to 20 percent of all missionaries, also undertake this calling as a privilege. The missionary identity is therefore an especially honorable one and the object of ongoing demands to meet missionary standards, recently emphasized by church leaders issuing a call to raise the bar (Ballard, *Ensign*, 2002).

At age 18, young women enter into adulthood by becoming members of the women's relief society, although the transition is marked by no ceremony (*Church Handbook of Instructions, Relief Society* 1998:206). On the Sunday morning after turning 18, instead of attending her young women meeting, she attends the relief society meeting. (Both convene at the same time.) As the 18th birthday also usually coincides with graduation from high school, the young woman may make plans in common with her age cohort of seeking a college education, finding a job, or getting married. Although marriage at 18 is not encouraged as an explicit duty for LDS women, it nonetheless has about it the sense of "the earlier the better."

Further, young women are not allowed to serve missions until age 19. Their missions last 18 months, rather than 24, which is standard for the men. And women generally do not take out their endowments until either a marriage or mission is pending, although older single women who manifest maturity and commitment are allowed to receive their endowments without either of these contingencies as a prerequisite. Going on a mission is essentially obligatory for young Mormon men between ages 18 and 25; in contrast, missions for women are allowed but not required or encouraged. On the other hand, motherhood for Mormon women has about it a sense of obligation and duty parallel to the priesthood.

Marriage, Family, and Kindreds

For both young men and young women, marriage becomes the next transition toward full adulthood in the church's culture (Church Educational System, *Achieving a Celestial Marriage: Student Manual* 1992 [1976]). In the cultural model of church standards, marriage is a temple ordinance that seals a husband and wife to each other for time and eternity under priesthood authority and also seals to them any children they may have. As a consequence, both partners must be worthy holders of temple recommends.

A civil marriage ceremony for an LDS Church member (at least in the United States) is simply an accommodation to the laws of the land and the short-term needs of couples who have chosen to marry on a secular basis; after a period of reflection and the attainment of worthiness, these couples may progress to a temple marriage. Traditionally, permission for such a temple sealing is not granted until at least a year has elapsed from the civil ceremony. Not surprisingly, church authorities exert considerable pressure on young people to seek a temple marriage from the very beginning, in which case the civil marital status is conjoined with the temple sealing, and the officiant serves as a representative of both the church and the state.

Given this strong emphasis on marriage and children as normative for full adulthood, those who do not marry frequently experience a burgeoning crisis of their LDS identity, mitigated somewhat by the church's sponsorship of singles' wards and special programs, and (primarily for women) reassuring discourses holding out the hope for marriage in the post-mortal world (but singleness and celibacy in this one).

The Birth of One's Own Children

Endowed and temple-worthy married members view the birth of their own children as the realization of full adulthood in the church and as increasing the blessings of a temple sealing. Children born of parents sealed in the temple are viewed as being born in the covenant, while children born to parents of a civil marriage do not have this status, but are much like investigators. If a couple who has married civilly and who has children later enter upon temple marriage, their children born before the temple marriage may participate in a special part of their parents' sealing ceremony and therefore acquire the retroactive status of being sealed in the covenant, which is automatically conferred on children born to a temple-married couple.

As the first presidency and council of the twelve make clear in *The Family: A Proclamation to the World* (1995), added blessings come to a temple marriage when the children themselves marry and bear children of their own. Then, an LDS can look across at least five generations in the building-up of the kingdom of God: their own grandparents and parents, their generational peers, and their children, and grandchildren. Family networks of even more than five living generations are not uncommon. The family network of kin, so real to members, also serves as a metaphor for all spirit selves as children of Heavenly Father (and, by implication, of Heavenly Mother) from eternity to eternity. This understanding is the basis for the church's extensive genealogical program and the performance of vicarious ordinances for the dead.

Divorce

A complication of this marital and kinship arrangement is divorce, which may involve either civil divorce or both civil divorce and a temple cancellation of sealing, if the circumstances are sufficiently serious to warrant it. A civil divorce may be obtained according to law, but only the president of the church has the power to cancel a temple sealing. A request for this cancellation is not to be undertaken lightly. According to Kristen L. Goodman (1992:159–163), under the president's authority, such a cancellation dissolves the sealing ordinance for time and eternity, thereby putting the celestial status of the parties at risk. Therefore, women especially are discouraged from seeking a cancellation of sealing in conjunction with a civil divorce; when and if they remarry, then they may obtain a cancellation of sealing in order to be sealed to their new spouse in the temple, if both parties are worthy. Because of earlier plural marriage practices and continuing vicarious marital ties, men who wish to remarry may receive a clearance to be sealed to their second wife without a cancellation from the first, because the doctrine of plural marriage allows multiple wives in eternity. This point has been underscored recently by the second temple sealings of members of the quorum of the twelve whose first wives had died (LDS Public Affairs, Elder Dallin H. Oaks, August 18, 2000; LDS Public Affairs, Elder Russell M. Nelson, April 6, 2006).

One explanation for this differential treatment of canceled sealings for men and women is that it assures women of an eternal marital relationship, which is necessary for entrance into the highest degree of glory in the celestial kingdom—but obviously (at least technically) leaves a woman paired for eternity with someone whom she no longer considers her husband (Goodman 1992:159–163; Duke 1992:304–307). Cancellations of sealing do not affect the parental sealing with children, regardless of the parents' marital status.

Issues of Sexuality

Currently, contention within the church regarding gender identity ("Are my self-feelings aligned as male, female, or what?") and sexual orientation ("Are my sexual preferences for persons of the same sex, the opposite sex, either, both, or neither?") is occasioned by the church's sexually restrictive morality (Oaks and Wickman, 2006; Hammarberg, 2008). Same-sex attraction (as a felt orientation) and homosexuality (as a behavioral propensity) are also construed as problems in the church. Because temple marriage as a sealing of husband and wife for time and eternity is viewed as the ideal marital form, civil marriage serves to accommodate the legal, sexual, and emotional needs of Mormons who are unprepared for temple marriage, choose to forego this ordinance, or do not meet the worthiness standard. Gay spokespersons argue that same-gender marriages or partnerships would constitute a similar accommodation as civil marriage for persons with same-sex attraction and would not intrude upon temple sealings (Affirmation 2006; Latter-day Saints for Civil Same-Sex Marriage 2006). The church, however, has taken a strong stand against such partnerships, opposes state and local laws allowing such an accommodation, and argues that the law of chastity prohibits all sexual expression outside the bounds of civil or temple marriage defined exclusively as a covenant between a man and a woman (First Presidency 2006).

The Proclamation on the Family (1995) may be seen also as part of a broad strategy justifying a definition of (secular or civil) marriage as involving only a man and a woman. This approach places the church within a coalition promoting "defense of marriage acts" (DOMAs) in state legislatures and in favor of a constitutional amendment using similar language (Hammarberg 2008). The proclamation is available on the internet at [www.lds.org/library/

display/0,4945,161-1-11-1,FF.html], in various poster sizes from the LDS Distribution Center, *Deseret News*, and in the LDS *2008 Church Almanac*. In addition, David C. Dollahite has edited a collection of essays under the title *Strengthening Our Families: An In-Depth Look at the Proclamation on the Family* (2000).

A recent statement on the issues of sexuality, marriage, and family was posted to the church's newsroom website under the title "The Divine Institution of Marriage" [//newsroom.lds.org/ldsnewsroom/eng/commentary/the-divine-institution of marriage, accessed September 2008]. The statement sought to balance two standards: (1) "The church has a single, undeviating standard of sexual morality: intimate [sexual] relations are proper only between a husband and a wife united in the bonds of matrimony;" and (2) "The church's opposition to same-sex marriage neither constitutes nor condones any kind of hostility towards homosexual men and women. Protecting marriage between a man and a woman does not affect Church members' Christian obligations of love, kindness and humanity toward all people."

Lives of Service

Adult life among the LDS is filled with myriad activities in church callings, temple work, and opportunities for service. To hold a calling means to be offered a specific position of responsibility by ecclesiastical officers and to accept it, to be sustained by a vote of the congregation, and then to be "set apart" by the laying on of hands by a priesthood officer accompanied by the pronouncing of a blessing (*True to the Faith* 2004:95).

Spheres of organized church life include the Aaronic and Melchizedek priesthood quorums enumerated above, auxiliaries such as primary, Sunday school, young women, young men, and the relief society, as well as any number of other committees, boards, and temporary assignments in wards, stakes, missions, and church-wide offices. If a man's calling is to a presiding office (e.g., a bishopric, stake presidency, or stake high council), then he will also be ordained a high priest if he is not already one. Bishops, patriarchs, seventies, and apostles are also ordained to those offices in addition to being ordained high priests. Men are released from these callings, usually after a traditional period of time—five years is standard for a bishop—at the discretion of his priesthood leaders. The ordination, however, remains unchanged, except to a higher office. The assortment of callings and releases is varied, without any necessary progression, and come in addition to members' occupational, family, and community roles, which are also seen as extensions of church service.

The General Authorities

Men who hold priesthood callings at the highest levels of the church are referred to as general authorities, men revered as worthy, holy, and wise. They include the first presidency, the council of the twelve, and the presidency and first two quorums of seventies (see table 2.3).

Table 2.3. LDS Church Organizational Structure

First Presidency		
The President, Prophet, Seer, and Revelator		
First Counselor		Second Counselor
Quorum of the Twelve Apostles		
General Officers	**Quorum of the Seventy**	**Presiding Bishopric**
Relief Society	Seven Presidents	Presiding Bishop
Young Women	First Quorum	First Counselor
Primary	Second Quorum	Second Counselor
General Membership		
Stake Presidencies	Stake Presidencies	Stake Presidencies
Ward Bishoprics	Ward Bishoprics	Ward Bishoprics
Aaronic Priesthood	Aaronic Priesthood	Aaronic Priesthood
Melchizedek Priesthood	Melchizedek Priesthood	Melchizedek Priesthood
Relief Society	Relief Society	Relief Society
Primary	Primary	Primary

Notes: Twice each year in the month following a general conference, *Ensign* magazine publishes the photographs of all general authorities, including the first presidency (the Prophet and his two counselors), the quorum of the twelve (lifetime positions), the seven presidents of the seventy, and the first and second quorums of the seventy, providing the church with a volunteer corps of upper-level management. There is, however, considerable turnover among these men. In the decade from October 1995 to October 2005, approximately 72 percent of members of the first quorum of the seventy either passed away, stepped down, or were otherwise replaced. Over that same decade, 100 percent of the second quorum of the seventy were replaced. The processes of replacement thus loom large as part of the structure of authority, requiring the circulation of new members from below to man the ramparts at the highest levels of leadership.

The First Presidency

The first presidency consists of the church president, who carries the title of prophet, seer, and revelator (as do all apostles); only one, however, is "the Prophet." Currently, the Prophet is 80-year-old Thomas S. Monson (*Ensign*, April 2008), the 16th church president from Joseph Smith Jr., the founder of the church, revered as the Lord's chosen one to "open the dispensation" known as "the fullness of time" (Allen and Leonard, 1992:181). In the eyes of LDS, Monson therefore stands in the succession of all prophets through whom Heavenly Father has spoken to all of the spirit children who have ever been born into mortality. For LDS, there is no greater authority on earth. The president of the church as prophet, seer, and revelator embodies the guiding rule of Heavenly Father and presides over the priesthood. What the president commands in his presiding authority is essentially the word and rule of God, which is considered as current and binding revelation for the church, although statements by the first presidency are considered more authoritative than statements by the president alone, and statements by the joint council of the first presidency and the quorum of the twelve are more binding than any other pronouncements except canonized scripture.

Supporting the president are his first and second counselors. Each president selects his own counselors, although he frequently carries over those from the previous presidency. Currently, these counselors are 74-year-old Henry B. Eyring, first counselor, a former educational administrator and college president (who also served with President Hinckley and was carried over by President Monson), and 67-year-old Dieter F. Uchtdorf, second counselor, a former pilot and international airline executive. Thus, the president does not serve alone but consults frequently with his counselors, to whom he delegates duties and responsibilities.

The Council of the Twelve

The twelve men who constitute the quorum (or council) of the twelve apostles are also prophets, seers, and revelators, but serve under the presiding authority of the president. They, too, hold lifetime callings, and are called to the council of the twelve by the first presidency. Together, the first presidency and the twelve are referred to as the brethren, whose utterances are a form of scripture to guide the faithful.

The church president serves until his death. By custom, the senior member of the quorum of the twelve then becomes church president upon a vote by the quorum of the twelve, reorganizes the first presidency, and fills any vacancies. Seniority within the twelve is determined by the date (or order) of calling to that quorum, so that the man who has the longest continuous period of service among the twelve serves as president of the twelve and president-presumptive of the church. If he is called into the first presidency as a counselor, then the next senior apostle serves as acting president of the twelve.

Presidency and the Quorums of Seventies

The seven-man presidency of the seventies and members of the first and second quorums of the seventies are also considered general authorities. Callings to these quorums usually go to men in the prime of their careers who bring considerable energy, experience, and expertise to their office, or to men who are recently retired from positions of high responsibility in the secular world. They are released at age 70 and thereafter have emeritus status.

Six additional quorums of seventies—which are world regional, rather than general, authorities—now augment the first two and are usually appointed for terms of five years, and are recruited from among men still active in their careers. The seventies therefore provide a large body of high-level administrators and managers who have operating responsibilities for all church-wide programs, and serve as area authorities around the world. They are not salaried but may have expense account budgets to cover any special costs associated with the performance of their duties. Essentially, they are a volunteer administrative corps. Stake presidents, ward bishops, and all other members of the priesthood serve the church on a part-time basis without pay, as do full time mission presidents and presidents of temples (though these latter officers may receive a living allowance).

Callings in the Auxiliaries

Women participate in the relief society under priesthood authority and are called to positions in the presidencies of the relief society, young women, and primary, similar to the men at general church levels, and in wards and stakes. Sunday school teachers and officers at the ward, stake, and general levels include both men and women, but the presidencies of Sunday school on the ward, stake, and general levels are always filled by men. Additional callings in the welfare program, seminary, the institutes of religion, ward mission programs, scouts, and other programmatic areas of the church provide opportunities for service. Participation in the church is largely keyed to these kinds of activity. In the Crystal Heights second ward, more than one-third of the membership held a position of teaching or leadership responsibility by virtue of callings within the ward, a not unusual proportion

within the wards of the church that is indicative of the high degree of organized activity among the LDS.

Temple Work

Temple work is a central feature of adult members' service activity. The LDS
Church (as of October 1, 2007) had 124 operating temples around the world,
with another 12 under construction or planned (*Church Almanac* 2008:506–
509). These buildings are not forums of congregational worship, but rather
places where temple-qualified members perform one-time ordinances on
their own behalf and subsequent repeated vicarious ordinances as work for the
dead. This work for the dead consists of proxy baptisms, anointings, endowments, and sealings for the deceased. It is guided by a belief that all persons
who have ever lived on earth, or who will yet live on earth, are the spirit off-
spring of divine parents to whom they may return as worthy of a heavenly
glory if these ordinances are performed on earth under priesthood authority
and their covenants honored. By virtue of individual agency, the spirit self
of the deceased person may accept the ordinance work that is done on earth
on his or her behalf. Temple work is the epitome of the forms of service that
occupy the adult lives of LDS, qualifying them for the highest degree of glory
in the celestial kingdom.

Church Discipline

Discipline is also a necessary part of priesthood responsibility in the church.
It is administered by priesthood officers as exhortation, private counsel, and
through formal disciplinary councils (Hammarberg 1996). The dark side of
mortal life is that Satan (the earthly manifestation of Lucifer) and his min-
ions are at work in the world, seeking to counter Heavenly Father and seduce
people into disobedience. Sin is a constant temptation to set oneself against
Heavenly Father in violation of God's rule. Satan falsely promises exaltation
(godhood) without effort and righteous living and, in his role as Satan, uses
deceit to entice followers. Thus, Jesus worked out redemption as a way by
which godhood can be achieved, even by those who have succumbed to sin, if
they will regret and abandon the sin, repent, make restitution, and return to
the true path. Jesus then pays the penalty of their sin for them. This payment,
called the atonement, is a sacrifice Jesus has already made by his death and
resurrection.

In the day-to-day working of the church, two kinds of sin seem to predom-
inate—apostasy (a form of disobedience to priesthood instruction) and sexual

sin (of various kinds). These are subject to disciplinary measures, administered by disciplinary councils of the bishopric or the stake high council, which
are intended to restore to the true path those who have succumbed to sin.
The disciplinary actions involve informal probation, probation, disfellowshipment, or excommunication—depending on the nature of the sin and need for
repentance.

Post-Mortal Existence

A funeral marks the completion of the mortal phase of existence for the spirit
self. The body is dressed in temple garments if the deceased was worthy of a
temple recommend at the time of death. Female relatives and/or relief society
sisters often assist in dressing deceased women, while male relatives and/
or Melchizedek priesthood holders assist for deceased men. A service is usually held in the ward chapel, followed by burial attended by family members
and close friends. (Cremation is allowed but discouraged except in countries
where it is legally mandated.) In LDS belief, the post-mortal spirit self then
enters a state of existence called either "paradise" (if the person lived a righteous life) or "spirit prison" (if their life was unrighteous according to church
standards).

Not all spirit persons will have completed their ordinance work or met the
conditions of righteous obedience necessary for progression to the highest
degree of glory in the celestial kingdom, and some will have actively opposed
the plan of salvation. However, those who have met conditions of obedience
can serve as missionaries to those in spirit prison, and all individual spirits
may progress along the path toward perfection by repenting and accepting the
vicarious temple work done on earth on their behalf, until all the ordinances
are completed. In this way, members of the church recognize and honor the
agency of the spirit self in its post-mortal existence. Then, members believe,
that with the first resurrection all spirits will be clothed with immortal bodies
of flesh and bones, and Christ will reign with the saints for a thousand years
(Underwood 1993).

The second resurrection will inaugurate the final destiny of all spirits. The
highest hope and glory of the plan of salvation, as foretold in the endowment
ordinance, is that these re-embodied spirit persons who have fulfilled their
covenants will return to Heavenly Father and Mother as married persons in
their own extended family. They will meet the Lord face to face in the highest
realm of the celestial kingdom. There, with their spouses and children, they
will become gods among the gods on the earth as it is transformed into the full
kingdom of God. This hope is the hope of happiness, joy, and perfection. It is

what LDS conceive as the ultimate goal of life, the achievement of exaltation, the culmination of their quest for glory in building the kingdom of God.

The Life Plan in the Church Today

Wendell H. Oswalt (1986) has shown in his classic anthropology text that all societies possess cultures that specify life cycles and life ways. I call this combination the life plan. The life plan of the LDS is just such a cultural model, a variant on the program outlined by Erik H. Erikson in his study *Identity and the Life Cycle* (1994 [1959]). This life plan informs the self-understanding and self-awareness of members of the church today. It elaborates schemas (or scripts) that guide Mormons in acquiring cultural knowledge so that they may make informed decisions, allowing them to reach their cultural goals. The highest of these goals are embedded in the temple ordinances of exaltation, which lift the nuclear family and its kinship connections to the status of eternal bonds.

The structure of the life plan involves three overarching life worlds, beginning with pre-mortal existence, unfolding in complex patterns through mortal existence, and culminating in a post-mortal existence that is viewed as "one eternal round." The key feature of the spirit self is agency, and the notion of personhood involves the immortal spirit as wrapped in a mortal body. The central stages of the life plan consist of birth, infancy, and early and later childhood when the basic framework of the life plan is taught and learned, including the chief virtue of obedience. This stage is followed by young adulthood, marked by distinctive gender roles for young men in the Aaronic priesthood (as deacons, teachers, and priests) and young women acquiring virtue and anticipating motherhood. The chief virtue for both young men and young women is chastity.

Adulthood is marked by the ordinance of endowment in the temple, with worthiness as the necessary condition for temple participation. Ideally for young men, marriage is postponed in order to undertake a two-year mission on behalf of the church, which offers a main gateway for the entrance of converts to the church's organizational structure and belief system. The strongest expectation of young adulthood is that both young men and young women will marry (though some young women also choose first to undertake a mission of 18 months). Temple marriage itself is given a distinctive church marking as a sealing "for time and eternity" under Melchizedek priesthood authority, in contrast to civil marriage, which is for "time only." The church opposes same-gender marriage while also seeking to affirm Heavenly Father's love for all persons. Raising a family is the highest form of service as members seek to exemplify the Christ-like life. In many other ways, members are called to serve their fellow members and the worldwide human community as well. Returned missionaries may draw aid from the perpetual education fund. Humanitarian service has increasingly seen the church acting to meet natural disasters in all parts of the globe.

Full adulthood is reached when a person may look to their partner in marriage, to their parents and grandparents for guidance, and to their children and children's children for the hope of the world to come. Death, in Mormon understanding, is the death of the body, because the spirit lives on, and even so the body will be transformed to immortal perfection by the resurrection on the model of Jesus as the Christ, while the whole world will become the kingdom of God in its celestial glory.

The epic journey of the saints from Nauvoo, Illinois, to the Great Basin kingdom was part of a westward movement culminating in what is now a global reach. This movement was led by the church's second president and prophet Brigham Young. He continued to guide the revitalization movement that Joseph Smith had begun. The current prophet, Thomas S. Monson, is the church's 16th president, prophet, seer, and revelator.

The ethos of the life plan is expressed through the challenges of the human journey, memorialized in William Clayton's anthem "Come, Come, Ye Saints," in which the first verse conveys the challenges to be faced with hard work and the promise of God's grace:

Come, come, Ye Saints, no toil nor labor fear;
But with joy wend your way. Though hard to you this journey may appear,
Grace shall be as your day. 'Tis better far for us to strive
Our useless cares from us to drive; Do this, and joy your hearts will swell—
All is well! All is well!

Hymn 30; Hymns of the Church of Jesus Christ of
Latter-day Saints (1985)
Text: William Clayton

3

Becoming a Latter-day Saint

ON SATURDAY AFTERNOON, May 31, 1997, McKenzie Mayne was baptized by her father Lonnie, who, like other worthy men in the Church of Jesus Christ of Latter-day Saints (LDS), held the Melchizedek priesthood. She was then confirmed a member of the LDS Church by the laying-on of hands to receive the gift of the Holy Ghost. These two ordinances, baptism and confirmation, signaled that McKenzie was old enough to make choices that really counted in the journey of life. She had just celebrated her eighth birthday, a turning point known in the church as the age of accountability. To members, McKenzie was now responsible for her own decisions and actions before her Heavenly Father and before the church. Endowed with agency from the preexistence, she now possessed accountability.

The decision to be baptized and confirmed, of course, had been fully discussed with her parents, and it was they who taught her what to expect and what these ordinances meant. Still, it was a big deal. This was a step of significant independence. Baptism and confirmation entitled her to claim identity as an LDS, no longer just a child of record. In the terminology of Arnold van Gennep (1960), these ordinances formed a rite of passage, and their structure and content marked several aspects of McKenzie's spiritual growth and her new identity as a member of the LDS Church.

The Gathering of Family and Friends for a Baptism

The Maynes were members of the Crystal Heights second ward, their local congregation, and of Highland stake, the larger grouping of adjoining wards in Salt Lake City. Beginning about 3:50 p.m. on Saturday afternoon, the family and friends began arriving at the stake center, talking softly with one another, their hushed tones indicating that the font room they had entered was to be used for a sacred purpose (otherwise, this was just a multi-use building of offices, meeting rooms, and a gymnasium). In keeping with the multi-purpose character of the stake center, the font room opened on one side to a conference room used by the stake high council. Four or five rows of chairs, seven or eight to a row, were arranged to face a set of closed folding doors. The baptismal font was behind those folding doors. A piano was set to one side opposite the conference room.

Preparations

Lonnie Mayne, McKenzie's father, emerged through a door from a changing room where he had donned a white one-piece baptismal suit, while McKenzie had changed into the special baptismal dress that her mother Darcie said was hand-sewn by an older woman in the ward for use by the young girls. Lonnie and Darcie greeted family members and friends as they took their places. One of the women cared for the Maynes' baby Colton, while McKenzie's other younger brother, five-year-old Schuyler, sat quietly in the front row with young friends.

Shortly after 4:00 p.m. most of the chairs were filled with 35 or 40 members of the ward, family, and close friends. Tori Thornock, one of the teachers from the ward primary, called McKenzie and her father aside to take a picture of them in their baptismal clothing prior to the actual ceremony, and I joined them to shoot a few images as well. After everyone returned to their places, the first counselor in the stake presidency welcomed those present and indicated the initial elements of the program. It began with the congregation singing "I am a Child of God," led by Sister Liane Bell, another member of the primary. The words of the song in the *Children's Songbook* gave a feeling of warm familiarity:

> I am a child of God, and he has sent me here,
> Has given me an earthly home with parents kind and dear
> I am a child of God, and so my needs are great;
> Help me to understand his words before it grows too late.
> I am a child of God; rich blessings are in store,
> If I but learn to do his will, I'll live with him once more.
> I am a child of God. His promises are sure;
> Celestial glory shall be mine if I can but endure.
> Lead me, guide me, walk beside me
> Help me to find the way.
> Teach me what I must do to live with him some day.
>
> (Children's Songbook 1989:2–3)
> Lyrics: Naomi W. Randall

The singing was followed by a prayer offered by one of the men, an elder in the Melchizedek priesthood. Like the words of the song, the prayer addressed God with the familiar "Our dear Father," but it also employed archaic forms of verbs like "art" and "hast given" and pronouns like "thou," "thy," and "thine" as a way of marking its sacred character:

> Our dear Father who art in heaven, we are grateful this day for the many blessings which thou hast given to us. We are thankful for thy son, Jesus Christ, and for the sacrifice that he made for us. We are thankful for McKenzie and her family. We are thankful for the priesthood which Lonnie holds, and we pray that thy spirit might be here today and that we might remember this day and think of it as a special day. We pray that we might all be touched by thy spirit. We ask these things in the name of Jesus Christ, amen.

Bishop Ennis Anderson, at this time the spiritual and temporal leader of the Crystal Heights second ward, spoke informally about McKenzie to those gathered and about the interview that he had held with her earlier regarding her baptism:

> McKenzie is a very special young girl. We met together and talked about various things, about her mom and dad. And she realizes how special they are, and the training that she has received. And she realizes how special this ordinance is, and the special responsibility that has been given and directed her to this point in her life. I don't know if I've met a young lady that is as versed in the reasons why we baptize as she is; she knows the Articles of Faith, so that she could pick them out one by one, and recite them. She's a fine young lady and knows the responsibilities she is taking on now.

Then turning directly to McKenzie, Bishop Anderson said, "This is your special day, McKenzie, as you make a covenant with your Heavenly Father."

The Teachings

The first counselor in the bishopric then introduced a 15-minute video (one of many indications that the church embraces modern technology) interpreting the role and meaning of baptism in the church's plan of salvation. The video's narrative was read by a seemingly older man representing the Melchizedek priesthood, accompanied by appropriate visuals. At several points in the video, children sang songs from the *Children's Songbook*. The narrative indicated that we human beings were spirits before our birth, and that we lived with our Heavenly Father. "We are his spirit children, and He loves us very much," the narrator said. The narrator was instructing us and reminding us of the plan by which our preexisting spirits were clothed in a mortal body, so that we might learn through earthly experience the difference between right and wrong, good and evil, and so choose the good and the right in order to grow more like Heavenly Father and return to Him.

Inevitably, however, we make mistakes and commit sins, we were told, and therefore need and seek a way to make ourselves right before Heavenly Father. This recognition of our wrongdoings opens the way for the role and power of Jesus Christ as the savior and redeemer of the world, to restore our relationship to Heavenly Father. In the narrator's words:

> When Jesus suffered and died for our sins, he paid for our mistakes. All the mistakes we make have been paid for by Jesus. Now you are eight years old. The Lord says you are old enough to be accountable for your mistakes and sins. After you have been baptized, you are responsible for your own decisions and will need to repent of your mistakes.
>
> Heavenly Father promises to forgive us of our mistakes, as we repent of them. Jesus taught, "Except a man be born of water and of the spirit, he cannot enter into the kingdom of God." Your baptism today is necessary to become a member of the Church of Jesus Christ. It is the first step towards returning to your Father in heaven. Even Jesus, who was perfect, was baptized, to set the example for us to follow (Hammarberg, Field notes, 1997).

The narrator tells us that John the Baptist had priesthood authority to baptize Jesus by immersion, "meaning he was buried completely under the water. The person who will baptize you has the same priesthood authority." The narrator continues:

> From this day on, the Lord will be able to forgive your sins, when you repent of them. You will want to live as worthily as you can, and keep yourself clean and pure. Following your baptism, you will be confirmed a member of the Church of Jesus Christ of Latter-day Saints. Being a member of Christ's Church will bring you many blessings.
>
> When you are confirmed, you will receive the gift of the Holy Ghost. This means that you can have the Holy Ghost to be your constant companion and friend. He can comfort you, guide you, and help you choose

the right. He can warn you when you are doing wrong. If you will listen with your mind and heart, you will hear his still small voice. The Holy Ghost will be with you for the rest of your life, as long as you keep God's commandments.

The concluding message of the video was from Stake President Justin Bell:

I want to be one of the first to congratulate you on your decision to join the Church of Jesus Christ of Latter-day Saints. Your baptism symbolizes your rebirth and your membership in the Savior's kingdom. Each Sunday, as you go to Church, you will be able to partake of the sacrament. In taking the sacrament, we renew our covenants—the covenants that you have made today. You promise to obey Heavenly Father's commandments, and to always remember him. Heavenly Father promises to bless you with his Spirit, and to forgive you of your sins (Hammarberg, Field notes, 1997).

Baptism by Immersion

As the video concluded, the folding doors to the baptismal font were opened wide. Behind them stood a pool of clear water in a rectangular font of blue-green tiles, above which a large mirror hung at a 45-degree angle, reflecting the inner pool to those assembled in chairs before it. On the congregation's right, McKenzie descended the steps into the pool while her father descended from the left, and the two met in the center. With a practiced set of movements, McKenzie's father grasped her right wrist with his left hand; she, in turn, grasped his left wrist with her right hand. Then lifting his right arm, Lonnie said, "McKenzie Mayne, having been commissioned of Jesus Christ, I baptize you in the name of the Father, and of the Son, and of the Holy Ghost. Amen." And with that, she raised her right hand and pinched her nose as her father laid her back in the water so that she was fully immersed, and then he lifted her up again, and she burst forth from the waters of baptism with a big smile and puffs of breath that blew away the droplets of water on her face.

A light ripple of laughter and awe swept through the small congregation. Then the father gently hugged his daughter, and the two participants returned to the changing rooms along separate paths. The doors to the font were again closed. The presiding stake official asked us to wait while the participants put on dry clothes in preparation for the ordinance of confirmation. For eight-year-old children of record, the ordinance of confirmation may follow immediately upon baptism, as in this case, or in a fast and testimony meeting as a separate occasion after baptism. Convert confirmations may follow baptism during any sacrament meeting, but not at the baptismal service itself (see *Preach My Gospel*, 2004, 63–65).

Confirmation by the Laying-on of Hands

After they had changed, McKenzie came forward. Her father, with other members of the priesthood who were present, gathered around her, each placing their right hand on her head and their left hand on one another's shoulder, forming a circle. Then her father confirmed her as a member of the LDS Church, saying, "Receive the Holy Ghost," adding his own words of benediction and promise.

In concluding these ordinances of the gospel, Bishop Anderson said:

> We are examples one to another. McKenzie will form patterns of thought, belief, faith and all that she will have in her own life by what she sees in her family, her friends, and all of us who share the Gospel. We have an awesome responsibility. And wherever she goes she will set a good example. I will leave that blessing with you that you may attain to that to which you aspire in the name of Jesus Christ. Amen.

One of the adult men then offered a closing prayer, and we were dismissed to continue this celebration at the Mayne home with a family backyard picnic.

Baptism and Confirmation as Rites of Passage

According to Immo Luschin, in "Ordinances" from *Priesthood and Church Government* (1992:221), the LDS view baptism and confirmation as "ordinances of the gospel," expressing the purposes of God as "laid out before the foundations of the world." Baptism, in particular, serves as an ordinance of salvation, a ritual act in mortality that the LDS view as necessary for immortal life in the celestial kingdom. Together with confirmation, baptism signifies formal entry into the church and bestows a new identity as a member of it—becoming a Mormon (or LDS)—for one who had previously been simply a child of record.

These two ordinances fit the structure and function that Arnold van Gennep laid out for rites of passage. As is well known, he identified three important sub-stages or ritual phases—*rites of separation* (when an initiate is set apart from others for a special purpose), *rites of transition* (which he also called *liminal rites*, a period between the old way and a new way), and *rites of incorporation* (when an initiate is recognized with a new identity and reference group). Van Gennep's model and metaphor was territorial passage across an international boundary or physical passage through a doorway. The emphasis in any given rite of passage might therefore fall upon one or another of its sub-component ritual phases, as in these ordinances of baptism and confirmation, which together change the social identity of a child who is reincorporated as a fully accountable church member.

Polysemy

These LDS ordinances are, of course, polysemic, possessing multiple meanings and conveying several effects. First of all, being baptized and confirmed involves a decision of individual commitment. That aspect epitomizes the exercise of what LDS call "agency," with its implications of choice, decision, and accountability. Second, the use of water suggests both a washing/cleansing/purification dimension, and also immersion as a burial with emergence for a new beginning or new birth. As among Christians generally, these too are implied in the new identity as an LDS.

Full immersion, modeled in LDS understanding of the baptism of Jesus by John the Baptist as recorded in the New Testament (Mark 1:9–11 and parallels; John 1:32–34), also signals a similarity to some Christian groups and differentiation from others that baptize infants by aspersion. Further, the distinction between baptism as an individual's symbolic purification, and confirmation as the church's bestowal of the Holy Ghost through the priesthood, makes clear the incorporative dimension of these two ordinances: It is the purified person who becomes a member. Finally, the words of the baptismal and confirmation formulas indicate the basis of their meanings and effects as grounded in priesthood authority to act on behalf of Heavenly Father (God). Baptism is an ordinance of the Aaronic, or lesser, priesthood, even though its performance among living members is usually done by members of the Melchizedek, or higher, priesthood.

Schema Analysis

We may also examine baptism and confirmation using schema analysis. In the words of psychological anthropologist Roy D'Andrade (1992:28–34), a schema "is a conceptual structure which makes possible the identification of objects and events...on the basis of simplified pattern recognition":

> To say that something is a "schema" is a shorthand way of saying that a distinct and strongly interconnected pattern of interpretive elements can be activated by minimal inputs. A schema is an interpretation which is frequent, well organized, memorable, which can be made from minimal cues, contains one or more prototypic instantiations, is resistant to change, etc. While it would be more accurate to speak always of *interpretations with such and such a degree of schematicity*, the convention of calling highly schematic interpretations schemas remains in effect in the cognitive literature (D'Andrade 1992:29).

As a pair of motivational schemas, the goal of baptism and confirmation is to acquire identity as a member of the LDS Church. Achieving this goal requires baptism and confirmation as identity-changing rites of passage. The candidate has an old identity as a child of record or an investigator (in the case of converts). The goal identity as an LDS member involves three steps: first, being recognized as a cleansed or purified soul or person (comprised of both a mortal body and immortal spirit), which is accomplished by full immersion in water under priesthood authority; second, subscribing to certain covenants (such as a promise to always remember Jesus Christ's atonement); and then third, receiving the Holy Ghost by the laying-on of hands under priesthood authority, so that this power is always available. Each of these primary elements subsumes further meanings: Full immersion symbolizes the cleansing and washing away of sins and a new birth as the candidate emerges from the water.

The covenants include promises to obey Heavenly Father's commandments, and to always remember him, while he is represented as blessing the candidate with his spirit and forgiving the sins of one who repents and asks his forgiveness. The laying-on of hands symbolizes physically the transmission of the power of the Holy Ghost from the priesthood to the candidate, accomplished by addressing Heavenly Father and bestowing the blessing in the name of Jesus Christ. As a schema, the cognitive components of baptism and confirmation leading to identity change may be diagrammed in figure 3.1.

This simplified identity transformation schema involves six or seven steps beginning either as a child of record or as an investigator under the care of missionaries. These old identities are subject to ritual transformation under priesthood authority in four steps from baptism by immersion to the laying-on of hands, and involving covenantal promises in order to receive promised

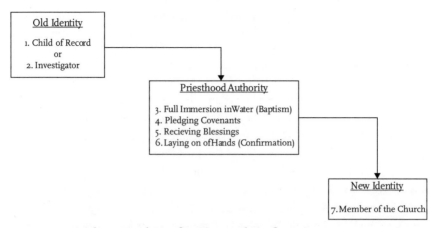

FIGURE 3.1 Schema Analysis of Baptism and Confirmation.
The process of bringing new members into the church involves an identity change from either a child of record or investigator status, through the liminal statuses governed by priesthood authority, to identity as a new member of the church, confirmed by the laying-on of hands.

blessings. The schema is completed in the acquisition of the new identity as a member of the LDS Church.

McKenzie Mayne, even at eight years old, grasped the essentials of this process in terms of symbolic content. I spoke with her briefly several days prior to her baptism, and asked her about it:

MEL [M]: Tell me a little about baptism. I'd like to know more about it.
MCKENZIE [MCK]: Well, it's really an exciting experience where you get to choose if you want to get baptized or not, and when you get baptized—I've seen lots of people—they just say it's an exciting event. You just get under the water once, and you have to go all the way under without anything sticking up.
M: Have you seen anybody get baptized?
MCK: Yes, I've seen about three people get baptized. My friend Rachel, my friend Lindsay, and my other friend Bergin....
M: I remember some things about baptism. First comes faith, then repentance, and then baptism for the remission of sins. Is that how you think about baptism?
MCK: Uhhuh. Washing away all your sins. And it's just like getting born again.
M: And the gift of the Holy Ghost? Can you tell me a little bit about that?
MCK: Well, he's a person that no one can see, but he's like a feeling inside, and if you ever are in danger you get this feeling and you look up and you realize what's happening. (Mayne, Interview, May 26, 1997)

Rituals, Sensations, and Feelings

Baptism by immersion involves certain forms of bodily or sensory experience along lines suggested by anthropologist Thomas Csordas in his introduction to *Embodiment and Experience* (1994:4–5). As far as I know, LDS do not conceive of the human sensorium in ways any different than other Americans—as involving the five basic senses of sight, taste, touch, smell, and hearing—except that LDS place a special emphasis on internally felt visceral signals, or internal bodily responses, as part of the meaning of feelings. As McKenzie makes clear, in baptism the initiate has to "get under the water once, and you have to go all the way under without anything sticking up." Immersion then is a sensory experience in several ways: holding one's breath and closing one's eyes while going under the water, feeling the water totally covering the body, and again feeling the release from the water and the restoration of air to the lungs and visual light to the eyes on emergence. And in the ordinance of confirmation—an ordinance granting the gift of the Holy Ghost through priesthood authority, the initiate feels the pressure of hands being laid on her head, a pressure that travels down her neck to the spinal cord and throughout the whole body as if a gentle but additional weight is being added. The ritual means that the individual LDS now has access to the Holy Ghost, a spirit "that no one can see," but whose presence can be felt. The Holy Ghost's presence, then, is "like a feeling inside you," a sign with many possible meanings, including as a warning of danger. "[I]f you ever are in danger, you get this feeling," McKenzie said. "And you look up and you realize what's happening." So, in these two LDS ordinances of baptism and confirmation, members observe, hear, and feel the embodiment of group identity in the physical actions that are part of the rituals (Csordas 1994:13–14).

These ordinances have further meanings in terms of the central LDS values of agency and accountability. However much parents and teachers may direct the learning process, these ordinances signify the first choice that is referenced to the initiate and for which he or she is held accountable in LDS belief. Thus, these two ordinances take place in a world that is a particularly LDS world, one in which identity as a member of the church is bestowed, and where the meaning of that identity itself entails agency and accountability within the constellation of LDS beliefs. Full identity as an LDS, then, is a group identity into which a person grows and yet acquires by choice, in the sense that acquiring it involves prior preparation but comes as a decision that anticipates further steps, while its full meaning will be realized only through elaborating and living out this identity over the whole life course (see Moen, Elder, and Luscher 1995; Erikson and Erikson 1997).

The Ward and Stake Structure of the Church

McKenzie's baptism and confirmation occurred in the Highland stake center, a place of offices and meeting rooms, including a basketball gymnasium that is used for activities of the members of seven wards and two branches of the church in the immediate Highland neighborhood. The LDS Church is organized both geographically and hierarchically. A ward (as in a political subdivision) is the LDS name for a local congregation, numbering approximately 400 to 700 members drawn from a particular neighborhood or geographic area. One of these wards is the Crystal Heights second ward, the congregation to which McKenzie and her family belonged. A stake (from Old Testament images of tents held fast by stakes) is the next larger geographical and organizational entity, generally containing five to eight wards, or local congregations. Wards are nested within stakes. A branch is a mission unit similar to a ward, but it is smaller and not yet fully organized as a congregational unit and is set within a mission district. Wards, stakes, branches, and mission districts provide the focal places for face-to-face associations, activities, and meetings in the church.

Crystal Heights Second Ward and Highland Stake

During my residency, the Crystal Heights second ward was part of the larger Highland neighborhood after which Highland stake is named. Highland stake serves as another form of congregation with semiannual stake conferences and a host of stake-level callings to which members were appointed. In commenting on this multilevel arrangement of wards within stakes, Jan Shipps, Cheryll May, and Dean May (1994:296) noted that "wards and stakes both function as congregations and…all Latter-day Saints are members of both," and that this integration of two geographic levels "is a signal that Mormon congregational life differs considerably from that in other traditions in the Judeo-Christian family of traditions." Any member of a ward, therefore, is also a member of the stake, and ward and stake activities are mutually coordinated. Hierarchy enters because ward bishops are recommended for their callings by the stake president, and when ordained and set apart, a bishop then chooses his own two counselors. The stake president is set apart by his area authority seventy, and serves with two counselors and a 12-member stake high council. The area authority seventy reports to the quorum of the twelve and the first presidency.

I came to know Bishop Justin Bell and Stake President Ralph Dewsnup through several interviews and participation in ward and stake activities, but knew the counselors and members of the stake high council only as an observer of them in their public roles. Shipps, May, and May (1994:296–297) noted:

> Whether by design or as a consequence of the frontier experience, wards are congregations that function according to a village-life model. The ward bishop and his two counselors fill roles not unlike those of village elders, presiding over and ministering to the members of the ward, managing and overseeing ward activities. They, in turn, owe allegiance to those in higher authority, their own stake presidents and those above them in the Church hierarchy. The ward leaders are also like village elders in that, as member[s] of the LDS lay priesthood, they are not professional clergy. In addition to discharging their duties in the ward, they must earn their own livings.

Most of my research activity, like the activity of church members generally, was focused at the ward level. The meeting house, or ward chapel, shared by the two Crystal Heights wards, stands as a symbol of LDS presence in the local Highland neighborhood, directly across the street from a Lutheran church. The ward meetinghouse is marked by a modest spire pointing toward the heavens, with the ward name posted in simple letters on the brickwork, beneath which is written "Visitors Welcome." The building complex includes a worship space, with overflow accommodations partitioned from the main sanctuary, a gymnasium with a stage and nearby kitchen, classrooms on two levels, larger meeting rooms on both the lower and upper levels, offices for the bishoprics of the two wards that share this building, and restrooms and storage areas. The design is entirely functional, with a minimum of symbolism (perhaps indicating Mormon austerity) in either the architecture or interior décor, and is one of the standard cookie-cutter designs of its 1970s period.

This ward building is located 25 blocks south and 22 blocks east of Temple Square in Salt Lake City, on the lower east "bench" or foothills of the Wasatch range of the Rocky Mountains. In the city, all locations are fitted to a grid system of coordinates running north and south, east and west, after a plan for the City of Zion offered by the founding prophet Joseph Smith; the city has as its zero-point the Temple Square corner of Main and South Temple streets. Any location can be specified by its coordinates from this intersection, whose distances span the Great Basin floor of the Salt Lake Valley and reach to the higher bench lands along the Wasatch mountain range. Because Salt Lake City is the ecclesiastical center of the church, LDS are denser there than any place else on earth, excepting only Bountiful, Provo, and Franklin County, Idaho. In the world at large, as represented in the *2009 Church Almanac* (2009:181), the LDS Church divides the globe into about 27 geographical areas, each under a three-member area presidency; these areas constitute about 2,818 geographic stakes (plus 348 missions), and the set of stakes (and missions) is subdivided into about 20,205 wards (and 4,103 branches). Thus, the church covers the earth and replicates itself around the world using the structure seen locally in the Crystal Heights second ward and Highland stake, Salt Lake City. This global church is the institution with which McKenzie now identifies when she refers to herself as an LDS.

The number and boundaries of areas into which the world is divided for purposes of church administration are subject to regular revision from church headquarters, as are the boundaries of wards and stakes in relation to population shifts; these changes also reflect centralized administrative authority. At the ward and stake level, the aim is to maintain a size commensurate with face-to-face activities, while world areas reflect dynamics of growth and other issues of general church membership distribution.

By good fortune, I was able to focus my fieldwork in the Crystal Heights second ward, and then extended it to other wards and stakes. Fifteen years earlier, in 1978, I was doing four to five months of research in the church archives and had rented part of a duplex that I shared with an LDS family, Bob and Kathy Fairbanks and their four daughters, Camille, Michelle, Jennelle, and Chantelle. We kept in contact over the years. In 1994, when I decided to do contemporary fieldwork in Utah, I told the Fairbanks family of my plans, asking their advice on selecting a local ward for intensive study. Kathy said, "Bob's in the bishopric in our ward, so why don't you study it?" I accepted that invitation gladly. Bob was the second counselor, and he provided an immediate introduction to Bishop Justin Bell and the first counselor, Steven Tingey. During my first Sunday attending sacrament meeting, Bishop Bell introduced me to the congregation and invited me to say a few words about myself and my plan of study in the congregation. I was warmly received, and many persons let me know they would help me understand how the ward worked and answer any questions I might have about the church.

Over the years the Fairbanks family had grown. The four girls had all become young women, and three boys were added to the clan, Daniel, Michael, and Nathaniel. I became a kind of "Dutch uncle" and was included in many family gatherings along with other relatives, including a Thanksgiving hosted by Kathy's parents, Richard and Myrle Dayhuss.

The Hierarchy of Authority at the Local Level

Although most of my primary relationships were with the people of the Crystal Heights second ward, there were two important moments when Stake President Ralph Dewsnup provided me with special support. One was the first time that I asked if I might attend a stake-level meeting of the high priests' quorum during the fall stake conference. Normally, this meeting is for those members of the priesthood who are members, generally men in their 40s and older who have served in a leadership calling. Bob Fairbanks explained to me that a leadership calling includes roles as "home teacher, primary teacher, scout master, custodian, Sunday school teacher, ward security, emergency preparedness coordinator, ward clerk, choir director" and other responsible positions. The high priests' meeting is one where priesthood leaders, including members of the stake presidency and high council, area authorities, and general authorities, speak to the men about their duties and responsibilities as members of the priesthood. When the stake quorum meeting was first announced, I asked Ennis Anderson, who was then the high priests' group leader in the Crystal Heights second ward, if I might attend this meeting, and he asked Bishop Bell. The bishop explained that he would consult with Stake President Dewsnup and let me know whether or not I could attend. On the day of the meeting, Stake President Dewsnup gave his approval, and so I joined the high priests' quorum for their meeting.

This small scenario was important in two respects. First, it made very clear how the structure of authority worked within the church—permission was requested up the chain of command and was granted down among file leaders. LDS Church authority is strictly hierarchical. Second, I believed that Stake President Dewsnup took my research program seriously and would provide guidance and access within his sphere of authority and would support Bishop Bell in giving me similar guidance and access within the ward. I took this to mean that at the local level, the doors were opened for me to seek an insider's understanding of the church's culture among local members based on their everyday experience in it. None of this was in any way secretive, and I wish to indicate my gratitude to both Bishop Bell and Stake President Dewsnup for granting me that access and letting me consult with them and interview them as my study progressed. The process of making requests upward and receiving (or not receiving) permission from above was repeated several times. Most often permission was granted, but the procedure clearly defined the structure of power and authority even at the most local level. During the course of this study, Justin Bell was released as bishop and was called, set apart, and ordained as stake president, and Ennis Anderson was called, set apart, and ordained as bishop. Such changes are a normal, taken-for-granted feature of life in a Mormon ward, and occur as part of activity and callings week by week and month by month. The iconic image of Utah as a beehive of activity certainly fits the church.

Neighborhood Composition

A second telling moment came in early winter when I sought permission to conduct a house-to-house survey of the Crystal Heights second neighborhood. I was aware that the LDS Church itself conducts a variety of focus groups, interviews, and surveys of its members through its Research Information Division (RID), and that the results of these interviews and surveys are used by church leaders and staff members as a basis for assessing church programs and making decisions. This church-sponsored internal social science research program is both important and sophisticated. It is a flexible planning and assessment organization used extensively in the effort of correlation, a program that seeks to integrate materials, programs, and activities. These church surveys are generally not available to outside researchers, not even social scientists at Brigham Young University. Thus, to learn about the social composition of the Crystal Heights second ward and its neighborhood, I needed to conduct my own survey, and this I set out to do.

I developed and planned to use a questionnaire for this survey—based in part on similar surveys within the church. Bishop Bell and Stake President Dewsnup reviewed the questionnaire with me, question by question, and helped me clarify terms and phrases. Neither, of course, could give official sanction to my undertaking. However, the bishopric did make a public announcement to members of the ward during a sacrament meeting that I would be doing a neighborhood survey as part of my research, and that each member could decide for himself or herself whether to participate, and that the ward leaders had no special position on the matter. When a few members who had not heard the public announcement called ward leaders about the questionnaire, the callers were reassured that their participation was purely voluntary, and that the survey was not an official ward undertaking. And ward leaders gave the same assurance to nonmembers, some of whom wondered if this was a ward activity. My own letter of introduction for the survey and its instructions made the same point and also indicated that the survey was being conducted under the auspices of the University of Pennsylvania Research Foundation, from which I had a grant for that purpose.

Opposition to the survey by ward leaders would surely have ended it. At the same time, they took it as their duty to review its contents because I was asking for their help with its public announcement as part of my research effort. The house-to-house delivery of the questionnaires and their return were entirely in my hands, though many members brought them to me at Sunday ward meetings during February of 1995 when this effort was in progress. For others, I returned to their homes as many as three and four times in my effort to secure wide participation. Nearly two-thirds of the residents of the Crystal Heights neighborhood, both LDS and non-LDS, completed questionnaires, and that substantial response rate was due, in part, to the indirect support of the ward and stake leaders.

The Neighborhood and Ward Census

Figure 3.2 is a map of the Crystal Heights second ward neighborhood. By my count, the neighborhood contained 321 dwelling units, including basement apartments. Nineteen units were unoccupied at the time of my survey, including six that were for sale. The ward membership directory listed members at 215 of these addresses, suggesting that about 71.2 percent of the dwelling units were LDS households. I obtained wholly or partially completed questionnaires from 191 households, a household response rate of 63.3 percent. This household sample included a total of 471 persons across all ages and backgrounds. Among the 455 who reported their religion, 71.7 percent identified themselves as LDS, which approximates the proportion of LDS households within the ward boundaries as noted above.

At the time of my residency, Highland neighborhood was a modest middle-class area on the lower east bench of Salt Lake City, and the Crystal Heights second ward partook of this same general character. Table 3.1 provides a demographic profile of the Crystal Heights second neighborhood, comparing LDS and non-LDS households. Among the 130 households whose members reported income, the 1994 mean household income was just over $39,000, with variation between the mean of approximately $34,800 among LDS households and the mean of about $45,500 among non-LDS ones, which was a statistically significant difference. Therefore, the non-LDS were a little better off in this neighborhood. There was also considerable variation around these figures, as indicated by the standard deviations, so that the two distributions overlapped. The ward neighborhood also showed significant variation in family size, with 118 LDS households having a mean size of 2.69 persons and 70 non-LDS households having a mean size of 2.04 persons. LDS households, on average, were just a little bit larger.

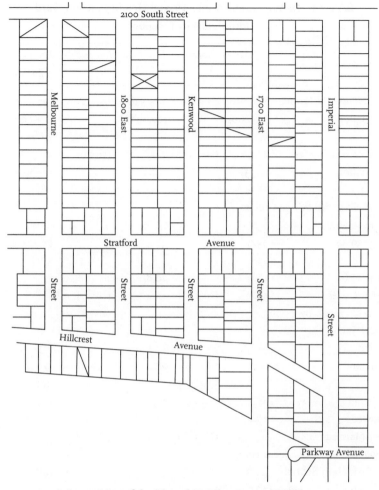

FIGURE 3.2 A Street Map of the Crystal Heights Second Ward.
The ward was bounded by 2100 South Street on the south, Hillcrest Avenue (and Parkway) on the north, Imperial Street on the west, and Melbourne on the east.

Other compositional differences among households included the age structure, with LDS households including a larger percentage of persons age 61 and over, while the non-LDS households held a larger proportion of persons in the younger working ages of 30 to 44. More LDS household heads were married or widowed and fewer were divorced than among non-LDS household heads. Nearly three-quarters of household heads in LDS homes attended church services twice a month or more, almost twice the percentage among non-LDS household heads. There were fewer single-person households and more multi-person households among the LDS households in this neighborhood

MELVYN HAMMARBERG

Table 3.1. Demographic Profile, Crystal Heights Second Ward, Households by Religion

	LDS Households		Non-LDS Households		Level of Significance
Mean Household Income	$34,756	(N=78)	$45,538	(N=52)	.002
St. deviation	(18,000)		(20,698)		(F=9.86, 1df)
Mean Household Size	2.69	(N=118)	2.04	(N=70)	.005
St. deviation	(1.73)		(1.01)		(F=8.24, 1df)
Household Heads by Age Groups					
Age 19 to 29	8.7%		7.6%		.004
Age 30 to 44	33.9		48.5		(χ=13.4, 3df)
Age 45 to 60	18.3		28.8		
Age 61 & over	39.1	(N=116)	15.2	(N=67)	
Household Heads by Marital Status					
Married	63.5%		54.5%		.03
Divorced	9.6		24.2		(χ=9.03, 3df)
Separated	.9		1.5		
Widowed	17.4		7.6		
Never Married	8.7	(N=118)	12.1	(N=70)	
Household Heads by Educational Level					
Less than High School	6.0%		– ·		differences
High School graduate	20.7		13.4		Not significant
Some College	28.4		31.3		
College graduate	15.5		20.9		
Post-graduate degree	29.3	(N=118)	34.3	(N=70)	
Household Heads by Church Attendance					
Twice monthly or more	74.1%		38.8%		.001
Monthly or less	25.9	(N=118)	61.2	(N=70)	(χ=20.5, 1df)
Household Heads by Gender					
Male	70.7%		59.7%		Differences
Female	29.3%	(N=118)	40.3%	(N=70)	not significant

	LDS Households	Non-LDS Households	Level of Significance
Family Size of Household			
Single-person	26.6%	34.2%	.02
Two-person	37.1	40.2	(χ =10.1, 3df)
3–4 persons	20.0	23.3	
5–8 persons	16.3 (N=118)	1.3 (N=70)	

than among the non-LDS, where nearly three out of four lived in single- or two-person households.

On two measures there was no difference within the neighborhood between the LDS and non-LDS households. The distribution of educational attainment was about the same among households in these two categories, and the proportions of households headed by a man or woman was about the same as well. My questionnaire did not ask explicitly about same-gender-headed households, but one questionnaire was returned with the notation that there were several same-gender-partner households in the neighborhood among persons who were raised both LDS and non-LDS.

The overall pattern of these households suggested a neighborhood comprised of young married and older widowed persons, where LDS households tended to be slightly larger due to the presence of more children. It was a starter neighborhood for new families and young singles and couples, with a notable number of divorced non-LDS household heads. About 75 percent had some college education, were college graduates, or had some post-graduate training. The Crystal Heights second neighborhood, then, was a modest, middle-class one, where many of its residents had experienced the benefits of higher education and were starting out on professional careers.

Extending My Reach

In addition to my participation in the Crystal Heights second ward, I also undertook observations and interviews in two other local wards elsewhere in the church, namely Alderwood second ward in Lynnwood stake (Seattle, Washington) and Country Club ward in Phoenix East stake (Phoenix, Arizona). I did not use questionnaire surveys in either of these wards. I suspect that each would show significant variation in its demographic profile from the Crystal Heights second ward. Alderwood second ward was located in an affluent

upper-middle-class suburban neighborhood near Seattle, likely to have a somewhat higher average household income than the Crystal Heights second ward
(by my subjective judgment). Country Club ward in Phoenix, in spite of its high
status name, had members who spanned the income range from poverty levels
to the very well-off, and I visited in homes across this range. I was told that the
diversity in Country Club ward was an intentional effect of constructing ward
boundaries in the Phoenix East stake to span the distance from the inner city
to the outlying suburbs like slices of an apple pie, a strategy for building community across ethnic and class lines. It is a ward and stake plan that would
merit study in its own right because of this strategy, but that was not part of my
research plan.

To these experiences in the West, I added research in the Philadelphia mission (from September 1995 through April 1997), and another four months
of follow-up research and writing during the summer of 1997 (May through
August), and again in 2002 during the Winter Olympics in the Salt Lake
City area (Hammarberg 2002b). The result was more than 80 tape-recorded
interviews and focus discussions with local members, former members (and
occasional nonmembers) in these several settings, each generally lasting an
hour or more. This fieldwork within the wards and stakes of the church was
augmented by attendance at general conferences, stake conferences, fireside
gatherings, and by participation in a variety of local activities.

Family Home Evening

For much of the early 20th century, LDS Church leaders had advised members to set aside one evening a week for family gatherings, a practice followed by the Mayne and Fairbanks families. This suggestion was an effort to
counteract increasing demands on the time of individual family members,
but it had modest success. Then in 1965, as part of the effort of correlation,
church leaders launched a set of teaching manuals with lessons and activities
for a program called "Family Home Evening," setting aside Monday evenings
for these family gatherings. All other church meetings were suspended on
Monday evenings. A general history of the church by James B. Allen and Glen
M. Leonard (1992:593–606) reported that this undertaking became one of the
"most successful of all the innovations" during the post-world-war-II period.
"The Monday family home evening quickly caught on throughout the church
and by the 1970s was an important and viable tradition.... In some areas
where the Latter-day Saints enjoyed a numerical majority, town and school
administrators even scheduled athletic and community activities to avoid family night" (Allen and Leonard 1992:599).

A Time and Place of Common Purpose

Regarding family home evening, Sally Jensen, who had just been released as primary president, recalled how she acquired the feeling that her family of origin had a common purpose, and that her place in it was important. She illustrated her point with a story:

> This one family home evening stands out in my mind. My mom took a ski pole and we each had a strand of yarn [tied to that pole]. And when we all pulled on the yarn, the ski pole went up quite straight. And then she told three of us on one side to let our yarn down, and the pole sagged. I couldn't have been more than about eight, but I remember when I pulled my string, I really realized "I'm part of this family." It was something physical and tangible to me. I could see that I was a part of the family and I had an influence on this family. I could make that pole stand up straight or I could pull it toward me or let it down. It was the first time that I really had the concept that I wasn't just an individual person, but I was part of a family. I remember the love that I felt that night, and how important our family was to me (Jensen, Interview, 8/2/1994).

The family, of course, has various configurations and forms in different cultures, but it is often one of the first groups with which individuals identify, as Sally so clearly indicated. And in addition, she also indicated her sense of agency and accountability within that family context. Increasingly, the LDS Church has come to recognize the family as the first teaching unit intermediary between the individual member and the face-to-face church groupings of branch, ward, and stake. Her story also notes the experiential impact of the physical demonstration of the ski-pole-and-string metaphor for showing the effects of individual agency within the family group.

The Kent Mickelsen Family

I joined a number of different families for their family home evenings. Among them was the Mickelsen family—Kent and Arleen, and their four children—Charlie (12), Megan (ten), Stephanie (eight), and Ashley (six). We gathered for a supper of hamburgers and potato casserole with broccoli on the side, hot home-baked rolls, and water, which is the ubiquitous Mormon beverage for meals and in-between snacks, except at church dinners where red or green punch is served. Prayer was offered by Kent, followed by mealtime chatter about the day's events while we passed the bowls of hot food, heaped our plates, and ate our fill. The children then cleared the dishes under Kent's supervision while Arleen collected the materials she had prepared for the evening's lesson.

When Arleen was ready, she called us together around the piano. As the ward pianist, she took her place comfortably at the piano and the family sang the evening's opening hymn with interest and fervor. We adjourned to the living room. Charlie read the pre-selected scripture, and Megan offered a prayer.

The evening program was conducted by Arleen using an instructional outline from one of the church's family home evening activity manuals. This night's program focused on the four main elements of prayer. Prayer, we learned (though I think everyone there already knew), should (1) be addressed to Heavenly Father, (2) offer him thanks for the good things of the day received from his bounty, (3) ask him for any blessings that were desired, and (4) be concluded in the name of Jesus Christ. Our activity was to show the different kinds of things for which to give thanks, and the kinds of blessings to request, by identifying illustrative cutout pictures. The prayer form is a simple schema learned as the most common mode of communication to Heavenly Father by everyone in the church.

Each of us received a handful of cutouts to sort and paste onto large red and blue poster boards titled "Thank you" and "Please Bless." Taking turns, we added cutouts to each poster and were then asked to describe in our own words what each picture was about. In all of this there was evident good fun, silly comments, requests from Kent and Arleen for the children to pay attention or prompts for more information, and occasional flouting by the children. When the cutouts were exhausted, Arleen again summarized the four elements of prayer as the standard LDS structure. We then gathered around the piano again; this time Kent sat at the keyboard to accompany the concluding song, followed by Stephanie's prayer (in fourfold structure, of course). Arleen and the children went to prepare a home-made ice cream dessert, while Kent and I began a discussion of his role as ward mission leader.

Several patterns are worth noting in this family home evening besides the important fact that family members gather weekly in a society that otherwise draws them apart into separate niches and activities. First, even when children serve as the presenters, these are adult-directed activities, but aimed toward inclusive participation, especially of the children. Sometimes the evening is used for a family council to discuss common issues (chores, vacations, conflicts) and make decisions that affect the whole family (sometimes including how those decisions will be made). Without children at home, spouses can arrange a date. A single person might use the evening to work on a genea-logical project or read a book. The church has no fixed rules for family home evening, but it encourages families to experiment in finding ways to use time together, and that time together constitutes a second observation about family home evening: Time together is important. Third, lessons and activities often explicitly direct attention to specific aspects of the belief system, even though that is incidental to the fact of family gathering as a value orientation stress-ing thoughtfulness, loving kindness, and consideration of others, as well as togetherness and learning.

McKenzie's Identity as an LDS

McKenzie Mayne's baptism and confirmation marked a rite of passage from her identity as a child of record born in the covenant to a new identity as a cov-enanted member of the church. At eight years old, she had already had a sub-stantial number of occasions to learn what it meant to be an LDS, including that she had the agency to make this choice. Along the way, like many others growing up in the church, she learned of the benevolent though authoritarian rule of Heavenly Father, the meaning of baptism and confirmation, the struc-ture of priesthood authority, and the construction of prayer as divine-human communication. She experienced the loving embrace of her family, the inter-est and support of her ward, and the consideration of stake (and neighbor-hood) teachers and friends. Family home evening was part of this learning process and identity formation.

McKenzie's identity as an LDS therefore was grounded in the family, but also supported in the ward teaching program. The task of becoming an LDS fell upon the individual, but it was supported by the family, the ward and stake communities, and the church as a whole, which sought to undergird the ear-lier and subsequent stages of lifelong learning. In the church, these stages begin in infancy and continue through the LDS Church's teaching program at all age levels.

4

I Am a Child of God

A NEWBORN CHILD is the initial responsibility of its parents but soon becomes an object of the church's interest as well. This occurs through the naming and blessing ordinance by which the infant becomes a child of record. From birth to 18 months, the infant accompanies its mother, father, and other family members to weekly ward sacrament meetings and monthly fast and testimony meetings. Babies are ubiquitous at Sunday Mormon ward gatherings, receiving considerable solicitous attention. And in all public places, it is common to see fathers holding and rocking the youngest ones present.

Primary is the earliest teaching program in the church, for children from age 18 months to 11 years and consumes an hour and 45 minutes of each Sunday's three-hour period devoted to church teaching and worship programs. In the course of those first 11 years, the content of belief is laid down in primary classes as a foundation on which subsequent roles, callings, and understandings will be built. The main division in primary occurs between junior primary (for children age four to seven) and senior primary (for children age eight to 11), with age eight (as the age of the beginning of formal accountability) marking this division. In a formal church-directed way, the children will be introduced to God as Heavenly Father, Jesus Christ as his literal son, the Holy Ghost, and Satan as among the immortals with whom humans have to contend, even as they learn of prayer, their own agency, and wider stories of revelation, scripture, and church history.

This teaching and learning process begins as a child enters primary through the nursery at 18 months and then takes up the formal learning program at age three in the first class, known as "Sunbeams." From that point on, until they reach age 12, the children will join in acquiring the knowledge, material manifestations, values, and actions that make them Latter-day Saints (LDS), or more popularly, Mormons.

Primary: Organization and Content

Barbara Jessee was called as primary president shortly after I arrived in the Crystal Heights second ward, replacing Sally Jensen and her two counselors who were released after several years in their callings. Sister Jessee's two counselors were Cathy Ipsen and Kim Brightwell, and these three young women constituted the ward primary presidency. In addition, Suki Cannon served as secretary; the chorister was Lisa Fuller, with Liane Bell serving as pianist.

The primary presidency was the leadership group responsible for directing and coordinating a team of 17 teachers in the Crystal Heights second ward, who taught about 95 children distributed across the age grades, including nursery (18 months until three years old, with three-year olds becoming the class of "Sunbeams"); junior primary (attending classes identified with the acronym CTR—"Choose the Right"); and senior primary (attending classes identified as "Valiant").

The administrative organization of the ward primary was mirrored at the stake level with oversight and supervisory responsibilities distributed among a stake primary president with two counselors and a three-person board. Clearly, the ward presidency was action-oriented toward teachers and ultimately the children, while the stake leaders held supervisory and training roles. This structure of primary is church-wide, modified very little even in the mission fields, among districts and branches not yet grown to stakes and wards (see the *Handbook, Primary* 1998:230–234).

Primary is also highly visible church-wide as a general church auxiliary. The first presidency of the church calls three women to serve as the general presidency of primary, who will teach and advise on all matters having to do with children. In addition, a general board is called to serve with the general primary presidency, providing resource personnel to assist in teaching and training local primary leaders throughout the church as invited by world regional area presidencies (*Handbook, Primary* 1998:229).

This hierarchy of leadership seeks to direct and teach the church's gospel to the children of the church who attend the local ward primary. Primary, therefore, provides the main linkage between the generations, next to the family, in the cognitive, organizational, and emotional exchange of "culture as given" (van der Elst 2003) that will lead the children to "culture as choice" beginning with baptism and confirmation.

Very early in my participation among the Crystal Heights second ward, I was able to attend a monthly planning meeting of the primary presidency and board as an observer, including teachers Dorie Olds and Shannon Pyne, along with Steven Tingey, first counselor in the bishopric. One of Tingey's assignments was as advisor to the primary presidency group. Part of this meeting was devoted to planning for the all-primary program that was to be presented in the ward sacrament meeting sometime in October, in which every child would have a part.

Children's Initial Spiritual Awareness

In one of my earliest interviews, I spoke with Cathy Ipsen, in her role as a counselor in the primary presidency, about what children know as they enter the church's teaching program, what they have learned from their homes. I was therefore interested to know how Mormon children were raised. How do their parents see them? How do they see themselves? As the church *Handbook* notes, parents bear the "primary responsibility for the welfare of their children" (see D&C 68:25–28). The bishopric and primary leaders and teachers support but do not replace parents in this responsibility (*Handbook, Primary* 1998:229). My initial questions concerned what the church calls pre-mortal existence (the preexistence) as the first estate or the initial condition of all spirit beings who have entered upon mortal life:

MEL (M): Talk with me about how kids are raised and when and how they come to understand things like being a "spirit child of God" in the pre-existence, and then through birth enter into mortality. How do children acquire this spiritual sense?

CATHY (C): I think they already have a sense of the Spirit when they're born. I believe they're very close to our Heavenly Father. . . . And it's said there's a veil drawn so that they can't remember, but I have heard stories of little children who have remembered some things about [the preexistence] like a family member or [that] . . . they saw a picture [of Jesus] down here on earth when they were maybe two or three and would say—"I know him, I've met him"—you know, something like that. So, I think they're already spiritually minded when they're born. And I think if, as they grow up, they're in the church, then [that] just reinforces what they already feel inside. And I think if they're not, if they're born into a family that's not [in the church], then I think they just learn another way. [Ipsen, Interview, 1994.]

For Cathy, the preexistence is part of the taken-for-granted structure of existence, and she finds evidence in her own and other mothers' experiences with their children that those children have "remembered some things" from the preexistence, and that growing up in the church may reinforce "what they already feel inside," while children from non-church backgrounds may "just learn in another way."

M: So, you believe that the knowledge [that they're a child of God] is already there.

c: I think it is. I mean I don't think they already know, "Oh, this is the plan for me; this is what I'm supposed to do down here on earth." I'm just saying I think they have a little bit of spirituality within them, because their—our bodies are patterned after Heavenly Father's, and our spirits come from him. And so I think [their spiritual awareness is] already present when they're born. I'm not saying they know everything, because they don't.

Clearly, Cathy acknowledges the limitations of what the youngest children may know in a cognitive sense while affirming by analogy "a little bit of spirituality within them" based on the fact that "our bodies are patterned after Heavenly Father's, [and] our spirits come from him."

m: Is it kind of like intuition?
c: Yeah. I think it's there. But I think they need guidance. One of the biggest things we're told is that up until the time they're eight years old, they're not accountable for mistakes they make. And in psychology I learned that they may do things that are wrong, but they really don't understand [the difference, for instance,] between truth and telling a lie. And so I think Heavenly Father has arranged the plan so that they don't get baptized until age eight, so they have that [earlier period of time] for their growing period—to really learn and practice making choices and really getting ready to know what it means, what Heavenly Father expects of us. So none of that do I think they know. But I think innately there's a spiritual sensitivity to them.

Then I pushed forward in our conversation from parents to teachers and from the notion of a preexisting spiritual base to filling in the unknown part in the course of mortality:

m: So, part of the task of a parent, and the task of teachers is to draw out and build upon a preexisting sensitivity or intuition, from a spiritual base that's already there, and to help the child fill in that unknown part [during] mortality. Because the veil has been brought down in the process of going from the preexistence....
c: Right. From preexistence to earth.
m: And so birth means that the veil really closes off all of the knowledge that they had, though they have the intuition of being spirit children of God.
c: Right. And to me, when you teach children that, it makes sense to them. And when they hear stories in the Bible that [God] created Adam and

Eve, and we came after them, you know, to me the whole plan just kind of…unfolds and it makes sense, and it's logical.

Clearly, we had reached a common understanding about the effect of the veil on the preexistent spirituality of children at the time of their birth. And for Cathy, this effect is logical and makes sense as part of a larger plan. But it also causes further reflection about the questions that arise later in life:

c: And maybe that's helped me. I'm looking at it from the perspective of that's how I've always been taught and told. Whereas I've often wondered, if I wasn't born a Mormon would I ever become one? Would I just think if someone told me the stories [of the church] later in life, would I just think they're really off-base, or up in the night? I mean, it's hard to know. And I think every child has to go through [that questioning]. Even if you're born in the church, you still go through this process of [asking]— is it true, do I believe it? And the big thing is when either you go away to school or when you get married, you're on your own. It's up to you to decide—am I going to go to church, am I going to be active, am I going to do the things that I'm supposed to do, or do I believe that they're true?

(Ipsen, Interview, 1995)

Age Three: Sunbeams

Cathy and I continued our conversation about primary in the Crystal Heights second ward and Highland stake. The age-graded segments of primary begin with nursery, using the teaching manual *Primary 1, I Am a Child of God* (1994).

c: Starting at eighteen months, we sing with the children. They do have a lesson, very rudimentary. And they start out basically just learning about the world around them, the trees, the earth, how Heavenly Father created the earth, how he created our bodies. It's all very basic. And then, when they turn three, they go to the first class that's actually in primary—Sunbeams.

I was very curious.

m: Are the kids at age three able to talk about being the spirit children of God? Does that make sense to them then?
c: They know that they're children of our Heavenly Father. We don't really get into the body and the spirit. I mean, we tell them that they're children of

God and there's the song we sing in primary, "I Am a Child of God." And my two-year old sings that song by heart; he knows the whole thing. So, I think they know—it's hard to say "know." That's a hard terminology to use for a two-year old. How do you know what they really know or what they're just repeating?

M: Some of it, sure, they're just repeating.

C: But the more they repeat it, then the more they come to understand it. So, I think having my child sing "I Am a Child of God"—yeah, I think if you ask him—where did you come from?—that he'd be able to tell you, for the most part.

(Ipsen, Interview, 1995)

Opening Exercises

Beginning at age three, then, the schedule of activities within primary repeats itself week after week as a pattern of opening exercises, sharing time for junior primary (ages four to seven) or senior primary (ages eight to 11), followed by separate age-graded class periods, and ending with closing exercises. The Sunbeams follow the pattern of junior primary. The variations are in content, level of participation, and the use of different teaching manuals for the nursery, junior, and senior age-grade levels. On one of the first Sundays that I attended primary, the opening exercises (lasting about 15 minutes) included a favorite opening song, one of the first songs in the *Children's Songbook* (1989:4) led by Sister Lisa Fuller, with initial words as follows:

> *I lived in heaven a long time ago, it is true;*
> *Lived there and loved there with people I know. So did you.*
>
> Children's Songbook 1989:4

This song is a capsule summary of LDS belief, geared for use by the youngest children, and so sets several of the central themes of the teaching program of primary: (1) our human goal in this earthly life is to return to our Heavenly Father; (2) we lived with him and our elder brother Jesus in heaven a long time ago [the preexistence]; and (3) Jesus was chosen to conquer evil and death, and to show us the way to that home in heaven again, "where Father is waiting for me." The song includes just a hint of opposition to this beautiful plan from "another who sought for the honor divine" that went to Jesus as Heavenly Father's chosen one. In cognitive terms, this song introduces a goal schema of a hoped-for return to our heavenly home (see D'Andrade 1992).

Following the song, one child read a scripture and another offered a prayer, each coming to the front of the room and using the microphone. From the very earliest ages, children are encouraged in public performance and group leadership roles of which this is one example. These activities were followed by words of welcome and announcements from Sister Jessee, who spoke with special emphasis on how reverent the children were. In fact, reverence had been emphasized several times as the children entered the room, with admonitions to "please sit up and fold your arms," or by direct reference to imitate one of the children whose reverent decorum was used as an example to the others. Because guests were present besides me, and someone had a birthday that week, a welcome song and a birthday song were sung next. Then a message was given by Steve Tingey, introduced by Sister Jessee as the first counselor in the bishopric, explaining and underscoring his special role in the ward; after Brother Tingey spoke, another song was sung. Then, Cameron MacLaclan, about age seven, gave a two to three minute talk on the heavenly plan, with assistance from one of the leaders who bent down beside him and helped him with quietly whispered prompts. He had prepared his talk at home on this previously assigned topic. Finally, a song to conclude these opening exercises was sung, and the senior primary children were dismissed for their classes, and the junior primary children plus the three-year-old Sunbeams remained for a period of sharing time. This division of primary between junior and senior age groups obviously reflects the fact that baptism and confirmation occur at age eight and essentially divides the children into those who are preparing for baptism and those who are already baptized and confirmed (or are eligible for these ordinances).

Sharing Time

Sharing time (about 35 minutes) was divided between a lesson, on this occasion presented by teacher Shannon Pyne, and learning a further series of songs. Sister Pyne's lesson focused on the theme: "I feel peace when I do the right." Holding a picture of a kneeling child in an upright posture, with the child's arms folded across her chest and eyes closed in prayer, Sister Pyne talked about the "good, warm feeling inside" that a child has "when you know what Heavenly Father wants you to do and when you are following his plan." She explained, "When we are following his plan, rather than doing what others might tell us to do, then we will feel peace in our hearts."

She distributed a series of cards to different class groups that depicted common problems that might arise in ordinary, everyday situations—for example, a small group of children were shown making fun of a minority child and another showed someone stealing a candy bar in a store. The children were asked to discuss "the right way to act in accord with Heavenly Father's wishes" in each of these instances, as opposed to doing what might be popular. After having discussed the problem in small groups, these social situations were then considered in the larger group to further assess possible right responses.

In this instance, the point of the exercise was to distinguish Heavenly Father's (and the church's) norms (or expectations) for good behavior from what might be popular or worldly norms held by others, and to choose right responses in accord with Heavenly Father's wishes; it also gave the children the experience of entering and participating in a group discussion.

The lesson was concluded by asking the children to color a line image of Jesus in the posture of prayer, again emphasizing the feeling of inner peace that comes from doing good. In cognitive terms, this exercise introduced and examined the church's schema for "choose the right," which involves (1) assessing the situation, (2) listening or praying for Heavenly Father's guidance, (3) seeking to sense the inner presence of the Holy Spirit, and then (4) acting according to Heavenly Father's (and the church's) norms without reference to popular opinion. What becomes clear to an observer is not so much the absence of opinion, but rather the identification of whose opinion counts—namely, the church's in the name of Heavenly Father, as interpreted by the teacher. The "good, warm feeling" inside is therefore associated with the proper alignment of one's own and Heavenly Father's desire for proper social action.

Sacred History as Prophetic Dispensations

The children were also making preparations for a coming group performance in a sacrament meeting. Therefore, Sister Fuller continued sharing time by teaching several new verses of the song "Follow the Prophet" to be used in that performance. One child after another was invited to come forward to choose a colored paper on the reverse side of which was the name of a prophet; the child was then given a picture of that prophet to hold before the assembly, while all the children together reviewed and sang the lyrics of a new verse about that prophet. On this particular morning, the prophets Adam, Daniel, Jonah, Samuel, and Moses were all reviewed as prophet leaders of different "dispensations" in the world's history. The world's history, described in terms of sacred history, is divided into different dispensations, each marked by the presence of a particular prophet. Obviously, there is a sub-schema for each of the prophets with associated meanings, and central roles for Adam as the "first man," Jesus whose earthly life represented the "meridian of time," and Joseph

Smith, whose prophetic career introduced the "fullness of time"—our present age in the modern world. This "dispensational history," marked by prophetic careers, is one basis for the prophetic authority and power by which the voice of God has been heard in preceding eras. Prophetic authority therefore serves as the interpretive ground for "sacred history," the story of God's dealing with humankind in the past, the present, and the anticipated future.

At the end of this lesson and song period, the junior primary students were dismissed class by class to go to their individual classrooms for an additional 40 minutes of instruction with their own teachers. About five minutes later, the senior primary children returned to the main assembly room for their period of sharing time, which was structured in a way that was very similar to what we have just described among the juniors. Thus, junior and senior primary children rotated sharing time and classroom learning, experiencing varying group settings, before everyone returned for the closing exercises.

Teacher Preparation and Curricular Content

Leslie Vernon, primary president in the Country Club ward, Phoenix East stake, conducted her first sharing time while I was there; it was focused on the church's 13 *Articles of Faith*. These articles were a set of basic beliefs written in 1842 by the Prophet Joseph Smith, who sent them in a letter to John Wentworth, a local newspaper editor. They are now canonized as a form of scriptural creed in the Pearl of Great Price. Leslie noted:

> I struggled all week as to what I was going to do with the children to reinforce the article of faith that we've been working on this month. With my typical insomnia, I sat in my recliner and started praying about what I needed to do. About 1:30 in the morning I knew. I got out my supplies and sat at the table and made a hidden word puzzle, took it to AlphaGraphics at two in the morning and had it blown up to about 16 x 20 [inches], so the kids could search out the words. With the younger kids I cut it into sections and worked with it that way. And the kids were quiet, they were reverent, and they were participating. And this was my goal, to get all of the kids, as much as possible, participating in the activity while they're learning the *Articles of Faith*.
>
> (Vernon, Interview, 1995)

Clearly, an important emphasis in the structure of primary was group activity where the children shared sets of activities. They also took turns as individuals and as classes in leading some activities, even as they responded to the adult supervision and the leader presentations that were guiding them. And they went to their classrooms in age-graded, mixed-gender small groups for learning under the close supervision of a particular teacher. And most teachers took their roles and responsibilities seriously. It was widely remarked among members that callings in primary were among the most enriching experiences in the church because the teachers were guiding the next generation. At the same time, primary teaching was frequently a first calling for a newly married woman or convert (including men), and turnover was high. In the case of absences, teachers were expected to arrange for their own substitutes, with occasional slips in this responsibility.

Children entered a new age-grade class on January 1 after they had reached a certain birthday. Sally Jensen (Interview, 1994) illustrated how this worked in the case of her three-year-old. "You have to be three before you leave nursery," she explained. "My little boy's birthday is June 26. He turned three last June [1994]. So, in January of 1995 he became a Sunbeam [the youngest age group]." Sally continued, "The system of change in age grades used to follow the school year, but when the church became more worldwide, the church leaders adopted the year-to-year system—January 1 to December 31. That's how it works now." Clearly, the increasingly visible worldwide scope of the church was being marked by the transition to annual age-graded change in assignments to primary classes.

Curriculum Materials in Correlation

New curriculum materials were being introduced in primary during the period of my research. In the new system, children were grouped according to their age on January 1, and advancement occurred with the beginning of the new calendar year, as shown in table 4.1. This new age-graded system and the publication of new teaching manuals have allowed for a standardized curriculum around the world, with all classes everywhere beginning on January 1; this also simplifies publication as teaching manuals are translated into more and more languages. Nursery and three-year-olds followed a single manual (*Primary 1*), and all children ages four through seven years (junior primary) followed one manual during even years (*Primary 2*) and a second manual during odd years (*Primary 3*), and then repeated. The junior class theme, "Choose the Right," symbolized as CTR, has given rise to an extensive lore in Mormon popular culture. Many children, for instance, are given a CTR ring as an important memento of these childhood years, which is then treasured into adulthood or passed on to younger siblings.

Children eight through 11 years (senior primary) follow a set of manuals that rotate annually in correlation with the four-year cycle of topics followed

Table 4.1. **Age and Class Structure of Primary.**

Age on January 1st	Class name	Teaching manual title
Nursery		
Eighteen months to three years	Sunbeam-Nursery	*Primary 1*
Three-year-olds	Sunbeam 4	*Primary 1*
Junior Primary (all 4–7-year-olds use the same manual on odd and even years)		
Four-year-olds	CTR 5	*Primary 3* (odd)
Five-year-olds	CTR 6	*Primary 2* (even)
Six-year-olds	CTR 7	*Primary 3* (odd)
Seven-year-olds	CTR 8	*Primary 2* (even)
Senior Primary (teaching manuals rotate for all 8–11-year-olds annually)		
Eight-year-olds	Valiant 9	*Primary 4* (Book of Mormon)
Nine-year-olds	Valiant 10	*Primary 5* (D&C/ Church History)
Ten-year-olds	Valiant 11	*Primary 6* (Old Testament)
Eleven-year-olds	Valiant 12	*Primary 7* (New Testament)

Notes: Instructions for priesthood and auxiliary leaders on primary 1996: 4 pages.

The class member after the class name corresponds to the age of the children on the subsequent December 31.

As the church has increasingly become a worldwide institution, the old academic class structure that followed the school year gave way to the system of annual class changes on subsequent years ending on December 31, and the next class year beginning on January 1, with a student's birthday associated with the annual class interval. The class name and teaching manual follow the same pattern, which means the whole church, worldwide, is on the same teaching and attendance schedule.

in the adult gospel doctrine course—Old Testament, New Testament, Book of Mormon, and Doctrine and Covenants/Church History. This standardization of grades and curriculum was part of a church-wide effort to simplify and rationalize the instructional effort around the globe, coordinating the content of lessons for older children, the young men and young women, and the older adults, while giving teachers at each age level, including primary, more latitude in adapting materials to the students they teach. Therefore, wherever in the world members of the church may go as new residents, converts, or visitors, they will find the same basic age-graded structure and curriculum content that they would encounter in their home ward.

The Heavenly Father and Child of God Relationship

The first lesson in *Primary 1* (1994) for the youngest children has as its stated purpose "to help each child understand that we are spirit children of Heavenly Father, who knows us and loves us" (Lesson 1:1). The implicit contrast with being spirit children is that we are also mortal (biophysical DNA) children of our parents. Among the suggested activities for learning who we humans are as spirit children is one in which the teacher tosses a beanbag or other soft object to them while she says: "I know a child of God named_____," and the children are prompted to add their own name to complete the sentence (Lesson 1:1). This activity is repeated with each child as the others look on. It is an activity that aims to establish an identity relationship based upon personal knowledge, using personal names, and connecting each young learner to God (who is identified as Heavenly Father) through the kin-relation of "Heavenly Father to spirit child." This father/child relationship is specified as meaning that "Heavenly Father is the father of our spirits, and we are his spirit children. We don't remember living with Heavenly Father before we came to earth, but we know we are his spirit children because we read it in the scriptures" (Lesson 1:1).

Further, the father/child relationship means "that Heavenly Father loves each one of us very much," and that "He knows our names and all about us. He knows what makes us happy and what makes us sad. He knows what is best for each of us (*Primary 1*, Lesson 1:2). This father/child relationship also means that "just as animals grow up to be like their parents, we will grow up to be like our parents," and by analogy, because "Heavenly Father is the father of our spirits, so [too] we can grow to be like him." This lesson of future similarity is made very explicit by attitudes that can be put into action: "Heavenly Father is loving, good, and kind, and he wants to help us. When we are loving, good, and kind, we are being like Heavenly Father" (Lesson 1:2). In this "family context," the absence of any reference to Heavenly Mother is notable.

Finally, this father/child relationship means that "Heavenly Father has important work for us to do." To emphasize that the relationship carries with it special duties and responsibilities, the teacher tells the story of Moses. As an infant, Moses was hidden in bulrushes along the bank of the Nile River to protect him from the Egyptian pharaoh who had issued a death threat against all Jewish infants. He was saved by Pharaoh's daughter and grew up to become "one of Heavenly Father's important helper's, a prophet" (Lesson 1:2).

Verses of scripture reporting this story are read to the children, both from the Old Testament (Exodus 2:1–10) and from the Pearl of Great Price (Moses 1:4, 6), in which Heavenly Father is portrayed as identifying Moses as his child and assigning him "work" to do. This work is identified as bringing "the Israelites out of the land of Egypt, where they were treated cruelly, into another land, where Moses taught them Heavenly Father's commandments" (Lesson 1:2). Again, the teacher is told to invite each child to come to the front of the class, and to help each one repeat the key phrase from scripture using the words attributed to Heavenly Father toward Moses, but substituting his or her own name: "I have a work for thee, (child's name), my son (or daughter)" (Lesson 1:2) Thus, both individual name recognition by Heavenly Father and personal responsibility for the children are made explicit as experiential components of a lesson teaching children about their relationship with Heavenly Father. In addition, stories from the Old Testament and the Book of Mormon as parallel scriptures are used as equally authoritative sources for identifying duties and responsibilities in this father/child relationship.

In the next lesson, Heavenly Father is portrayed as a "real person, with a perfected body of flesh and bones, and that we are made in his image." The difference between a real person and an image of a person is developed by asking each child to draw a picture of himself or herself and noting the difference between themselves as actually possessing bodies and the picture. The point of this exercise is that "[w]e can see pictures of Heavenly Father, but they are not the real Heavenly Father. The real Heavenly Father has [an immortal] body of flesh and bones" (Lesson 2:4), and we have bodies made in his image; thus, he looks like us, and we look like him.

Furthermore, the parent/child relationship is then employed to introduce Jesus Christ as Heavenly Father's son, and to point out that Jesus looks like Heavenly Father. In turn, "because we are spirit children of Heavenly Father, we also look like him" (Lesson 2:4). A further activity associated with this point is to have the children take turns looking at themselves in a mirror, or at another child, and to "name a part of the body he or she sees, such as arms, legs, eyes, or ears." The teacher then explains that "Heavenly Father and Jesus also have those body parts" (Lesson 2:4). Further, the teacher explains that "we know what Heavenly Father and Jesus look like because some prophets (leaders of the church) have seen Heavenly Father and Jesus (in visions) and have written about them in the scriptures" (Lesson 2:4). The point being established here is the physical body-like similarity between these members of deity and us mortals, as well as our kin-like relationships to them, and that prophets have testified to these similarities (as depicted in a painted rendition of Joseph Smith's "First Vision").

Heavenly Father's Plan

Lessons three and four are about Heavenly Father's plan for us and prayer as the means of our communication with him. Lesson four involves the space-time context within which the most important relationships of the LDS worldview occur, including the human spirits' presence in the preexistence and their continuing relationship to Heavenly Father. The lesson unfolds in the form of an abbreviated story of what it means to be Heavenly Father's spirit children who were sent "to live on the earth" and that he "wants us to return to him someday" (Lesson 3:7). The teacher is instructed "[t]o help each child understand that we lived with Heavenly Father as spirit children before we came to earth and that we can live with him again after this life" (Lesson 3:7).

The first task then is to consider what it means to be alive as "spirit children of Heavenly Father." The possession of a spirit self is the condition for anything being alive, which the teacher can demonstrate by placing a doll on one of the chairs used by the children and asking the children "to stand up, turn around, and sit back down." The obvious questions are: "Why didn't the doll stand up?" and "Why can you stand up?" And the answer is that the doll is not alive, but the children in the room are, which is interpreted to mean that "[t]hey each have a spirit inside their body that makes them alive so they can see, hear, stand, move, think, and talk" (Lesson 3:7). The spirit is therefore the vitalizing center of selfhood that vitalizes the body so all of its parts work. Dolls do not have spirits, except in make-believe. They are not alive. We are alive and therefore have spirits. Furthermore, the teacher explains, a spirit "looks like a physical body but does not have flesh and bones" (Lesson 3:7).

Second, the children are then told by the teacher that each of them "lived with Heavenly Father before being born on earth, and [that] he or she is a spirit child who is loved by Heavenly Father" (Lesson 3:7). The teacher explains that out of his love, Heavenly Father prepared a plan for his spirit children before the world was created, and "[a]ll of us, our parents, and our brothers and sisters were there" as spirits in the preexistence (Lesson 3:8). The plan also has several more components. One part is that the plan included the creation of the earth. The teaching manual proposes that "[u]nder Heavenly Father's direction, Jesus Christ created the earth for us. We were sent here to be born here and receive a physical body" (Lesson 3:8). Again, the experiential aspect of this teaching involves asking the children to feel their own bones, skin, and muscles, with the reminder that "our spirits inside our bodies give us life, but we cannot see or touch our spirits. [Only] our physical bodies can be seen and touched.... [I]t is a great blessing to have a physical body" (Lesson 3:8).

Furthermore, because Heavenly Father wants each of us to return to live with him, and with "our parents, and all our families" when our earth life is finished, he has established certain things for us to do that will make this possible. The teacher is instructed to explain "that to live with Heavenly Father and Jesus again, we must be baptized and keep all the commandments," and "that the scriptures teach us about Heavenly Father and Jesus and what they want us to do." Among other things, Heavenly Father "wants us to love our families, be unselfish, go to church, receive the sacrament, pray morning and night, have family prayer and family home evening, be baptized, be confirmed and receive the Holy Ghost, be married in the temple, learn about the prophets, and become like Heavenly Father and Jesus" (Lesson 3:8). This series of attitudes, actions, and aims is the cultural program of the church in an abbreviated form.

Children are thus introduced to several critically important ideas and concepts within the church's worldview—(1) that "persons" (or souls) "like me" (the teacher says) are spirits with bodies, (2) that their spirit is distinct from their body but is integrated with it and vitalizes it after birth, (3) that their spirit existed with Heavenly Father and Jesus prior to the creation of the earth, (4) that Jesus created the earth, (5) that the aim and goal of earthly life is for our spirit self to return to live with Heavenly Father and Jesus, (6) that it will be newly clothed in an immortal body, and (7) that certain conditions must be met to attain this goal.

These elements are presented and developed as experientially grounded logical and psychological concomitants of the way things are from the point of view that is being established within the cultural worldview. One may wonder how much of this framework a child at age three to four grasps, but clearly a set of attitudes and experiences is being developed, along with a vocabulary and set of concepts that will become freighted with further meanings through successive teachings in primary and beyond. The groundwork of the worldview is being laid, which may be conceived as the farthest reaching (or most general) frame of reference within which the world as presently known from an LDS perspective can be described.

Prayer as Conversation with Heavenly Father

As in the family home evening lesson introduced earlier, prayer is again highlighted in a primary lesson as a means of communication with Heavenly

Father while we are on earth, and that Jesus taught us to pray by folding our arms, bowing our heads, and closing our eyes (Lesson 4:10). These are characteristic elements of the LDS posture for prayer, particularly the folding of arms across one's chest, which may be combined with sitting, standing, or kneeling with one's head bowed. Prayer itself involves the four elements previously noted: to begin by (1) saying "Dear Heavenly Father" as a form of address, then (2) thanking him for the blessings he sends, followed by (3) humbly asking for things that are needed, and (4) concluding with "In the name of Jesus Christ, Amen." The point of the lesson, aside from the mechanics, is that Heavenly Father listens to our prayers; prayer is the primary personal means of communication with him, spirit to spirit.

The teacher explains "that we can pray to Heavenly Father whenever we want; the most common times are when we wake up and when we go to bed, at mealtimes, with our families, and when we need special help" (Lesson 4:10). The teacher may also remind the children "that when we pray we are talking to Heavenly Father, who loves us and listens to us" (Lesson 4:12).

Jesus Christ as the Son of Heavenly Father

The following two lessons present and focus on Jesus Christ as a separate being and the literal son of Heavenly Father, and that both Heavenly Father and Jesus Christ express their love for each of us. Again, an experiential demonstration in the classroom is a planned part of learning. With the approval of the primary president, the teacher is instructed to "invite the father of one of the children to come to class to talk about his child when he or she was a baby. Ask him to bring photos and a favorite toy, if possible. Encourage him to express love for his child" (Lesson 5:13).

At the beginning of class, the teacher invites the visiting father's child to introduce his or her father to the class, and asks the father to tell the children about his child and "each child to tell something about his or her father, such as the color of his hair or his occupation" (Lesson 5:13). Then the teacher explains that each of us "has two fathers: an earthly father and a Heavenly Father. Our earthly father is the father of our physical bodies. Heavenly Father is the father of the spirits inside our bodies. Jesus has only one father, because Heavenly Father is the father of Jesus' spirit and his physical body. That is why Jesus is called the Son of God" (Lesson 5:13). Thus, similarity to Jesus and now also difference are introduced. Jesus, in particular, is someone special, who has only one father while we have two.

Pictures and scripture readings are used to add further dimensions to this basic narrative, including a nativity scene with Mary, the mother of Jesus, and

Joseph, "a good man chosen by Heavenly Father to take care of Mary and Jesus" (Lesson 5:13). The story is elaborated further with a picture of Jesus as a young boy going to the temple "because he loved Heavenly Father and wanted to teach people about him" (Lesson 5:14). Another picture shows Jesus being baptized by John the Baptist "because he loved Heavenly Father and wanted to obey him. Jesus also wanted to set a good example for us" (Lesson 5:14). The relationships and themes of love, obedience, service, and being a good example are thus introduced within LDS understandings as important values associated with Jesus. Further, an older Jesus (after his death and resurrection) is portrayed as blessing both Israelite children in the ancient Near East (Mark 10:13–16) and Nephite children in America (3 Nephi 17:11–12, 21–24). Experientially, each child is invited to look in a mirror held by the teacher, who says: "This is (child's name), and Heavenly Father and Jesus love (child's name) very much" (Lesson 6:16).

Throughout each of these lessons, and as part of the continuing process of learning in primary, teachers are encouraged always to "bear your testimony that Heavenly Father and Jesus Christ live and that they love each of us. Share your feelings of gratitude for the many blessings Heavenly Father and Jesus have given you" (Lesson 6:16). Thus, in addition to experiential learning and the building of spiritual awareness within each child, the teacher bears witness to his or her own spiritual awareness and beliefs.

The Holy Ghost

A central issue in building a child's spiritual awareness is how they acquire and deepen their understanding and commitment to the church's way of conceiving and perceiving the world. This issue involves the experiential confirmation of personal belief to the point of being able to say "I know that something is true" and hold to that belief. Within the LDS worldview, the theory of how belief is confirmed as personal and social knowledge involves conceptions of spirit and the action and influence of the Holy Ghost as a distinct spirit and companion to Heavenly Father and Jesus Christ. Some of the elementary ideas about the Holy Ghost are introduced in the seventh lesson in *Primary 1*, the purpose of which is, at the simplest level, to "help each child understand that the Holy Ghost helps us" (Lesson 7:19).

In order to capture children's attention, the teacher whispers something in each child's ear about the Holy Ghost, such as "The Holy Ghost helps Heavenly Father and Jesus," and then asks the class "if they know who you are going to talk about today." The children are shown a picture of the Prophet Joseph Smith Jr. as a young man who is being visited by Heavenly Father and

Jesus in his first vision experience. The teacher points out that in the picture, Heavenly Father and Jesus have physical bodies that look like ours, as does Joseph Smith. He or she then explains that the Holy Ghost is like them in many ways, in that "[h]e loves us and helps us. But he does not have a physical body like Heavenly Father and Jesus. He is a Spirit so he can quietly put ideas into our minds and give us feelings of happiness and comfort" (Lesson 7:19), and sometimes of warning. Essentially, the Holy Ghost is a non-embodied spiritual messenger of Heavenly Father and Jesus, with his own role as comforter, guide, and protector.

The lesson proceeds by analogy and Socratic questioning. "When you are hurt or sad, how does your mother or father comfort you and make you feel better?" "Tell the children that Jesus knew that the disciples, his helpers, would be sad when he died, so he told them that he would ask Heavenly Father to send a comforter to help them not feel so bad." "[T]his comforter is the Holy Ghost, and he can comfort us, too. [W]hen we are sad or upset, Heavenly Father will help us by sending the Holy Ghost to comfort us." Further, "the Holy Ghost can also warn us and guide us when we need help," which is illustrated by a life-story event recounted (in Lesson 7:19–20) by Harold B. Lee, 11th president of the church:

> Young Harold was probably about eight years of age, or younger, when he was taken by his father to a farm some distance away. While his father worked young Harold busied himself with things around the farm yard. An old shed happened to catch his eye and attracted his attention. Beyond a fence there was a broken-down shed that looked very interesting to him. In his mind he thought of this broken-down shed as a castle that he wanted to explore, so he went to the fence and started to climb through it in order to go over to that shed. But there came a voice to him that gave this very significant command not to go over there.
>
> He looked around to see who was speaking his name. His father was way up at the other end of the field and couldn't see what Harold was doing. There was no speaker in sight. Then young Harold realized that someone that he could not see was warning him not to go over there. What was over there, he never came to know, but he also learned early that there are those spirits beyond our sight that could talk to us.
>
> (Conference Report, Mexico City Area Conference 1972, 48–49)

Instructions to the teacher tell her (or him) to explain that "sometimes the Holy Ghost whispers out loud, like he did to President Lee, but often he just gives us a feeling about what we should or should not do" (Lesson 7:20). The illustration is a personal experience narrative and assumes that most, if not all, of us have experiences of hearing an inner voice, which is here identified as the voice of the Holy Ghost who sometimes "whispers out loud." The contrast being established is between "hearing an inner voice" identified as "the voice of the Holy Ghost" and the psychological experience of "self talk," a form of inner dialogue in which we talk to ourselves (see Burns 1980:28–49; Beck 1976:24–46).

But the story is also used to suggest that the action of the Holy Ghost may not always be heard as a verbal instruction, but instead as "a feeling about what we should or should not do." Thus, attention to our bodily feelings can provide us with signals or promptings from the Holy Ghost as much as might be provided by verbal whisperings. Spirit acts upon spirit in forms of both whisperings and bodily feelings, among other ways. And as pure spirit, the Holy Ghost comforts, guides, teaches, and warns us in accord with promptings from Heavenly Father and Jesus. And President Lee's story, both in form and content, models a personal experience narrative as a form of testimony.

The teaching manual *Primary 1* lays the foundation for an understanding of the most important relationships within the LDS spiritual world, including the relationships of our spirit self (clothed in a mortal body) to Heavenly Father (a spirit being of immortal flesh and bones), Jesus Christ (his begotten son, also a spirit being of immortal flesh and bones), and the Holy Ghost (a pure spirit being). It indicates the role of prayer as a primary means of communication between us in our mortal condition and Heavenly Father, and shows that the relationship involves values of love, gratitude, happiness, obedience, and service, manifested by being a good example to others as Jesus is to us. And it asserts that we can share our experiences of these relationships and practices in the form of a personal experience narrative testimony, thereby bearing witness to others of this divine world.

The threat to these relationships and each person's own standing as a child of God is posed by another spirit being, Lucifer, who seeks to realize his own self-centered plan, for which he was cast down from heaven (without a body) along with one-third of the heavenly hosts who were his evil followers (also without bodies). Because we humans have bodies, we know that we accepted Heavenly Father's plan and that we are not, in the earthly state of things, among the followers of Lucifer. But exploring this dark side of the worldview of the LDS is not the purpose of *Primary 1*; rather, its purpose is to provide the divine inoculation against personal threats.

Instruction, based upon the manual, is highly experiential as the divine/human relationships are introduced and the identities of Heavenly Father,

Jesus Christ, and the Holy Ghost—and their attributes—are established. First, then, spiritual knowledge is experiential knowledge; our experiences of self, other, and the world provide evidence for how the LDS conceive this world to be. Second, teachers are encouraged throughout to provide personal testimony of their own spiritual experience and knowledge, which both models that experience and knowledge and also provides social support for its acquisition by the children. Third, the LDS' understanding of spiritual relationships includes a view of how personal knowledge of spiritual matters is brought to awareness and confirmed as true through the action of the Holy Ghost, in verbal whisperings and bodily feelings, among other ways.

In addition to these foundational matters, *Primary 1* also includes separate lessons, beginning with Lesson 8, about reasons for giving thanks to Heavenly Father and a range of normative interpersonal matters representing essential values. To summarize, these include giving thanks for my home and family, food and clothing, all the parts of my body, my senses and feelings, day and night, water, and all the plants and animals. Lessons on values include affirmations that I can be obedient, say I'm sorry, forgive others, be a friend, love others, be kind to animals, be a good example, be honest, and be reverent.

The foundations for spiritual growth occur both in families and in the teaching program of the church, which begins in primary and continues in different forums through the rest of a member's life. Primary is a fully didactic undertaking—to teach the ways of the church and their rationale in the linkage of the self and its behavioral environment, including the relationship between the self as spirit and other spirit selves, such as Heavenly Father, Jesus, the Holy Ghost, and other immortals (including those who have died) who are now beyond the veil separating mortality from immortality. Thus, the foundations of LDS spirituality have their beginnings both in the home and, more systematically, in primary, ensuring that knowledge is continuous from the earliest years and throughout life. Joseph Smith said, "One is saved no faster than he gets knowledge" (quoted in Joseph Fielding Smith 1958:74). And, "the glory of God is intelligence" (D&C 93:36).

5

Choose the Right

JUNIOR PRIMARY ENCOMPASSES children in the age group from four to seven years old and has as its central theme making the right choices, symbolized by CTR ("Choose the Right"). The church curriculum presents making right choices as an exercise of agency by which the individual acquires personal and social virtues using the life of Jesus Christ as a standard and example. Learning to make right choices also serves as preparation for baptism and confirmation, where identity as a member of the church is the first goal for the individual as an embodied spirit (a "self," "person," or "soul") upon reaching age eight, which is the beginning of accountability before Heavenly Father and others in the church.

The lessons of junior primary reinforce making right choices in accord with Heavenly Father's plan that all humankind, by their own efforts, should return to his celestial kingdom worthy of a kingdom of their own. The teaching manuals *Primary 2* (1995) and *Primary 3* (1994) pay particular attention to the council in Heaven and the emergence of Lucifer as an immortal, subversive force and personality among Heavenly Father's spirit children. Lucifer stands in direct opposition to his older brother Jesus as the Christ, and directs one-third of the hosts of heaven against Heavenly Father's plan. In the mortal earth life of humans, Lucifer is widely known as Satan (or the Devil), the father of lies and author of evil. Lucifer, therefore, represents a threat to every person's identity as a child of God by presenting temptations in opposition to Heavenly Father's desire.

The Spirit Self and Agency

In the worldview of Latter-day Saints (LDS), the central attribute of the spirit self is agency. Agency is both the capacity of the spirit self to choose and the fact of accountability in its exercise of choice during pre-mortal, mortal, and post-mortal experience. Choice implies the existence of alternatives among which a decision must be reached. Even seeking to avoid a decision is to make

a choice, and LDS believe that all choices have positive or negative consequences. This leads to questions: How shall right choices be made? Are there
better ones rather than worse? What constitutes a right choice, perhaps a better choice? Presented with a choice between alternatives A and B, can one
reject both in favor of creating a new alternative C? Is that what is meant by
freedom of choice?

These questions are difficult because human beings often cannot foresee all
of the consequences to which their choices will lead, or their ramifications in
the interpersonal social world as others also make their own choices. Further,
individual choices usually have social, not just individual, consequences, and
therefore affect groups, institutions, societies, and the world order at large. As
anthropologist Ward Goodenough (2003) pointed out, in the face of multiple
choices, human beings seek forms of direction and guidance by learning from
one another over time. And as members of society, we humans often grant to
political institutions of governance and law the authority to limit our choices
for the sake of the common good. Such institutions may command our allegiance and activity insofar as we recognize their legitimacy. It is not surpris-
ing, then, that we will often turn to other people for guidance, advice, and
feedback based on their experience, which is how a shared culture comes into
focus. And our shared values and goals will certainly enter into our choices,
both individual and social.

The teaching manuals *Primary 2* (1995) and *Primary 3* (1994) are each
used twice during a child's progression through the church's junior primary
program. Several topics are woven into these lessons that depend on the
quasi-logical connections between making choices, awareness of social norms
regarding what is expected, good, or right behavior, the acquisition of certain
personal and social virtues, and individual awareness of consequences (blessings or penalties) for following or violating social norms. These themes are
presented within the framework of Heavenly Father's plan (the plan of salvation) involving Heavenly Father, Jesus Christ, the Holy Ghost, and Lucifer,
along with other immortals in relation to human individuals, families, the
church, and society (*Primary 2*, 1995, 3:11–15; *Primary 3*, 1994, 2:4–8).[1]

Teaching in Primary as a Church Calling

Teachers in primary are called to their teaching responsibility by the bishopric
and are usually set apart with a bishop's blessing. Susan Wade, one of the

---

1. The full citation is the book/manual title, date of publication, lesson number, pages:
Primary 2, 1995, 3:11–15; *Primary 3*, 1994, 2:4–8.

teachers in Country Club ward, Phoenix East, told me how she felt empowered when set apart in a calling like primary, as opposed to simply being called without being set apart under a priesthood blessing. She explained:

> When you get a calling, you're set apart. Now, I've had callings in the church where I've accepted the calling, but was never set apart in it, and I've had callings where I'm sustained and set apart immediately. The callings in which I had not been set apart had been horrible. I was unable to do them [properly] and by nature I tend to be a very organized person....I just couldn't function. My family would argue, the kids would get on each other's nerves, my husband and I would argue, big time. We would get into arguments, not necessarily related to the calling, but just with him and [me] arguing. I wasn't able to do the calling.
>
> [However,] with going in [to the Bishop] and being set apart, and receiving that blessing, there's a comfort that comes with that...I don't let things get on my nerves as easily....[My husband] and I simply have not fought....
>
> [This time] we were both set apart in our callings. My husband and I have not had an argument. We'll joke with each other....I'll call him a "Neanderthal" and he calls me an "insensitive cave woman." But we're really joking.
>
> (Wade, Interview, 1995)

The contrast that Susan identifies relates to her own sense of empowerment by being set apart, which she then sees manifested in family relationships. The result of being set apart was to give her the feeling that she had proper authority. Everything was much calmer, especially during a period when both she and her husband were each set apart in different callings. She said it was as if Heavenly Father was watching over each of them and their family, with no opportunity for Satan to intrude. Still, the demands were notable. Here's how she described them:

> A primary calling takes a lot out of you—you're on the phone, you're trying to get teachers, there's a lot of stuff that goes on in there. And [my kids] were angels all this time, which tells me Heavenly Father was watching over us. There was no intrusion in our family of Satan at all during my calling.
>
> Then the time had come for me to be released. And I was sitting in sacrament meeting and I felt the mantle leave me. I'd been primary

president for about five years and had taught in primary about eight years. And I could remember every one by name. When that mantle left me, I'd look at these kids and go "I know this face, [but] I cannot remember the name."

(Wade, Interview, 1995)

In her view, being set apart bestowed a form of authority referred to as receiving the mantle of that office. She noticed that even her memory for the names of primary children was much better under the mantle of the Bishop's blessing. And she felt the shift in power when she sensed that the mantle left her. She said, "The children still know me as 'Sister Wade.' [But] it was just like night and day. When I felt this mantle leave me—whoa!—away went all of the things that helped me do my calling. So, it really does make a difference. Being set apart is crucial; it's the crucial part of receiving a calling" (Wade, Interview, 1995).

Age-graded Characteristics of Children

The front matter of the manuals reminds the teachers of their responsibilities. "Your calling to teach children the gospel of Jesus Christ is a sacred trust given to you through your bishopric or branch presidency. These priesthood leaders have called you by inspiration from Heavenly Father. You can greatly influence the children in your class to follow the Savior throughout their lives." Further, this introductory matter provides general guidelines for the "age characteristics" of children that reflect attention to "why the children behave as they do and how to teach them in ways that they can best learn" (*Primary 2*, 1995, x).

Social Science Research Information

The church's general primary presidency conducts research on children's learning that helps fit primary lessons to children's learning needs and abilities. I met with a team of five or six social science researchers in the Research Information Division (RID) of the church, which conducts social science research on the content, structure, and understanding of the lesson materials used in primary in an effort to make these materials age-appropriate for the students. This research effort is conducted on a cross-cultural basis. Kristen Goodman, a member of the RID staff, indicated that this research is not generally available in the public domain except as used in the front matter of the LDS teaching manuals or through occasional publications in professional peer-reviewed journals. As an indication of their own work, Goodman referred me to a survey and review of non-LDS empirical research on children's religious learning by Kenneth E. Hyde (1990), titled *Religion in Childhood and Adolescence*. The RID is now expanding its own research in wards and branches around the world in keeping with the church's international scope (Cunningham, Goodman, Cooper, and Payne, Group Interview, 1994).

In the front matter of *Primary 2* (1995) and *Primary 3* (1994), and based on current LDS in-house research, four-year-olds are characterized this way: "Four is the age of finding out. *Why* and *how* are two of the words most frequently used by four-year-olds. Four-year-olds are very active." And then specific examples follow of their more typical activities, actions, and questions. For example, one pertinent observation indicates that "since their experience has been mainly in the home, they talk mostly about home and family. Children this age love to tell the teacher about their families. They would often rather tell their own stories than listen to the stories of other children. They love lessons and activities that focus on the family" (*Primary 3*, 1994, xi).

Descriptive characterizations of five-, six-, and seven-year-olds follow a similar reportorial pattern in an effort to help teachers understand some of the age-related features of the children they teach. For instance, the front matter reports: "At seven, children are still close to their parents and still appreciate their love, attention, and sympathy, but they are beginning to relate more to people and situations outside the home. They have individual tastes and want to be allowed to make some of their own decisions. They are lively, eager, and tremendously interested in life about them. They explore many activities and like to repeat those that give them pleasure" (*Primary 2*, 1995, xii–xiii).

Further specific characteristics follow: "They are beginning to interact less with members of the opposite sex"; "[t]hey are becoming more independent and more logical in their thinking"; "[t]hey are looking forward to baptism"; "can pray alone"; and "take pride in the fact that they can fast [by foregoing] at least one meal...and that they pay tithing" [ten percent of childhood allowance as a contribution to the church] (*Primary 2*, 1995, xiii). This introductory matter provides special guidelines for teaching those with disabilities and suggests "counsel[ing] with your bishop" when dealing with emotional or physical abuse (*Primary 3*, 1994, xiv). Some lessons suggest that teachers should be especially sensitive to variations in family arrangements that the children of the church are experiencing involving absent parents, stepparents, and single-parent families. These and other social aspects of the church's personal and family culture are to be examined in the light of the proclamation on the family (Dollahite 2000:206–241).

Jesus Christ as Exemplar

The central theme of junior primary is announced in the first lesson in both manuals. *Primary 2* (1995) emphasizes "that happiness comes from choosing the right" (*Primary 2*, 1995, 1:1), while *Primary 3* (1994) indicates "that choosing the right can help them follow Jesus Christ" (*Primary 3*, 1994, 1:1). In both lessons, Jesus Christ becomes the exemplar whose life pattern is to serve as the template for the lives of the children. The second lesson in *Primary 2* (1995) focuses on choosing the right by asking, "What would Jesus want me to do?" (*Primary 2*, 1995, 2:6). This "framing" of Jesus as the basis for action implies an identification of the self with Jesus. But the lesson also cautions the teacher to explain that the teachings of Jesus "do not tell us exactly what to do in every situation. Jesus wants us to learn to make wise choices ourselves. He wants us to learn how to think and to show love and kindness" (*Primary 2*, 1995, 2:8).

Heavenly Father's Plan

Both manuals introduce the idea of Heavenly Father's plan for mortal life as the central meaning of the gospel. The scriptural foundation of this heavenly plan (the plan of salvation) is found in the Book of Moses and the Book of Abraham in the Pearl of Great Price, as revealed to the prophet Joseph Smith in his continuing efforts at a retranslation of the Bible [see Smith *History of the Church*, 2nd ed. (1978) vol. 2:235–236, 348–351]. These two books are compendia of foundational stories with Joseph Smith as the interpreter.

The Book of Abraham (chapter 3) reads as follows:

22. And there stood one among them [Jesus as Jehovah at the beginning of creation] that was like unto God, and he said unto those [immortal spirits] who were with him: We will go down, for there is space there, and we will take of these materials, and we will make an earth whereon these [spirits] may dwell;

23. And we will prove them herewith, to see if they will do all things whatsoever the Lord their God shall command them;

24. And they who keep their first estate [promises in the preexistence] shall be added upon; and they who keep not their first estate shall not have glory in the same kingdom with those who keep their first estate; and they who keep their second estate [promises in mortal life] shall have glory added upon their heads for ever and ever.

25. And the Lord said: Whom shall I send? And one answered like unto the Son of Man: Here am I, send me. And another answered and said, Here am I, send me. And the Lord said: I will send the first.

26. And the second was angry, and kept not his first estate; and, at that day, many followed after him.

(Pearl of Great Price, Abraham 3:22–26)

And the Book of Moses (chapter 4) tells how Moses learned of the conflict between Heavenly Father and Lucifer (Satan):

1. And I, the Lord God, spake unto Moses, saying: That Satan, whom thou hast commanded in the name of mine Only Begotten, is the same which was from the beginning, and he came before me, saying— Behold, here am I, send me, I will be thy son, and I will redeem all mankind, that one soul shall not be lost, and surely I will do it; wherefore give me thine honor.

2. But, behold, my Beloved Son [Jesus], which was my Beloved and Chosen from the beginning, said unto me—Father, thy will be done, and the glory be thine forever.

3. Wherefore, because that Satan rebelled against me, and sought to destroy the agency of man, which I, the Lord God, had given unto him, and also that I should give unto him mine own power; by the power of mine Only Begotten, I caused that he should be cast down;

4. And he became Satan, yea, even the devil, the father of all lies, to deceive and to blind men, and to lead them captive at his will, even as many as would not hearken unto my voice.

(Pearl of Great Price, Moses 4:1–4)

Agency, Obedience, and Worthiness

The lessons begin by characterizing all people who are born on earth as children of Heavenly Father who are able to exercise choice, but who are commanded by Heavenly Father to "choose the right" in order to return as worthy to live with him in heaven again. Obedience to Heavenly Father's commands is therefore equated with choosing the right. To achieve the goal of being worthy to return to heaven, each person must overcome obstacles and meet the tests that are placed in his or her way by Lucifer (Satan) who, as a fallen spirit, led his followers among the host of heaven into disobedience and opposition in an effort to subvert Heavenly Father's plan in favor of his own. Thus, a measured portion (one-third) of the spiritual forces is arrayed against Heavenly Father's wishes and plan, and create evil in the world.

The Great Council in Heaven

The initial step in the plan of salvation is the recognition that our first choice as a spirit child was to accept Heavenly Father's plan for us, which is marked and confirmed by our human existence on earth today in physical bodies as persons (or souls) distributed around the world in many different societies. This expansion of the LDS cultural world unfolds as the story of a great meeting in heaven—a heavenly council—to which all spirit children of Heavenly Father were invited, and in which Heavenly Father presented his plan: "that we needed to go away from him for a time [on earth] in order to get a physical body and learn to choose the right" (*Primary 2*, 1995, 4:17). Since we would not remember living with him, we would need someone to help us return to heaven to live with him again" and that person would be Jesus Christ, "the firstborn of our Heavenly Father's children" (*Primary 2*, 1995, 4:17), and the eldest brother of all human beings.

The conflict that emerges during the council in heaven (which becomes a war in heaven) introduces what may be called the agency-obedience-worthiness schema, a central script of the church's model for the spirit self as interacting with others in its environment. Teachers are told (in *Primary 3*, 1996, vii) that each manual contains lesson materials "to help you teach the children that by following Jesus Christ's example, they can choose the right, be baptized, and become members of the Church of Jesus Christ of Latter-day Saints" (*Primary 2*, 1995, 12:55–59; *Primary 3*, 1994, 11 and 12:50–60). Thus, the agency-obedience-worthiness schema of these lessons is preparation for and is directly connected to the baptism-confirmation ordinances as rites of passage.

When Heavenly Father presented his plan to all those gathered in this great council, everyone shouted for joy, and when he asked "whom he should send to teach us" the way of return, Jesus answered [in the words of the book of Moses]: "Father, thy will be done, and the glory be thine forever" (Pearl of Great Price, Moses 4:2). He promised to do whatever Heavenly Father asked of him, all to the glory of Heavenly Father. At the same time, another spirit son, Lucifer, called out—"Here am I, send me," and said he would "force all of us to do what is right," and asked Heavenly Father "to give him [Lucifer] all the honor and glory." When Heavenly Father said that he chose Jesus, "Lucifer became very angry" and "caused a great war in heaven," not of guns, bullets, and bombs, but of alluring talk, deception, seduction, and intimidation in trying to get [other spirits] to follow him (*Primary 2*, 1995, 4:18). In this effort, Lucifer convinced one-third of the heavenly host to follow him. In consequence of this rebellion, Heavenly Father did not allow these spirits "to be born on earth and receive physical bodies." Therefore, "we [humans] know we followed Jesus because we are here on earth [now]" (*Primary 2*, 1995, 4:18). Our own birth represents a consequence of this important first choice. Essentially, the same story is told in the second lesson of *Primary 3*, under the title "Heavenly Father Trusts Us to Follow His Plan" (*Primary 3*, 1994, 2:4):

> Heavenly Father's plan included the creation of an earth for us. On earth we would learn the difference between right and wrong and choose for ourselves what we would do. Our Heavenly Father knew that we would make mistakes. But he would send Jesus Christ to help us overcome them.
>
> We had another brother named Lucifer. He wanted us to follow him instead of Heavenly Father. But following Lucifer would not have been good for us.
>
> Heavenly Father knew that and chose Jesus to carry out his plan. That made Lucifer very angry.
>
> Heavenly Father wants us to choose to follow his plan here on earth so we can return to live with him (*Primary 3*, 1994, 2:6–7).

The Amplification of Agency

The central theme of this story of the council in heaven is the exercise of choice among spirit children between opposing alternatives represented by Jesus' affirmation of Heavenly Father's glory and plan of individual agency and Lucifer's use of force, coercion, and self-conceit. At the same time, Heavenly Father's plan establishes Jesus as the model older brother and pathfinder for the return to heaven, where his way is the way of obedience to Heavenly Father's commands. Thus, two schemas are conjoined, one focused on choice and agency and another focused on obedience and worthiness, resulting in the imperative to choose the right.

If the first choice of a spirit child of God was to follow Jesus in the pre-existence and therefore to be born into mortal existence, the second choice arises in the story of Adam and Eve, who chose to eat the fruit of the tree of the knowledge of good and evil, and the third choice arises upon attaining the age of accountability, being faced with baptism and confirmation and membership in the LDS Church, which is now a personal choice in mortality. Thus, junior primary is directed toward learning those lessons that will allow children to exercise their agency and make this third choice on the path of their own worthiness.

Many of the lessons in *Primary 2* (1995) and *Primary 3* (1994) are extensions and amplifications of the lessons already introduced in *Primary 1* (1994), with an emphasis on children's increased abilities. It is a pattern that begins from "I am a child of God" and proceeds to a further series of personal affirmations, such as "I can choose the right" (*Primary 3*, 1994, 1), "I can pray" (*Primary 2*, 1995, 10, 18; *Primary 3*, 1994, 34), "I can show gratitude" (*Primary 2*, 1995, 24), "I can follow Jesus Christ" (*Primary 2*, 1995, 4), "I can be a good example" (*Primary 2*, 1995, 29; *Primary 3*, 1994, 45), "I can pay tithing" (*Primary 2*, 1995, 33; *Primary 3*, 1994, 42), and "I can repent" (*Primary 3*, 1994, 10). These are choices that expand upon abilities, actions, and values that are important to the church's program. Other lessons similarly amplify characteristics, attributes, and features of Heavenly Father, Jesus Christ, and the Holy Ghost as members of the godhead with whom a spirit child may continue to build a relationship.

Therefore, Heavenly Father "watches over me" (*Primary 2*, 1995, 8), "helps when we pray" (*Primary 3*, 1994, 19), and "helps us obey his commands" (*Primary 3*, 1994, 18). Jesus Christ was once "a child like me" (*Primary 2*, 1995, 9), has the "power to heal" (*Primary 2*, 1995, 16), "loves me" (*Primary 2*, 1995, 19; *Primary 3*, 1994, 30), "is our savior" (*Primary 2*, 1995, 41), and "lives forever" (*Primary 3*, 1994, 46). The Holy Ghost "helps me" (*Primary 2*, 1995, 13), "helps us" (*Primary 3*, 1994, 26), comes as a "gift" (*Primary 3*, 1994, 12), and "helps us know the truth" (*Primary 3*, 1994, 20).

Introduction of Heavenly Mother

Among the new elements that begin to expand the children's understanding of the preexistence is the presence of "our heavenly mother." In one of the first lessons of junior primary, the teacher is told to explain to the children that "we all lived in heaven with Heavenly Father before we came to this earth. We are his children. That is why we call him Heavenly Father. We also lived with our heavenly mother and all the rest of Heavenly Father's children.... Everyone who has been born on the earth is a child of Heavenly Father."

This image of a heavenly mother introduces gender to the order of heaven, though her role is not explained or elaborated. The focus remains on Heavenly Father—that "everyone who has been born on the earth is a [spirit] child of

Heavenly Father," though we "do not remember" this prior experience but only "read it in the scriptures." Still, heavenly mother remains hidden and subordinate (*Primary 2*, 1995, 3:12), with her identity marked by lowercase initials.

At the same time, other lessons introduce new persons, organizations, objects, and ideas. Among immortals, Lucifer is given a position and role that places him in opposition to the godhead (*Primary 2*, 1995, 4; *Primary 3*, 1994, 2). Joseph Smith as the prophet is introduced with lessons on his childhood (*Primary 3*, 1994, 4), the first vision (*Primary 3*, 1994, 5), and the coming forth of the Book of Mormon (*Primary 3*, 1994, 15). The establishment of the "church on earth" (*Primary 2*, 1995, 42) and the role of the priesthood are addressed (*Primary 2*, 1995, 17), along with "prophets" (*Primary 3*, 1994, 8), "ordinances" (*Primary 3*, 1994, 9), "temples" (*Primary 3*, 1994, 35) and practices such as "fasting" (*Primary 3*, 1994, 41), "tithing" (*Primary 3*, 1994, 42), or being "a missionary" (*Primary 3*, 1994, 25). But the central focus remains the development of the agency/obedience schema as central to the spirit self's action in the world of the LDS.

Agency: Choice, Accountability, and Consequences

While acknowledging that children change at different rates in cognitive, social, and physical development, age eight is established by the church as the spiritual benchmark for accountability. It is a temporal milestone. One of the lessons for junior primary under the subtitle "When We Are Eight, We Are Accountable" instructs the teacher to remind the children that Heavenly Father is wise: "He knows that we must learn what is right and wrong. When we have grown enough and learned enough about right and wrong, we become accountable for what we do. Being accountable means that we must take responsibility for what we do wrong, and we are blessed for what we do right" (*Primary 3*, 1994, 27:129). Accountability means that choices have consequences.

Baptism and confirmation are important, in part then, as the first accountable actions of our mortal lives within the plan of salvation, as part of the cultural model that shapes and governs social action from the preexistence to the final judgment (Hammarberg 2002a:8–9). And junior primary becomes the formal arena for learning about the kinds of choices in the world of everyday life that children will be called upon to make and about agency and obedience as the most important attributes of the spirit self as a child of God. In its simplest formulation, the plan of salvation provides Heavenly Father's vision of our happiness: that through mortal experience and our own choices, we humans might grow in righteousness and return worthy to be with him in our heavenly home.

The Elements of the Agency Schema

The elements of this agency schema involve (1) a *person* faced with (2) *alternative choices*, who responds with (3) a *decision* that is either (4) *right* (by following a commandment of Heavenly Father, or patterned on the example of Jesus Christ, or reached through personal revelation after prayerful consideration and confirmation by the Holy Ghost) or (5) *wrong* (in response to the wiles of Satan, or personal willfulness, or succumbing to worldly temptation), which (6) entails *consequences* of temporal and eternal import as (7) based on *personal worthiness*. We proceed to break down this schema according to lessons in the *Primary* manuals that address each of its components.

The first element is the *person*. In LDS understanding, the person is either a spirit child of God (in pre-mortal existence) or a soul in mortal existence who is possessed of both a physical body and an immortal spirit. This "body and spirit" person is an independent agent who possesses the capacity (agency) to choose. Each of the first several lessons in the *Primary* manuals supports one or another of these views of the person, but especially the lesson on "I Am a Child of God" (*Primary 2*, 1995, 3). Specifically, it addresses the distinction between "spirit" and "physical body" as forming a "flesh and bone" unity of thought, action, and person.

In posing the question, "What is a spirit?"—the teacher explains that "our spirits are the part of us that makes us alive," and using a mirror for each child to look into, explains "that our spirits look like our physical bodies" and "have eyes, ears, arms, and legs" (*Primary 2*, 1995, 3:12). A further analogy is for the teacher to "put your hand into a glove and wiggle your fingers," explaining that "the glove is like a physical body, and the hand is like a spirit" (*Primary 2*, 1995, 3:13). Thus, body and spirit have the same form and are integrated with each other.

The element of *alternative choices* is represented by lessons on choice, such as obeying civil law (*Primary 2*, 1995, 31:162), choosing to be baptized (*Primary 2*, 1995, 12), and many examples of moral self-expression already cited. The primordial choice, of course, is cast in the story of the heavenly council as to whom to follow, Jesus or Lucifer. A *decision* may involve obedience to a commandment of Heavenly Father, such as receiving an ordinance. It may also follow examples drawn from the life of Christ, or by employing prayer for communication with Heavenly Father in anticipation of receiving help or guidance from the Holy Ghost in new circumstances, or by following examples and directions issued by church authorities, especially the president of the church as prophet, seer, and revelator. The use of these resources leads to a *right* decision. Knowingly violating such examples and expectations in all likelihood will lead to a *wrong* decision. Thus, the obedience schema is embedded in and linked to the agency schema, and entails *consequences* that will play themselves out. Guidance from parents and church authorities can help each individual make beneficial choices and avoid costly mistakes, so that they may gain in worthiness through eternal progression. (See table 5.1.)

Mothers' Views of their Children's Spiritual Awareness

In order to explore parental perspectives on this stage of their children's lives, I invited a small group of seven mothers to meet on Thursday evening, November 3, 1994, in the home of Kathy Fairbanks for a focused conversation about childrearing and the spirituality of their children. They gave me permission to tape-record our discussion and to use their real names. The participants in this focus group included Wendy Kiefer, Tori Thornock, Kathy

Table 5.1. Worship Attendance by Age Cohorts for Members of the Crystal Heights Second Ward.

Age Cohorts	Almost every week or 2–3 times a month	Every few months or less	A few times a year or almost never	Total	Percent
Age 1 to 7	94.7	1.8	3.5	100	17.5
Age 8 to 11	91.3	4.3	4.3	100	7.1
Age 12 to 18	76.5	8.8	14.7	100	10.5
Age 19 to 29	82.6	6.5	10.9	100	14.2
Age 30 to 44	75.7	7.1	17.1	100	21.5
Age 45 to 59	83.3	0.0	16.7	100	9.2
Age 60 plus	76.9	3.1	20.0	100	20.0
Total	82.2	4.6	13.2	100	100.0 N=325

Fairbanks, Cathy Ipsen, Lynette Rich, Kim Gillette, and Nancy Tingey. From the tape recording I could not always identify who was speaking. Still, one of the advantages of a group interview is that the participants can respond to each other, enriching the discussion.[2]

One of my first discoveries in talking with these mothers was that the term "spiritual development," which I initially proposed as a cover term for our discussion, reminded some mothers of a model of physical or social development that did not fit their idea of the spiritual domain. Nancy Tingey expressed her dissatisfaction with the "development idea" in the following way:

> We've talked about children's spiritual development as if they're start-
> ing from a clean slate, but to me they already know a lot of what we're
> talking about. It's just that the veil has been drawn at birth. That's why
> I have a hard time with the idea of "development" as what's expected;
> it's not that there's a checklist or an expectation like physical or social
> development. It's more what's uncovered and what children are able to
> express to us that we then understand.
>
> (Mothers' Focus Group, Interview, 1994)

These and other comments led to a discussion of birth as passing through the veil, involving a clouding over of pre-mortal experience, and that spirituality involved an uncovering or recalling of events and relationships that were grounded in the preexistence. Kim Gillett urged "that there's something deep inside of our spirit that's eternal, that we know. We know [certain] truths. We know Heavenly Father. We know Jesus. We know that they're real, that they're our friends, and we know that families are important." Another mother indicated that "[a]ll the spirits that were coming here [to earth] were together and had a say in the plan of salvation," which involved the decision to be tested in mortal experience as Jesus was. So, in the process of this discussion, they searched for a better word to describe the spirituality of children—if not "spiritual development" then perhaps "uncovering," or "re-awakening," or "awareness." "Yeah," Nancy said, "awareness would be a better word, as children become able to communicate spiritual things in more and more ways, their spiritual awareness increases."

---

2. On individual and group interviews, see Glynis M. Breakwell, *Interviewing* (1990), chapter 4; Paul Bohannan and Dirk van der Elst, *Asking and Listening: Ethnography as Personal Adaptation* (1998). On intra-cultural parental ethno-theories about their children's learning, see *Parents' Cultural Belief Systems*, eds. Sara Harkness and Charles M. Super (New York: Guilford Press, 1996).

Tori Thornock agreed that the term spiritual awareness summed up her experience with her 18-month-old. "In the beginning you think she's just doing things out of the example of the other children. She's always so busy and intense. And then you start to realize that she has that spiritual awareness—that [she's aware that] this is a time to be reverent and kneel and fold her arms."

Kim picked up the idea of a re-awakening and applied it to adults: "Missionaries go out and teach adults who have never even heard of the church. They'll be taught principles. And it will seem familiar to them, like— 'I knew this, this makes sense'—because I firmly believe that we all knew it [the gospel or plan of salvation] before we came here, and sometimes there's something deep in the spirit that comes to awareness."

Birth as Passing through the Veil to Mortality

Birth is viewed by LDS as "passing through the veil" from preexistence into mortality. I proposed that perhaps there was a "forgetting" involved in this process. But this notion was clearly too strong. Kim said, "I don't think that it's a forgetting so much as it's that [memory] is clouded." Nancy added, "It's clouded by the influence of the world, and the busyness of life, and other things." Clearly, as this discussion unfolded, I was being told that spiritual awareness of the preexistence remains intact, though clouded, as a spirit self enters mortality in the form of an infant, and that this awareness may be encouraged to emerge and increase into adulthood. Kim noted: "As an adult I'm sometimes frustrated because I'm limited because I'm mortal, and yet spiritually I want to do certain things. I'm frustrated that I can't progress, maybe, as fast as I want to—that I can't reach [my spiritual] potential as fast as I want to reach it."

Age and Spiritual Awareness

I asked these young mothers what they noticed about their children's spiritual awareness in the period before they learned to talk. Someone said they noticed their child's spiritual origins from the moment they first put their child on their shoulder or first held them. Kim noted that in their home they had a picture of Christ in their daughter's bedroom, and that when she asked Alex at 6 months where Jesus was, Alex looked right at that picture: "[T]he expression that she had on her face when she met [his] eyes—to this day I won't forget it—she came out in a full smile, like 'I recognize him,' 'I'm familiar with his face.'" And she added, "If you're asking what sorts of things we do, we try to make [the children] more aware of pictures in our home that deal with Christ or that deal with the gospel. We try to make sure that we involve them with prayers. When we pray we are reverent with our arms," Lynnette Rich said, "There's a lot of singing, too, songs that have to do with Christ and with Heavenly Father."

These mothers agreed that children seemed to be aware of a difference between right and wrong in their preverbal stage, but do not have the mental or physical ability to exercise self-control. Tori noted: "I can see, with my 18-month-old right now, that when she does something wrong, she knows it's wrong, and when I tell her to stop, she doesn't yet have the self-control necessary to stop doing what's wrong." Someone else commented that self-control is "a discipline," because the eternal spirit is "trying to get along in a mortal body, which that spirit has never before experienced. And so it's trying to overcome the mortal."

I asked if that meant that there was a tension between the spirit self and the mortal body. "It's not really a tension," I was told, "because...it is an eternal union...and after this life, through the resurrection of Jesus Christ, it will be body and spirit together, eternal, inseparable. So, at some point they start working together." Someone else commented, "It goes back to self-control," and added an example of learning to skate. "As a child, or for any of us even as adults, [getting] on ice skates for the first time, or rollerblades, it was almost impossible to get along. But, after awhile, with experience, you're able to create beauty on ice." Another added, "Or that you feel comfortable, and that you're not going to fall." And another added further, "But there's a lot of falling that goes on." To which another expanded even further, "That's right. There's a lot of falling that goes on even when you're comfortable. No matter how good you are on ice skates, you'll still fall." Clearly, the group was developing a potent and expansive metaphor for learning through agency and experience.

Language, Prayer, and Spiritual Awareness

To these parents, the idea and gestures of prayer also seemed rooted in preexistent spirituality and came into a child's awareness very early. I suggested that this awareness may be a product of social learning, which occurs as children observe others and then do what they observe. My words were, "[I]f they try it out, and if it's comfortable for them, or if it fits the circumstances, then they continue to do it." In response to these comments, Tori remarked:

> Well, that hits it right on the nose—that is, most children pick up the concept of prayer because it is comfortable; because they are familiar with it; before they came here they were familiar with it; they know it; it's part of their spirit; it's part of their whole existence. And that's why, for me, we have never had any trouble teaching them—or not even that

we've had to teach them—it's just been part of them. You know, one
child may be more shy than another, but the language is still there for
all of them. And that's been our experience with our three [year old],
and even now with the 18-month-old, who says "Amen" at the end of
the prayer. She doesn't give the "Jesus" part yet, but she's got "Amen"
in there, and folds her arms and is very reverent through the whole
prayer.

(Mothers' Focus Group, Interview, 1994)

Thus, it seems clear that parents have concepts in their minds that lead them
to look for signs of their children's spiritual awareness. They then perceive
their child's recognition of and familiarity or comfortableness with Heavenly
Father, visual representations of Jesus Christ, songs and gestures like kneeling
and folding one's arms, and reverence during family prayers. Parents hold a
belief that these gestures and responses are indicative of preexistent experience that has been clouded over by the spirit child's passing through the veil
at birth and assuming a mortal body. Even before their children begin to talk,
parents will help focus their children's attention on what the parents consider
are important spiritual matters. "It's not hard to get kids' attention and have
them focus if you're focused on them; it's when mom gets distracted then
they get distracted. If it's something serious that you need to teach them, and
you're looking them in the eye, they pick up on it." To LDS parents, it is as
if the signs of a preexisting spiritual awareness are coming from inside the
infant to an outer expression, and therefore, to the parents, these signs con-
firm their belief in the preexistence.

A whole new world opens up when a child begins to talk. When I asked
what changes occur then, the responses came rapidly. "You really get to
see yourself," one mother said. "Is that ever true!" added another. A third
said, "My two-year-old said, 'I want to go visit Jesus.' No, no, that was my
four-year-old....I can't remember which, anyway one of them said, 'Ya, let's go
visit him tomorrow.' So the time factor—they don't have any understanding
of time, but they do recognize that Jesus is somebody that's familiar and comfortable, and a friend." Lynnette reported that the television news was showing
the new Bountiful temple, and three-year-old Kelton said, "That's a house they
built for Jesus."

With their new language abilities, children want to pray and will compete
with other family members for this opportunity. Tori reported:

Sometimes we almost have knock-down drag-out fights over who gets
to say the prayer. And I say that in all seriousness. I don't want to

take away from the reverence of prayer, but they often argue with one another as to who gets the opportunity to pray. And for awhile there it was so bad that we were allowing both of them to say a prayer just because it was better to do that than [have them fight.] They weren't quite old enough at the time to [grasp the concept of taking turns]. Michael Ted says it now: "You get to say it in three hours, at lunch"— but...until they got a little older, we did have quite a few prayers at our house.

(Mothers' Focus Group, Interview, 1994)

Lynette added: "My boy is about two, and he couldn't understand why we had to take turns. He'd cry because he wanted to talk to Jesus. So, if we actually called on Kelsey to say the prayer first, she'd do the prayer and then he'd cry and cry, and when he'd stop crying, he would ask if I'd let him say the prayer too, and so we'd have two prayers."

Bedtime prayers also tended to enter the repertoires of children about this time, or as Nancy said, "from the time you move them out of the crib, when they can kneel by the side of the bed, so maybe about [age] two." Wendy Kieffer added, "Sometimes I'll pray every night with Logan, and then other nights we'll forget and he just goes to bed. Then sometimes he'll just drop down [to his knees], and he's not quite two and is still in the crib." At the time the children were acquiring the ability to talk, they had not yet begun to distinguish between Jesus and Heavenly Father. As Lynette reported, "Kelton doesn't really distinguish between Jesus and Heavenly Father. He's only three. And this was when he was two. Right now, for Kelton, everything is Jesus."

Social Relations and Spiritual Awareness

The active use of language offers children a new form of control and brings them into an increasingly social world. Lynette reported:

My three-year-old has a friend who is three, and his family are not members of the church. He came over to my house a few weeks ago, and asked me to teach him how to pray.... He's had dinner or lunch at our house and we have a prayer, but he's only seen us pray a few times. So I was surprised that he even asked me, and then I worried about forcing my religion on him. But at three, this is someone who doesn't attend any religion, and he asked me how to pray.

(Mothers' Focus Group, Interview, 1994)

Through language, parents are also able to help their children recognize and identify categories of events, persons, places, and things with appropriate labels, and therefore to begin a differentiation of kinds of objects and social experiences. One of these categories has to do with feelings as distinct from thoughts and actions. Spiritual awareness to LDS seems primarily to be a matter of recognizing and correctly identifying feelings. Kim said,

> Even for me, as an adult, part of the constant struggle of life is developing your spiritual self, and learning to recognize the spirit in your life, and to have that be the stronger part of your life versus the mortal part. And I think that part of the challenge of raising children is helping them feel it [the spirit] and know that's really what it is and what they're feeling, so that they have that independently apart from you, so that they can develop themselves spiritually. And I agree that children in one sense are more spiritually susceptible—in that they haven't been tainted by the world or were recently with Heavenly Father. But I also think that as you develop, you develop cognitively, and you're able to really expand yourself even more spiritually; then, if you can grow with that you can become even more deeply spiritual than maybe even the innocence of the child.
>
> (Mothers' Focus Group, Interview, 1994)

Learning in Family and Primary

From about age five, these LDS mothers believe that the "expansion of [spiritual] awareness" continues as "a kind of natural process." Children are ready to give lessons in primary, and they want to do some leading in family home evenings. They are full of questions about life and death, and once they start school, of questions about what it means to be LDS, since they become aware of non-LDS "others" in their midst. And they are beginning to differentiate Jesus and Heavenly Father as well as the Holy Ghost, and perhaps even Satan. With respect to Jesus and Heavenly Father, one mother said her children would distinguish them as "father and son—two different people." Another said, "Jesus is the baby that grew up," and Heavenly Father is "Jesus' father." And when they pray, they pray to Heavenly Father. I asked what role Jesus has in their children's prayers, and the answer came back that by age five, prayer is "in Jesus' name." To which Wendy added, "I'm sure they don't grasp the concept of the mediator yet." But praying in Jesus' name is "really way down there, three- or two-year-olds."

Then I asked if five-year-olds distinguish the Holy Ghost or Holy Spirit. Tori responded:

> Maybe not the Holy Spirit, per se. But they keep talking about the warm, peaceful feeling. Michael Ted, at least, does equate that with the Holy Ghost, although I think he still pictures the Holy Ghost as a ghost in his mind. I think that's what he's seeing, but he equates the feeling of peace [with that name]... because he talks all the time about how he's going to do what's right because he wants to feel good and he wants to feel peace, and that's definitely a product of what he's been taught in primary. It's helping him to identify.
>
> (Mothers' Focus Group, Interview, 1994)

Tori also reported that the family was reading in the New Testament where Satan tempts Jesus, and said, "I don't think Michael Ted quite grasps it yet...the notion of the 'bad.' And then we talked about the story of the man who was possessed, and how the evil spirit went into the pig—and that went right over his head." Lynette added that her daughter at six and a half understands Satan. "Not that she knows about being possessed or anything, but she knows that Satan wants us to do bad things so that you can't live with Jesus again. So, whenever she sees things that are about smoking or drinking, she'll say that that's what Satan wants us to do so we can't return to live with Heavenly Father. So, at six she understands that, but I'm not sure she did at five."

Social situations also become more complicated with each increase in age. Different rules seem to apply in different circumstances, but to the children it's not always clear why that should be the case. For instance, Tori reported that in their home they have a rule that when the children have a guest, the guest gets to decide what games the children will play, and another rule that the children are to work out their differences. "Yesterday," she said,

> Michael Ted was playing with a friend and got upset and came home, and I had to talk to him and make him go back and work out their differences. I was trying to teach him that you work out your differences rather than just leaving—and he said, "Well, he [his friend] won't play what I want to play." And I said, "Well, it's his home, and it's his rules in his home [that you have to abide by]." And he said, "But in our house it's the guest—the guest—mom." And I said, "But that's his home." And I think it's a hard thing to grasp for a child. That's what we're

working on. And it doesn't mean that the rules are bad somewhere else, or that they're wrong, but that they are different from your situation.

(Mothers' Focus Group, Interview, 1994)

Some notions, like that of "the one true church," or that evil refers to something deeper and more pervasive than just being bad, still appear to be beyond the cognitive grasp of five-year-olds. But they are responsive to verbal control and "threats" from their parents, as well as the very rare physical spanking; they feel anxious about the unknown and experience fear in the face of events that are beyond their control. And they want to feel loved and to know that home is a place of refuge and security.

Aggression and Self-Control

By age seven, two important issues seem to have emerged. One has to do with a child's cognitive control of feelings of anger leading toward aggression, and the other with what parents identify as spiritual feelings. Both are involved with the development of self-control and the idea of the preexisting knowledge of right and wrong. Tori argued that self-control has to do with knowledge or awareness of right and wrong on the one hand, and with physical and mental development on the other hand. "The knowledge of right from wrong is there, it's just that their body isn't quite ready to express it, or they don't have the language [yet], and so therefore they don't have the self-control. And as they get older, they gain that self-control—as they learn to use their body, as they learn to walk, as they learn to pick up things."

Overt forms of aggression are to be channeled and limited. When I asked about hitting and fighting among kids as a "chance to work off some steam," Tori said, "I feel like fighting is wrong. Whether you're Catholic or Mormon or Jewish or atheist, you probably know that. I believe there's an innate sense...that has to do with that spirituality that we have all been given from the very beginning." I pushed the idea of aggression a little further by commenting, "There are some parents who would say that you've got to stand up for yourself, protect yourself, defend yourself." Nancy replied, "Those are all true. You do have to do those things. But...hauling off and hitting somebody is not acceptable. I mean, you've got to be aggressive; you've got to work hard; what this world is made for is to learn how to work; and there is a literal fight on this earth—but it's between good and evil, not between one person and the next. It's not a pecking order like hens."

Another mother said, "It's okay to be angry, but it's not okay to slug your brother." And another indicated that angry feelings are "natural feelings, and they're good feelings; but it's also a matter of channeling [them], and [asking] 'why am I feeling this way and how should I react?' " Another added, "And to be able to talk about it when you get angry. Rather than screaming and yelling, you can say 'I'm angry' and say why you're angry, and try to understand it." Another indicated what she says to her child: "You can be as angry as you want, but you go sit on your bed while you're doing that." This comment received knowing laughter from the group—as if that were the right thing to say, but that it didn't always work. The issue, Nancy suggested, went back to self-control—"just being able to control the spirit and [getting] the spirit to control the body—because the flesh is gonna want to haul off and hit somebody."

Development and Spiritual Awareness

The other aspect of control has to do with spiritual feelings and the role of mortal experience in bringing those feelings to awareness. The conception of mortal life as a period of testing is one of the background assumptions employed by parents. As one mother said, "Well, our life is about a test, really. And it's helping that child to always be prepared for the daily test, to go out and to function in the world. . . . From the minute you have that baby in your arms, you know that that child is going to leave your home some day, and you're not going to have as much influence over the child to help them, [so you had better help prepare them now]."

These parents are distinguishing between physical and cognitive development on the one hand, and spiritual awareness on the other. Spiritual awareness is both an identification of the working of the spirit as distinct from simple inner thoughts or cognition, and a recognition of when and how the spirit acts. This identification and recognition are most clearly equated with feelings. Wendy Kiefer said, "I served a mission, and when we were teaching people, one of the things you had to do is to point out when they were feeling the Holy Spirit, because so many people don't recognize what that good feeling is inside, the good feeling that we're given in order to recognize what is good. And I think it's the same way with a child. Sometimes you need to identify what they're feeling because they don't necessarily have the words or the vocabulary to identify it. And that's just the same principle in teaching the gospel to people who've never heard the gospel."

Over the course of a child's first five to seven years, parents are encouraged to be very solicitous of their child's well-being—holding, cuddling, rocking, and gently quieting infants and calmly and patiently talking with young children in efforts to explain to them whatever it is that needs explanation at a given moment—and they generally succeed in these efforts, at least in a middle-class ward like Crystal Heights. The care and concern for their children is evident in the demeanor of the parents, who clearly guide and direct but also respect the choices their young children make. The process of childcare is clearly an adult-guided one, in which parents see evidence of their own children's preexisting spiritual awareness, give it recognition, and continue to build on it as this natural unfolding of the spirit-self in mortality. Physical and cognitive development opens the door to language and the ability to recognize and identify feelings that are linked to spiritual awareness.

This focus on warm, peaceful feelings is associated with Jesus and Heavenly Father, with prayer, with Jesus as a friend, with parents and family as providing a safe and secure haven, and with the presence of the Holy Ghost. And it leads to baptism and confirmation as choices that a young person may make at age eight, initiating formal membership in the church and the beginnings of responsibility for continuing his or her own life journey.

6

We Thank Thee, O God, for a Prophet

SENIOR PRIMARY (KNOWN in the church as the valiant classes) provides the church's teaching program of prophetic and scriptural history for children in the age group of eight to 11 years old. Most of these children will have been baptized and confirmed (or continue to consider these steps) and will anticipate entering "mutual" at age 12, a set of organizations that was once called the Mutual Improvement Association but is now known as young men (for boys) and young women (for girls). At age 12, the young men will also enter the Aaronic priesthood. Senior primary therefore sets the stage for the coming adolescent transition in life experience of boys and girls as LDS.

During the four years of senior primary, the children receive formal church instruction regarding both scriptural and revelatory authority. This four-year cycle will consider, in turn, the most important texts of canonical scripture:

(1) The Old Testament and the Books of Moses and Abraham (in the Pearl of Great Price) as "a prophetic record of Heavenly Father's earliest dealings with human kind," using the teaching manual *Primary 6* (1996) (see Lesson 1:3);

(2) the New Testament as an apostolic record of Jesus Christ's life, teachings, and atonement, using the teaching manual *Primary 7* (1994) (see Lesson 9:29–32);

(3) the Book of Mormon as "another testament of Jesus Christ" in his dealings with the people on the American continent, using the teaching manual *Primary 4* (1995); and

(4) the Doctrine and Covenants and Joseph Smith-History (in the Pearl of Great Price), which "teaches about the restoration of the Church of Jesus Christ in the latter days through the Prophet Joseph Smith," using the teaching manual *Primary 5* (1996) (see Lesson 22:115–120).

One of the enrichment activities in *Primary 5* stresses, in the simplest terms, the different foci for each of these texts, known collectively as the "standard works":

- The Bible [Old and New Testaments] tells us about prophecies of Jesus Christ and about the Savior's life and teaching when he was on earth.
- The Book of Mormon is another testament of Jesus Christ and tells us about the Savior's dealings with the people on the American continent.
- The Doctrine and Covenants (D&C) is a collection of revelations from Jesus Christ for the latter days, or our times.
- The Pearl of Great Price gives us teachings and testimonies of Jesus Christ from ancient prophets as well as Joseph Smith's history and testimony of Heavenly Father and Jesus Christ. (*Primary 5*, 1996, 22:118)

These standard works are the basis for a similar cycle of topics that is followed simultaneously by the adult Sunday school classes for those 12 years old and older (but with different study materials). Thus, all members of baptismal age and older follow a correlated program of study over a four-year cycle that is also supported by the Monday family home evening program and the monthly periodicals *Ensign* (for adults), *New Era* (for young adults), *The Friend* (for children), and *Liahona* (in several different languages internationally).

The rationale for this correlated curriculum is to provide continuity of teaching content and greater depth and enrichment at different age levels while encouraging cross-generational conversations and a similar structuring of lessons wherever the church gathers in wards or branches around the world. Thus, wherever members live or travel—for example, Hong Kong, Mexico City, Montgomery (Alabama), London, Copenhagen, Johannesburg, Lima, and Philadelphia (Pennsylvania)—they will discover the same teaching program covering the same material adapted to different age levels and local use.

The church's approach to these materials is most fully expressed in its lessons concerned with the Doctrine and Covenants and the Pearl of Great Price, which provide a set of lenses through which the other standard works are taught and learned, and through which scriptural, priesthood, and continuing prophetic authority are viewed. The teaching manual for these materials is *Primary 5* in the new curriculum for older children. And the first ten to 12 lessons of the 46 contained in this manual focus on the text of "Joseph Smith-History" (JS-H), an autobiographical account of the rise of the church written by Joseph Smith (with the assistance of others) and first compiled in 1838, some eight years after the church was established. This "Joseph Smith-History" is contained in the book of scripture titled the Pearl of Great Price.

In a structural analysis of this history, anthropologist Steven L. Olsen (1980, 1996) has proposed construing it as comprised of three (I suggest five) separate mythic vignettes that he identified as (1) the first vision (verses 1–26), (2) the visits of the angel Moroni (verses 27–54), and (3) the recovery of gold plates by Joseph Smith, their translation and publication as the Book of Mormon (verses 55–67), plus (4) what might be considered a fourth vignette dealing with the establishment of priesthood authority, and (5) a fifth dealing with the founding of the church (verses 68–75). The whole account, in Olsen's view, forms a basic cultural charter for the church, "provid[ing]...its ultimate metaphysical and ontological foundations," "defining an ideal relationship between man and God," and "providing models for understanding the natural world and relating to the social world" by these young LDS.

Olsen's analysis, indebted to the structural approach of French anthropologist Claude Levi-Strauss and the ethnographic approach of Emile Durkheim, is a richly detailed reading of this text. Olsen suggested that sacred stories such as these have a "truth value for a people [that] lies beyond question or critical analysis." Although this approach to truth value may hold true for many believers, the meaning of these texts may not be so self-evident for those outside of the church's cultural purview or who have been exposed to alternative approaches to, or versions of, "manuscript truth." I enter this caveat because it is important in the search for symbolic meanings that the question of "symbolic to whom?" be addressed if the "meaning" is to be generalized to persons other than the interpretive author. Clearly, Olsen's reading of the text assumes an LDS readership and the Mormon worldview.

By introducing these young learners to Joseph Smith's personal history of the rise of the church in *Primary 5* (1996), they are being taught some of the fundamentals of the church's beliefs about Joseph Smith's life and role as they are understood within the church today.

The First Vision

The first lesson in *Primary 5* concerns what LDS refer to as the "first vision" (JS-H, verses 1–26), which finds the 14-year-old Joseph Smith in 1820 wanting "to know which Church was true" (*Primary 5*, 1996, 1:1). His resolve to search out this question was intensified by his recollection of a New Testament passage from the Epistle of James—"*If any of you lack wisdom, let him ask of God, that giveth to all men liberally, and upbraideth not; and it shall be given him*" (James 1:5). Consequently, Joseph retired to the woods near his home to ask God directly which sect he should join. As young Joseph set out to pray, he reported that he was "seized upon" by some enemy power that sought his destruction. Then, at the moment of his greatest despair, he said, "I saw a pillar of light exactly over my head…, which descended gradually until it fell upon me." He continued, "When the light rested upon me I saw two Personages, whose brightness and glory defy all description, standing above me in the air. One of them spake unto me, calling me by name and said, pointing to the other—'*This is My Beloved Son. Hear Him!*'" When Joseph asked "which of all the sects was right—and which should I join"?—he said, "I was answered that I must join none of them, for they were all wrong."

This "telling" represents the standard account of Smith's vision experience, now known as the first vision and published in 1838 and 1842. But at least two other earlier published accounts of the first vision were offered by Joseph Smith that differ in several details, and they have led to controversy regarding the nature and dating of this event and the representation of divine figures in it, as discussed by LDS scholars James B. Allen (1966) and Dean C. Jessee (1969).

The purpose of the first lesson in *Primary 5* (1996) then is to "strengthen each child's testimony that the Prophet Joseph Smith saw Heavenly Father and his Son, Jesus Christ" (*Primary 5*, 1996, 1:1). The key elements of the lesson focus on Joseph's family, his own birth in 1805 in Sharon, Vermont, and the family's migration to upstate New York in the Finger Lakes area near the town of Palmyra. Joseph learned only the basics of reading, writing, and arithmetic, and to his mother "seemed just like other boys his age until the time of his vision" (*Primary 5*, 1996, 1:2). The contextual characterization continues: Joseph's family loved God and wanted to keep his commandments. They read the Bible and prayed together often. Like Joseph, they were confused about which church was the true Church of Jesus Christ. After Joseph received his first vision, his family believed him and supported him in the great work he was called to do (*Primary 5*, 1996, 1:2).

In the lesson, the emphasis derived from this account falls on the choice among contending sects or religious denominations. As preparation prior to class, the teacher is asked to acquire "two empty containers, such as boxes or paper bags, that appear to contain something," and to label each with the words "Choose Me!" During class, a child is asked to leave the room while the other students are divided into two groups (each associated with one container) and coached to try to persuade the child to choose "their" container upon reentering the room. Obviously, this is a social experiment. After a choice is made, questions may be asked: "Why did you choose that container?" and "How did you feel when others were trying to tell you what to do?"

The point of the exercise is then driven home: "Explain that when Joseph Smith was 14 years old (or 15, in the JS-History text), he was confused

[in]...trying to decide which Church he should join. Other people tried to help him choose a Church, but he only became more confused. He felt that he needed more information to make a wise decision: he wanted to know which Church was true" (*Primary* 5, 1996, 1:1). The teacher can explore the issue of choice among competing religious groups further with the aid of maps of upstate New York and an account of historical conditions during Joseph's boyhood, which are included in the lesson plan.

In addition to the focus on choice, the other elements that receive emphasis in this lesson include the inner feelings of the chooser in response to the social pressures of competing persuaders, as well as the chooser's desire for more information, wisdom, and a standard of truth. Joseph Smith is represented as the exemplary chooser of this schema. The choice schema of this lesson is a variant on "choose the right," as applied here to Joseph Smith. Further elements as reported by Joseph are taken from scripture readings and become material for discussion, including the threat posed by Satan ("some actual being from the unseen world") and the appearance of "two Personages," which is taken as evidence for a lineal descent relationship between Heavenly Father and Jesus as two separate beings, a literal father and son.

The final question to be posed in this lesson is: "Why is it important that we each have a personal testimony of Joseph Smith's first vision?" Answer: "Once we believe that Heavenly Father and Jesus Christ actually appeared and talked to Joseph Smith, then we can be sure that everything else the Prophet taught or restored to us is also the truth" (*Primary* 5, 1996, 1:3–4). From an outside perspective, this conclusion does not follow. Smith is reporting his personal perceptual experience, which is an individual perceptual judgment, and like all such judgments, it is the basis from which inquiry begins. In the words of philosopher of history Murray G. Murphey (1994), "perceptual judgments are reports of what our experience is or was at a particular time...[and] are attempts to formulate in language the character of our experience" (53), and this "reporting" (I believe) is what Joseph sought to do.

Thus, we may accept Joseph Smith's report of his vision experience as a statement of fact about his perceptions without any further necessary implications about how we should view the world independent of our own (or others') further knowledge. In fact, since there are other accounts that may be earlier versions of the same experience, a full analysis would then involve accounting for their differences in much the manner that cultural historian Richard Lyman Bushman (2005:35–41) does in his account of Joseph's experience. Within this lesson in *Primary* 5, Smith is shown comparing his vision to the

New Testament vision of the Apostle Paul on the road to Damascus, for which Paul, like Joseph Smith, was persecuted. Joseph wrote:

> So it was with me. I had actually seen a light, and in the midst of that light I saw two Personages, and they did in reality speak to me; and though I was hated and persecuted for saying that I had seen a vision, yet it was true; and while they were persecuting me, reviling me, and speaking all manner of evil against me falsely for so saying, I was led to say in my heart: Why persecute me for telling the truth? I have actually seen a vision; and who am I that I can withstand God, or why does the world think to make me deny what I have actually seen? For I had seen a vision; I knew it, and I could not deny it, neither dared I do it; at least I knew that by so doing I would offend God, and come under condemnation
>
> (Pearl of Great Price, Joseph Smith-History 1:25).

Visits of the Angel Moroni

The second vignette in the Joseph Smith-History account in the Pearl of Great Price involves visits by the angel Moroni. Three years passed following Smith's first vision. During this time, Joseph said that he was persecuted for continuing to affirm his visitation experience (*Primary 5*, 1996, 3:12–13). In his vision, he had been forbidden to join any of the religious sects of the day.

> I was left to all kinds of temptations; and, mingling with all kinds of society, I frequently fell into many foolish errors, and displayed the weakness of youth, and the foibles of human nature; which, I am sorry to say, led me into divers [sic] temptations, offensive in the sight of God. In making this confession, no one need suppose me guilty of any great or malignant sins. (JS-H 1:28)

In consequence, through prayer and supplication Joseph sought "forgiveness of all my sins and follies" from Almighty God, "and also a manifestation to me that I might know of my state and standing before him." His prayer was answered by the appearance of another "personage" at his bedside "standing in the air, for his feet did not touch the floor" (1:29–30). After a momentary fright, Joseph's fear soon left him:

> He called me by name, and said unto me that he was a messenger sent from the presence of God to me, and that his name was Moroni; that

God had a work for me to do; and that my name should be had for good
and evil among all nations, kindreds, and tongues, or that it should be
both good and evil spoken of among all people.

He said there was a book deposited, written upon gold plates, giving
an account of the former inhabitants of this continent, and the source
from whence they sprang. He also said that the fulness [sic] of the everlasting Gospel was contained in it, as delivered by the Savior to the
ancient inhabitants;

Also, that there were two stones in silver bows—and these stones,
fastened to a breastplate, constituted what is called the Urim and
Thummim—deposited with the plates; and the possession and use of
these stones were what constituted "seers" in ancient or former times;
and that God had prepared them for the purpose of translating the book
(JS-H 1:33–35).

Joseph wrote that three times during the night of September 21, 1823, he was
visited by this angel, who offered him an apocalyptic warning, the announcement of a restored priesthood, and a promise linking the children's generation
to that of their fathers'. Joseph also reported that

the vision was opened to my mind that I could see the place where the
plates were deposited, and that so clearly and distinctly that I knew
the place again when I visited it. [Furthermore, Moroni also cautioned
him] that Satan would try to tempt me (in consequence of the indigent
circumstances of my father's family), to get the plates for the purpose
of getting rich. This he forbade me, saying that I must have no other
object in view...but to glorify God, and must not be influenced by any
other motive than that of building his kingdom; otherwise I could not
get them (JS-H 1:42, 46).

A fourth visit the next morning resulted in the angel telling Joseph to share
his experiences with his father, which he did; he then went to the place of the
plates and made an attempt to secure them, but was told that he should return
again at the same time and to the same place each year over the next four
years, until "the time should come for obtaining the plates" (JS-H 1:53).

Lessons 3 and 4 of *Primary 5* (1996) build upon this portion of the
account of Joseph's vision experiences with the angel Moroni. The teacher
is instructed to present one of the children with a microphone, while asking
him or her to give an important message to the whole world. He or she is
prompted with the question, "What message would you give?" After taking

turns, the children are shown a picture of a gold-covered statue of Moroni blowing a trumpet on a spire of an LDS temple in order to ask about the message and the messenger. "Who was Moroni?" the teacher is instructed to ask. The teacher then will show the children the book of Moroni in the Book of Mormon and explain that he was the last of the Nephite prophets; that he lived about 400 A.D.; was a son of the prophet Mormon; and buried the gold plates in the Cumorah hill when he had finished writing on them. Thus, this account of Moroni introduces the Book of Mormon as the channel for the work that Joseph was called by Heavenly Father to do. The lesson concludes with three assertions to be used for discussion about the message of the Book of Mormon: The Book of Mormon is true; it tells about the people who lived on the American continent long ago; and it contains the fullness of the gospel of Jesus Christ (*Primary 5*, 3:14).

The fourth lesson emphasizes Joseph's preparation to undertake his assigned role as a prophet and expands upon the intervals between the first vision, the visitation visions of Moroni, and the four years that were to elapse before the plates could be recovered. One elaboration in the lesson is taken from the account of Joseph Smith's mother, Lucy Mack Smith, who wrote that after the first visits of Moroni,

> Joseph continued to receive instructions from the Lord, and we con-
> tinued to get the children together every evening for the purpose of
> listening while he gave us a relation of the same.... During our eve-
> ning conversations, Joseph would occasionally give us some of the
> most amusing recitals that could be imagined. He would describe
> the ancient inhabitants of this continent, their dress, mode [method]
> of traveling, and the animals upon which they rode; their cities, their
> buildings, with every particular; their mode of warfare; and also their
> religious worship. This he would do with as much ease, seemingly, as
> if he had spent his whole life among them (Lucy Mack Smith, *History of
> Joseph Smith*, 1979 [1853]:82–83).

In the lesson, Joseph was given a task to do; therefore, his first duty was to pre-pare himself for it. One aspect was the decision to obey divine instruction. In the fourth lesson, Joseph's preparation included having faith in the message he had received, being obedient and prayerful, studying the scriptures, and trusting Heavenly Father and Jesus. Thus, preparation was linked to obedi-ence, with Joseph Smith's following the angel Moroni's directions serving as an example to be emulated by these young learners in their identity as mem-bers (or investigators) of the church (*Primary 5*, 1996, 4:18).

Joseph Smith Receives the Gold Plates and Translates the Book of Mormon

The third vignette of the JS-History begins by tracing several events that occurred during the four-year interval prior to Joseph's receipt of the gold plates. In 1824, his eldest brother Alvin died; he had been a strong supporter of Joseph's quest. A year later, Joseph assisted an acquaintance by the name of Josiah Stoal in digging for an old Spanish silver mine in the vicinity of Harmony (now Oakland), Pennsylvania, that gave rise to "the very prevalent story of my having been a money-digger" (JS-H 1:56). At this time, he boarded with Mr. Isaac Hale and there met his future wife Emma (Isaac Hale's daughter). Joseph and Emma were married on January 18, 1827, though Emma's father's family "were much opposed"; so they eloped and were married in another town at the house of Squire Tarbill. Joseph left his employment with Mr. Stoal and returned to farm with his own father near Palmyra, New York.

September 22, 1827, was the fateful day for obtaining the plates, [and special instruments known as] the Urim and Thummim, and the breastplate. Joseph reported that he went to "the place where they were deposited, [and] the same heavenly messenger [Moroni] delivered them up to me" with a charge to guard them carefully until he called for their return. Then Joseph said,

> [N]o sooner was it known that I had them, than the most strenuous exertions were used to get them from me.... But by the wisdom of God, they remained safe in my hands, until I had accomplished by them what was required at my hand. When, according to arrangements, the messenger called for them, I delivered them up to him; and he has them in his charge until this day, being the second day of May, one thousand eight hundred and thirty-eight.
>
> (JS-H 1:59–60)

The continued "falsehoods" and persecution in Palmyra forced Joseph to return to his wife's father's house in Harmony, Pennsylvania, where, he said, "I commenced copying the characters off the plates...and by means of the Urim and Thummim I translated some of them" by February 1828 (JS-H 1:62). He was initially aided by Martin Harris, a friendly gentleman who not only provided him with $50 on his journey to Pennsylvania, but also took some of the characters to a Professor Charles Anton in New York City to have the translation certified. Having received the certificate, Harris reported that Anton called him back to ask where Joseph found the plates. When Harris told him that an angel of God revealed the place to him, Anton thereupon took back his certificate "and tore it to pieces, saying that there was no such thing now as ministering angels" (JS-H 1:65).

Lessons 5, 6, and 7 of *Primary 5* are concerned with Joseph's receipt of the gold plates and their translation, and the lessons that these young students might learn from Joseph's experience. One lesson is that "when we are obedient and do our part [like Joseph], Heavenly Father will help us" (*Primary 5*, 1996, 5:20). Joseph had promised to guard the plates once they were in his possession, only to discover that many other persons sought to steal them. Joseph's mother, Lucy Mack Smith, recorded several of these stories. The teacher is advised to draw illustrations of a fallen log, a fireplace, a log cabin, and a wooden barrel as different places where Joseph hid the gold plates against the evil intentions of others—first in the decayed inside of a fallen log, under the floor stones of a fireplace, in the loft of a log cabin, and finally in the bottom of a barrel of beans while in transit to Pennsylvania. The lesson to be learned: "Because Joseph did his best to protect the plates as he had been commanded, Heavenly Father helped him keep the plates safe and also sent help in other ways" (*Primary 5*, 1996, 5:22), such as the gift of $50 from Martin Harris. The implication is that as we do our best to be obedient, Heavenly Father will also help us.

The story of Martin Harris and Professor Charles Anton is also employed in the lesson as a problematic situation to further support the idea that "Heavenly Father will help us with our problems and difficulties when we do our part" (*Primary 5*, 1996, 5:23). Four steps are outlined: (1) "Pray about the problem or difficulty," (2) "Live worthily and follow the promptings of the Spirit," (3) "Do all you can to solve the problem," and (4) "Leave the final result to Heavenly Father."

Among the most interesting problems during the translation process was the loss of the first 116 pages, when Joseph allowed Martin Harris to take them home to Palmyra to show his wife. This episode, recorded in D&C, sections 3 and 10, forms part of Lesson 6 in *Primary 5*. It serves as a negative proof "that when we pray, we should seek Heavenly Father's help and follow his guidance" (*Primary 5*, 1996, 6:26), and if we don't, then untoward events may follow.

When Joseph asked God whether he should let Martin take the first 116 pages, the Lord said "no." But Joseph repeated his plea again and again (at Martin's insistence), and then violated his earlier pledge not to show this work to others until it was finished by letting Martin take those pages to show his wife. When he learned that Martin lost the 116 pages, "Joseph exclaimed, 'All is lost! All is lost! What shall I do? I have sinned—it is I who tempted the wrath of God. I should have been satisfied with the first answer which I received from the Lord; for he told me that it was not safe to let the writing go out of my possession' " (Lucy Mack Smith, *History*, 1979:128).

The angel Moroni then took the plates and Urim and Thummim, and returned them only after Joseph repented of his disobedience. "Joseph learned that Satan and wicked people could not stop Heavenly Father's work" (*Primary 5*, 1996, 6:28). And the lesson the children are to learn is that we should "pray for what is right for us rather than just for what we want" and that "answers to prayer may come in many ways, such as through counsel from a parent or Church leader, from reading the scriptures, or from listening to a lesson or talk in Church" (*Primary 5*, 1996, 6:28).

Lesson 7 focuses on the role and influence of the Holy Ghost in the process of translating the unknown inscriptions on the gold plates into a manuscript in written English. As a demonstration, the teacher uses a radio that first must be turned on and then tuned to a station in order to clearly hear the messages that are being transmitted. So it is with the Holy Ghost. "Before we can hear what Heavenly Father wants us to know, we must be tuned in to the Holy Ghost" (31). Joseph records the arrival in Pennsylvania of a schoolteacher named Oliver Cowdery in early April of 1829. When Joseph resumed translating, Oliver joined him as scribe. Oliver had been teaching school while boarding at Joseph's father's house and there learned of the plates, which he came to see for himself in Harmony, Pennsylvania. By the 7th of April, Joseph began to dictate his translation from the plates while Oliver served as his scribe, and the process went forward more rapidly. Oliver himself said, "These were days never to be forgotten—to sit under the sound of a voice dictated by the inspiration of heaven.... Day after day I continued, uninterrupted, to write from his mouth, as he translated with the Urim and Thummim . . . the history or record called 'The Book of Mormon'" (JS-H, 1:71 note).

In teaching the children about the process of translation, the teacher can indicate that Joseph learned that he could not translate without the help of the Holy Ghost. Among other things, he had been upset with Emma (who also acted as a scribe) and needed to make peace and ask her forgiveness before he could continue translating with the help of the Holy Ghost (*Primary 5*, 1996, 7:32). Thus, the aim of Lesson 7 is to "help the children understand and recognize the influence of the Holy Ghost and desire to be worthy of his companionship" (*Primary 5*, 1996, 7:31).

Current practices of translation presume equal language facility by the translator in the different languages at issue, one as a written "source language" text and the other as a "target language" text. The translator works from one language source to the other. But this is not the meaning of translation as applied to the process by which the Book of Mormon was brought into existence. Historian Richard Bushman (2005:131) noted that over Joseph's lifetime, he produced three inspired translations: the Book of Mormon, the Book of Moses, and the Book of Abraham, plus the revision of the Bible, a form of translation. Bushman (2005:132) noted that "Joseph did not translate in the sense of learning the language and consulting dictionaries. He received the words by 'revelation,' whether or not a [source] text lay before him," and sometimes by using a seer stone while looking in a hat (Bushman 2005, 71–72).

In teaching Lesson 7, the teacher outlines the decision-making process presumably used by Joseph Smith when faced with a problem, like the translation problem, as follows:

1. Study the problem or question in your mind. Think about how you could solve the problem or question.
2. Decide what you think you should do.
3. Ask Heavenly Father if your decision is right.
4. Listen with your heart and mind. If your decision is right, the Holy Ghost will give you a good feeling about it. If your decision is wrong, you will not feel good about it, and you need to make a different choice.
5. If your heart and mind are settled, put your decision into action. (*Primary 5*, 1996, 7:32–33)

This outline is proposed as a model for decision-making, one that Oliver Cowdery should have used when he wanted to translate. As a schema, the critical element is the role of "feeling," which is an internal visceral response. The teacher is told to "[r]emind the children that answers to our prayers often come as "peaceful feelings" (*Primary 5*, 1996, 7:33). The children can then build two lists of what they can do that "invites the spirit" on the one hand or "offends the spirit" on the other, and check their feelings against these expectations of a bodily response. A further activity is for the children to stage part of the translation process reported for Joseph Smith, where he sat on one side of a curtain and his scribe sat on the other side. In the role-play, one or more children can serve as scribes on one side of a blanket or curtain that is held between two other children while another child on the other side reads ("dictates") a short verse from the Book of Mormon, which can then be read back from the child/scribe to check for accuracy. The point of these activities is to show "that the Holy Ghost will teach us, comfort us, protect us, strengthen us, and guide us … but to receive his help we must do things that will invite him to continue to be with us" (*Primary 5*, 1996, 7:34).

The Priesthood and Church Are Restored

In mid-May 1829, Joseph and Oliver "went into the woods to pray," concerned about understanding a passage "respecting baptism for the remission of sins." And as they prayed, they reported that another "messenger from heaven descended in a cloud of light, and having laid his hands upon us, he ordained us...." (JS-History, 68–72). The messenger said that his name was John, known as the Baptist, and that he acted under the direction of the Apostles of Jesus—Peter, James, and John [now immortals]—"who held the keys of the [p] riesthood of Melchizedek." Under the direction of this "valiant" prophet messenger, Joseph first baptized Oliver and ordained him to the Aaronic priesthood, and then Oliver did the same for Joseph. This messenger said that in due course the priesthood of Melchizedek would also be conferred upon these two, and that Joseph should be the first elder and Oliver the second elder of the restored church (*Primary* 5, 1996, 9:37).

Shortly after this visitation by John the Baptist, Joseph Smith and Oliver Cowdery took a trip to Colesville, New York. As they were returning to Harmony, Pennsylvania, Joseph later reported that the Apostles of Jesus— Peter, James, and John—appeared to them on the banks of the Susquehanna River. As recorded in D&C (27:12), these apostles conferred the "keys" of the Melchizedek priesthood on Smith and Cowdery, restoring the power of the priesthood to the earth following its long absence during the centuries known as the period of apostasy. The teacher notes, "The power of God (through the priesthood) was on the earth again: Joseph and Oliver now had the priesthood authority to act for the Lord upon the earth" (*Primary* 5, 1996, 7:38).

Publication of the Book of Mormon and Organization of the Church

The final steps in the restoration were the publication of the Book of Mormon and the organization of the restored Church of Jesus Christ. These foundational events are the subject matter of *Primary* 5 (1996), Lessons 10 and 11, and conclude the third (and fourth) vignette of JS-History. In the front matter of the Book of Mormon are two sets of testimonies, first of the three witnesses who were close participants in Smith's "translation process"—Oliver Cowdery, David Whitmer, and Martin Harris—and second, a group of eight witnesses who were also close companions of Joseph Smith. The first three declared "with words of soberness, that an angel of God came down from heaven, and he brought and laid before our eyes, that we beheld and saw the plates, and the engravings thereon...and bear record that these things are true" (Book of Mormon, front matter). The second eight also "bear record with words of soberness, that the said Smith has shown unto us, for we have seen and hefted, and know of a surety that the said Smith has got the plates of which we have spoken" (Book of Mormon, front matter). The teacher is told to have "the children think of ways they can be witnesses of the Book of Mormon and its teachings" and to list them on the chalkboard.

The Book of Mormon was published in March 1830 by Egbert B. Grandin, a printer in Palmyra, New York. This signal event presaged the organization of the restored church led by Joseph Smith as a prophet of God. The children, therefore, are to "be grateful that the Book of Mormon is available for them to read and study" (*Primary 5*, 1996, 10:47) and "to strengthen each child's testimony that through revelation the true Church was restored to the earth" (*Primary 5*, 1996, 11:52). Much of the attention in the tenth lesson focuses on the mechanics of printing and the security of Cowdery's complete copy of the manuscript. Joseph Smith also referred to the Book of Mormon as "the keystone of our religion," prompting a lesson activity that would expand upon this metaphor (*Primary 5*, 1996, 10:49). Another activity focuses on how the book's 16-page signatures were composed as part of the typesetting process (*Primary 5*, 1996, 10:50). The point to these exercises is that the Book of Mormon as an intelligible material object entered into the world of the LDS, providing the material basis for what its subtitle now claims: that it is another testament of Jesus Christ, establishing Mormonism firmly in the orbit of non-orthodox Christianity (Bushman 2005, 108; Shipps 1985:ix–xiv).

On Tuesday, April 6, 1830, an organizational meeting was held in the home of Peter Whitmer Sr. in Fayette, New York. Lesson 11 suggests that about 60 people attended this meeting, conducted by Joseph Smith. Six official members were recognized in accord with state law. "All of these men had seen the gold plates and had testimonies that Joseph Smith was a prophet and the person through whom Jesus Christ would restore his Church" (*Primary 5*, 1996, 11:53). The lesson continues:

> After a prayer, Joseph asked the people at the meeting if they accepted him and Oliver as their teachers and spiritual leaders. Everyone said yes by raising their hands (as [members] do in the Church today when [they] sustain people to callings). Joseph Smith and Oliver Cowdery then ordained each other to the office of elder. (*Primary 5*, 1996, 11:53)

Thereafter, Joseph Smith was recognized as the first prophet who received revelation on behalf of the restored church and its priesthood.

The cultural charter represented by the Joseph Smith-History of the events leading to the organization of the church provides five important vignettes that inform the initial lessons in *Primary 5* (1996). These include the first vision; the visits of the angel Moroni; the recovery of the gold plates, their translation, and their publication as the Book of Mormon; and the bestowal of the Aaronic and Melchizedek priesthoods. These vignettes are presented as important foundational stories introduced in senior primary for children ages eight to 11. The events these stories recount led to the organization of the church, the establishment of authority through the priesthood, and the recognition of Joseph Smith as the first prophet in these latter days. Out of these events was born the modern LDS Church.

Apostasy and Restoration

Given a question as to which is the true church, the second lesson in *Primary 5* focuses on the presumed characteristics or attributes that the true church should possess, as a basis for exploring the idea that "Jesus Christ's Church was taken from the earth because of apostasy and had to be restored to the earth" (*Primary 5*, 1996, 2:7). Five features of the true church, with supporting scriptural references, are identified:

(1) Ongoing revelation (Matthew 16:17);
(2) Priesthood authority from God (Luke 9:1–2; John 15:16);
(3) Living prophets and apostles (Amos 3:7; Ephesians 2:20);
(4) Ordinances done as Jesus taught (Matthew 2:16; Acts 2:38); and
(5) Heavenly Father, Jesus Christ, and the Holy Ghost [understood as] three separate personages (Acts 7:55–56).

Clearly, these criteria are designed to point to and fit the LDS Church. As the lesson develops, the children are told that the true church had once existed on the earth, but after Jesus Christ was crucified and his followers were killed, there was a falling away from Jesus' true church. This falling away is known as the apostasy. Subsequently, several church reformers such as John Wycliffe (in England), Martin Luther (in Germany), and Roger Williams (in America) sought to reestablish the church but "did not have authority from Jesus Christ to correct the problems" that each reformer had identified (*Primary 5*, 1996, 2:10). The true restoration occurred when "Heavenly Father chose Joseph Smith to receive authority for restoring Jesus Christ's Church on earth again" (*Primary 5*, 1996, 2:10). This reestablishment is known as the "restoration," when the five key features came to characterize the LDS Church through revelations to Joseph Smith following the first vision.

However, the foundational stories of the restoration would not be worth very much if they did not connect to the present operation of the church and its members. That connection is rooted in the doctrine of continuing revelation through a living prophet, which is developed in Lesson 15 of *Primary 5*, 1996, 15:76–79. The purpose of this lesson is "to help the children understand that revelation for the whole Church comes only through the living prophet and that we should follow him." The fundamental issue in this matter is authority: How shall authority be conceived? The answer is that authority for the whole church resides with the living prophet who stands in the order of succession among the prophets traced from the death of Joseph Smith in 1844 to the present.

Lesson 15 indicates that in the early days of the church, "a few other people besides the Prophet Joseph Smith claimed they were receiving revelations for the whole Church." This led to conflict over revelatory authority and confusion among members regarding to whom they should listen to hear the voice of Heavenly Father or Jesus Christ. In one instance, Oliver Cowdery, along with members of the Whitmer family, sought to correct the wording of a revelation given through Joseph Smith. The story is recounted as follows:

> While Joseph and Emma Smith were living in Harmony, Pennsylvania, a few months after the Church was organized, Oliver Cowdery disagreed with the wording of one of the revelations Joseph had received from the Lord. Oliver wrote to Joseph Smith and said, "I command you in the name of God to erase those words!" Joseph immediately wrote back to Oliver and asked him "by what authority" he undertook to command Joseph "to alter or erase, to add to or diminish from, a revelation of commandment from Almighty God" (*Primary 5*, 1996: 15:77).

A few days later, Joseph visited with the Whitmer family to discuss this subject and convinced Christian Whitmer that the meaning of the sentence was reasonable (as given by Joseph), and then reported, "I succeeded in bringing, not only the Whitmer family, but also Oliver Cowdery to acknowledge that they had been in error, and that the sentence in dispute was in accordance with the rest of the commandment" (see Smith, *History of the Church*, 2nd ed., vol. 1 (1978), 105).

A second episode involved Hiram Page, one of the eight witnesses to the golden plates, who claimed to use a "seer stone" to see revelations such as the location of Zion (where the church would be established as the kingdom of God on earth); this was also influencing Oliver. Just prior to a planned conference of the church at Fayette, New York, in September 1830, Joseph conveyed a message from the Lord to Oliver Cowdery; it said "that Joseph Smith was the only one authorized to receive revelation for the whole Church" (*Primary 5*, 1996, 15:79):

> 2. But, behold, verily, verily, I say unto thee, no one shall be appointed to receive commandments and revelations in this Church excepting my servant Joseph Smith, Jun., for he receiveth them even as Moses.
>
> 3. And thou shalt be obedient unto the things which I shall give unto him, even as Aaron, to declare faithfully the commandments and the revelations, with power and authority unto the Church.
>
> 4. And if thou art led at any time by the comforter to speak or teach or at all times by the way of commandment unto the Church, thou mayest do it.
>
> 5. But thou shalt not write by way of commandment, but by wisdom;
>
> 6. And thou shalt not command him who is at thy head, and at the head of the Church;
>
> 7. For I have given him the keys of the mysteries, and the revelations which are sealed, until I shall appoint unto them another in his stead (D&C 28:2–7).

The content of this revelation establishes the relationship between Joseph and Oliver as parallel to that between Moses and Aaron, as the one chosen by God for a special purpose and the other to serve and follow in obedience. At the same time, the revelation allows Oliver to speak or teach by way of wisdom and commandment, but not to command in writing, nor to command Joseph, who holds "the keys of the mysteries, and the revelations which are sealed, until I [the Lord] shall appoint unto them another in his stead." Thus, the revelation establishes an ordering of authority in the church in which the prophet stands at the top.

The lesson material indicates that others may also have claimed to receive revelations and that "Joseph Smith prayed to Heavenly Father about the problem and received D&C 43 as an answer. This revelation says that the prophet of the Church, whether Joseph Smith or someone who would be called to be prophet after Joseph, is the only one who receives revelation for the entire Church" (*Primary 5*, 1996, 15:78). The enrichment activities associated with this lesson include a further corollary that is canonized as D&C-Official Declaration 1 from Three Addresses by President Wilford Woodruff: "The Lord will never permit me or any other man who stands as president of this Church to lead you astray."

Another corollary is that every member of the church may receive revelation in regard to their own life or sphere of responsibility: a husband and wife for themselves and with respect to the family, a teacher with respect to his or her class, a bishop with regard to the ward, members of a stake presidency with respect to the stake, and so on as related to the hierarchy of offices in the church or vocations in the world. But the church president alone holds the keys of revelatory authority for the church as a whole.

The retelling of these foundational stories is intended to teach each new generation what their predecessors believed to be the chartering events of the church, their implications for today, and the basis of the church's authority in their lives. The stories come to life through the church's organization and leaders, its ordinances, rituals, and social practices, and its ongoing inculcation of fundamental beliefs. My own firsthand experience of the church began with a solemn assembly sustaining a new prophet when, as an anthropologist, I first began visiting the Crystal Heights second ward in Salt Lake City.

The Standard Works

Over the course of four years of study, senior primary children from ages eight to 11 are introduced to a sacred history embodied in the church's standard works: the Old Testament, New Testament, Book of Mormon, D&C, and the Pearl of Great Price. The interpretative Christian core of this history is recorded in the D&C and the Pearl of Great Price, which serve as the lenses through which the remainder of the canon is viewed.

The young learners in senior primary are introduced to the chartering stories of Joseph Smith, his first vision, the visits of the angel Moroni, the translation and publication of the Book of Mormon, and the bestowal of priesthood authority and the founding of Church of Christ (as the Church of Jesus Christ of Latter-day Saints was first known). In the expansion of study to the whole canon over the course of four years, the authority to speak through revelation to the whole church for Heavenly Father and Jesus Christ remains with the president of the church, whose words, along with those of the council of the twelve, direct the church and its members. The church's orientation to prophetic authority is well captured in the following hymn:

> We listen to a prophet's voice and hear the Savior too.
> With love he bids us do the work the Lord would have us do.
> The Savior calls his chosen seer to preach the word of God,
> That men might learn to find the path marked by the iron rod.
>
> Hymn 22, Hymns of the Church of Jesus Christ of
> Latter-day Saints
> Text: Marylou Cunningham Leavitt

7

For the Strength of Youth

DURING STANDARDS DAY in Lynnwood Stake, Seattle, Washington, Dean Bennion, one of the youth advisors, was leading a session on the theme "control thyself." He told of an experience reported earlier at a church fireside (an informal Sunday evening meeting) by Eugene R. Cook, who was his area mission president in Ecuador, South America. Elder Cook was flying from Ecuador to Houston. When he boarded the plane, he sat down next to a craggy-faced character in an open-buttoned shirt and faded blue jeans. Elder Cook didn't recognize this person, so he introduced himself:

"Hi, I'm Gene R. Cook of the Church of Jesus Christ of Latter-day Saints."
And the person next to him says, "Hi, I'm Mick Jagger."
And Gene says, "Nice to meet you, Mick."
And Mick says (louder), "No, I'm MICK JAGGER."
And Gene says, "Like I said, I'm Gene Cook; nice to meet you."
AND JAGGER OPENS UP A COPY OF *Rolling Stone Magazine* AND SAYS, "THAT'S ME ON THE COVER!"

Elder Cook figured out that he was talking to the rock star featured in this magazine and understood that this person sitting next to him was that real live person. Mick Jaggar was one of the kings of rock 'n' roll music. They proceeded to have a conversation that went something like this:

Elder Cook says, "Mick, I travel the whole world and speak to young people quite often, and some of them say to me that 'rock music has no effect on me at all,' and others say that your music has a very real negative effect. What do you think?" And Mick Jagger said—and I quote: "Our music is calculated to drive kids to have sex."

And Jagger proceeded to say that he thought the deterioration of the family was a good thing, that children should be liberated from their parents, that parents should have no say in their children's lives.

In telling this story, Elder Bennion went on to say:

But I testify to you, as Elder Cook did in that Fireside, that some people just don't care about what happens to the young people they seek to influence. You should be very careful about who or what you let into your lives, because some people are there for one main reason, to make a buck. They don't care about you. They're not like a loving father or mother, or Heavenly Father. They could care less what happens to you in your lives. They just want to make a buck. And they found that by making things crude and immoral, they could make a lot of bucks![1]

I don't want you to misunderstand me. I love music, all kinds of music, including rock 'n' roll. I hesitate to say things like this, by pointing to rock music. I don't think that any particular style of music is bad (though some lyrics may be), but what I'm suggesting to you is that you have a Heavenly Father who loves you. You have been—most of you—baptized into the Church and have the gift of the Holy Ghost. You have the right to have the Holy Ghost with you. And you have to be concerned with what enters your mind, what you let impact you, because what goes in has an effect on what you think and how you act (Bennion 1995, "Control Thyself").

Bennion's point, and one of the main points of standards day, is that a young person's identity as a member of the church is always under threat from others using worldly standards, including the threat that what enters a person's mind via the media may affect them in ways they may not want. Choice—agency—begins with "what you let impact you," because "what goes in has an effect on what you think and how you act."

Church Worthiness Standards for Youth

Standards day is an annual program in many stakes that brings together the young men and young women from the several wards of the stake in order to discuss and underscore the differences between LDS Church standards for behavior and the standards of contemporary popular culture. Psychoanalyst Erik

---

1. An earlier version of this story, taken from a talk given by Elder Cook at Ricks College (now BYU, Idaho) on October 25, 1988, "to illustrate an important point about selecting wholesome music." The text given here is not verbatim and does not fully convey either Elder Cook's words or Dean Bennion's interpretation. I found this text on the Internet while doing a search of church standards. Elder Cook bore testimony that good music can have a great impact on you and evil music surely is of the devil. Elder Bennion's warning was that "[y]ou should be very careful about who or what you let into your lives, because some people are there for one main reason, to make a buck. They're not like a loving father or mother, or Heavenly Father." My point was to understand church standards and how they are learned in the LDS family and church settings.

Erikson (1968) has suggested that the adolescent years are an important period for identity consolidation among young people. Erikson's view fits very well with the church's effort to establish alternative programs for LDS group and individual identity, self-discipline, and service that lays a foundation for adulthood as the next stage in the church's life plan (compare Erikson's chapter on "Growth and Crises of the Healthy Personality," 1980 [1959], 51–107). The standards day program at which Dean Bennion spoke was one way of underscoring the importance of what the church calls "worthiness" among church youth.

Purity, Chastity, and Fidelity as Primary Values

The primary values that the church standards program emphasizes are personal purity, chastity before marriage, and fidelity in marriage. These three values are linked together in a pamphlet titled "For the Strength of Youth" (2001), which seeks to support actions in accord with these values. The purity ethic focuses on the body as a tabernacle for the spirit (or spirit self), aiming at what the LDS consider moral cleanliness, wholesomeness, and good health. A key code of the purity ethic is provided by the "word of wisdom," which identifies actions that may affect the body in negative ways, phrased as taboos: Do not smoke, drink alcohol, or use drugs, and avoid coffee, tea, and other stimulants. On the positive side, the word of wisdom encourages a healthy diet and adequate exercise, and makes water the Mormon beverage of choice.

The chastity ethic for youth specifically concerns sexuality and is summarized under sexual purity. "Physical intimacy between husband and wife is beautiful and sacred. It is ordained of God for the creation of children and for the expression of love between husband and wife. God has commanded that sexual intimacy be reserved for marriage" ("Strength of Youth," 2001:26). Marriage and family therefore are the twin pillars of this ethic, underscoring sexual abstinence for everyone outside of marriage, whether a civil marriage or a temple marriage. The injunction is clear and specific: "Do not have any sexual relations before marriage, and be completely faithful to your spouse after marriage" ("Strength," 2001:26). Marriage is the fulcrum and norm of this ethic, and sanctions for this ethic grant considerable power to church authorities as matters of discipline and social control requiring confession, remorse, and repentance.

Worthiness Criteria

Worthiness is established by priesthood interviews regarding several normative aspects of beliefs and practices in the church. Each bishop and stake president is considered "a judge in Israel" and is considered to represent the Lord in conducting worthiness interviews. These local leaders are expected to seek the power of discernment in order to bless members and help them live according to the gospel. I constructed figure 7.1 to reflect the opposition of worthiness and unworthiness as church standards in relation to choice, discernment, and agency. These are centered around the concept of agency,

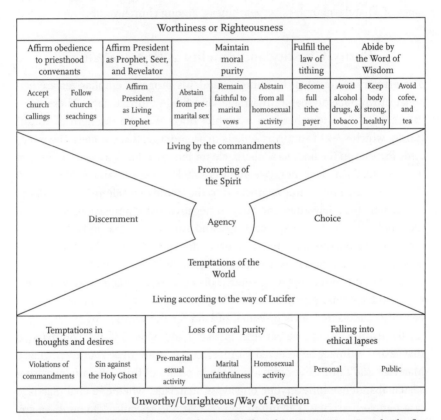

FIGURE 7.1 Chart Representing the LDS Church's Normative Standards for Youth.

This chart provides a set of panels and dimensions showing opposing social tensions. At the top of the chart is the category of worthiness or righteousness, which stands in contrast to the category of unworthiness, unrighteousness, or the way of perdition at the bottom of the chart. Then the more specific categories at both the top and bottom panels come together in the triangle of living by the commandments under the promptings of the Spirit on the one hand, over against living by way of Lucifer and the temptations of the world in the lower triangle. "Agency" by way of discernment and choice represents the central "norm" shown in this chart, surrounded at top and bottom by the specific contrasting norms—in positive terms of affirming covenants or commandments, honoring the prophet, living with moral purity, fulfilling the law of tithing, and practicing the word of wisdom.

which is bracketed on one side by the discernment of alternatives and on the other side by the making of choices among them.

The further elaboration involved in making worthy choices is represented as ascending upward from agency by following the prompting of the Spirit, and living according to the commandments of Heavenly Father, which encompass the specific categories of personal righteousness or worthiness, namely, obedience to priesthood covenants, affirming the church president as prophet, seer, and revelator, maintaining moral purity, fulfilling the law of tithing, and abiding by the word of wisdom. Each of these categories is then comprised of even more specific subcategories.

The descending elaboration of unworthy choices is like a mirror image that represents threats posed by the temptations of the world as a manifestation of living according to the way of Satan, by succumbing to his temptations in thoughts and desires, the loss of moral purity, and falling into ethical lapses. This personal unrighteousness also has its more specific subcategories that manifest the larger polarity of "opposition in all things" as a key feature of mortal life (2 Nephi 2:11–13).

Worthiness is considered an individual, confidential, and private matter beginning with a bishop's informal baptismal interview of eight-year-old children, and the more formal interviews related to advancement for 12-year-old boys preparing to receive the Aaronic priesthood and girls preparing to enter the young women program. The bishop also interviews each young man and young woman annually thereafter, and twice annually for those reaching the ages of 16 and 17. These interviews provide teaching opportunities regarding the church's doctrines and practices, including regular prayer, scripture study, honoring parents, paying a full tithe, modesty in dress, refraining from any sexual activity or reading, listening to, or viewing pornographic material, obeying the word of wisdom, refraining from the use of illegal drugs, using vulgar expressions or taking the Lord's name in vain. The church's booklet *For the Strength of Youth* (2001) may be used to guide discussions about obeying commandments, building a testimony, and preparing to serve a mission.

In the background of these worthiness standards and interviews among the youth are the worthiness standards for receiving a temple recommend to receive the endowment ordinance or a calling as a full-time missionary. The interviewing instructions to the bishop and stake president are as follows:

> Exercise great care when interviewing applicants for recommends to enter a temple. Make it clear that you represent the Lord in determining worthiness to enter his holy house. No unworthy applicant should

receive a recommend. Be certain that each applicant is worthy as a result of living up to Church standards and principles. Acceptable answers to the recommend interview questions ordinarily will establish worthiness to receive a recommend. Do not assume that worthiness to enter the temple at one time is reason for a casual interview later. Discuss the interview questions with each applicant, and keep each interview private.

Require an applicant who is not living up to Church standards and principles to demonstrate true repentence [sic] before receiving a recommend to enter a temple.

When interviewing an applicant for a recommend, do not inquire into personal, intimate matters about marital relations between a husband and his wife.

Generally, do not deviate from the recommend interview questions. If, during an interview, an applicant asks about the propriety of specific conduct, do not pursue the matter. Merely suggest that if the applicant has enough anxiety about the propriety of the conduct to ask about it, the best course would be to discontinue it. If you are sensitive and wise, you usually can prevent those being interviewed from asking such explicit questions (www.lds-mormon.com/veilworker/recommend.shtml; accessed 2008).

For young people, worthiness is established mainly by the chastity ethic and by the prospect and promise of forgiveness through repentance. The enforcement of chastity is modulated to some extent by age and maturity in the sense that full-fledged adults are held to stricter standards than teens, because adults ought to know better and are better able to control themselves. But worthiness also depends on a personal testimony of the truth of the Book of Mormon, that the church is the one true church, that the president is the living prophet, and that obedience through the priesthood is the requisite for good order in the kingdom of God on earth. Teaching and learning in the church has prepared young people for these fundamentals of worthiness, kept salient and visible in regular interviews with priesthood leaders as young men and women enter their teenage years.

The Two Priesthoods

There are two priesthoods in the church, the Melchizedek and Aaronic priesthoods (*Handbook, Melchizedek Priesthood*, 1998, 161). The Melchizedek priesthood is known as "the higher or greater" of these and "holds the right of presidency." This priesthood has "power and authority over all the offices in the Church" (D&C 107:8) and "holds the keys of all the spiritual blessings of the Church" (D&C 107:18). The Aaronic is the "lesser" priesthood, beginning at age 12.

The Aaronic priesthood is comprised of the offices of deacon, teacher, and priest. The Melchizedek priesthood includes the offices of elder, high priest, patriarch, seventy, and apostle. These offices represent divisions of authority with different rights, duties, and responsibilities for the operation of the church in the world, and each successive office includes all the duties and responsibilities of those that go before it, beginning as a deacon. Worthy brethren may be ordained elders when they are at least 18 years old. The title "elder" refers to the first Melchizedek quorum group and is used in addressing a missionary; adult men refer to each other as fictive kin known as "brethren" or as "brother so-and-so." A man holding the office of high priest may have authority to preside over a unit or activity of the church; thus, a priesthood holder is ordained to the office of high priest when called to a bishopric, stake presidency, stake high council, or when otherwise determined as worthy by the stake president (*Handbook, Melchizedek Priesthood*, 1998:162). "Patriarch" is also a stake level office wherever the church is organized, and provides for a senior Melchizedek priest whose authority is to give special one-time blessings to other church members (Mortimer, "Patriarchal Blessings," 1995:255–257). The office of a seventy is reserved for both area and general authorities, and apostles serve as the highest officers of the church. At the local level, members of the ward bishopric, stake presidency, and high council are all ordained as high priests in the Melchizedek priesthood.

The Aaronic priesthood is known as "an appendage to the Melchizedek priesthood" at the local level (D&C 107:14) and is generally reserved for young men ages 12 to 18; older male converts may also begin their priesthood progression in the Aaronic priesthood. Its authority includes "the key of the ministering of angels and the preparatory gospel," which is also known as "the gospel of repentance and of baptism, and the remission of sins" (D&C 84:26–27). The Aaronic priesthood is comprised of three age-graded offices—deacon (ages 12–13), teacher (ages 14–15), and priest (ages 16–17)—not to be confused with the office of high priest in the Melchizedek priesthood. Aaronic priesthood members meet in their three groups, referred to as quorums, under the presiding office of the bishop. The ward bishop serves as president of the Aaronic priesthood, and the three-member bishopric serves as its presidency (*Handbook, Aaronic Priesthood*, 1998:175–176).

By being ordained a deacon in the Aaronic priesthood, a boy is becoming a young man in the structure of the church. Two statements about the priesthood are particularly important: (1) "Although the priesthood is bestowed only on worthy male members of the [c]hurch, both men and women partake of its blessings" (*Handbook, Melchizedek Priesthood*, 1998:161), and (2) "No priesthood keys exist on earth except with the offices of the [c]hurch" (*Handbook, Aaronic Priesthood*, 1998:175). The first of these statements makes clear that priesthood is restricted as a male prerogative, though women are considered to be "co-equal with men" (Hawkins, et. al, 2000:63–82), while the second claims exclusive presiding authority on earth for priesthood leaders of the church, which undergirds the claim of the church to be the one true church for the administration of the kingdom of God on earth.

These statements also make clear that priesthood in the LDS Church is the fundamental structure of power. In formal terms, "the priesthood is the eternal power and authority of God. Through the priesthood He created and governs the heavens and the earth. Through this power He redeems and exalts His children, bringing 'to pass the immortality and eternal life of man' (Moses 1:39)" (*Handbook, Melchizedek Priesthood*, 1998:161).

Ordination to the Aaronic Priesthood and the Young Men Organization

Bridger Jensen was ordained a deacon in the Aaronic priesthood within days of his 12th birthday. With his parents' permission, he had been interviewed for worthiness by Bishop Justin Bell, and during sacrament meeting was presented to the members of the congregation for their sustaining vote. On this occasion, five or six Melchizedek priesthood holders gathered with the bishop in a small classroom following sacrament meeting. They formed a circle around Bridger and placed their right hands on his head and their left hands on one another's right shoulder. Bridger's father Clint performed the ordination of his son, conferring upon him the Aaronic priesthood, ordaining him to the office of deacon and bestowing its rights, powers, and authority, and then blessing him under the inspiration of the Spirit in the name of Jesus Christ. Bridger's mother Sally was also present to witness the ordination of her son. Bridger, his parents, and the bishop had given me permission to observe and photograph this ordination, which clearly signaled a rite of passage into young adulthood.

Having been ordained a deacon, Bridger joined others in the Aaronic priesthood for their opening exercises as part of the Sunday meetings, but then continued to meet with his senior primary class for the remainder of the year. Thereafter, he would meet with other Aaronic priesthood holders in their regular Sunday meeting classes.

The Role of Bishop

At the local level, the ward bishop is the focal point of power and authority. He is the central figure in the ward—the president of the Aaronic priesthood, the presiding high priest, a "common judge," the one who administers the church's local welfare program, and who oversees finances, records, security, and use of the ward meetinghouse. He delegates many assignments associated with these duties to one or the other of his two counselors, to the ward secretary, the ward clerk(s), and quorum and auxiliary leaders, but serving as bishop is really a second full-time job—though all ward callings are voluntary and unpaid, including serving as bishop. At the general level, the president of the church as prophet, seer, and revelator is the presiding apostle. The LDS believe that through him all power and authority flows from Heavenly Father and Jesus Christ into the ranks of the priesthood.

One difference between these organizational structures is that the bishop (rather than a member of the age-group quorum) serves as president of the priests quorum (in the Aaronic priesthood), and calls two age-group priests as assistants to join him. In a sense, the bishop in his person embodies the linkage between the Aaronic and Melchizedek priesthoods, because as bishop he is a high priest in the Melchizedek priesthood, as well as president of the Aaronic priests in the ward. In addition, because the young men organizational structure is an overlay on the Aaronic priesthood, each young men quorum president receives keys of presiding authority that the young women president does not. Like young men/Aaronic priests, the young women group also operates under the presiding authority of the bishop. Among other things, this also means that positions are filled by appointment from above, and nominees are sustained by a vote from below as part of the church's hierarchical ordering. This ordering makes clear the hierarchy of presiding power along with the church's claim of priesthood exclusivity under the concept of "keys":

> The exercise of priesthood authority is governed by those who hold its keys (see D&C 65:2; 124:123). These keys are the right to preside over and direct the Church within a given jurisdiction.
>
> The Lord Jesus Christ holds all the keys of the priesthood. He has given His Apostles the keys that are necessary for governing His Church. Only the senior Apostle, the President of the Church, may use

(or authorize another person to use) these keys for governing the entire Church (see D&C 43:1–4; 81:2; 132:7).

The President of the Church authorizes presidents of temples, missions, stakes, and districts; bishops and branch presidents; and quorum presidents to hold the priesthood keys they need to preside. A person who serves in one of these positions holds the keys only until he is released. Counselors do not receive keys, but they do receive delegated authority by calling and assignment.

No priesthood keys exist on earth except with the officers of the Church.

(*Handbook, Melchizedek Priesthood*, 1998:161)

As president of the priests' quorum in the ward, the bishop has direct responsibility for and oversight of the Aaronic priesthood and young women. His responsibility includes conducting an annual personal worthiness interview with each young man and young woman in the ward, and semiannual interviews with each priest and each 16- and 17-year-old young woman. In addition, at the six-month mid-cycle, the first counselor and second counselor interview each young man and young woman in the quorums and groups for which they are responsible.

Duties of the Aaronic Priesthood and the Coming of Age of Young Men

As a 12- and 13-year-old deacon in the Aaronic priesthood, Bridger was expected to share certain duties and responsibilities with his young men age mates. These expectations are spelled out in the *Handbook, Aaronic Priesthood*, 1998:175–176, which specifies duties as follows:

- He is to follow the counsel and instruction of the bishopric, quorum presidency, and quorum adviser.
- He passes the sacrament.
- He is a standing minister appointed to "watch over the Church" (D&C 84:111). He is also to "warn, expound, exhort, and teach, and invite all to come unto Christ" (D&C 20:59). Some ways he does this include notifying members of Church meetings, speaking in meetings, sharing the gospel, and bearing testimony.
- He assists the bishop in "administering...temporal things" (D&C 107:68). This [duty] may include gathering fast offerings, caring for the poor and needy, and caring for the meetinghouse and grounds. He also serves as a messenger for the bishop in Church meetings.

- He participates in quorum instruction (see D&C 38:23). He serves in quorum leadership positions as called and on quorum committees as assigned.
- He fellowships quorum members and other young men. He encourages them to participate in quorum meetings and activities. He supports each quorum member with sincere concern for his spiritual and temporal welfare. He also sets a good example for quorum members and encourages righteous behavior.
- He may be baptized and confirmed for the dead.
- He assists the bishopric in other ways consistent with this office. He also assists teachers "in all [their] duties in the Church...if occasion requires" (also see D&C 20:57).

This formal listing of duties in relation to members of the ward, the bishop, other Aaronic priesthood members, and members of his quorum is intended to help him take himself seriously by defining expectations for him in this priesthood role and giving him real responsibilities in relation to specific others in terms of their roles. In his identity as a deacon, he is now not only a baptized and confirmed LDS, but also a member of the priesthood within the church. And he can begin to envision his own future in the church through the succession of roles in the priesthood that he will take after beginning as a deacon, and then in the subsequent offices of teacher, priest, and elder in the Melchizedek priesthood.

Each of these offices will give him new powers and responsibilities while being inclusive of those of the prior offices. When he is ordained to the office of teacher at age 14, he will then help prepare the sacrament, serve as a home teacher, a peacemaker, and participate in seminary as he enters his high school years. At age 16, he will be ordained to the office of priest, adding further responsibilities to "preach, teach, expound, exhort...and visit the house of each member" (D&C 20:46–47). He may then "administer the sacrament" at the sacrament table and be authorized to offer the sacramental prayers (D&C 20:46), and also may baptize new members and "confer the Aaronic [p] riesthood and ordain deacons, teachers, and priests when authorized by the bishop" (see D&C 20:48), and in these and other ways will assist the bishopric in administering the ward (*Handbook, Aaronic Priesthood*, 1998:176).

Bestowal of ordination as a deacon on Bridger as a member of the Aaronic priesthood is therefore the first gender-based rite of passage for members of the church and opens the pathway to increasing power, authority, and responsibility for men in the church. This ordination also automatically brings boys into the young men organization.

Young Men Organization

The young men organization is largely the "temporal" aspect of the Aaronic priesthood, focused on learning more about the priesthood, participating in skill-building activities like boy scouts, and undertaking service projects on behalf of the church. The young men organization of priests, teachers, and deacons is led by a young adult presidency, modeled on the first presidency of the church and replicated throughout church organizations.

Steve Tanner was 28 years old when I talked with him about his role as president in the young men presidency in the Crystal Heights second ward, a position he had occupied for the previous year and a half. He was a returned missionary, an investment broker, and with his wife Kimi, was about to begin his family. Kimi was working as a physical therapist at the University of Utah Hospital. Steve's first counselor was Brian Fuller and his second counselor was Kerry Pyne, while David Sandberg served as secretary and Clint Jensen and Phil Meidel worked with the scouts. In many ways, Steve and his counselors worked in parallel with the bishopric, and I asked him about the relation of the Aaronic priesthood and young men. He explained that his calling was to oversee the temporal activities of young men, including the boy scouts, as a non-LDS function. "My position would be to oversee that activity, and in combination [with other responsibilities] to make sure that the activities we have and the lessons we teach meet the spiritual side, even though we're doing things like camping, service projects, things like that—just to make sure there's a spiritual side to all of the activities that we have." In his view, the young men organization includes the spiritual, but puts the emphasis on the temporal, and his presidency is responsible for making sure that there is a spiritual purpose to their activities:

> There are five or six different purposes that the young men organiza-
> tion tries to fulfill. What it boils down to is preparing young men to be
> good fathers and worthy missionaries, and that's through five different
> things—to help young men become converted to the gospel of Jesus
> Christ and live by its teachings; to magnify their priesthood callings; to
> give meaningful service; to prepare and seek the Melchizedek priest-
> hood; to commit to, worthily prepare for, and serve an honorable full
> time mission; and to live worthy to make temple covenants and prepare
> to become a worthy husband and father. So that's the bottom line of
> what the young men's organization is about (Tanner, Interview, 1995).
> (These six items are listed and expanded in the *Handbook, Aaronic
> Priesthood*, 1998:177–178.)

As shown in table 7.1, within young men groups, the Aaronic priesthood quorums (priest, teacher, deacon) each have an age-group presidency (president, first counselor, second counselor, with a secretary) plus a young adult quorum advisor and other specialists who may be needed, such as the scoutmaster and varsity coach, or others that the young men presidency deems necessary. Appointments to these presidencies and specialties are made by the bishop as a calling for which the recipient is set apart. This very full organizational structure makes clear that the young men of the church receive considerable attention, responsibility, and support in their lessons, activities, and church participation.

Table 7.1. Structure of the Bishopric and Young Adult Leadership

Bishopric	
Bishop	
First Counselor	
Second Counselor	
Young Men/Aaronic Priesthood	*Young Women Class Organization*
Priest (Ages 16–17)	Laurel (Ages 16–17)
Teacher (Ages 14–15)	MIA Maid (Ages 14–15)
Deacon (Ages 12–13)	Beehive (Ages 12–13)
Adult Leadership	
Young Men Presidency	*Young Women Presidency*
President	President
First Counselor	First Counselor
Second Counselor	Second Counselor
Secretary	Secretary
Scout Master	YW Camp Director
YM Sports Director	YW Sports Director
Stake YM Representative	Stake YW Representative

Notes: The office of bishop is complex, responsible for "comprehensive pastoral and administrative responsibility" at the ward (congregational) level. He is the "presiding high priest," a "common judge," and "president of the ward's Aaronic priesthood holders, and therefore particularly attentive to the youth of the congregation. He is assisted by two counselors, usually high priests, and these three men together form the bishopric to which others may be called by the bishop to assist in clerical, financial, and other administrative work.

Scouting

Scouting is viewed as part of the activity program of the church for boys and young men, and operates under the direction of the priesthood. "The ideals of scouting—to foster good citizenship, physical fitness, and moral integrity, all based upon a firm belief in God—are in harmony with the objectives of the church" (*Scouting*, 1985:2). The program begins with cub scouting for boys ages eight and nine organized as a pack that includes one or more dens. Ten-year-old boys are called Webelos. The dens meet weekly under adult leaders, with an adult leader like den mother Teresa Sadler, and packs meet monthly. Cub scouts employ an activity badge system to recognize achievement under the group names of Bobcat, Wolf, and Bear, culminating in Webelos and the Arrow of Light Award. The program involves overnight experiences as well as day camps, before graduating into the 11-year-old program of scouting prior to receiving ordination to the Aaronic priesthood.

The full scouting program is then integrated by age levels with the church's young men program and the Aaronic priesthood, pairing priesthood offices with troop groupings of deacons and scouts (ages 12–13), the team pairing of teachers and varsity scouts (ages 14–15), and the post-group pairing of priests and explorer scouts (ages 16–17), with adult Melchizedek priesthood leadership at each level. Clint Jensen served as scoutmaster in the Crystal Heights second ward, assisted by Kerry Pyne. Organized activities and a system of achievement recognitions culminate in the Faith in God Award and the On My Honor Award (*Handbook, Scouting*, 1985).

Recognition of Coming of Age for Young Women

In parallel fashion to young men entering the Aaronic priesthood, at age 12 girls are inducted into the young women organization, though without ordination or priesthood. The *Handbook, Young Women* (1998:211) indicates that the "purpose of the [y]oung [w]omen organization is to help each young woman 'come unto Christ' (Moroni 10:32). By following the Savior's example and teachings, she can fulfill her mortal mission and return to live with her Heavenly Father." Following a worthiness interview with the bishop, a young woman is publicly recognized during sacrament meeting as entering young women and joins the Beehive class (the youngest group) for opening exercises during Sunday school (as a transition from primary), but remains with her primary class until the next coming January, similar to a young man who becomes a deacon.

Young men and young women have similar leadership and group structures, as shown below. The ward bishop and his two counselors oversee both
young men and young women organizations, with one bishopric counselor
providing direct oversight to each. In turn, the young women organization is
led by a women's adult presidency that includes the roles of president, first
and second counselor, with an associated position of secretary. In the Crystal
Heights second ward at this time, Michelle Williams served as young women
president, and Michelle Hansen as first counselor and Celeste Sorensen as
second counselor, with Jennifer Merritt as secretary. Within young women,
three age groups are recognized as classes—Beehive (ages 12 and 13), MIA
Maid (ages 14 and 15), and Laurel (ages 16 and 17). These classes are not
attached to roles in the sense of priestly offices but simply provide ways of
aggregating young women in age structures similar to the young men. Each
of these classes has its own age-related presidency, and in consultation with
the young women presidency, may seek additional advisors for music, sports,
camp leadership, and other specialties. Appointments to these presidencies
and specialties are also made by the bishop as a calling for which the recipient
is set apart.

The Personal Progress Program

The young women leaders meet with each 12-year-old girl and introduce her
to the "personal progress program" based on young women values. This program of individual personal growth requires a young woman to keep journal
records of selected projects, experiences, and responsibilities under the guidance of parents and group leaders. The projects emphasize preparation for
the future as a temple-worthy and faithful young woman able to make and
keep covenants (promises). To be temple-worthy means following the church
standards outlined for both young men and young women in the booklet *For
the Strength of Youth* (2001), with a particular emphasis on moral purity. The
projects range over the three classes of young women programs and encourage developing leadership skills and personal talents and abilities, including
the skills of a faithful wife, mother, and homemaker. In consultation with
her mother and young women leaders, a young woman will set goals and
aim to accomplish them while keeping a record of her progress. This progress is recognized from class to class upon completion of all requirements in
Beehive (truth recognition), MIA Maids (promise recognition), and Laurels
(faith recognition), culminating with the awarding of the Young Womanhood
Recognition certificate and medallion, presented publicly in sacrament
meeting.

Young Women Values

The central theme (or mission) of young women includes learning to act upon seven key values that each young woman is ideally expected to embody. At each meeting or gathering of young women, a theme statement is repeated in unison:

> We are daughters of our Heavenly Father, who loves us, and we love Him. We will "stand as witnesses of God at all times and in all things, and in all places" as we strive to live the [y]oung [w]omen values, which are: Faith, Divine Nature, Individual Worth, Knowledge, Choice and Accountability, Good Works, and Integrity.
>
> We believe as we come to accept and act upon these values, we will be prepared to make and keep sacred covenants, receive the ordinances of the temple, and enjoy the blessings of exaltation (*Handbook, Young Women*, 1998: 211).

Each of these values is given a brief definition (and associated color and scripture) as a help for internalizing the meaning of the different values:

- **Faith** *(white):* I am a daughter of Heavenly Father, who loves me, and I will have faith in His eternal plan, which centers in Jesus Christ, my Savior (see D&C 14:7).
- **Divine Nature** *(blue):* I have inherited divine qualities which I will strive to develop (see 2 Peter 1:4–7).
- **Individual Worth** *(red):* I am of infinite worth with my own divine mission, which I will strive to fulfill (see D&C 18:10).
- **Knowledge** *(green):* I will continually seek opportunities for learning and growth (see D&C 88:118).
- **Choice and Accountability** *(orange):* I will remain free by choosing good over evil and will accept responsibility for my choices (see Joshua 24:15; 2 Nephi 2:27).
- **Good Works** *(yellow):* I will nurture others and build the kingdom through righteous service (see 3 Nephi 12:16).
- **Integrity** *(purple):* I will have moral courage to make my actions consistent with my knowledge of right and wrong (see Job 27:5).

(*Handbook, Young Women*, 1998, 212)

In addition to learning the young women values, each young woman is expected to hold to a set of standards of personal worthiness as a witness for

Christ. These standards expand upon those that are part of one-to-one worthiness interviews that have been a regular part of advancement in the church from before baptism to the present for each young woman and young man.

Field notes from Girls Camp, June 27, 1997

I joined Stake President Lynn Payne for a visit to girls camp at Wallsburg, Utah, at the end of June 1997. He was invited to give a talk that evening as part of an official visit to camp. We arrived earlier in the day at the camp, which consisted of many groupings of multi-person tents spread across a variety of niches under the forest canopy. The young women, from ages 12 and 13 to 16 and 17, were organized into ten or 12 named units generally taken from the Book of Mormon (the names chosen by the girls), each emphasizing a different theme. A number of family campers were distributed among the clusters of tents.

Throughout the morning and afternoon, the girls gathered under large canopies erected over wooden platforms holding chairs and tables. On the tables were many varieties of construction paper, leatherette, cloth, beads, banner material, paints, glue, wooden slats, hammers, nails, and other materials with which to fashion displays, cutouts, and visuals for their programs, as well as to make items of personal adornment. They were looking forward to performances and theatrical events that were scheduled for later in the week, and this was the work in progress. So, the girls, their young women advisors and scatterings of parent volunteers were busy under these canopies, while others were cleaning campsites or swinging from a rope suspended from a tree limb, and then plunging into a small stream. It was a scene of great variety, a multitude of projects, and activities that kept everyone busy.

In the early evening, we joined one of the campfire groups for a supper of beef stew, roasted potatoes, cooked carrots, and hot biscuits—with green punch as the beverage. Then, after a brief cleanup, everyone made their way to a hillside bowery fronted by a small wooden platform that served as a stage where a small singing group had assembled. The sun was just setting, and the girls were singing rounds of songs, including "Rise, Shine, Give God the Glory," "Give, Said the Little Stream," and "Singing, Singing, All the Day," with the chorus "Give Away, Oh, Give Away!"—and then Stake President Lynn Payne was introduced to provide the evening's message.

He began by offering public thanks to the stake and ward young women's leaders and the parents and advisors who had accompanied the girls to camp. He reminded them of the time six months earlier when snow was falling and these leaders had made telephone calls to each of the girls reminding them of the June girls camp and inviting them to sign up. "And wasn't this a great time!"

He then turned to the reason he was there, indicating his intention to draw their attention to the diaries of pioneer women whose journal entries, he said, spoke to the hardships and sufferings of an earlier time. And he asked his listeners to keep three criteria in mind as he recounted some of these pioneer stories. He said that the young women today could learn three important lessons that he wanted to highlight from these diaries: Keep your eyes on the prophet, put your shoulder to the wheel, and keep your feet firmly planted in the faith. And then he began reading from those diaries and journals some of the past stories of danger and loss, suffering and heroism, and determination and constancy. And, of course, he spoke too long, but the young women listeners indulged his enthusiasm as he told one last story. And then he concluded:

> You are as strong as were these pioneer women you've heard about tonight. You have great opportunities in your life. And just as God sent angels to those young pioneer women, God sends angels to you today, as we are reminded whenever we read the Book of Mormon.
>
> I bear witness that it is not in the nature of God to leave you alone. He will help and bless you in your own struggles. I am grateful to be with you at camp and hope you will remember those three things—to keep your eyes on the prophet, put your shoulder to the wheel ('til it hurts), and keep your feet firmly planted in the faith. God bless you in the name of Jesus Christ. Amen.
>
> (Field notes, June 27, 1997)

As the closing prayer was called, someone also announced that a pocket knife was lost should anyone happen upon it. After the prayer, we all dispersed—everyone heading for her tent as President Payne and I got in his car for the drive back to Salt Lake City.

Gender, Age, and Power

The parallel but different organizational structures for young men (Aaronic priesthood) and young women make clear the gender differentiation that is characteristic of church organization and authority from this point onward in the life course. Young women will increasingly prepare for the primary roles of wife and mother in the church, while young men will prepare for the primary roles of husband, father, and priesthood holder (including roles of leadership). Both men and women, of course, may take up other church roles, as well as careers beyond the church, but activity in church roles will consume considerable portions of time and energy, a process that begins in the young men and young women organizations.

Worthiness Interviews

The personal worthiness interviews are not meant to be intrusive but rather to offer opportunities for discussion of the pressures that young people face. This frequent one-to-one interaction ensures that each young person has regular adult priesthood guidance regarding the performance of positive duties on the one hand and the avoidance of proscribed activities on the other, and a chance to talk with an adult outside the home.

The positive duties include praying regularly in private and with one's family; honoring parents; speaking and acting honestly; treating others with kindness and respect; being morally clean; paying a full tithe; obeying the word of wisdom; doing one's duty in the church and living according to its rules and doctrines; fulfilling assignments given by the quorum presidency; attending priesthood and sacrament meetings and participating in other church meetings and activities. Taboos include sexual behavior beyond holding hands and a quick kiss (the "slippery slope" problem); reading, listening to, or viewing pornographic material; using tobacco, alcoholic drinks, coffee, and tea; using illegal drugs and similar substances; using the name of the Lord in vain; and making vulgar references and using other forms of degrading language (*Handbook, Young Women,* 1998:212).

The bishop confers with the parents or guardian, prior to the interview at age 12, with each young person (or when a boy advances in the priesthood) before he presents each young person's name in sacrament meeting for the sustaining vote of members. In case of a dissenting vote by a member in good standing, the objection is to be heard in private by the bishop or other presiding officer, or someone assigned by them, in order to ascertain the basis for a negative vote that might disqualify the person from the position. A negative vote is a rare occurrence.

Meetings and Activities of Young Men and Young Women Organizations

The young people's program of the church aims to counter mainstream teenage pop culture by providing a different set of challenges and experiences for adolescents than is offered by many other churches, most non-church social groups, the secular media, and the schools. And the church program appears to work well for most of those teenagers who stick with it; they generally leave young adulthood with a solid, if narrow, platform for new challenges in their early adult years. Those teen years also include pervasive threats to their youthful identity as LDS, and the church programs are designed to help these young men and young women cope with those threats to their identity as LDS.

Countering Threats to Social and Personal Identity

In his discussion of social and personal identity, anthropologist John Caughey (2006:14–20) links social identities with various traditions and institutional forms, such as regional variants of national cultures, racial and ethnic cultural differences, social class, religious, family, educational, occupational, political, philosophical, military, sports, media, and artistic cultural traditions. In each of these areas, people take roles, or social identities, in relation to one another (see Merton 1968 [1957; 1949]; Nadel 1957; Goodenough 1965). To claim identity as an LDS is to make just such a social identity claim in the American (and international) religious landscape, while providing a context for being a deacon in the Aaronic priesthood or a member of the MIA Maids in the LDS young women organization. "Personal identity" on the other hand has to do with "the kind of person one presents" to others (and reflexively to oneself)—for example, warm, aggressive, distant, kind, stubborn, and other ways of describing personality display within social identity contexts (Caughey 1980:173–177). Because these two aspects of identity—the social and the personal—become more or less integrated in the course of development, each person seems to acquire a unique and individual personality that revolves around their "master" identities. It is this integration of the social and personal to which Glynis Breakwell (1986) refers in her discussion of coping with threatened identity, where the threat may be to either the "content" or "value" aspects of identity as these contribute to what she considers the identity principles of self-continuity, personal distinctiveness, and self-esteem.

From the perspective of LDS Church leaders, the very first threat facing members of the church is loss of interest, leading to dropping out of church programs during the course of the teen years or later, or as a convert. Although the church keeps very good records of eligibility and participation in church activities, those records are not publicly available, so actual rates of declining interest and dropouts are unavailable. But informal observational and anecdotal evidence suggests that inactivity is not an uncommon problem among converts internationally, as well as domestically (Stewart 2007). Brian Fuller, who was serving as first counselor in the young men presidency (and teachers quorum advisor) in the Crystal Heights second ward, suggested from his experience that if young men "start out active and stay interested and there's encouragement from home, then they generally stay active in their priesthood quorum." Having "active parents makes a big difference," in his view. If young men drop out, he said, it was most likely to occur between being a teacher and a priest at age 16, about the time when they start to drive:

> Usually, the teachers are the ones that start to lose a little interest, and then turn 16 and become a priest, and start driving a car, and doing all the things they can do with a car. They become less active, wanting to find out what's going on [outside the church]. And a lot of times, priests will remain [in that office] until they go on their mission [at age 19] (Fuller, Interview, 1994).

Sunday Meetings of Young Men and Young Women

Both young men and young women meet twice weekly, once during the Sunday sacrament meeting quorum and auxiliary segments and each Wednesday evening from 7:00 to 9:00 p.m. The Sunday three-hour-block system for church meetings includes a 50- minute period during which young women and the relief society meet separately from, but parallel to, the Aaronic and Melchizedek priesthood quorums. The two priesthoods share a common opening exercise before gathering in their separate quorums. These Sunday meetings are devoted to studying the gospel, learning church and priesthood duties, and conducting business as necessary. They also share a Sunday school segment.

Wednesday Evening Mutual

The Wednesday evening meetings known as "mutual" are largely devoted to social activities, including one meeting each month combining young men and young women. In the Crystal Heights second ward, this combined meeting was usually the first Wednesday of each month, planning for which was rotated among the quorums and classes. The remaining Wednesday evenings were planned separately; for the young men, this activity was devoted to the scouting program (including scouts, varsity, and explorers). These programs often involved physical challenges like hikes, bike rides, bowling, or golfing—where costs are kept low and paid from the ward budget. Scouting involves the merit badge system for learning a variety of skills and progresses to the physical challenges of the varsity and explorer programs. In both young men and young women, the third Wednesday evening involves opening exercises with a prayer, a teaching thought, a song, and a brief "all about me" talk given by one of the youth focusing on hobbies, interests, and other facets of selfhood. Clearly, the aim of these programs is to build individual self-esteem and group solidarity through a variety of group activities.

The activities on Wednesday evening were highly varied, especially for the combined programs. They focused on service projects, social events, games, or other activities that arise from brain-storming among the class or quorum responsible that month. Michelle Williams's class of Laurels took the lead one Wednesday evening in organizing *Book of Mormon Feud*, based on the popular TV game show *Family Feud*, but using tests of Book of Mormon knowledge as the basis for team competition. Brian Fuller's teachers quorum group, on another Wednesday evening, planned a "road rally," a team competition scavenger hunt employing Book of Mormon clues to find specific historical and contemporary church history sites around Salt Lake City. For this activity, parent drivers were recruited to assist the five-member teams, as the rally clues were distributed in different parts of the city and required automobile transportation. Service projects involved cleaning the ward building, bundling quilts for distribution to the needy, helping at the Ronald McDonald House, and doing yard work or shoveling snow for elderly persons in the neighborhood.

Firesides

In addition to these ward meetings, Sunday evening quarterly stake-level "firesides" brought young men and young women together for special programs featuring a variety of guest speakers—usually general authorities in the church, but also popular authors and instructors, and others who could provide an inspirational message. And tri-stake dances, usually held on a Friday or Saturday evening, offered occasions for larger social gatherings beyond the borders of the local ward and stake. These gatherings took place under close adult supervision and according to church standards.

Seminary

In addition to young men and young women programs, the church also seeks to engage secular education at the high school and college levels and to supplement secular learning with programs of seminary (high school level) and institutes of religion (college level) that emphasize church teachings. Seminary, in particular, is addressed to young people ages 14 through 17 for purposes of religious education that involves studying the standard works and teachings of the prophets, supporting student efforts to live by gospel precepts, offering a spiritual and social climate of association, and encouraging them in church service.

The Crystal Heights second ward youth attended Highland High School; the early morning seminary program was held in a local ward building nearby. The seminary class started at 6:15 a.m. each school day and ran for an hour before regular 7:30 a.m. classes at the high school, about a block away. On one of the days when I was present, the seminary teacher, a specialist in financial planning, was seeking to teach the students about the value of money, its meanings, uses, and implications in their lives and the life of the church, tying this message to a scripture lesson about the Nephites in the Book of Mormon.

The seminary space in the ward building offered a gathering area of chairs and tables, with a ping-pong table off to one side, where a game was already in progress. On the other side was a hallway and door that opened into the classroom, which had chairs with writing tablet arms. At the back of the room were honeycomb shelves partitioned for individual student "cubbies" that could hold schoolbooks, notebooks, and "quads" (three-inch-thick combination scriptures of the Bible, Book of Mormon, D&C, and the Pearl of Great Price). The kids picked up their quads and left their schoolbooks in the cubbies, and then sprawled into the chairs half asleep (except for some super-attentive ones). In teen talk, the teacher was "awesome" in the sense that his enthusiasm was contagious, and even at this early hour in mid-winter, he was able to elicit comments, observations, and a modicum of occasionally heated discussion.

Seminary classes are run by the Church Educational System (CES) from its own budget, and no fees are charged. Students are expected to attend each school day during the four years of high school, with lessons rotating among the Old Testament, New Testament, Book of Mormon, and D&C, in correlation with senior primary and Sunday school courses. The class began abruptly when the instructor wrote two Book of Mormon references on the chalkboard and asked one young woman to read Jacob 3:11: "O my brethren, hearken unto my words; arouse the faculties of your souls; shake yourselves that ye may awaken from the slumber of death; and loose yourselves from the pains of hell that ye may not become angels to the devil, to be cast into that lake of fire and brimstone which is the second death."

Then the teacher asked the question: "What was Jacob saying to the Nephites about prophets?" And a young man volunteered that Jacob said prophets were calling them to repentance. The teacher asked, "What does the reference to 'hell' mean in the scriptures?" Another student suggested that suffering the

pains of hell meant spiritual death, and the teacher added, "And spiritual
death means separation from Heavenly Father." And then the class session
went forward, considering this scripture narrative verse by verse, including
the teacher's conceptual commentary about the difference between "prophets" and "profits," and the moral problems associated with the sole pursuit
of money, a particular problem for some of the Nephites, just as "fornication
and lasciviousness" were for others of them. Seminary, therefore, is another
way in which the church aims to engage its youth in study and practices that
serve as alternatives to current popular culture (Hammarberg, Seminary field
notes, 1995).

In terms of youth group religious experiences as reported in Christian
Smith's *Soul-Searching* (2003), the National Study of Youth and Religion
(NSYR), Mormon youth appear to be quite distinctive. They had the highest
rate of current religious involvement (72 percent) and an ongoing participation rate of 75 percent. The youth ministry was conducted overwhelmingly
by volunteers (85 percent), and 57 percent of participants reported attending
their current youth group once a week or more, which was more than double
the rate among all U.S. teens. And leadership within the youth group was
more widely distributed among the youth (36 percent) than was the case generally among all youth group participants (13 percent) according to the NSYR
report.

In many ways, the young men and young women who comprise LDS
youth are among the most religiously active young people in the contemporary United States. Smith notes that comparisons "across the religious traditions...reveal a noticeable pattern of religiosity, ranging from Mormons at
the high end, to conservative and black Protestants, further down to mainline
Protestant and Catholic teens, and then to Jewish and nonreligious teens on
the lower end" (Smith 2005, 70). The author does not seek to explain this pattern so much as to make note of it.

For the Strength of Youth

In an effort to minimize the impact of what leaders perceive as an overly
sexualized, secular, general American public culture, the first presidency
published a newly revised version of the pamphlet *For the Strength of Youth*
(2001). In turn, the church promotes the alternative of sexual abstinence and
chastity before marriage through a variety of channels including the church
magazine for teens and young adults, *New Era*, and "standards" gatherings
that emphasize positive interpersonal relationships in the context of the law
of chastity.

Agency, Adolescence, and Accountability

The opening paragraphs of the pamphlet *For the Strength of Youth* underscore the conditions of choice, agency, and accountability:

> Your Heavenly Father has given you agency, the ability to choose right from wrong and to act for yourself. You have been given the Holy Ghost to help you know good from evil. While you are here on earth, you are being proven to see if you will use your agency to show your love for God by keeping his commandments.
>
> While you are free to choose for yourself, you are not free to choose the consequences of your actions. When you make a choice, you will receive the consequences of that choice. The consequences may not be immediate, but they will always follow, for good or bad. Wrong choices delay your progression and lead to heartache and misery. Right choices lead to happiness and eternal life. That is why it is so important for you to choose what is right throughout your life.
>
> You are responsible for the choices you make. You should not blame your circumstances, your family, or your friends if you choose to disobey God's commandments. You are a child of God with great strength. You have the ability to choose righteousness and happiness, no matter what your circumstances.
>
> You are also responsible for developing the abilities and talents Heavenly Father has given you. You are accountable to Him for what you do with your abilities and how you spend your time. Do not idle away your time. Be willing to work hard. Choose to do many good things of your own free will (*For the Strength of Youth* 2001:4–5).

The Law of Chastity

This booklet then lists a series of topics for further discussion—gratitude, education, family, friends, dress and appearance, entertainment and the media, music and dancing, language, dating, sexual purity, repentance, honesty, Sabbath day observance, tithes and offerings, physical health, service to others, faith—and concludes with "THE LIVING CHRIST: The Testimony of the Apostles, and The Family: A Proclamation to the World."

Under "dating," the booklet indicates that those who date "are responsible to help each other maintain their standards and to protect each other's honor and virtue." Dating too early (before age 16) "can lead to immorality." In an effort to reduce what might be viewed as an early form of dating pressure, the booklet notes: "Not all teenagers need to date or even want to," and suggests that young people who begin dating should plan "activities that are positive and inexpensive and that will help you get to know each other" (*Strength of Youth*, 2001:24–25).

The section on sexual purity in *Strength of Youth* anticipates the physical intimacy between husband and wife as "ordained of God for the creation of children and for the expression of love between husband and wife." However, the command is clear: "God has commanded that sexual intimacy be reserved for marriage." This statement underscores the law of chastity as a purity code of premarital sexual abstinence. Further discussion provides a rationale for this commandment as a form of preparation "to make and keep sacred covenants in the temple," "to build a strong marriage and ... bring children into the world as part of a loving family," and to "protect yourself from the emotional damage that always comes from sharing physical intimacies with someone outside of marriage" (*Strength of Youth*, 2001:26).

From leaders of the church, the command is clear: "Do not have any sexual relations before marriage." This law of chastity seeks to counter the ways that "Satan may tempt you to rationalize," and advises, "Do not do anything to arouse the powerful emotions that must be expressed only in marriage. Do not participate in passionate kissing, lie on top of another person, or touch the private, sacred parts of another person's body, with or without clothing. Do not allow anyone to do that with you. Do not arouse these emotions in your own body" (*Strength of Youth*, 2001:26–27).

As these further instances illustrate, the standards are quite explicit. Under "music and dancing," for instance, is the injunction: "Choose carefully the music you listen to. Pay attention to how you feel when you are listening. Don't listen to music that drives away the spirit, encourages immorality, glorifies violence, uses foul or offensive language, or promotes Satanism ...," and another: "[w]hen dancing, avoid full body contact with your partner. Do not use positions or moves that are suggestive of sexual behavior" (*Strength of Youth*, 2001:20–21). Under "entertainment and the media," young people are told to choose only those media "that uplift you." "Do not attend, view, or participate in entertainment that is vulgar, immoral, violent, or pornographic in any way" (*Strength of Youth*, 2001:17). These standards—both virtues and prohibitions—are normative ideals against which individuals may judge their own thoughts, feelings, and actions, and by which others may judge them too. They also have the social effect of binding adherents as a group who live together under these standards, which serve as criteria for group participation. Brian Fuller summarized these standards by saying,

They talk about dressing modestly, maintaining cleanliness, friendships, and relationships with the opposite sex. The main thing that's taught is chastity. You don't have any sexual relationships with anyone before you're married, to keep yourself morally clean for marriage, and that's something sacred.... That's a big concern in the Church, not only from local leaders, but all the way up to the prophet. The President of the Church is concerned about the youth. The pamphlet was written by the First Presidency. It's used as a teaching tool by youth leaders, who encourage the youth to keep the small one with them all the time.... I keep mine with me (Fuller, Interview, 1994).

Brian Fuller also gave me one of the wallet-sized pamphlets that are distributed to young men that summarize the church's worthiness standards for youth as listed below. The complete set of standards spells out a code of conduct that applies to all youth. Young men are encouraged to keep a copy in their wallet for ready reference at any time of temptation. Indeed, one of the "tests" during the standards day session I attended in Lynnwood stake occurred when the leader of the session asked the young men to hold up the copies of the code that they carried in their wallets, and all who did received a candy bar as a reward.

Worthiness Standards for the Strength of Youth[2]

Agency and Accountability

Choose righteousness and happiness, no matter what your circumstances. Take responsibility for the choices you make. Develop your abilities and talents, and use them for good. Avoid idleness and be willing to work hard.

Gratitude

Have a spirit of gratitude in all you do and say. Thank God for your blessings, and express appreciation to others who help you.

Education

Prepare to be an influence for good in the world. Obtain an education, and be enthusiastic about learning. Attend seminary.

Family

Do your part to build a happy home. Honor your parents, and strengthen your relationships with your brothers and sisters.

Friends

Choose friends who share your high standards. Treat everyone with kindness and respect. Invite friends of other faiths to Church activities. Reach out to new converts and those who are less active.

---

2. Source: *For the Strength of Youth*, wallet-sized version (Intellectual Reserve, 2001).

Dress and Appearance

Dress modestly to show respect for God and yourself. Never lower your dress standards for any occasion. Do not disfigure your body with tattoos and body piercing.

Entertainment and the Media

Choose uplifting entertainment. Avoid anything that is vulgar, immoral, violent, or pornographic in any way. Commit to keeping God's standards.

Music and Dancing

Listen to music that helps you draw closer to Heavenly Father. Do not listen to music that encourages immorality, glorifies violence, or uses offensive language. When dancing, avoid full body contact or suggestive movements.

Language

Use language that uplifts, encourages, and compliments others. Use the names of God and Jesus Christ with reverence and respect. Do no use profane, vulgar, or crude language or gestures.

Dating

Do not date until you are at least 16 years old. Date only those who have high standards. When you begin dating, go in groups or on double dates. Plan activities that help you remain close to the Spirit of the Lord.

Sexual Purity

Keep yourself sexually pure. Do not have any sexual relations before marriage. Do not participate in talk or activities that arouse sexual feelings. Do not participate in homosexual activities. Seek help if you become a victim of rape, incest, or other sexual abuse.

Repentance

Through the Savior's atonement, you can receive forgiveness and be cleansed from your sins, when you repent. Confess your sins to the Lord and to those you have wronged. If the sins are serious, you also need to confess them to your bishop.

Honesty

Be honest with yourself, others, and the Lord. Do not rationalize that dishonesty is right.

Sabbath Day Observance

Use the Sabbath to worship the Lord, attend church, draw closer to your family, and help others. Do not seek entertainment or spend money on the Sabbath. When possible, avoid working on Sunday.

Tithes and Offerings

Willingly pay a full tithe. Attend tithing settlement. Obey the law of the fast.

Physical Health

Keep the word of wisdom. Eat nutritious food, exercise regularly, and get enough sleep. Do not use hard drugs, alcohol, coffee, tea, or tobacco products. Do not abuse prescription or over-the-counter medications.

Service to Others

Serve others in your church assignments and in your home, school, and community. Seek daily the guidance of the Holy Ghost to know whom to serve and how to help meet their needs.

Go Forward with Faith

Be true to the Lord and to His Church. Regularly pray in private and read the scriptures. Keep your covenants and listen to the whisperings of the Spirit. The Lord will help you meet your trials and challenges.

As shown above, the 1990 categories of the "wallet code" (like the 2001 "Strength of Youth" version) included dating, dress and appearance, friendship, honesty, language, media, mental and physical health, music and dancing, sexual purity, Sunday behavior, repentance, and spiritual help. The standards within these categories emphasize both positive virtues and negative prohibitions, and occasionally statements of belief or knowledge.

From early childhood and early adolescence onward, the church becomes a partner with parents in directing and valuing sexual beliefs, feelings, and behavior, but knowledge in this area has lagged. The 1985 booklet *A Parent's Guide*, which focused on intimacy, provided a minimal guide to physical aspects of human sexuality. It was the first and remains the only guide to sexuality that the church has produced. On its basis, parents were encouraged to monitor public school sex education as supplementary to their own and the church's efforts. In the meantime, the cross-cultural and biomedical study of sexuality has made some important strides (Money 1988; Francoeur 1991; Suggs and Miracle 1993; Miracle, Miracle, and Baumeister 2003). The church has cautioned its members to "go slow" as it has sought to develop a different program.

The Problem of Sexual Identity and Orientation

Same-gender sexual activity is forbidden to members of the LDS Church and in the past was the object of harsh criticism. Homosexual behavior remains categorized as a serious sin (Oaks 1995; 2006) that results in excommunication, even as same-gender attraction has come to be understood as a biological and psychological component of gender identity and gender orientation. The church's position appears to have softened somewhat in the last ten years, though that may be more a softening of rhetoric than of any real change in principle or policy (Oaks and Wickman 2006). The church's opposition to homosexuality causes considerable anxiety within many families and under-cuts the church's most fundamental doctrine that all human beings are sons and daughters of heavenly parents, who love and nurture them in the hope of a return to their eternal home.

The Role of Scriptural Precedence

The scriptural references that are often interpreted as condemning homosexu-ality occur primarily in the Old Testament book of Leviticus, especially the story of Sodom and Gomorrah, and in the New Testament writings of the Apostle Paul. In addition, church presidents since the 1950s have opposed same-sex relationships. On the other hand, Jesus did not speak to this issue, and in canonical LDS scriptures such as the Book of Mormon, the D&C, and the Pearl of Great Price, there is no guiding commentary. The prophet Joseph Smith did not address this issue. Thus, the church's current position appears to be largely derived from the earlier norms of the wider society that have been characterized as homophobic and lacking an adequate biomedical foundation.

A Recent Statement of the First Presidency

The church released a first presidency statement regarding same-gender mar-riage on October 19, 2004:

> As a doctrinal principle, based on sacred scripture, we affirm that mar-riage between a man and a woman is essential to the Creator's plan for the eternal destiny of His children. The powers of procreation are to be exercised only between a man and a woman lawfully wedded as husband and wife.
>
> Any other sexual relations, including those between persons of the same gender, undermine the divinely created institution of the family. The Church accordingly favors measures that define marriage as the union of a man and a woman and that do not confer legal status on any other sexual relationship. (News Release: <www.lds.org/newsroom/ showrelease>, accessed October 2004)

Thus, the law of chastity applies to gays and lesbians, while heterosexual cou-ples may seek a civil marriage to realize legitimate sexual activity as members of the church. A temple sealing in marriage, rather than a civil marriage, is the church's highest form of marriage according to its own standards.

Multi-Stake Standards Day and Evening Dance

As a way of bringing group sentiment to bear in support of church standards for youth, a program called "standards day" was organized for Lynnwood stake around three themes—"Know Thyself" (meaning as a child of God), "Control Thyself" (meaning self-control according to church standards), and "Give Thyself" (meaning in service to the church and other people). The program offered the youth of six or seven wards and branches an opportunity to meet one another in a context where adult leaders directed activities and conducted discussions according to the normative beliefs of the church. Similar standards programs are organized in stakes throughout the church.

The codes of conduct for young men and young women are "behavioral" in the sense that they focus mainly on actions, though occasionally on thoughts and feelings, with a particular emphasis on the ability and responsibility of the individual person to bring their thoughts, feelings, and actions under personal control in accord with church standards. Thus, personal choice serves as the situational contingency for expressing agency, making the individual responsible for his or her actions. And the individual is characterized as morally accountable across a wide range of personal and social experience.

As an observer in Lynnwood stake in Seattle, Washington, I attended a multi-stake dance for the youth. These teenage members of the church were encouraged to bring their nonmember friends with them to this event with the understanding that member and nonmember youth alike were to be bound by the same church standards. These standards were underscored and reinforced through one-on-one interviews conducted by members of the ward bishoprics, the stake presidencies, and members of the stake high councils as the young people arrived at the stake center.

The interviews were provided for both members and nonmembers, who were asked to sign a pledge to abide by those church standards. Kids came in groups, as well as singly, and parents knew in advance that the dance ended promptly at 10:00 p.m. At the dance, there was plenty of excitement. The music was highly varied forms of rock 'n' roll, selected by DJs who were also pledged to uphold church standards. And the leaders of young women and young men mingled easily with the crowd, joining in some of the dances, standing and talking during others, and generally encouraging those attending to have a good time.

Testing the Limits: A Model of Sin, Repentance, and Forgiveness

Life, from birth to death, is viewed as an arena of "testing" within the church, with the recognition that people may make mistakes or commit sins, and that they can learn from those mistakes within a framework of sin, remorse, repentance, and forgiveness. The code itself makes repentance as a process clear and explicit: "If you have made mistakes, you can be cleansed through proper repentance" (*Strength of Youth*, 1990, "Repentance," 29). Speaking in a personal note, Jane Hawley, a young women leader I interviewed in the Phoenix East stake, summarized her own experience of repentance a decade or so earlier as a teenager:

> It had been about five or six months since I had gone to the bishop. I said to him: "This is what I've been doing in my life, and I'm not happy, and I want to get things right with the Lord. I know I need to come to you to do that, and talk to you about these things." And that's what I did, and it was a very healing experience for me. I was terrified for months ahead of time, [saying to myself:] "I've got to tell the bishop everything I've been doing!" And I went and I did it and felt such a healing. It was beyond what he had done for me that day. It was like he was the mediator between me and Heavenly Father.
>
> He said, "Yes, what you've been doing isn't good, but you'll be okay; here's what we need to do—A, B, C—to get you feeling better again." And it worked. I followed his counsel and began to feel peace come into my life again (Hawley, Interview, 1995).

In terms of its component steps, this account led to a sense of forgiveness and personal renewal. Jane expressed (1) an awareness of having breached or violated one or more of the church's worthiness standards, saying "I'm not happy, and I want to get things right with the Lord"; next (2) she reached the decision to make a full confession to the bishop and the Lord [though for serious sin, confession might jeopardize membership or standing in the church]; (3) she then received emotional support and attentive listening from the bishop; and (4) together they worked out a plan of restitution and healing (characterizing the bishop's intervention as if he were a mediator between her and Heavenly Father) and as a way of "making right" the wrong that had been done; (5) taking into account any other persons who might have been harmed; then (6) accepting a penalty authorized by the bishop as the presiding authority [implied by "I followed his counsel"]; and finally (7) a promise to the Lord (and bishop) not to repeat this wrong in the future [unstated, but implied by "it worked"]. The result was a deep sense of forgiveness that renewed individual commitment to the normative standards of the church ["I began to feel the peace come again"].

Therefore, exhortations and the wallet-sized *Strength of Youth* (1990) pamphlets and other sources of instruction may rightfully proclaim that spiritual guidance is available: "You are never alone. Rely on the Holy Ghost. Knowing what is right and wrong is always possible" (under "Spiritual Help"). "Forgiveness is available." The goal, then, for LDS youth is personal "moral cleanliness" according to church standards attained through personal control of one's own actions according to those standards, which are intended to consciously differentiate LDS from others in the wider society.

Coming of Age: Acquiring the Personal Identity of LDS Youth

Among LDS, the shaping forces of age and gender are given cultural primacy as Mormon young people enter the young men and young women organizations. The initial thrust is to ordain young men with the power of the Aaronic priesthood at age 12, inaugurating a series of offices to be enacted as role identities. Thus, to the spiritual identity of a child of God and the LDS identity as a baptized member is added a priesthood identity as a deacon, teacher, and priest in relation to other role identities in the church. Among others, the identity of deacon was also linked to maleness and manhood, in contrast to femaleness and womanhood. From the moment of ordination, young men and young women are not only aware of, but also must deal with, this gender distinction and the power that an adult male priesthood identity brings to its bearer.

From Culture as Given to Culture as Choice

The symbolic movements that begin with the Aaronic priesthood ordination track a three-step set of male offices as deacon, teacher, and priest. The reciprocal movement among female members is the structured set of three classes (not role identities or offices) for young women in an organization that divides them into Beehives, MIA Maids, and Laurels. That symbolic movement reverberates to the young men, as an organization that is an overlay on the Aaronic priesthood and linked with scouting. The young men organization is not an auxiliary as are primary, young women, and Sunday school, because the young men organization is rooted in the Aaronic priesthood.

The young men program emphasizes an incremental public presence as a young man becomes a deacon, teacher, and priest, providing opportunities to give blessings, opening avenues of leadership, and fostering the right to preside. A young man will learn what it means to represent the church as a missionary, and later to be a good husband and father as complementary to his priesthood roles and career. Scouting provides opportunities for the development of skill-sets within a merit-badge system of outward recognition and reward. The young women program focuses on the cultivation of value orientations, nurturance, and personal recognition in the domestic spheres of wife-to-be, mother-to-be, and homemaker. Family issues become her primary domain somewhat disconnected from educational and career considerations. Nonetheless, young women are entering employment in about the same proportions as non-LDS women, a reality that is not yet fully recognized in church programs.

For both young men and young women, the church establishes the fundamental standard of chastity before marriage and fidelity in marriage, and develops this as part of the church's core morality in relation to its other standards of personal worthiness. The worthiness standards come to be regarded as constituting a good Mormon as a baptized and virtuous young woman or a baptized, valiant, and ordained young man. And in the young men and young women organizations, the dimension of service to others receives its first programmatic implementation through participation in home teaching and visiting teaching.

8

Endowed from on High

THE AIR WAS cold and crisp with light snow falling on an evening in January 1995 when I toured the Bountiful Utah Temple. This tour was during the public open house prior to the temple's dedication. With my escorted group, I went to see the baptismal font set on the backs of 12 sculpted oxen and passed through several places of assembly and ordinance rooms leading to the celestial room, a space decorated to mark the special glory and elegance fitting its name. Cameras are not allowed in the temple, so I left mine at home. But I was very much struck on this occasion by the actions of the young men and young women outside the building, who were assisting visitors in donning slippers worn to protect the interior carpeting. This activity was a small measure of service by these young people. So I returned a few days later with my camera to take pictures of their work outside the building itself; this seemed to me to be symbolic of the roles of service all members are asked to take. I also took pictures of the lines of the faithful and the visitors who came to learn more about the meanings among the LDS of the temple as a sacred edifice (see figure 8.1).

Nearly 20 years earlier, I had made a similar journey to the newly constructed Washington, D.C., Temple in Silver Springs, Maryland, bringing with me a class of graduate students from the University of Pennsylvania. That dedication was the first time I observed temple architecture both inside and out. Soaring exterior walls and massive, high spires gave me the mistaken impression that LDS temples enclosed a large congregational area, like a cathedral or mosque, but what I discovered was that the temples actually had several interior stories, with sequences of rooms and spaces that serve quite specific ritual purposes—baptisms for the dead, sacred washings and anointings, endowments, and sealing ordinances for both the living and the dead.

The Meaning and Purpose of the Temple Ordinances

The temples of the LDS are not used for congregational worship. That style of collective worship occurs in local ward meeting houses and stake centers, and

FIGURE 8.1 The Salt Lake City, Utah, Temple.
The Salt Lake Temple was the third Utah temple constructed after the Kirtland, Ohio, and the Nauvoo, Illinois, temples. A fully illustrated memorial book, *The Salt Lake Temple: A Monument to a People* (Salt Lake City, UT: University Services Corporation, 1983) is readily available and provides an interpretation of its architectural background. Photograph courtesy of the author.

for semiannual general conferences, now held in the 21,000-seat conference center and broadcast via satellite to locations around the world. These are the times and places where Mormons gather as congregations.

Mormon temples serve an altogether different purpose than other places of gathering. The temples are focused on the redemptive work of individuals in their purest religious roles, as temple patrons undertaking temple ordinances for themselves and as proxies doing vicarious temple ordinances for those who have died. Janet Kincaid (2000:28) defined this individual form of worship as "extraordinary worship," requiring the use of the temple as its own designated sacred place. This kind of worship is a form of religious work. Seattle Temple President Brent Isaac Nash (1995) explained to me that "a temple is a place where we work each week day. It's not even open on the Sabbath. It's closed on the Sabbath. We work here five days a week, Tuesday through Saturday, and Sunday it's closed. And people go to worship in their [ward] chapel. So [the temple] is a house of labor, for working."

The temples of the LDS and the temple ordinances performed within them hold a central place in the church's life and in the spiritual life of its members. Once dedicated, only worthy LDS may enter the church's temples, and members who undertake the endowment ordinance as part of their temple work make solemn promises not to reveal certain keywords, signs, and tokens associated with the covenants and promises that form the central features of this ordinance, keeping those keywords, signs, and tokens hidden from profane eyes and therefore sacred (Packer 1980:28). As part of members' work of vicarious service, these rituals are repeated time after time in temple work for the dead as part of "the new and everlasting covenant" (D&C 132).

The *Encyclopedia of Mormonism* defines the central role played in the life of members of the church by the temple ordinances:

> The privilege of entering the House of the Lord, the temple, and participating in its ordinances is a spiritual apex of LDS religious life. Through temple ordinances, one receives a ceremonial overview of and commitment to the Christlike life. Temple ordinances are instruments of spiritual rebirth. In the words of President David O. McKay, they are the "step-by-step ascent into the eternal presence." Through them, and only through them, the powers of godliness are granted to men in the flesh (D&C 84:20–22). Temple ordinances confirm mature discipleship; they are the essence of fervent worship and an enabling and ennobling expression of one's love for God.
>
> (Rozsa, "Temple Ordinances," 1992:407–410)

Background of the Temple Ordinances

In his study of the historical development of the temple ordinances, *The Mysteries of Godliness* (1994:35–58), David John Buerger showed that the ritual elements upon which Joseph Smith drew for the temple ordinances came largely from Masonic rites and scriptural sources, as well as personal revelation. In Nauvoo, Joseph Smith had been inducted into the Masonic order and subsequently suggested that its rituals represented corrupted forms of the rituals of Solomon's temple, which he then sought to restore. Sociologist Armand Mauss (1987:80), commenting on the temple ordinances, noted that "prophets and religions always arise and are nurtured within a given cultural context, itself evolving," and that "even the most original revelations have to be expressed in the idioms of the culture and biography of the revelator." These features certainly seem to have been present for Joseph Smith as he constructed the temple ordinances.

Religious studies scholar Douglas Davies, in his *Introduction to Mormonism* (2003), distinguished between the earliest "Book of Mormon Mormonism" practiced under Joseph Smith early in his career and later "Doctrine and Covenants Mormonism" as reflecting a second stage in his prophetic revelations, the latter focusing on the temple. These two distinctive scriptural sources—the Book of Mormon and the Doctrine and Covenants—serve as records linked to the doctrines of salvation in early Mormonism on the one hand, and the doctrines of exaltation in the Nauvoo period on the other, that emerged just before the LDS moved West. These differences, Davies has suggested, were even reflected in the architectural differences between chapel and temple in the further development of Mormonism (Davies 2003:222–224).

Sealing as the Power of the Priesthood

In spite of the differences between earlier and later Mormonism, there are significant conceptual continuities between these periods that knit them together. The most important of these is the concept of "sealing," associated with the bestowal of the high priesthood on June 3, 1831. Buerger (1994:2–3) considers this conferral of a sealing power to be one of the most important developments in Book of Mormon theology, which certainly undergirded later ceremonial developments in Nauvoo.

In Buerger's view, the Book of Mormon story of Nephi, son of Helaman (Helaman 10:7), shows how the word "seal" was substituted for the biblical word "bind" (Matthew 16:17–19) as the form of God's power that was bestowed upon the Apostle Peter. Thus, in LDS interpretation, the Book of Mormon story represents Helaman as a human agent who is the recipient of a super-natural power, one that must be ratified by Heavenly Father as it is fulfilled through individual righteousness. This shift in power from the divine to the human agent opens the way for members of the Melchizedek priesthood to "seal [people] up unto eternal life" (Buerger 1994:5; D&C 68:2, 12; also 1:8–9). Temple ritual therefore comes to be increasingly centered in priesthood authority, and its sealing power carried out through the spiritual effects of temple ordinances.

As Buerger (1994:35–44) indicates, the endowment was constructed by Joseph Smith from preexisting materials of Masonic origin together with his own prophetic insight during the church's settlement in Nauvoo, Illinois, in the 1840s, and was intimately linked to the building of the Nauvoo temple. The endowment was modified subsequently by Brigham Young and others, before and after the LDS had moved to Utah territory (Buerger 1994:73–85; 97–102). And it was subject to further modifications in the 20th century to adjust to the changing internal communication needs of a church that had grown to international stature (Buerger 1994:133–171).

The Ritual Attribution of Agency to Both the Living and the Dead

Anthropologist Anthony F. C. Wallace (1966) argued that ritual is the primary phenomenon of religion. In his words:

> Ritual is religion in action; it is the cutting edge of the tool. Belief, although its recitation may be a part of the ritual, or a ritual in its own right, serves to explain, to rationalize, to interpret and direct the energy of the ritual performance.... The primacy of ritual is instrumental: just as the blade of the knife has instrumental priority over the handle, and the barrel of a gun over the stock, so does ritual have instrumental priority over myth. It is ritual [that] accomplishes what religion sets out to do.
>
> (Wallace 1966:102)

Wallace's emphasis on ritual as embodying what religion seeks to accomplish allows us to consider the special meaning and effects of LDS temple ordinances.

In the first place, temple ordinances are initially performed for and by the living to meet their own spiritual needs, as in the case of baptism and confirmation. These ordinances are acts of agency exercised by and for oneself under priesthood authority, which together are the ingredients of identity that make a person a member of the church. Second, as a baptized member of the church, a person may stand as "proxy" for a deceased person, where the concept of proxy allows for the action of a living person to be extended to the dead as a vicarious transformation.

The Meaning of Ordinances by Proxy

In LDS belief, the "dead" are dead only by virtue of the deaths of their bodies, but otherwise continue to live as immortal spirits. A hymn, expressing this sentiment, written by President Gordon B. Hinckley (1988) with music by Janice Kapp Perry (2007) was sung at his funeral. It contains as its opening line, "What Is This Thing That Men Call Death," and its last verse begins "There is no Death, but only Change." This is a direct expression of transformation within the worldview of the LDS in which the spirit of a person is released and lives on even as the body is buried. It is the spirit of a person that has agency to commit to, and act according to, the covenants and promises made on its behalf by living proxies. Thus, without knowing the ultimate outcome of temple work for the dead, except as divine promise, a living member may nonetheless stand as a proxy for the deceased, with the promise that the person dead in body is alive in spirit and can accept (and act on) ordinances performed by a living member according to the church's priesthood authority.

The Temple Ordinances as Rites of Passage

All of the temple ordinances may be considered rites of passage that have in common a change in the status and identity of the patron. As in the case of baptism and confirmation, change involves the threefold sequence of separation from the old status, transition as a liminal process between the old and the new, and reincorporation in terms of the new status. The temple ordinances afford this transformation through the vicarious work of living members "standing in for" the living spirit of a person whose body has died and is not yet resurrected. Due to this vicarious work, the temple itself is considered a sacred place and is so dedicated.

Baptism and Confirmation of the Dead

The first of the temple ordinances is baptism for the dead. This ordinance is patterned directly on baptism for the living by immersion of the proxy under the authority of the priesthood to bind on earth and seal in heaven, providing a necessary entrance into the church as the kingdom of God on earth. Although baptism for the living may be performed wherever convenient, it is now most frequently done in a stake meetinghouse, whereas the ordinance of baptism for the dead is performed only in the temple by living proxies who have received their own baptism. A proxy therefore must be a member of the church (and at least 12 years old) who stands in place of the deceased person on whose behalf the ordinance is being performed. Apostle James E. Talmage indicated that baptism is required of all who would enter the church beginning at age eight, also known as the age of accountability. Only children who might die in infancy or before age eight should not be baptized, because of their innocence, in which case they are covered by the atonement of Christ, and their redemption is fully assured. The atonement also covers those who lived prior to Christ's time on earth and afterward as well, thus providing a sanctuary on earth for all persons past, present, and future (Talmage, 1978 [1912]:75–76).

In the temple setting, the baptismal font is placed in the lowest level of assembly, as in the basement of the Salt Lake City Temple. Talmage notes that the baptismal font serves as a facsimile of the grave, and is to be a gathering place where the living and the dead might assemble (Talmage 1978 [1912]:156). In Joseph Smith's words, baptism for the dead was "ordained and prepared before the foundation of the world, for the salvation of the dead who should die without knowledge of the gospel" (D&C 128:5). A proxy confirmation for the dead follows directly upon baptism for the dead. The transformational effect of baptism and confirmation of the dead was to bring deceased spirit persons into the church, which they may choose to enter by their own agency, so that they may bear the identity of an LDS in the last days.

Ordination of a Deceased Man into the Melchizedek Priesthood

Ordination to the Melchizedek priesthood for a living man aged 18 or older is also a rite of passage into adult status in the church and a prerequisite for other temple ordinances, and may be performed for the living in a variety of settings. An ordination to the Melchizedek priesthood for the dead by proxy must be performed in the temple for the deceased member who has been previously baptized and confirmed under the authority of the priesthood. A proxy must, in all cases, hold the ordinance to which the deceased is being ordained, so that only a living holder of the Melchizedek priesthood may stand as proxy in the ordinance for one who is dead. Again, the effect of the ordinance as a transformation in status is not automatic, but is held to depend upon the agency of the living spirit of the deceased person.

Initiatory Washings and Anointings

Both men and women receive washings with pure water and anointings with pure olive oil before receiving one's endowments while living and subsequently for someone who has died. Some changes were introduced to these initiatory ordinances during the period of my research, so I will describe these rituals first as they had been performed and then indicate the more recent changes. The washings and anointings are purification and blessing rituals in which male anointers administer to men and females to women. As rites of passage, these ordinances served as enactments of liminal purity. In a locker room, members removed their worldly clothing and donned a "shield" with openings on the sides so that modesty could be preserved during the actual washing and anointing. The ritual concluded with members putting on a special garment that was to be worn next to the body ever afterward, now covered by a robe.

Worthy members first performed the washings and anointings for themselves as part of their own initiatory preparatory to receiving the endowment, before they were permitted to do so as a proxy in a group (or "company") for the dead. In the ordinance for the dead, a living female proxy stood vicariously for a deceased female baptized member just as an ordained Melchizedek priest stood vicariously as proxy for a deceased Melchizedek priest. The ritual actions of washing and anointing were traditionally directed toward specific body parts taken to serve specific purposes—head, ears, eyes, nose, lips, neck, shoulders, back, breast, stomach, arms and hands, loins, legs and feet. One earlier version of the wording was as follows:

> Brother [or Sister], having authority, I wash you that you may be clean from the blood and sins of this generation. I wash your head that your brain may work clearly and be quick of discernment; your eyes that you may see clearly and discern the things of God; your ears that they may hear the word of the Lord; your mouth and lips that they speak no guile; your arms that they may be strong and wield the sword in defense of truth and virtue; your breast and vitals that their functions may be strengthened; your loins and reins that you may be fruitful in the propagating of a goodly seed; your legs and feet that you may run and not be weary, walk and not faint (quoted in Brodie 1971 [1945]:279).

The general meaning is that the members of the company have been so washed that by their faithfulness they may be clean from the blood and sins of the current generation, that they may become kings and queens, priests and priestesses to the Most High God. These purification actions and meanings are confirmed and sealed with the laying-on of hands by two temple workers, who also serve as witnesses. Because women serve women and men serve men in these rituals, they are one instance where women carry out a (male) priesthood duty (Talmage 1978:79; 156).

As a consequence of the washings and anointings, the living or proxy participant may put on the garment of the holy priesthood, symbolic of the clothing given to Adam and Eve when they discovered their nakedness in the garden of Eden (Genesis 3:8–24; Moses 4:13–27). The garment is to be worn next to the body day and night for the rest of one's life as a shield against pollution and danger, and as a reminder of the further covenants of the endowment (see McDannell 1995:198–221; Douglas 1966:217).

The Giving of a New Name

As the garment is given, a new name is also given, not to be revealed except at a later point in the endowment ritual. The new name may be almost any given name from the Bible or Book of Mormon and is specific to the company, or assembled group, with which a member undertakes these rituals. This brief new name ceremony completes the initiatory ordinances. The members are now ready to put on the robes of the holy priesthood for the endowment proper. These robes are carried in a bundle or large cloth envelope.

Changes to the Initiatory

To forestall any possible legal challenges (such as charges of sexual touching), the initiatory washing and anointing ceremony was revised in January 2005 so that now "only the forehead is touched with water and oil" as symbolic of all other body parts (//home.teleport.com/~packham/endow05.htm; accessed January 2006). The members also put on the garments and robes themselves in the privacy of a locker room.

LDS historian Dean May, as the father of a 19-year-old newly called missionary, Tad May, spoke with me about their preparation for his son's receiving of (or "taking-out") his endowments, indicated that "on a first visit it is customary for a father to accompany his son when the father is a holder of the Melchizedek priesthood; otherwise the guide will be another close relative or friend who is a priesthood holder. A missionary, of course, must be endowed. And a returned male missionary is held in especially high regard as having fulfilled an important duty within the church, and—because already endowed— is a prime candidate for a temple marriage. "Similarly," Dean noted, "mothers and daughters often will attend together the first time, if the mother is already endowed; otherwise, a temple-worthy older woman who is a family friend will guide a young woman" (May, Interview, 1997).

The Three-Part Structure of the Endowment

The temple ordinances of washing and anointing, the endowment, and sealings for time and eternity are most commonly understood in Arnold van Gennep's (1960 [1908]) conception as rites of passage. Armand L. Mauss, for instance, in commenting on Buerger's earlier paper on the historical development of the endowment noted that "one of the more obvious functions of the temple endowment...is that of a rite of passage, signifying to the whole church that the endowed individual has become a 'spiritual adult'" (Mauss 1987:78). Similarly, American studies scholar Colleen McDannell (1995:210) suggested that going on a mission and getting married are each major rites of passage into adult Mormon culture, and that "[t]he wearing of garments physically marks [the endowment as a ritual of] transition into social adulthood."

This way of framing the temple ordinances makes obvious sense. The process of receiving one's endowment usually occurs for young men just prior to going on a mission as McDannell indicates, or for those who don't go on a mission, occurs sometime after they turn 19 years of age and have entered the Melchizedek priesthood. For young women, receiving their endowments usually occurs either before a temple marriage or prior to going on a mission after age 19, whichever comes first.

Contrary to the view of Douglas J. Davies, the endowment ordinance always precedes a temple marriage. Davies (2003:211; 215) wrote: "The endowment follows after temple marriage and presupposes it." And again, "Having been sealed for time and eternity, a married couple who meet the moral, doctrinal and economic demands of the Church may take their endowments." This depiction is incorrect. The actual sequential relation of these two ordinances is precisely the reverse; a sealing in temple marriage may be performed only after the completion of the endowment, and even where they are linked together in a single performance, the endowment always precedes a temple sealing in celestial marriage. The endowment involves promises and covenants that are to be held inviolate for the rest of a person's life, meaning that a young man or woman has committed himself or herself, as Mauss indicates, to full adult responsibility within the community as a keeper of the sacred. Among other privileges, this new adult status entitles a person to perform the vicarious (proxy) washings and anointings, endowments, and sealings for the dead.

The endowment is also a precondition for a person to serve a mission and to undertake a temple (celestial) marriage.

The elements of separation, transition, and reincorporation can certainly be recognized in the endowment. In one sense, going to the temple is itself a form of physical separation from the normal activities of the community. But other elements also emphasize the geography of separation, as recognized in the preparatory washing and anointing ordinances immediately prior to the actual endowment ceremony. Mary Douglas notes how washing may have the ritual force of cleansing a candidate of prior worldly pollution (see Douglas 1966:33–36). Furthermore, consciousness of the garment as something a person puts on and wears thereafter is a lifelong reminder of one's identity as an "endowed temple-worthy LDS" and, in that sense, marks separation and difference from others in the world who do not share and remain unaware of this hidden aspect of LDS identity. As this high priest father noted, his son had purchased his garments before going to the temple and "had even put his 'boxers' away since he wouldn't be needing them anymore" (May, Interview, 1997).

Van Gennep (1960:10–13) called the liminal transition a moment on "the margin," regardless of its duration, or a period of liminality, or a liminal rite. Victor Turner (*Ritual Process*, 1969:94–97) examined this psychosocial "threshold" period in considerable detail as one of being "betwixt and between" a prior status while not yet fully incorporated into a subsequent one, marked by a psychological state of what might be called the "suspended animation" of normal, ongoing everyday commitments.

In the endowment, this liminal period ranges from 90 minutes for some film versions to the eight or so hours of earlier live performances, as noted by Herbert Howe Bancroft in his *History of Utah* (1890:357). The live performances in the Salt Lake City Temple have been shortened today to a relatively manageable two hours or less from entry to the creation room to the moment of passing through the veil at the endowment's conclusion. And a mission, to take another example of liminal transition, may be considered a two-year liminal period of intensive work on behalf of the church in the world. Given the richness of van Gennep's formulation, I see no reason not to continue thinking about baptism and confirmation, and the endowment ordinance, along with the mission experience and sealings in marriage and other life transitions, as rites of passage, augmented by Turner's emphasis on the liminal quality of the transition period itself. In the temple, with the initiatory ordinances completed, members can turn their attention to the central endowment ordinance for both the living and the dead, and its complex ritual expression.

Rituals and the Issue of Polysemy

Wallace (1966:105–107) pointed out that a second major category of ritual, called rites of intensification, was proposed by anthropologists Eliot Chapple and Carleton Coon (1942). They indicated that rites of intensification were centered on groups rather than individuals, and often had a cybernetic effect, countering a tendency for group commitments to atrophy over time by providing periodic refreshment. A classic LDS example of a rite of intensification is the ward sacrament meeting, where the sacrament is received as a reminder and intensification of the meaning of the atonement and of a member's own baptism (with its covenants and commitments). And the hymns sung and the talks and testimonies given also serve to refresh and intensify prior commitments among attending members.

But the distinction between individual and communal rituals that Chapple and Coon make cannot be too strictly drawn, for the LDS find personal renewal or intensification in group rituals, and rituals intended for individual transformation also intensify group commitments through repetitive LDS baptisms, endowments, and sealings for the dead. Repetitions themselves are important experiences because meanings are recalled, renewed, and expanded, as well as intensified.

Furthermore, these two are not the only categories by which to classify rituals, as Wallace (1966:106) recognized. He suggested that "all ritual is directed toward the problem of transformations of state in human beings or nature," and proposed a taxonomy that included about 13 minimal categories of religious behavior that might be combined in various ways to comprise modules the themes of which involve five main categories for transformations of state: (1) rituals as technology aimed at the control and exploitation of the natural environment; (2) therapeutic and anti-therapeutic rituals seeking control of human health through forms of therapy and forms of sorcery; (3) rituals of social control intended to have cybernetic effects, with rites of passage as prototypical, but also involving role change, ideology, and group ceremonials; (4) ritual as salvation that aims toward the powers, identities, and well-being of the individual person; and (5) rituals as revitalization movements involving some identifiable social group.

Thus, by expanding his list, Wallace was proposing a classification of varieties of ritual in a relatively complete taxonomy for use in cross-cultural studies (Wallace 1966:102–166). The last type, revitalization, tends to erupt when a crisis of identity affects an entire community where "the customary individualized procedures for achieving personal salvation may no longer be effective"

(Wallace 1966:157). The origins and rise of the LDS Church may be considered a prototypical instance of a Christian revitalization movement.

It is not my purpose to explore this taxonomy further; I simply wish to underscore the fact that rituals are polysemic and may carry many meanings, not simply one. The same set of ritual behaviors may be classified under more than one category in Wallace's taxonomy (or any other), depending on the frame of reference employed. At the same time, I wish to propose an additional category to this taxonomy—namely, *rituals of anticipation*—a form of social and experiential confirmation of beliefs based on expectations about the future that are realized in the present in ritual form. Similar ideas about anticipation have been proposed by psychologists in relation to the experience of time (Cottle and Klineberg 1974) and planning for the future (Miller, Galanter, and Pribram 1986 [1979; 1960]). I have inferred this additional kind of ritual from an examination of the temple ordinances of the LDS of which the endowment is the central one.

By definition, a rite of anticipation involves a current experience, in the form of ritual behavior and its interpretation, of what is hoped will be a future process or state. The behavioral aspect is the current ritual drama itself; its cognitive component is the proffered forward-looking anticipatory interpretation; and the emotional dimension is a feeling of hope, security, and happiness that is recognized in abstract terms as joy. In combination, these elements provide for a goal-directed orientation toward the future based upon present ritual experience. The ritual in that sense confirms a structure of belief about the future and anticipates its realization, as we can see in LDS temple ordinances.

Endowment and Sealing Ordinances as Rites of Anticipation

In the church's terms, an ordinance may be defined as "a sacred ceremony that has a spiritual meaning and effect" (*Endowed from on High*, 1995:15). Not all ordinances are viewed as essential for entrance to the celestial kingdom; some simply bestow a priesthood benefit, such as a father's blessing of a newborn infant, or much later, a patriarchal blessing. Other ordinances, including baptism under the authority of the Aaronic priesthood and confirmation under the Melchizedek priesthood, are viewed as necessary for entrance into the celestial kingdom, and are known as ordinances of salvation. Finally, some priesthood ordinances affect the degree of glory that may be attained in the celestial kingdom, and are known as ordinances of exaltation; these are the central ordinances of the temple. As Stake President Ralph Dewsnup explained to me:

Under the direction of the Twelve, you need to repent of your sins; you need to be baptized and receive the gift of the Holy Ghost; then you've entered through the gate. You're now on the strait and narrow way. Have you reached the destination? No. There's still more to be done....

Baptism is an entry into the highest kingdom, but there are other ordinances that may qualify you for still greater blessings within that kingdom....There are other ordinances to be accomplished before one can enter into the presence of God (Dewsnup, Interview, 1995).

Anointings, endowments, and sealings are performed in the temple for both the living and the dead. This means that, on the first occasion, the ordinance serves as a personal rite of passage, while on subsequent occasions, it serves as a rite of intensification—and on both occasions, also serves as a confirmatory rite of anticipation (see Maslow 1964 with respect to "peak experiences").

Describing the Endowment

The endowment ordinance is a complex ritual of several interlocking parts. The *Encyclopedia of Mormonism* summarizes the temple endowment as follows: The temple endowment is spoken of in scripture as an "endowment," or outpouring, of "power from on high" (D&C 84:20–21; 105:11; 109:22, 26; cf. Luke 24:49). Participants in white temple clothing assemble in ordinance rooms to receive this instruction and participate in the unfolding drama of the plan of salvation. They are taught about pre-mortal life; the spiritual and temporal creation; the advent of Adam and Eve, and their transgression and expulsion into the harsh contrasts of the mortal probation; the laws and ordinances required for reconciliation through the atonement of Christ; and a return to the presence of God. The endowment is a series of symbols of these vast spiritual realities, to be received only by the committed and spiritual minded.

During the endowment, solemn covenants are made pertaining to truthfulness, purity, righteous service, and devotion. In this way, the temple is the locus of consecration to the teaching of the law and the prophets and to the ways of God and his son. One does not assume such covenants lightly. Modern commandments relating to temple building have been addressed to those "who know their hearts are honest, and are broken, and their spirits contrite, and are willing to observe their covenants by sacrifice—yea, every sacrifice which I, the Lord, shall command" (D&C 97:8–9). As with Abraham of old, LDS revelation says that to obtain "the keys of the kingdom of an endless life" one must be willing to sacrifice all earthly things.

In one of my conversations with Ennis Anderson, then the high priests' group leader in the Crystal Heights second ward, I asked if he would take me through the steps of the endowment as far as it was comfortable for him to talk about them. He indicated that there was "no way to explain it all," but he would provide an overview:

> We get dressed in our white clothes; and we have other pieces of cloth-ing that we carry with us. These other clothes are symbols of the priest-hood. For example, the robe signifies the priesthood that Solomon had in his temple.
>
> As we go through the sessions, we put this robe on and then talk about the things that the Lord has given us to remember, to keep our-self [sic] clean from the world, and those types of things. We put on these clothes to signify the promises that we make, to keep ourselves clean and pure.
>
> We gather in the chapel beforehand, just waiting to start. It's a good time to ponder things. Then we're taken into what we call the creation room. We sit down and go through [a dramatic performance] where the Lord created the worlds, and where we were in the preexistence. Then we go from there into the garden room and we talk about Adam and Eve and the things that happened there. And that's how it begins and continues from there (Anderson, Interview, 1994).

As Ennis Anderson's comments make clear, there are limits to what may be described; at the same time, he indicates that the endowment employs several different settings in telling its story. These settings represent the creation of the heavens and earth in the context of eternity, the garden of Eden as a place within that creation, the telestial world of human mortal experience in its vari-ous epochs or dispensations, the terrestrial world of ministering angels, and finally the celestial world or highest realm in the kingdom of God, which, in turn, includes several degrees of glory leading to the very presence of God himself. The division between the celestial world and all others is represented by a veil separating mortality from immortality and the eternal worlds.

The kingdom of God is inclusive in this telling; it is part of the eternal world—often spoken of metaphorically as a place of "one eternal round"—without beginning and without end, within which all other worlds are mani-fested, and those other worlds are differentiated and ordered temporally and spatially into the telestial, terrestrial, and celestial kingdoms, each with its degrees of glory (see D&C 76). This eternal universe of deity, an LDS version of what Mircea Eliade (1957) has called "the sacred," manifests itself in mate-rial forms, and is comprised of and built from the primal elements identified by the prophet Joseph Smith as matter (or "element"), spirit, and intelligence (D&C 93:33–34). From these elements, everything else has been shaped and has acquired its form and substance.

The Plan of Salvation as the Conceptual Core

The endowment presents the conceptual core of the LDS worldview, the framework of beliefs held fast by the LDS. This conceptual core is presented in a dramatic narrative as the plan of salvation. In this plan, all spirits who chose mortal experience may, by their own effort and good works, and in faith and dependence upon Christ's atonement, pass through the veil at birth into mortal life, and again at death return through the veil to their spirit home in the kingdom of God, and there, if worthy, achieve a place in glory before Heavenly Father as a god among the gods.

Talmage places the atonement of Christ at the center of this plan. "The vicarious effect of the atonement of Christ is twofold; it is seen to have wrought a universal redemption of all men from the mortal death incident to the transgression of Adam; and it has been proffered to provide a means of propitiation for individual sin whereby the sinner may attain salvation through obedience" (Talmage 1978:66).

The plan of salvation itself is the framework of belief that is taught from birth onward to all members born in the covenant and to all converts in the missionary lessons that are part of their preparation for baptism. In greater and lesser detail, the plan of salvation shapes the way LDS understand themselves and their world, including their notion that the church is the kingdom of God already being realized in the world today.

The Endowment as a Rite of Anticipation

The most succinct description of the endowment was provided by Brigham Young at the dedication of the Salt Lake Temple, a description that has been published widely by the church:

> Your *endowment* is to receive all those ordinances in the House of the Lord, which are necessary for you, after you have departed this life, to enable you to walk back to the presence of the Father, passing the angels who stand as sentinels, being able to give them the keywords, the signs and tokens, pertaining to the Holy Priesthood, and gain your eternal exaltation in spite of earth and hell.
>
> (Widtsoe, *Discourses of Brigham Young* 1977:416; cited in Packer 1980:153)

John D. Charles, without authoritative standing in the LDS Church, has written an insightful interpretation of the scriptural images reenacted in the endowment, within the framework provided by Brigham Young's description above. Charles "deconstructed" Young's image as follows:

> *Note the image that President Young paints: after we have*
> *"departed from this life" (presumably, after we have been res-*
> *urrected), we must physically "walk back" to God's presence.*
> *On the way, we will be met by guards, "angels who stand as*
> *sentinels." To pass these guards, we must show that we are*
> *authorized to live with God by presenting certain celestial*
> *passwords—what President Young calls "keywords," "signs,"*
> *and "tokens." Only after we have given these passwords*
> *and signs will the sentinels allow us into God's presence,*
> *where we will be exalted. The purpose of the endowment,*
> *President Young says, is to teach us those passwords (Charles*
> *2004:20).*

My discussion of the endowment does not seek to teach those passwords. I do rely upon the 1990 transcript of the endowment in presenting some narrative elements, updated from the 1984 version (Tanner and Tanner 1990), published online at www.lds-mormon.com/compare.shtml. A chronological list of these and other published sources constitutes appendix 2 in Buerger's (1994:203–227) account. My intent is to focus on the scriptural images and temple settings that embody the endowment ceremony.

The actual endowment performance is quite specific as to which elements are not to be revealed except under certain conditions, as indicated by the quotation from Brigham Young given earlier, while most of the endowment is an enacted set of lectures that reflect core LDS doctrines cast as covenants made by the patron in relation to promises from Heavenly Father.

Some sources provide relatively unrestrained interpretations (e.g., Deborah Laake, *Secret Ceremonies* 1993:74–91); others link the development of the endowment to Joseph Smith's interest and participation in Masonry (Brodie, *No Man Knows My History* 1971:280–281); and still others focus on positive personal and scriptural aspects of temple participation that aim to aid spiritual understanding (Allen H. Barber, *Celestial Symbols* 1989; S. Michael Wilcox, *House of Glory* 1995; Janet M. Kincaid, *Temple Participation* 2000; and John D. Charles, *Endowed from on High* 2004).

In most respects, the endowment brings together the core beliefs of the LDS, and provides members with a means of grounding their faith in a sacred story and its ritual. In order to narrate the endowment as a sacred ordinance,

I draw upon several published church sources dealing with the Salt Lake City Temple, including C. Mark Hamilton with C. Nina Cutrubus, *The Salt Lake Temple: A Monument to a People* (1983), James E. Talmage, *The House of the Lord* (1978 [1912]), Boyd K. Packer, *The Holy Temple* (1980), and the *Encyclopedia of Mormonism* (1992).

Members of the church receive their endowments only once for themselves during their lifetimes, but may go through the performance of this ordinance many times for the dead. Also, different family members, or others, may complete different portions of the composite set of ordinances for the dead at different times; the church keeps a computerized record documenting this work. In "work for the dead," where the initiatory washing and anointing has previously been done by proxy, the vicarious endowment begins with the brief new name ceremony.

Many of the new temples have a single "endowment room" in which the endowment is presented using a film/video presentation as a quasi-participatory screening. Only the Salt Lake City Temple and the Manti Temple now present the endowment as a live performance with actors taking the key parts. My approach follows the room-by-room outline used to describe the Salt Lake City Temple as a series of architectural settings for the endowment, and refers to fundamental doctrinal understandings as a means of interpreting those settings apart from the restricted keywords, signs, and tokens.

Setting: The Creation Room

The presentation of the endowment in the Salt Lake Temple begins in the creation room, where an assembled company of temple-worthy members is reminded of their washed and anointed status, receive the special name, and hear the central purpose of the endowment as previously described by Brigham Young.

The company then hears and observes a reenactment of the work of creation in six periods of time in which Elohim (God, the Heavenly Father) commands Jehovah (his immortal spirit son, Jesus Christ), and Michael, the archangel (who becomes Adam, the first man) to carry out the actions that bring an organized universe into being. The use of two names of reference for these immortals indicates that they may act within two different worlds. Furthermore, the organization of the universe during these six "days" establishes a hierarchy among these immortals based upon the chain of command and reports about the conduct and effectiveness of their shaping of creation. The sequence of the creation process is similar to the accounts in the Bible (Genesis 1:1–2:3) and Joseph Smith's account in Moses 2:2–31.

This sequence of creative periods concludes with Elohim (God) instructing Jehovah (Jesus) and Michael (Adam) to form mankind "in our own likeness and in our own image, male and female," putting into them their spirits, telling them to multiply and replenish the earth and giving them "dominion" over all things on the face of the earth. In this setting, Elohim and Jehovah put the angel Michael into a deep sleep from which he awakens as the first man, Adam; and while asleep a rib is taken from him to form Eve, the first woman, as his companion. But Adam and Eve have no deep memory of their preexistence. They therefore represent the innocent condition of humankind at the time of birth into mortality.

Setting: The Garden Room

The company moves to the garden room. In the Salt Lake Temple, this room is "furnished with rich continuous wall-through-ceiling oil murals that represent the 'earth as it was before sin entered and brought with it a curse; it is the Garden of Eden in miniature.' Cast in pervading greens, yellows, and subtle blues, the mural depicts a luxuriant landscape with birds, insects, and beasts living in harmony, an idealized image" (see Hamilton and Cutrubus, *Salt Lake Temple*, 1983, which provides the photographic image and description, 92–93).

The story of "the Fall" unfolds, in which Adam and Eve are commanded not to eat of the tree of knowledge of good and evil. Lucifer enters the scene as Adam and Eve's spirit brother, questioning Eve about the meaning of Elohim's command to them to refrain from eating this fruit. Adam initially resists, but Eve chooses to partake of the forbidden fruit and uses a logical argument to persuade Adam to follow her, considered as a means of "testing" humankind.

As Elohim (God) calls out to them, Adam and Eve recognize their nakedness. Adam, because of his guilt for eating the fruit of the tree of knowledge of good and evil, blames Eve, and Eve blames Lucifer (also known as Satan), who is identified as the rebellious spirit son of Elohim. Rather than obey Elohim, Lucifer became defiant and threatened havoc on the earth, while Jehovah continued to obey Elohim's commands. Elohim places a guard around the tree of [eternal] life to protect Adam and Eve from eating of its fruit and therefore living forever in their sins. However, as a penalty for Adam's disobedience, Elohim curses the earth and requires that henceforth Adam shall labor for food until his body dies and returns to dust, though his spirit lives on.

In the garden, a chain of obedience is established. This chain of obedience reflects the idea that, where there are two persons who are unequal, there will also be a third, thereby establishing a hierarchy of three. Thus, Eve agrees to obey the law of the Lord under which she will follow Adam's counsel as Adam obeys Elohim. Then a savior (Jesus as the Christ) will guide Adam and Eve to help them return to the divine presence, enabled to receive eternal life and exaltation by the law of obedience and sacrifice.

The law of obedience thus establishes the hierarchy of obedience in familial/kinship terms: Eve to Adam, Adam to Jehovah, Jehovah to Elohim, and through Adam and Eve to all their progeny and descendants. All persons in the company may therefore identify with Adam and Eve (and with a "witness couple" who symbolize all of the other members) in making their covenantal promises of obedience before an altar in this room. The holy garment that each member of the company wears is interpreted as symbolic of the protective coats of skins worn by Adam and Eve.

A lecture on the law of sacrifice establishes vicarious service to others as a pattern of obedience modeled on the atonement of Christ. This atonement is interpreted as ending blood sacrifice and overcoming the death of the body through resurrection; it also symbolizes the sacrifice of everything that humans possess in order to sustain and defend God's kingdom, including giving their own lives if necessary.

Setting: The Telestial or World Room

In the Salt Lake Temple, at the landing of the grand staircase between the first and second levels, "is a Tiffany stained glass window depicting the expulsion of Adam and Eve from the Garden of Eden. This image symbolically reinforces the lecture of the Garden Room and prepares the patron for entrance into the Telestial Room, representing the world in which we live." . . . "In contrast to the Garden Room, the Telestial Room is embellished by a continuous mural of the earth in a fallen rather than an exalted state" (Hamilton and Cutrubus 1983:94). It represents mortal experience of the "lone and dreary world."

The scenes are typical of the world's condition under the curse of God. Nevertheless, there is a certain weird attractiveness in the scenes and in their suggestiveness. The story is that of struggle and strife, of victory and triumph, or defeat and death. From Eden man has been driven out to meet contention, to struggle with difficulties, to live by strife and sweat. This chamber may well be known as the room of the fallen world, or more briefly, the world room.

The telestial or world room is the world of mortality in which Adam and Eve are tested by the intrusion of the rebellious and evil Lucifer (who becomes Satan), who challenges the covenants that Adam and Eve have made with Elohim. At the same time, Elohim, Jehovah, and the Apostles Peter, James, and John, as "true messengers" of Elohim and his earth-born son Jesus Christ, are seeking to defeat Lucifer. Thus, the scenes change from the abode of Elohim in the celestial kingdom (with Jehovah, Peter, James, and John) to the telestial world, where Lucifer makes his own claims of divinity against Adam and Eve and all of the others in mortality (including the present company).

In this lone and dreary world, Adam builds an altar and offers a prayer, asking God to hear him. Lucifer, usurping God's status, answers by offering Adam the chance to hear about the religions and philosophies of the telestial world. At the same time in the celestial kingdom, Elohim commands Jehovah (Jesus) to send Peter, James, and John to surreptitiously monitor the actions of Adam and Eve in order to assess their commitment to the covenants they made in the garden. Adam is cast as a seeker of truth. Lucifer interjects a question about the value of the promises to which Adam and Eve are pledged. Peter states firmly that the promises are not for sale. Adam then rejects Lucifer's offer, even as Lucifer continues to relish the power he holds in the telestial world.

Peter reports to Jehovah who reports to Elohim that Satan is striving to lead Adam and Eve astray—and everyone else as well—but that Adam remains faithful to his covenants while awaiting further knowledge that would lead him to truth. As a consequence, Elohim instructs Peter, James, and John, through Jehovah, to present themselves before Adam and Eve as true apostles of Jesus Christ with the power to cast Satan out of their midst and to instruct their posterity in the law of the gospel as given in the holy scriptures.

Lucifer (Satan), in his self-centeredness, presumes that the apostles have returned to the lone and dreary world in order to take possession of it, and voices the threat that Adam's posterity will be in his power if they fail to fulfill every covenant that they may make this day. Peter commands Satan to depart. Lucifer asks him by what authority he gives this command. Peter answers that his authority resides in the name of Jesus Christ, and indicates to Adam that the three apostles are true messengers of their Father in heaven, Elohim, who will give them further light and knowledge.

In response to Adam's question of how they shall know the true identity of the apostles, Peter answers that they shall know by means of the symbols that Adam and his posterity have received in the Garden of Eden. Questioned further by Adam about his name, Peter indicates that it is a "new name," but that his covenant requires that it should not to be revealed until the proper moment. Then, by receiving a certain sign, Adam knows that Peter and the others are indeed true messengers of the Father who will counsel, teach, and lead them and all who follow to salvation and eternal life.

Peter, represented by an officiator at the altar, invites the assembled company to identify with Adam and Eve and their posterity, and again with a witness couple who comes before the altar. The officiator indicates that the law of the gospel is contained in the holy scriptures and charges them to avoid all impure practices. This covenant and promise is affirmed by the company. Further, Peter instructs Adam and Eve and their posterity to put on the robes of the holy priesthood, with the robes flowing over their left shoulders, and to add other accoutrements, including a cap, green apron, and slippers as part of their temple clothing (which was carried in and removed from the clothing bundle). The company is told that the robes of the holy priesthood are a sign of the authority of the Aaronic priesthood to officiate in the ordinances of salvation.

Setting: The Terrestrial World

In the Salt Lake Temple, the terrestrial room is classically appointed in muted colors, and is symbolically elevated one step to mark the change in the heavenly kingdoms from telestial to terrestrial as a progression toward the highest or celestial kingdom. As an architectural and artistic matter, "[t]he carnage and strife of the Telestial Room give way to a room completely devoid of such images. The architectural intent was to illustrate the marked doctrinal and environmental differences between the rewards of these two kingdoms. A new, indirect lighting system, crystal chandeliers, and mirrors enhance the effect of increased spirituality" (Hamilton and Cutrubus 1983:97). Talmage (1978:159) says:

> In this room, lectures are given pertaining to the endowments and emphasizing the practical duties of a religious life. It is therefore commonly known as the upper lecture room, but in view of its relation to the room that follows, we may for convenience designate it as the Terrestrial Room. At the east end is a raised floor reached by three steps, across which springs an arch of thirty feet span. The arch is supported by five columns between which hangs a silken portiere in four sections. This is the Veil of the Temple.

Once again, the scene shifts to the celestial kingdom, where Elohim instructs Jehovah to send Peter, James, and John to visit Adam and Eve and their posterity, requesting that they change the flow of their robes to the right shoulder in preparation for administering the ordinances of the Melchizedek priesthood in the terrestrial world. The company follows these and further instructions. The officiator, representing Peter, invites a witness couple to come to the altar and asks the company to affirm the law of chastity. The assembled company affirms this covenant and promises to obey it.

Elohim again instructs Jehovah to send Peter, James, and John to Adam and Eve and their posterity in the terrestrial world to teach them the law of consecration. Again, the officiator taking the role of Peter invites a witness couple to kneel at the altar. The law of consecration is contained in the D&C (42:30; 78:7) and is a comprehensive pledge to the LDS Church of time, talents, and everything received as a blessing from the Lord, to be used for building up the kingdom of God on earth, and for establishing Zion (the Holy City). The assembled company affirms this covenant and promise.

The Prayer Circle

Peter, in the person of the officiator, requests that the whole company arise and repeat in unison Adam's prayer three times; this anticipates a ritual component known as the prayer circle (Quinn 1978:79–105).

The prayer circle and the true order of prayer begin with an invitation for an equal number of brothers and sisters to come forward, including couples, to form a circle around the altar. They are instructed that good feelings should exist in the circle.

As Adam's prayer is repeated, the officiator places a white cloth pouch upon the altar containing the names of persons who are sick or afflicted, for whom requests have been made to be remembered in faith and prayers. The sisters in the room as well as in the prayer circle are asked to veil their faces, perhaps as a sign of purity. The brothers, alternating between the sisters, with their right hands take the right hands of the sisters at their left and bring their left hands to their shoulders. Then they all together repeat after the officiator, phrase by phrase, the words of his prayer inspired by the Holy Ghost. At the conclusion, the sisters unveil their faces, and all members return to their seats.

Setting: The Veil of the Temple

Behind the altar [in the Terrestrial Room] is a raised platform and the Veil. Both were later enlarged to accommodate the movement of a greater number of people between the Terrestrial and Celestial Rooms. The Veil is in similitude of one in the Tabernacle of Moses and the temple of Solomon. To pass through it into the Celestial Room is to symbolize one's passage and acceptance into the Kingdom of God or the highest degree of spiritual reward.

(Hamilton and Cutrubus 1983:97)

A curtain is drawn aside to reveal the veil. It is comprised of multiple segments. The officiator uses a pointer to focus attention on the seven markings of each segment and to explain them briefly. Four of the markings correspond to marks on the individual garment that each patron wears. On the right of the veil segment is the mark of the builder's square, which is also over the right breast of the garment, interpreted to mean exactness and honor in keeping the covenants of the endowment. On the left of the veil segment is the mark of the compass, which is also placed over the left breast of the garment, interpreted to mean that one is following a straight path to eternal life. It is also a reminder that the Lord has placed bounds on emotional passions and has circumscribed truth as a single whole. The navel mark of the segment is related to the navel mark of the garment, indicating the need of regular refreshment for body and spirit. And the knee mark is placed on the right leg of the garment, to symbolize the biblical injunction that every knee shall bow and every tongue confess that Jesus Christ is Lord (see McDannell 1995:209–210).

The three remaining marks are related to the work at the veil. One allows the person behind the veil, representing the Lord, to put his right hand through the veil to test for personal identity and symbolic knowledge of the holy priesthood. A mark higher on the right allows the Lord to ask certain questions, and through the mark on the left, the member can give his or her answers, such as the identifying name.

A demonstration of the "work" at the veil is rehearsed by the officiator representing Peter before the veil and a temple worker as the Lord on the other side. Peter and the Lord then conduct a dialogue on behalf of Adam (for the member), where Peter demonstrates the proper responses of the Aaronic priesthood and then of the Melchizedek priesthood. This demonstration continues to a point where the Lord intervenes.

At this point, row by row, the members in the company come to the veil to be introduced by a veil worker to the "Lord" (a temple worker) on the other side. The worker in front of the veil taps a mallet three times to indicate that a patron is at the veil, which initiates an exchange of questions, answers, and symbolic gestures as part of this drama at the veil, culminating in the member requesting entry to the celestial kingdom, which is granted by the Lord who parts the veil, taking the member by the right hand and gently ushering him or her into the celestial room.

Setting: The Celestial Room

In its entirety, the endowment is a performative ritual in which meanings are expressed directly as covenants and promises and indirectly as gestures and dramatic action. The sacred and taboo aspects provide a picture of the particular norms and commitments that will identify a person as a worthy LDS, one who is entitled to enter the celestial kingdom.

> The endowment ritual concludes upon entrance into the Celestial Room. The symbolic importance of the room is evident from its increased size. The most obvious dimensional change [in the Salt Lake temple] is its [34]-foot-high ceiling. The spatial expansion was a deliberate effort to express visually a feeling of exaltation and a spiritual terminus. The concept of a terminus is suggested by the absence of an altar and the accustomed attached and oriented row seating. Instead, luxuriously appointed chairs and couches are placed in formal conversational arrangements. The furniture is set within an environment designed to imply the majesty that one would associate with the Kingdom of God.
>
> (Hamilton and Cutrubus 1983:98)

In this rite of passage, the member moves from a status as a baptized and confirmed member of the church to being an endowed temple-worthy member who qualifies for all of the further blessings of the church. Because this ritual may be repeated many times as work for the dead, it is also a rite of intensification. Throughout, the member is reminded of covenants and promises.

In addition, the endowment may be viewed as a rite of anticipation. Under this interpretation, the final entry into the celestial room provides a present experience of an anticipated future reality, an immortal status of eternal duration in which a member comes face to face with many gods, including those who are now present in the kingdom. Experientially, then, the endowment ordinance confirms this anticipated future. It provides an experience for the member of the celestial kingdom that is a real, tangible experience worth striving for. The image is recorded in scriptures known as "the vision" (in D&C 76):

> For thus saith the Lord—I, the Lord, am merciful and gracious unto those who fear me, and delight to honor those who serve me in righteousness and in truth until the end.
> Great shall be their reward and eternal shall be their glory....
> And again we bear record—for we saw and heard, and this is the testimony of the gospel of Christ concerning them who shall come forth in the resurrection of the just—

*They are they who received the testimony of Jesus, and believed
on his name and were baptized after the manner of his burial,
being buried in the water in his name....
They are they who are the church of the Firstborn.
They are they into whose hands the Father has given all
things—
They are they who are priests and kings, who have received of
his fullness, and of his glory;...
Wherefore, as it is written, they are gods, even the sons of
God—
Wherefore, all things are theirs, whether life or death, or things
present, or things to come, all are theirs and they are Christ's
and Christ is God's....
These shall dwell in the presence of God and his Christ forever
and ever.*

(D&C 76:5–6, 50–51, 54–56, 58–59, 62)

9

Preach My Gospel

THE ANNOUNCEMENT BOARD in the Crystal Heights second ward meeting house reminded members to pray for Justin Schroepfer, who was serving in the Danish mission. Justin had been gone for nearly a year and a half of his two-year mission when I arrived in the summer of 1994. He would return during my fieldwork in the ward. Over the next year, I spoke with him and several other young men and women in this and other wards who left for missions, and later, still others, who returned from them. Justin, and others before him, had trained using a missionary manual called the *Missionary Guide*, which had been the "Bible" of LDS missionary work since the mid-1980s. Then, late in 2004, church leaders launched a new missionary program using a new manual titled *Preach My Gospel* (2004). This shift in teaching materials was publicly announced in the January 2005 issue of *Ensign* (35[1] 2005:74–75).

Since the 1950s, the practice of going on a mission has been an important cultural and spiritual experience for young LDS, involving a change in status to "elder" and "sister" in the informal transition from child (boy or girl) to young adult. Undertaking a mission has often been a turning point in the lives of young men and women, preparing them for lifelong service in the church, as well as citizenship. At age 18[1] for young men and 19 for young women, the mission physically separates a young person from their family, friends, and neighbors and relates them to a mission president, a new ward or branch either foreign or stateside, with peer missionaries, investigators, and new converts.

The Farewell of Rich Parry

Along with the members of the Crystal Heights second ward, I was a witness to missionary farewells, including one for Rich Parry that took place during the

---

1. President Thomas S. Monson announced "effective immediately" that all young men will have the option of being recommended for missionary service beginning at age 18, instead of age 19. Furthermore, able, worthy young women who have the desire to serve may be recommended for missionary service beginning at age 19, rather than age 21 (see *New Era* 42, 2012, November, p. 6).

sacrament meeting of March 19, 1995. After other members of his family had spoken, it was Rich's turn. He invited the congregation to listen as he reflected on his preparation for his mission. "It was three years ago that my brother had his farewell," he began. "This is a different experience for me this time. I've seen all my cousins get ready to go and every time I saw them, I said to myself, 'Hey, wait, I'll be up there some day; that's gonna be me,' and now it is, and I'm really nervous." But then he started at the beginning, talking first of being born of "goodly parents," drawing on the image and words of Book of Mormon prophet Nephi. So, Rich began his account by referring to his mother and father and then his teachers and friends. He was measuring himself publicly now, with some tongue-in-cheek irony, as he told of learning to follow the commandments:

> When I was growing up there were times when my mother or father would ask me to do something. It would not be easy, because I was playing basketball or football or watching TV at the time—you know, all these important things. But then I'd remember Exodus 20:12, and it's just one of the Ten Commandments: 'Honor thy father and thy mother that thy days may be long upon the land which the Lord thy God hath given thee.' In the footnote, 'honor' means to respect or value what they're saying. So, against my better judgment [and injecting a little humor], I'd go and do what they asked me to do, and it worked out for the best (Field notes, Rich Parry Farewell, 1995).

"Most of the time, keeping the commandments is pretty easy," he said, "unless you really let Satan in, and then he starts telling you little things like 'Don't go to Church; you don't really need it.' Or, 'forget to pay your tithing this month; it's your money, you should keep it.'" But then Rich admitted that the commandments are good to keep and concluded by talking about prayer and loving your enemies.

He anticipated encountering some enemies on his mission (as well as friends) and would need to pray. He shared a brief personal story: "One day when I was in junior high, I was picked on by a much bigger guy, and while he was picking on me all I had to do was just ignore him and let him have his fun, because in a few minutes we'd be in class and I knew after that, that the Lord would watch over me and take care of me, and he did. And that was an answer to prayer."

His talk filled all of ten or 15 minutes. He testified that he would rely on prayer to keep him close to his Heavenly Father on his mission and knew the Lord would always be there for him. And then he thanked all his friends in the Crystal Heights second ward and concluded with his own "Amen." (Field notes, Rich Parry Farewell, 1995)

A Voluntary Decision

Going on a mission is a voluntary undertaking by members of the church, with a strong obligatory component for the young men. For them, the expectation to undertake a mission is especially powerful. The obligation is taught in primary and Sunday school, emphasized in fireside talks by church leaders, recounted in testimonials, and used to illustrate one of the most important forms of service on behalf of the church. A mission is considered optional for young women, though increasing numbers are taking up the mantle. Both young men and young women are encouraged to begin saving for their mission as early as middle childhood and, as folklore scholar William Wilson (1981) has noted, mission tales recount the spiritual benefits of missionary service in story after story.

The ideal time for serving a mission for young men is a two-year period between the ages of 18 and 25. Young women may not begin a mission until age 19 and then serve for 18 months. About one-third of age-eligible young men go on a mission and somewhat more than ten percent of the young women. These proportions increase in Utah and are somewhat smaller in newer areas of the church outside the United States (Shepherd and Shepherd 1998:xiii; Ostling and Ostling 1999:210). As of October 11, 2009, the total number of proselytizing missionaries serving in the church's mission program was 52,109 (*2010 Church Almanac* 2009:4). Older adult couples whose own children are grown are included in missionary service roles rather than proselytizing roles, as are some older single adults who seek to serve others on behalf of the church.

To undertake a mission is to invest a sustained period of one's life in joy and anguish, testing and solitude, and the company of fellow LDS who are seeking to build and enlarge the select company of the church. It is preparation for leading and living in the kingdom of God on earth, and it was portrayed quite realistically (I thought) in Richard Dutcher's commercial film *God's Army* (1994). A signal sociological study of missionary experience is the personal account of two brothers, Gordon and Gary Shepherd, as they each kept journals and exchanged correspondence during their respective missions in Mexico in the mid-1960s (Shepherd and Shepherd 1998).

Opportunities and Effects

Undertaking a mission has many effects. It gives missionaries goals and purposes beyond their own immediate self-interests. It teaches them personal discipline and social responsibility. And it offers opportunities to deepen and broaden their spiritual awareness through prayer, scripture study, personal testimony, bonding with others, direct challenges to their fundamental beliefs, and encounters with temptation, injustice, calamity, and evil. They see the effects of their beliefs in their own lives and how beliefs and practices affect the lives of others. Thus, the mission experience changes the missionaries themselves while expanding the church as the kingdom of God on earth, which is its primary purpose. Clearly, the missionary program of the LDS Church is a massive and expensive effort.

A *Missionary Recruit*

Annie Turner was working in Sam Weller's Zion Bookstore in downtown Salt Lake City, one of my first stops on my return to the valley of the LDS for fieldwork in the summer of 1994. I was seeking an out-of-print book on the Mormons. As we spoke to one another in the store, Annie asked if I was LDS. Because the bookstore caters to many "outsiders," I doubt she was surprised when I said, "No," but I also added, "I've been studying them for quite some time." As we talked, she said that she was soon leaving on a mission. With that brief introduction, I asked if I might interview her about how she was preparing for her mission. Of course, she said, "Sure."

Briefly, Annie grew up in Orem, Utah, while her mother attended Brigham Young University (BYU). Following a year in Wyoming, Annie returned with her mother to Salt Lake City for junior and senior high school, and then also attended BYU. Following graduation she went to work at Sam Weller's Zion Bookstore. At Weller's, Annie worked in the out-of-print section, mostly LDS and Western Americana literature, and helped run the out-of-print search service, attending to both LDS and non-LDS customers. "We'd get anti-Mormon people, and we'd get—I call them 'tunnel-vision' Mormons—who are complete 'letter-of-the law' members, and everything is black and white for them. But life isn't so black and white for me."

Neither of Annie's parents grew up in Utah, but both served missions for the church in the north-central states; their missions overlapped by about two months and that's when they met. Then her father began a correspondence with her mother, and it wasn't too long before they married. They both earned advanced degrees, also an aim of Annie's. At the moment, she was involved in a singles ward and noted that many young women in the ward were returned missionaries, which perked her interest.

Experience in a Singles Ward

A singles ward is for single adults between the ages of about 18 and 26, but is organized without a primary; there are few high priests or seventies and an abundance of elders (young men holding the Melchizedek priesthood). Annie attended the singles ward so that she could be with her peers. She ended up going to her home ward within the church's geographical ward boundary system where she played the piano for primary every Sunday, but then she also went to the singles ward Sunday school and relief society with members of her own age who were not yet married. Some single parents also attended. Annie recounted her own parents' divorce after 20 years of marriage, when Annie was about four. She was raised by her mother as a single parent, even as both her father and mother remained committed to the family ideal. Annie said:

> I only got to see my dad about once a year, but we kept in touch, and it was always known that if anybody in the family called his office, regardless of what meeting he was in, they were to be put through. So, Annie said she always knew that her dad was available to her. And the same with her mom, wherever she was—if she was at work, if I needed her to come home she would be there.
>
> And also, when I first talked about going on a mission, she and I talked about some side reasons for going—not my main reasons—but bonuses and pros and cons, and whether I was going for the right reasons and that sort of thing. One thing I told her was that when I got married I didn't want to get divorced. I feel like my generation of the family is supposed to break the [divorce] cycle. So that's an added bonus of going on a mission; it's not that going on a mission guarantees that such things won't happen, but it helps build your spirituality and makes divorce less likely (Turner, Interview, 1994).

Annie and I met three times for working lunches in the next two weeks, and then she invited me to her ward farewell and the luncheon hosted by her mother Colleen afterward. Though her parents were divorced, Annie's father George was also invited to the farewell, along with her brothers, grandmother, and many friends. Within a week, she left home for the Missionary Training Center (MTC) in Provo, Utah, for eight weeks of intensive preparation for proselytizing in the Texas, San Antonio, Spanish-speaking mission.

The Mission: Worthiness and Putting in Your Papers

As young men in the church approach their 19th year, one question becomes increasingly insistent: "Have you put in your papers yet?" Putting in papers to request a mission assignment involves making an appointment to see one's local ward bishop. As Elder McConaghie reported, "We first talk with our bishop and tell him where we'd like to go on a mission. And from there he'll interview us, and see what are our thoughts and feelings about a mission, and what makes us decide, you know, why we want to go on a mission" (McConaghie, Interview, 1996).

In the LDS Church, young people are regularly invited to assess and discuss what the church calls worthiness (as reported in chapter 7). Church standards of tithing, chastity, the word of wisdom, and following the prophet are the basis of this assessment process, but it is also understood that young people may have tested the boundaries set by these standards. Confession, repentance, and restitution are therefore part of worthiness, and those who sincerely repent the trespassing of church norms will generally not be kept from undertaking a mission. Sexual issues, however, are a critically important part of worthiness for young people, and the violation of those standards can be a reason for a leader's refusing to call someone to a mission.

The discussion of worthiness takes place under priesthood authority. It is confidential and falls under the mandate of obedience. It is a serious undertaking that also serves as the basis for a temple "recommend," enabling members to receive their endowments prior to going on a mission. Both parties, the bishop and the prospective missionary, are expected to treat this interview as involving a combination of temporal and spiritual issues, no matter how routine it may be as a matter of church governance. For purposes of putting in papers to undertake a mission, the interview with the bishop goes beyond earlier personal or Aaronic priesthood interviews, and is itself part of the preparation for going to the temple, as well as undertaking the mission. In the words of Elder McConaghie, this interview involves "counsel" and suggestions about "forming habits" preparatory to the mission experience itself, including temple worthiness.

Temple-Worthiness Interview Questions

The content of the temple-worthiness interview is structured by a set of suggested questions. These guidelines are used by the bishop and stake president to establish worthiness to enter an LDS temple:

Interview Questions for Recommends to Enter a Temple

1. Do you believe in God, the Eternal Father, in his Son, Jesus Christ, and in the Holy Ghost; and do you have a firm testimony of the restored gospel?
2. Do you sustain the President of The Church of Jesus Christ of Latter-day Saints as the prophet, seer, and revelator; and do you recognize him as the only person on the earth authorized to exercise all priesthood keys?

3. Do you sustain the other General Authorities and the local authorities of the Church?

4. Do you live the law of chastity?

5. Is there anything in your conduct relating to members of your family that is not in harmony with the teachings of the Church?

6. Do you affiliate with any group or individual whose teachings or practices are contrary to or oppose those accepted by The Church of Jesus Christ of Latter-day Saints, or do you sympathize with the precepts of any such group or individual?[2]

7. Do you earnestly strive to do your duty in the Church; to attend your sacrament, priesthood, and other meetings; and to obey the rules, laws, and commandments of the gospel?

8. Are you honest in your dealings with your fellowmen?

9. Are you a full-tithe payer?

10. Do you keep the Word of Wisdom?

11. Have you ever been divorced or are you now separated from your spouse under order of a civil court? If yes, (a) Are you current in your support payments and other financial obligations for family members, as specified by court order or in other written, binding commitments? (b) Were there any circumstances of transgression in connection with your divorce or separation that have not been previously resolved with your bishop?

12. If you have received your temple endowment—(a) Do you keep all the covenants that you made in the temple? (b) Do you wear the authorized garments both day and night?

13. Has there been any sin or misdeed in your life that should have been resolved with priesthood authorities but has not?

14. Do you consider yourself worthy in every way to enter the temple and participate in temple ordinances? (Source: www.lds-mormon.com/veilworker/recommend.shtml; accessed 2008)

In practice, the bishop adapts this template of questions to the individual. He is not to probe, but simply to offer opportunity for discussion. If the bishop is satisfied by a candidate's serious intent and worthiness, he invites the candidate to a second interview, this time with the stake president. These interviews, therefore, serve a dual purpose. First, they are interviews that assess worthiness for issuance of a recommend for entry to the temple to receive one's own

---

2. The reference of this question has to do with fundamentalist plural marriage group membership, advocacy, or other practices that violate the stance of the Salt Lake City-based church, which discontinued plural marriage in the period from 1890 to about 1915.

endowment, and subsequently for endowments to be undertaken vicariously for the dead. Second, they are the basis for sending the papers requesting a mission assignment to church headquarters. In Elder McConaghie's words:

> We go to the stake president after the bishop. He has the final "say" before the papers actually go in. There's a reasonable time [after that], so you can go to the temple. We go to the temple before we come out in the missions. So the interview is about more than just the mission, or being a missionary; it's to have us "live to enter into the temple." And at that point, the stake president issues us a temple recommend. Then our papers are sent to the Church mission committee.
>
> (McConaghie, Interview, 1996)

"Raising the Bar"

Church leaders have been concerned to maintain (or "raise") church standards of worthiness among missionary recruits, issuing a statement on "raising the bar" in 2002 for those seeking to undertake a mission. In the April 2002 priesthood meeting at general conference, Apostle M. Russell Ballard warned that "the day of the 'repent and go' missionary is over.... Some young men have the mistaken idea that they can be involved in sinful behavior and then repent when they're 18 ½ so they can go on their mission at 19. While it is true that you can repent of sins, you may or you may not qualify" to serve a mission (*Ensign*, 2002, 32(11):46–49). In the course of the previous two-year period (2003–2004), approximately 6,000 fewer missionaries were approved than had been the norm during the preceding four years (1999–2002), declining from about 36,000 accepted recruits to about 30,000 (2006 *Church Almanac*, 655).

As I settled into my own routine in the Crystal Heights second ward, I joined members anticipating the return of Justin Schroepfer from his mission to Denmark, while other young people like Jim Fenton, Jarrod Schroepfer (Justin's brother), and Jennie Fairbanks anticipated their missions. I was also invited to the farewell of Tad May in Emerson Ward, as well as Annie Turner in Granger 12th ward. They each had received their missionary callings and were sent forward to the MTC with farewells. The farewell made clear that each missionary recruit's experience was part of a personal and individual decision while also being part of the church's culture. This ongoing process of recruitment contributed to discussions of the pattern of mission experiences that was expressed in conversations before, during, and following this special undertaking.

About a week and a half before the date of reporting to the MTC, the missionary recruit would have a local ward farewell. Elder McConaghie explained the family-centered practice:

> We have either mom or dad speak, or we have brothers and sisters speak also. There's usually a musical number, maybe friends will come and sing, and then the missionary is the very last speaker that day. The missionary speaks for about ten or fifteen minutes, gives a talk, and it's always very neat. When I was growing up, missionary farewells were special for me, to see someone else go off on a mission. It's always very intriguing to see a young man that you've grown up with, who you knew all about, just start to change, start to mature and have more responsibility. You can begin to see the change even before they leave. And then when they come back, it's really a different story, they are a totally different person. Yeah, it's good to see someone go off. It's a good experience doing it.
>
> (McConaghie, Interview, 1996)

Tad May's Farewell

On June 15, 1997, I attended sacrament meeting in the Emerson ward for Tad May's farewell. Once again members of the family spoke, including Tad's father Dean, who expressed thanks on his own behalf and on behalf of his wife Cheryll to the ward members. "You are the ones who should be proud," Dean said, "because you are the ones who did as much as we did in bringing Tad to maturity. I would like to express my love for him, my appreciation for his being such a fine, worthy son, and as I said, my appreciation to all of you for making that possible." And then it was Tad's turn:

> My talk will be a little bit jumbled at best. I have to warn you, I have a severe allergic reaction to Church microphones. If I cry, it's not really me, it's just my medication acting up.
>
> The theme for today is "faithful journeys," so I'll talk to you about my journey and the reasons why I've decide to go on a mission, the reasons why I want to be a missionary. I'd like to start out by thanking my Heavenly Father. He's the first reason and the most important one. I've had lots of ups and downs in my life, and like my mother said, in the last year I've really made some changes, and remade my life to the point where I consider myself worthy to serve a mission. I'm so thankful that my Heavenly Father was always there for me when I was

making mistakes and doing wrong things, and I could kneel down and know that he was there. I'm really thankful for that.

I'm thankful for the whole process of repentance. I've been on both sides of the fence and, believe me, the grass is greener over here. It's so wonderful to come back and feel the spirit every week. It's really amazing. I would like all of you to know that if you're having any problems, or any concerns, you can repent as much as you need to. And just as often as you ask you will be forgiven. We're taught in Alma—don't ever give up. Don't think the mountain is too high to climb.

I'd like to thank all of you people.... You truly made it so easy to be a member of this Church. I was always surrounded by good friends. I never, ever was at a party where any bad things were going on. It just never happened. And I'm so thankful for that. I never had to say "no" to drugs because they were never offered to me. I've got so many friends that are just neat guys.

And another reason I want to serve is because I know there's somebody in the Philippines right now who doesn't know what life is all about. But I know this Church is true. I know a lot of people who love to be together. This is real. It's true. The gospel of Christ shows us that there's a prophet, and that we can grow to know these things. And I bear a strong testimony of the power of the temple. I've been there three or four times...three times...in the last couple of weeks, and there's truly a Spirit that's there.

This last week I went with a few of my buddies, and I couldn't help but think of Alma, where he meets his brothers and says, "I was so delighted to see them, that they were still brethren in the Lord." And I know that when I return from my mission, all of my friends are still going to be in the Church. They're so strong. I can't wait until that day when I return and they're all still brethren in the Lord. That's my prayer to you. I love you all, and I love my Savior.

(Field notes, Tad May Farewell, 1997)

As becomes clear in these farewells, growing up in the church is the single most important influence shaping the lives of young men and women who go on a mission. It begins in the naming ordinance shortly after birth, when an infant is given a name and a blessing. Two important blessings are a regular part of that ritual. One is that a boy may grow up to serve a mission, and the other for both boys and girls is that they may enter into a temple (celestial) marriage. Thus, as an infant, Gus Kefalopoulos, one of my Penn students, received a blessing as follows: "We bless you, Gus, that you will prepare yourself to serve a mission, and that your testimony [of the gospel] may be used to convert the people of your father...and that you may seek a mate whom you can take to the temple to be sealed for time and all eternity" (cited in Miles Family Records, 1976; see Kefalopoulos 1996). In the context of a Sunday sacrament meeting, this blessing of a newborn infant expressed the expectation that those present, along with parents and family members, would work to ensure the results that the blessing conveys.

The aspiration, duty, and privilege of serving a mission is nurtured in many ways during the first 18 to 20 years of life, helping to prepare, motivate, and encourage young men to anticipate their mission, while granting the mission as a privilege to young women. Parental involvement is certainly an important ingredient in motivating missionary service, and family home evening lessons often reinforce the idea of serving a mission. Annie Turner's mother, for instance, had served a mission in the 1950s when it was much more unusual for a young woman to do so than it is now. And certainly uncles and aunts, cousins, brothers, and sisters often provide family models and traditions of missionary service.

Often, the family of the missionary recruit will hold an open house later on the day of the farewell. The church has sought to de-emphasize the giving of gifts (and money) to the missionary in favor of a simple social hour. Annie Turner's farewell social was a backyard barbeque with family and friends, symbolic of well wishes for this special undertaking, coupled with emotional partings before a separation that would last 18 months. The farewells of Rich Parry and Tad May were very similar, a chance for family and friends to gather and offer their good wishes prior to each young man's departure for two years.

President Hinckley, in his October 2002 report to the men of the priesthood, announced "after most prayerful and careful consideration" that the first presidency and the twelve "have reached a decision that the present program of missionary farewells should be modified." A departing missionary would still have an allotted time to speak in sacrament meeting, but parents and siblings would not be invited to do so. Further, the meeting would be "entirely in the hands of the bishop and will not be arranged by the family," nor would there be special music or "elaborate" open houses (though families may wish to get together without a large public reception). President Hinckley remarked, "We know this will be a great disappointment to many families. Mothers and fathers, brothers and sisters, and friends have participated [during sacrament meeting] in the past. We ask that you accept this decision. Where a farewell has already been arranged, it may go forward. But none in the traditional sense should be planned for the future" (Hinckley, *Ensign*, November 2002:57). Clearly, this was one of several decisions made to simplify and focus family and church resources in a church grown large, complex, and with a worldwide reach. The aim was to integrate the missionary farewell into the regular sacrament meeting as part of the congregation's sacrament celebration, rather than allowing it to become solely a family undertaking.

The Mission as a Church Program

Beyond the family, the church provides strong and consistent institutional support that contributes substantially to this directive missionary effort. This support occurs through lessons in primary and Sunday school and other parts of the church's program. In primary, for instance, songs reinforce and sustain this missionary orientation. One begins this way:

> *I hope they call me on a mission,*
> *When I've grown a foot or two.*
> > (*Children's Songbook, 1989:168*)

One anticipating the mission affirms:

> *I want to share the gospel while I'm young,*
> *For I have a testimony of my own.*
> > (*Children's Songbook, 1989:169*)

Lesson plans within the primary curriculum also focus on missions and missionary- related topics. The emphasis continues through social involvement of the youth in church activities, the Aaronic priesthood, scouting, young women, the seminary program during the high school years, and through continual idealized calls to all members by the president of the church for "missionaries to match our message," as it once was phrased by President Ezra Taft Benson. He requested as missionary candidates youth who sought to meet the church's ideals in moral terms and in terms of activities, church meetings, including priesthood and seminary programs, while developing a strong personal testimony of the truth of the Book of Mormon and other scriptural repositories (Ezra Taft Benson 1986:43).

Individual Decisions

I explored contacts with missionaries in a number of contexts beyond the Crystal Heights second ward, especially in the Philadelphia Mission, where I met with a half dozen missionary companionships during the years of the mission presidencies of Frank E. Wagstaff (1995–1998) and Joseph V. Cook (2001–2004).

Though a mission may begin at age 18 for young men, individual missionaries identify significant earlier turning points in their own lives leading to the decision to seek and accept a mission assignment. For instance, I interviewed Jeremy Arndt while he was on his mission in Philadelphia; he said that he began thinking about a mission as a high school freshman newly enrolled in the church's seminary program:

> That was my first spiritual "kick in the pants." That was the start of my decision to go on a mission. Then, I just followed up with hanging around the right crowd, those that wanted to go on missions, too. Most of my friends—all of my friends that I'm really close with are in different places in the world, so it's kind of like a big happy family of missionaries.
>
> (Arndt, Interview, 1996b)

Elder Arndt's missionary companion at that time was Patrick McConaghie, who indicated that the example of his two older brothers influenced him (McConaghie, Interview, 1996c). They had served foreign missions and that was what he expected to do. Kim Stone (Interview, 1995a) said that at age 14 she decided to do a mission if she hadn't married by the time she was 21. Annie Turner had pointed to the example of her mother, who had served a mission 20 years earlier (Turner, Interview, 1994a). Thus, within the context of family and church, those who serve missions find a variety of more specific influences on their individual journeys, often redirecting their lives within the church by undertaking a mission.

Receiving Mission Assignments

Usually two to six weeks will elapse between submitting the papers requesting a mission assignment and receipt of a first presidency letter indicating the mission location and the date to report to the MTC. Elder Arndt said that receiving word about one's mission call is "one of the most exciting times in a family, a pretty big event, to find out where you're going." Friends and family members speculate on the timing of receipt of the manila envelope and the location of the mission assignment. Elder McConaghie expected to "go foreign," because his two brothers were assigned overseas. The alternative is a mission in the states. Many missionaries-to-be play a guessing game with their friends as to the place of assignment, even putting a world map on the wall and letting others place pins in what they believe are locales of likely assignment. No one bets on these guesses, but they add to the anticipation.

Elder Arndt recounted how he learned of his mission assignment:

> I didn't know it was going to be a special dinner, [but] my mom was really cooking, like a lot, and I'm going, "wow, what's this for?" And she had put the manila envelope underneath my place mat, and I had no clue. Then my parents said something to the effect that "You need to look underneath your place mat," really tactfully and smooth. And I said, "What?" And I looked under my place mat and there was my manila envelope. And I'm going, "What's this?" From that point I just ripped it open as quickly as I could and started reading. You know, I just read it line by line and I knew that part was coming up, where it tells you where you're going. (Arndt, Interview, 1996b)

Elder McConaghie then reported his experience:

> Yeah, I forgot about it, too. You know, it was a hard day at work and I came home and I was exhausted, I was tired, and I usually take a nap when I get home from work. And I walked in and my parents were acting really strange, really peculiar. They took me out to the backyard. I was working on the car at the time, taking pictures of my car and me, and I had no idea—they just toyed with my mind. And finally they said, "Go into the living room," and I'm, like, "what's going on?" And they pulled out the manila envelope, and it was pretty exciting, yeah, I was a little nervous, a little excited, mixed feelings.
>
> (McConaghie, Interview, 1996c)

The church's notification of a mission assignment requires a letter of acceptance from the missionary-to-be in response, acknowledging the assigned report date for the MTC about six weeks later. The notification also includes a packet of instructional materials. Before reporting to the MTC, another letter usually arrives from the mission president in the place of assignment; this spells out more specifically what needs to be brought from home and what can be obtained on site.

Reporting to the Missionary Training Center

Then comes the day to report to the MTC in Provo, which is the largest of 17 such MTCs operated by the church in different parts of the world. Both parents and missionary recruits are instructed to prepare for a brief joint meeting and then a swift separation, because the recruit will be on church assignment for the next two years. Elder Arndt recalls arriving at the MTC with his parents:

> It was a pretty big room with lots of parents and other missionaries in it. They have one speaker or a couple of speakers, and a film. Then I guess the most dreadful part of that whole situation is where you have to....They tell you, "Okay, parents go out one door and missionaries go out the other, so you're going to say your good-byes now, and then be on your way."
>
> (Arndt, Interview, 1996b)

And generally, that's the last time the missionaries will see their parents for two years. In about five or ten minutes, the departures at the MTC are over, the missionaries are on their way to their dormitory rooms, and the parents leave. But Elder Arndt reported a brief exception:

> You don't usually see your parents after you separate. We went out separate doors. And when I came out I looked to see where my parents were going. My dad, he looked too, and he just came walking back down the hallway and gave me a big hug and told me he loved me for the first time in my entire life, and like, said those words exactly, and I just crumbled, just about fell down that day. And see, he's my step-dad, so it was hard for him to do that, and it was the first time that he called me his son in my whole life, too. It was just everything at once. So it was pretty eventful. I was about six or seven years old when he became my step-dad. So, it's like I call him "dad" because to me that's who he is. That was a tough day, for sure. I had to pick up my heart, you know, and put it back in place, and then walk away. But that was how it was. It was a really big separation. But the long walk to my room kind of helped me just wipe away my tears. And my journal got a lot of good writing that night.
>
> (Arndt, Interview, 1996b)

Elder McConaghie flew from Phoenix where his parents said goodbye, and then drove with his sister, who was living in Provo, to the MTC. She brought a video camera to videotape the proceedings for his parents. The separation is hard, he said, "real hard."

> You know it will be two years before you see them again, and it's a struggle. It's real hard to think about that; you have mixed emotions.

You're excited for the mission, excited about what's going to take place, but it's your family you're leaving, who you grew up with for [19] years. You've been around them your whole life. Leaving for the mission was the first time I left home, so it was really hard for me. (McConaghie, Interview, 1996c)

Life in the MTC

Rooms at the MTC are like old college dorm rooms, six missionaries with three upper and three lower bunks and three desks and six small closets. Very close quarters. Most missionaries arriving at the MTC are aware of the companion rule: You are never to be out of sight of your companion at any time. But a few are unaware that the rule begins in the MTC. McConaghie said he walked into the dorm room, and "the other Elders were in there unpacking, and I found out that my spot was—my bed. I didn't know who my companion was at the time. I didn't realize we had companions at the time. I knew we had companions in the field, but at the MTC I didn't think we had companions. I just thought it was a big, you know, school" (McConaghie, Interview, 1996c).

Little time is wasted at the MTC. Teary-eyed companions who have just parted from their families and who have met one another for the first time moments earlier are quickly absorbed in a round of orientation meetings, and discover that they will spend precious little time in their rooms. New missionaries enter one of three different tracks. The briefest is a three-week immersion in the full daily round of classes and lessons for those going to missions in the states. A second track adds two weeks of mission work at the church's telecenter, responding by telephone to inquiries about the church that arise from advertisements, TV commercials, and other invitations to learn more about the Book of Mormon or the church. The third track involves an additional five weeks of intensive language training for those missionaries going foreign. About 40 different languages are being taught at any one time in the MTC. The church likely has the most intensive and diverse set of language training programs of any institution in the world, the envy of businesses, the government, and much of academia. The church almanac for 2003 reported that 173 different languages were spoken by members of the church and that the Book of Mormon had been translated into printed editions in 68 languages (*Almanac*, 2003:6).

Approximately 30,000 new missionaries are trained annually in order to maintain or increase the current number of nearly 54,000 missionaries who are in the field. This massive training program is rigidly structured, yet highly personalized, through the use of small-group teaching modules conducted almost entirely by returned missionaries. On average, each year about 700 returned missionaries, almost all BYU students, serve as part-time instructors. The director of training at the MTC during my time in the Crystal Heights second ward was Allen C. Ostergar, who identified for me what he considered as the most important consideration at the MTC:

> If a person wants to help someone else understand that what we [receive] in the Church is true, and to feel it in terms of the Spirit, then they first must feel it themselves. If a person doesn't have that feeling then they can't maintain the enthusiasm and commitment—so it's very important, in my opinion that missionaries in training have experiences that give them that feeling of the Spirit. The primary source for that would come from personal prayer and personal—I don't want to use the word "study"—but from reading, honoring the scriptures. I think the strength of the Church is based, not only for missionaries but for every member, on the fact that each person as an individual can know for themselves that something is true in terms of the testimony of the Spirit. That's what we all seek with our internal mind. And it's especially true for missionaries. (Ostergar, Interview, 1995)

He emphasized that the "great secret of this place" is the teaching provided by the returned missionaries. "Those who have been on a mission are selected as the very best teachers in terms of their own conviction, spirituality, and ability to help others. And there's great empathy. It's unique. It's very credible."

Thus, there is a personal, highly dynamic feedback of field experience from prior missionaries to the new missionary recruits at the MTC, with all of the personal face-to-face motivation that arises from this close personal engagement in a common enterprise.

The MTC Routine of Companions

The daily routine involves awakening between 6:00 and 6:30 a.m. in order to assure time for private personal prayer, prayer with one's companion, and personal study time. Some missionaries shower before, and others after, their spiritual exercises. "At first, you have the macho day, where you don't want to ask someone to say a prayer with you, but after a while that all gets situated," Elder McConaghie said. Soon, missionaries learn to kneel by the bed or a chair and fold their arms for prayer. And each will find a half hour for reading the Book of Mormon. One missionary noted that the showers are "primitive" and "down the hall," like group showers in a

locker room at high school. Breakfast is served starting at 7:00 a.m., with
the first class beginning at 8:00 a.m. So, being ready for morning classes
always means calculating time, because breakfast lines are long with so
many people to feed. And breakfasts are "all you can eat!" (McConaghie,
Interview, 1996c)

Classes are "a.m.," "p.m.," and "evening," each about three hours in
length, with a short break midway, and each class has a different teacher.
The morning break allows a half hour for additional Book of Mormon reading, with the expectation that each missionary will have completed the entire
book by the end of training (and, of course, most do, some for a second or
third time). Lunch is served from 11:30 a.m. to 12:30 p.m., with afternoon
classes beginning at 1:00 and going until 4:00 p.m. Almost universally,
missionaries complain that the class right after lunch "just drags because
your stomach is full, you're tired, and it's really difficult to stay awake—so
it's very good to have a nice, very upbeat teacher" (McConaghie 1996c). An
early dinner is served between 4:30 and 5:30 p.m. And then evening classes
and meetings resume at 6:00 and go until 9:00 or 9:30 p.m. Lights-out is
10:30 p.m.

The evening time block varies in several ways. For instance, as preparation
for the field, missionaries at the MTC are organized into districts and zones
with leaders of each, much as they will be in the mission field. Some evening
meetings are designed to give missionaries experience preparing talks in front
of their peers on different subjects. Most Tuesday evenings are given over
entirely to a meeting of the whole MTC in the new auditorium with songs and
a special speaker who is often a general authority.

In addition, all missionary companions have a "P-Day," meaning a personal preparation day to do laundry, shopping, and recreation, until 4:00 p.m.
Then it's back to work. Sunday was also different, when district groups met for
sacrament meeting and perhaps an evening meeting with a general authority,
or a "victory" conference in support of the mission enterprise. The MTC gym/
auditorium has a portable stand and bleachers that fold out to seat up to a
thousand people.

From the *Missionary Guide* to *Preach My Gospel*

The *Missionary Guide* was published in 1988 as a training manual for the
missionaries. On the first page it identified clearly the purpose and practices
of a missionary as "help[ing] people come to Christ through the ordinances
of baptism and confirmation." It suggested that investigators "will be converted when they feel the Spirit and act on the promptings they receive."

The missionaries' task, then, is to "help people become converted by using a process identified as the commitment pattern."

> To use this pattern, first, you *prepare* others to feel the Spirit. When they are feeling the Spirit, you *invite* them to make and keep the specific commitments found in the missionary discussions [itemized in six discussions in the *Missionary Guide*]. After they accept your invitations, you *follow up* to help them keep the commitments they have made. If an investigator expresses concern or doubt during the [teaching] process, you help him [or her] *resolve the concern*. Then he [or she] will be better able to make and keep the commitments that lead to conversion. (*Missionary Guide*, 1988:1)

Although the immediate aim or goal is to motivate investigators to make commitments to be baptized and confirmed, the key factor in this process is to *resolve concerns*. This resolving of concerns lowers the barriers to making commitments and aids in mutual understanding.

On a personal level, the missionaries were urged to model themselves on the life of Christ while also developing proselytizing principles and skills. This part of the process was a form of training the self in the use of the image of Christ as a personal model:

> There are many Christ-like *attributes* that you should strive to develop during your mission and throughout your life. No doubt you already live righteously. You understand the importance of gospel knowledge and testimony, faith and hard work, and charity. As you carefully study the *Missionary Guide*, you will further develop these attributes and your ability to bring others to Christ.
>
> There are [also] a number of proselytizing *principles and skills* that you should use to help others accept the gospel. These include building relationships of trust, helping others feel and recognize the Spirit, finding out what people understand, presenting the message, inviting people to make commitments, following up on those commitments, resolving concerns, and planning. (*Missionary Guide*, 1988:1)

The Six Discussions

The central teaching materials were the "six discussions," companion materials to the *Missionary Guide* as part of the *Uniform System for Teaching the Gospel* (1986). These six discussions introduced sets of principles, presented in the form of six concise brochures, and were organized to lead to specific commitments, outlined as follows:

1. The Plan of Our Heavenly Father:
Principles of the Plan.
Commitments: Read the introduction to the Book of Mormon,
Moroni 10:3–5, and 3 Nephi 11.
Pray to know that Joseph Smith was a prophet of God.
2. The Gospel of Jesus Christ:
Principles of the Gospel.
Commitments: Establish a date to follow the example of Christ by
committing to be baptized under priesthood authority at a certain
date. Read 2 Nephi 31:4–7.
3. The Restoration:
Principles of the Restoration.
Commitments: Attend sacrament meeting each Sunday
before baptism.
Read 3 Nephi 11–18; Mormon 7–9.
4. Eternal Progression:
Principles of Eternal Progression.
Commitments: Live the law of chastity.
Live the Word of Wisdom.
5. Living a Christ-like Life:
Principles of a Christ-like Life.
Commitments: Pay tithing.
Review all prior commitments.
6. Membership in the Kingdom:
Principles: The Goal of Exaltation.
Commitments: Actively join in fulfilling the mission of
the Church.
Commit to the baptismal date.
                                                (See the Discussion Pamphlets, 1986.)

The Trainer's Role

The manual is organized in terms of a teaching relationship between a trainer (a teacher in the MTC or a senior companion in the mission field) and a learner in the MTC (and the missionary as the junior companion in the mission field). Their interactions are presented in a two-column format on each lesson page in the *Missionary Guide*, where the investigator (a nonmember or potential convert) is the largely *absent* object of their concern at the MTC. Once in the mission field, methods of finding potential investigators lead to the interpersonal concerns that are to be the focus of the actual teaching situations.

The first 11 chapters explore all of the elements highlighted above. Chapter 12 is about finding people to teach; chapter 13 deals with teaching directly; and chapter 14 alone deals with baptism and "fellowshipping" the convert. The major thrust throughout the *Missionary Guide* is how to apply the commitment pattern as the main means by which to persuade investigators to become converts, by helping them feel the Spirit. If investigators feel the Spirit, the likelihood of their becoming a convert is dramatically increased. The manual concludes with a chapter on leadership. Thus, the entirety of the *Missionary Guide* is a study book that guides the formation of the missionary identity as a key component of LDS identity.

The Role of Investigator

I invited several companion missionaries to engage me in the missionary discussions so that I could experience the role or identity of an investigator. Elder Kenneth Benson was Elder Jeremy Arndt's companion at this time, and Elder Benson undertook to demonstrate the process of building a relationship of trust with me. (Building a Relationship of Trust is known as "doing BRT" among the missionaries.) Here's how this role-play unfolded:

ELDER BENSON [EB]: It's good to be here today.

MEL [M]: I'm glad to be here, too. And I'm interested in the Church and would like to learn more about it.

EB: What first caught your interest in the Church? How did you come into contact with the Church?

M: My first contact was probably in college as an undergraduate when I wrote a paper on the life of Joseph Smith. I was fascinated by his story. And much later I wanted to learn more about the Church because I knew members were the people who settled Utah.

EB: What college was that?

M: Gustavus Adolphus College, a Lutheran school in St. Peter, Minnesota. Much later, after I had finished my own graduate work, I was involved in helping build a graduate curriculum in American Civilization at the University of Pennsylvania.

EB: And as an undergraduate they taught you about religion?

M: Yes, Gustavus had a course in the Religion department on different religions and I had to compose a research paper. I chose Joseph Smith

because the professor [Robert Esbjornson] made him sound like a very
interesting leader and prophet.

EB: I wasn't sure that different colleges would give comparative religion
classes, but if they did I never really expected that one on our Church
would be offered.

M: It was the late 1950s, way back then.

EB: And then you wrote the paper and became interested?

M: Yes. But I don't remember anything too specific other than that Joseph
reported a vision experience. I thought that was an interesting story that I
could compare to the vision experience and conversion of the apostle Paul
in the New Testament, so that was in the back of my mind.

EB: And when did it start to come to the front?

M: Well, actually now, because I'm in the process of writing a book on the
Latter-day Saints today, so Joseph Smith's experience is an important part
of the background of the Church.

EB: That's good. I'm glad we could be here to share our beliefs with you.
I know some things that will help you understand and increase your
knowledge of the Savior, and provide peace and happiness as it evolves
with experience.

Clearly, the conversation up to this point involves "getting to know you," in
which the missionary seeks to build personal interest and interpersonal trust.
But very shortly, I offered a challenge:

M: Let me ask a more direct question. How do you know that the things
you're sharing with me are true?

EB: How do I know?

[He repeats my question, which indicates that he's actively listening, but this
repetition also buys time.]

EB: I know because of the peace and happiness the Church has brought into
my life; because the Spirit has been with me as I learn these things and
teach them to other people like you.

M: Because you feel happy and good inside, does that mean that what you're
teaching is true?

[This probe is a question that "pushes" further, but Elder Benson is ready.]

EB: I believe that it does. I believe the gospel of Jesus Christ and knowing the
truth can bring peace to our hearts.

M: What if I told you that in logic that's the fallacy of affirming the
consequent?

EB: I'm going to have to ask you what that means.

M: It means that one event (feeling happy) has occurred after another event (learning about Jesus' gospel); you then posit that learning about Jesus' gospel is the cause of the good feeling, simply because the gospel learning precedes the happy feeling. You treat the second event as a consequence of the first. Essentially, you've picked one preceding event to serve as "the cause" out of many other events that could also have been a cause.

EB: What would I say if you told me that? I guess I really don't have an answer.... But, I feel I'm a witness to the Spirit time and time again by living the gospel, by beginning to learn the gospel, and by trying to teach it.

[At this point, I wanted to join with him to see where that would lead.]

M: Is it possible for me to have the kind of experience you've had?

EB: Yes, and we hope you would. That's really our purpose as missionaries, to share the gospel with you and to help you recognize the Spirit in your own life.

M: How can I go about it?

EB: Well, that's one of the things we'd like to share with you today. We'll teach you about the prophet Joseph Smith and about the Book of Mormon, and ask you to do certain things as you fulfill commitments that we will ask of you. And if you are sincerely seeking the truth, our Heavenly Father will bless you.

M: What kind of commitments?

EB: We're going to ask you to read from the Book of Mormon and to pray to Heavenly Father to know that it's true.

M: All right, now, is that the kind of role playing that you would do at the MTC, and that you would carry out in your mission?

EB: Yes, except at the MTC we would have a third person as an observer writing down comments about the exchanges, and we'd go over them in comparison to the commitment pattern. (Benson, Interview, 1996)

From the *Missionary Guide* to a New Manual: *Preach My Gospel*

A new training manual was introduced in 2004 titled *Preach My Gospel* to guide and support the efforts of missionaries during their time in the field, replacing the older *Missionary Guide* (1988). The new *Preach My Gospel* places a central focus on the core doctrines of the church in what are now called the "five lessons." This core material is situated in the third chapter of the new manual and preceded by two introductory chapters directed to the missionary purpose and how to study and prepare to teach. The third chapter, with its five lessons, follows this introduction and is supported by subsequent chapters on recognizing and understanding the Spirit, the role of the Book of Mormon, and the development of Christ-like personal attributes. The central focus of chapter 3, however, remains on inviting interested investigators to seek baptism and confirmation.

The next four chapters address a variety of important missionary skills, such as learning a language, organizing time and planning, finding new investigators, and improving teaching skills. The concluding three chapters focus on helping investigators keep commitments, preparing them for baptism and confirmation, and showing how missionaries can support and integrate their work with the stake and ward structure of the church. The most important change, however, involves "teaching by the Spirit" from the missionaries' own personal backgrounds, rather than teaching by what seemed like rote memorization. Nonetheless, the new manual also provides material to guide the missionary through the five lessons.

Beginning in 2002, this new manual was field-tested in 14 missions, then reviewed, modified, retested, and finally approved for publication in 2004 by the first presidency and quorum of the twelve. *Preach My Gospel* was intended to serve missionaries over the course of two years of proselytizing as they would study, grow, apply, and evaluate their work.

The new manual began with a message from the first presidency that offered what they called an "eternal framework": "We challenge you to rise to a new sense of commitment to assist our Father in Heaven in His glorious work. Every missionary has an important role in helping 'to bring to pass the immortality and eternal life of man'" (Moses 1:39)" (*Preach My Gospel*, 2004:v). The text of the manual also integrated suggestions for personal study, study with one's missionary companion, weekly district meetings, and larger zone conferences under the direction of the mission president. These relationships were also supplemented in the mission field by regular interviews with the mission president.

Each chapter of the new manual started with a set of questions to be considered and information boxes underscoring important points, references for scripture study, suggestions for related activities, and flagged "red boxes" for especially significant information. In addition, each missionary was encouraged to keep a separate personal journal: "Spiritually sensitive information should be kept in a sacred place that communicates to the Lord how you treasure it. ... Review your study journal to recall spiritual experiences, see new insights, and recognize your growth" (*Preach My Gospel*, 2004:x). Thus, the manual established personal self-reflective exercises as a normal part of missionary experiences.

The central purpose of missionary work, repeated throughout the new manual, is to "invite others to come unto Christ by helping them receive the restored gospel through faith in Jesus Christ and His Atonement, repentance, baptism, receiving the gift of the Holy Ghost, and enduring to the end" (*Preach My Gospel*, 2004, 1). This purpose was offered to meet the needs of people in the world today as "children of God, your brothers and sisters." "They want to feel secure in a world of changing values. They want 'peace in this world, and eternal life in the world to come'" (*Preach My Gospel*, 2004:1). "[T]hey need relief from feelings of guilt that come from mistakes and sins. They need to experience the joy of redemption by receiving forgiveness of their sins and enjoying the gift of the Holy Ghost" (*Preach My Gospel*, 2004:2).

Striving to Teach Families

In particular, the missionaries were told time after time that the gospel "blesses families" in accord with a first presidency proclamation on the family: "The divine plan of happiness enables family relationships to be perpetuated beyond the grave. Sacred ordinances and covenants available in holy temples make it possible for individuals to return to the presence of God and for families to be united eternally" (see "The Family: A Proclamation to the World," *Ensign*, November 1995, 102). This emphasis on the family and its eternal significance goes hand in hand with the church's focus on temple work, which leads to the missionary directive: "Strive to find and teach families—a father, mother, and children—who can support one another in living the gospel and eventually being sealed as a family unit by restored priesthood authority" (*Preach My Gospel*, 2004:3).

Every missionary had been ordained to the Melchizedek priesthood under church worthiness standards. These standards have received renewed emphasis as the brethren announced they were "raising the bar" for the "greatest generation" receiving a missionary calling (Ballard 2002:46–49). Priesthood authority meant that missionaries had "the right and privilege to represent the Lord," and had received a "ministerial certificate that verified their authority to the world." Missionaries are expected to "live worthy of your calling" and "to exercise power in your work" (*Preach My Gospel*, 2004:4).

The "Restoration" and "Teaching by the Spirit"

The new *Preach My Gospel* shifted the emphasis away from memorized lessons toward the missionary's presentation of a conceptual understanding of the central gospel of Jesus Christ. The missionary was encouraged to use his or her own experience of the gospel as what was taught, and reduce the teaching material to the five lessons by emphasizing teaching from the heart and "by the Spirit." It used the theme of "the restoration" as the primary framework for understanding the gospel and the action of the Spirit in the LDS story of the gospel.

In a letter on expectations for missionary work, the first presidency stressed the relationship between the missionaries and those who were investigators of the church, urging the missionaries to put the gospel in their own personal terms by speaking from their hearts, as prompted by the Spirit. As the missionary learns of the interests and needs of the investigator, he may even depart from the order of the lessons in order to speak from his personal convictions and in his own words.

Some of the introductory matter reflected a change in the narrative voice that framed *Preach My Gospel*. The shift was from the interactive trainer/missionary roles, on which the narrator comments in the *Missionary Guide*, to a more authoritative, partly omniscient narrator who provides instructions and directions to the missionary and through the missionary to the investigator in *Preach My Gospel*. The missionary is still responsible for covering the core doctrines and principles as a basis for the work of the Holy Spirit. For instance, in the introductory matter of chapter 3, the narrator gives this instruction:

> Make sure you teach all the doctrines in these lessons. Unless directed by the Spirit, for each of the first three lessons, you should give the full content in the order in which they are written. A few of the commandments [from chapter four] may also be included as appropriate or be taught as lessons of their own.
>
> Each lesson outlines the baptismal interview questions, commitments, and doctrines that you are to teach. Thoroughly learn the doctrines. Consistently focus on helping those you teach make and keep the commitments. Use the baptismal interview questions to prepare those you teach for baptism and confirmation. (*Preach My Gospel*, 2004, 30)

Since 2005, the main focus of training in the MTC has been the five lessons contained in chapter 3 about life in the church as the kingdom of God, which the missionaries will draw upon in teaching potential converts. The five lessons answer the question for the missionary: "What do I study and teach?" The topics are arranged in the following order:

Lesson 1: The Message of the Restoration of the Gospel of Jesus Christ
Lesson 2: The Plan of Salvation
Lesson 3: The Gospel of Jesus Christ

Lesson 4: The Commandments
Lesson 5: Laws and Ordinances

The first three lessons (The Message of the Restoration, The Plan of Salvation, and The Gospel of Jesus Christ) are comprised of foundational doctrines and principles that outline the core beliefs of the church, together with the commitments that missionaries encourage investigators to make. In particular, framing the story of the LDS gospel as "the restoration" encourages the missionaries to identify the foundations of the church as being rooted in the origin story of Adam and Eve, which anticipates the Gospel of Jesus Christ. On the basis of learning and affirming the first three lessons, the investigators can then be baptized and confirmed as members of the church, and this is the immediate goal of missionary labor.

The foundational beliefs are related most directly to the doctrinal qualifications for baptism, whereas the commitments deal with such practices as attending sacrament meetings and giving testimonies about coming to know the truth of the gospel. The fourth lesson concerns commandments that all members and missionaries are expected to follow—obedience, prayer, scriptural study, keeping the Sabbath day, following the prophet, chastity, the word of wisdom, tithing, fasting, and obeying secular laws.

The fifth lesson on laws and ordinances builds upon and adds to the foundational doctrines and commandments, and considers missionary work, eternal marriage, temple work, family history, service activities, teaching and learning, and enduring to the end.

Missionaries are told to teach the first four lessons before baptism. After baptism, new members will be taught the first four lessons again, as well as laws and ordinances (29). This structure of the mission program aims to provide a substantial amount of doctrinal teaching as church membership spreads around the globe and provides a way to craft and share basic common understandings. *Preach My Gospel* expresses a global awareness of the whole earth in a system of galaxies, not just an international church.

During their period of instruction at the MTC, missionaries practice ways of presenting these lessons in order to gain and reinforce their own familiarity with the fundamental doctrines and commitments of the church and their justification. They continue this practice in the field with their missionary companions and in district meetings as well. The MTC is simply an introduction to the full program of study and its applications that will continue through the entire 18-month to two-year mission enterprise, and carry over to daily life in the branches, wards, and stakes of the church. Personal identity as a missionary may then be expected to carry over to identity as a Mormon, an LDS, and a member of the restored church.

Thus, the main task at the MTC is for the missionaries-in-training to become fully immersed in these doctrinal lessons and the commitments they entail. The aim for the missionaries is to be better able to present the materials to investigators in a positive and persuasive manner that makes sense from the investigator's point of view and can be confirmed by feelings intimately linked to the Holy Spirit.

Becoming a Convert

MORE LATTER-DAY SAINTS acquire their LDS identity by conversion than by birth and coming of age. The LDS mission system nourishes this church growth. From the perspective of the church, potential converts are drawn from among the world's non-Mormon population as if into a funnel that narrows their identity from random strangers to "seekers" and from seekers to "investigators"—persons who desire to "learn more about the church and its mission." This sequence is the process that missionaries refer to as "finding," when they go knocking on doors or preaching on street corners to discover and encourage someone's interest. Once a seeker is identified, he or she is invited to become an investigator, take the lessons, and seek baptism under priesthood authority in order to be confirmed a member of the true church. For converts, as for children of record, the ordinances of baptism and confirmation are the church's basis by which they come to claim identity as LDS.

Converts, of course, are faced with the daunting task of learning the church's culture in a brief, condensed form through the missionary lessons. For the most part, these lessons are focused on doctrines, commandments, and ordinances, and provide a rationale for newly baptized LDS to be brought into activity within the church. For converts, the process of acquiring an LDS identity is thus "telescoped" or collapsed and abbreviated. Jan Shipps (1994) has suggested the term "Saintmaking" as the general name for both the lifespan process of learning to be an LDS (a process of enculturation) and the intensive and focused conversion process of learning experienced by investigators (known as assimilation). The lifespan process emphasizes "descent" within an LDS family lineage or kin group as a pathway to baptism and confirmation at age eight, while the conversion process focuses on "consent" as the pathway to these same ordinances after age eight under the auspices of the missionaries.

Becoming a convert by conversion is thus a different process than becoming an LDS from the childhood status of a member of record, though both involve what Shipps has described as Saintmaking. This process includes conversion, even for the eight-year- old, but is more general, and refers to the formation or construction of Mormon ethnicity, denoting the mechanisms by means of which individuals, whether born outside the faith or to LDS parents, come to be perceived and come to perceive themselves as Mormon, identifying themselves as members of the group both ecclesiastically and culturally (Shipps 1994:64). Over the life course, these two processes converge in the experience of children of record and new converts as both groups actively acquire the personal feelings and social identities of the LDS.

Conversion, as William James demonstrated in *The Varieties of Religious Experience* (1958 [1902]), is a notoriously varied phenomenon among religions and churches and individuals, ranging from deep experiential transformations of personality to slow but often highly rationalized commitments. Shipps's account of Saintmaking draws upon selected Quaker concepts in her analysis of the LDS processes, such as referring to those socialized under the lifespan model as "birthright Saints." I have not heard this term used by LDS members to refer to themselves, though it is a common Quaker term and certainly makes sense in the LDS context. Similarly, she suggests that core LDS religious experience involves a moment of "quickening," a Methodist term for an inner confirmatory revelation common among LDS members, though as she notes, membership in the LDS Church does not require such an experience. Rather, membership depends upon the formal ordinance criteria of baptism and confirmation under priesthood authority, and the beginning of a "testimony." The gaining of a more complete testimony may then be a lifelong process, with or without a "paradigmatic" confirmatory emotional experience.

In this chapter, I focus on what LDS members view as the conversion process by which a new social identity component is added to, or comes to cover an individual's sense of self, or is substituted for a prior social identity component such that the individual claims to be an LDS, a Mormon, and an active member of the church subject to priesthood authority. These identity claims are different pathways to the same membership social identity, as Shipps's analysis makes clear.

The Background of Consent

Our first task, then, is to understand what Shipps's analysis proposes, using concepts of descent and consent to describe "how individuals acquire group membership" (Shipps 1994:64–65). She focuses first on the earliest period of Mormon history when Joseph Smith emphasized the New Testament link between Christ and his church as a covenant similar to the Old Testament covenant between God and Abraham. The promises of the gospel as Smith proclaimed them were linked to Abraham and were fused with obedience to God's commands under priesthood authority as revealed by Smith, resulting in consent to acquire an LDS and Mormon identity. Followers *chose* to become active LDS. They *consented* to being embraced by the reference to themselves as Mormons, followers of the Book of Mormon. Consent also involved a lineage doctrine of descent from Abraham. As Rex Cooper has argued, those who received the gospel were also "*adopted* (rhetorically) into the lineage of Abraham" (Cooper 1990:70) under Malachi's promise "that Elijah would come 'to turn the hearts of the fathers to the children, and the hearts of the children to their fathers'" (Cooper 1990:137).

Furthermore, historian Dean May (1983:56) showed that during the period from 1830 to 1880, more new members joined the church as converts than acquired their identity by birth. The building of the Nauvoo temple (1841–1846) and the introduction of plural marriage (1842) reinforced the "symbolic underpinnings" of Abrahamic descent. After Smith's death in 1844, Brigham Young led the LDS westward to Utah in 1847, reinforcing their consent decisions as LDS and as members of the new Israel.

Brigham Young died in 1877, and the church was forced to give up the practice of plural marriage between 1890 and 1904 (Quinn, 1985). Regarding Mormon ethnicity in the pioneer period, Shipps wrote:

> Beyond any question the rhetorical construction of blood descent was a factor contributing to...the creation of Mormon ethnicity. There were other, equally significant factors, however: geographical isolation; cultural distinctiveness produced by the practice of plural marriage; the external perception of the community as an ethnic body; and the development of intrastructural [role] differentiation within the community. In addition, the practice of gathering continued throughout the nineteenth century ("Making Saints," 72).

In the second period, from 1880 to 1960, Shipps suggests that the Saintmaking process was gradually altered to increase the prominence of *descent* from the pioneer families. In addition to conversion to the LDS gospel, technically still a matter of consent, the new situation required "fitting into the LDS religio-ethnic community." This "fitting in" was the assimilation process. A convert's identity "was no longer measured by how well they could continue to integrate radical new theological claims...or accept prophetic direction....Instead converts became Saints when and if they managed to fit into the LDS world." This process was more "evolutionary," similar to how immigrant Europeans became Americans (73).

Thus, beginning around the turn of the 20th century, a modified Saintmaking mechanism emerged that structured the process of identity acquisition among those born to LDS parents in ways similar to the maturing of Presbyterians, Roman Catholics, Lutherans, Jews, or adult members of other well-established religious groups seeking to perpetuate their kind. (See table 10.1.) Shipps notes:

The developmental Saintmaking process resting on *descent* that became the norm in the eighty years between 1880 and 1960 continues to operate unimpeded along the Wasatch Front and throughout the Mormon culture region, as well as in LDS families located in areas where the Church's program is fully elaborated. At the same time, the process of making Saints that rests on *consent*, along with the necessity of fitting into the lifestyle and adopting the cultural ethos of the LDS community,

Table 10.1. Church Attendance in the Crystal Heights Second Neighborhood

	Attends Church Regularly	Attends Church Periodically	Rarely or Never Attends Church	Totals
Non-LDS	32.0%	36.7%	31.2%	100% (128)
LDS	82.2	11.4	6.5	100% (325)
Youngest to age 7	94.7	5.3	0.0	100% (57)
Age 8 thru 11	91.3	4.3	4.3	100% (23)
Age 12 thru 18	76.5	20.6	2.9	100% (34)
Age 19 thru 25	82.6	15.2	2.2	100% (46)
Age 26 thru 45	75.7	10.0	14.3	100% (70)
Age 46 thru 60	83.3	13.3	3.3	100% (30)
Age 61 and Over	76.9	12.3	10.8	100% (65)

Notes: This table is comprised of two parts: the LDS distribution, which shows that 82.2% of the neighborhood citizens attended church regularly as compared to 32.0% of the non-LDS neighborhood residents.

The non-LDS residents distribute across the three categories of church attendance in approximately similar percentages: 32.0%, 36.7%, and 31.2%. On the other hand, the LDS residents are clearly concentrated, showing 82.2% among the regulars in church attendance. In addition, the younger LDS residents show the higher proportions of residents in attendance, and those levels were maintained across all age groups. These figures suggest an acculturation process in which the older residents show sustained regular church attendance that remains high across all age categories. These percentages also reflect a "descent" model of acculturation.

also continues to function, not only in the United States in areas out-side the Mormon culture region but throughout the world. Yet without a physical gathering place and with growth threatening to overwhelm what might be called normative Mormonism, the making of Saints is currently posing problems for Mormonism that have not yet been addressed (80).

In the most recent phase of Saintmaking, the church has sent well-trained young people around the world in search of new investigators. To many people among the world's populations, the LDS are a newly visible religious group on the world stage by virtue of mass media images and through such activities as distribution of the Book of Mormon in hotel rooms, LDS social messages on radio and television, and cultivation of the image of young men in white shirts wearing badges proclaiming their LDS identity. The stories of conversion among the LDS are personal and highly varied, yet demonstrate how different individuals become investigators preparatory to their own baptism and confirmation.

The Conversion of Maxine York

In the summer of 1958 following her sophomore year of high school, Maxine York attended a two-week daily vacation Bible school in Big Piney, Missouri, held at the Hopewell Baptist Church (York, *Memoir*, 1962). The following week this church was having a revival, and Maxine prayed that someone would help her and her sister attend. Her prayer was answered when the Baptist preacher and his family drove by her home on the way to church, stopped, asked for her father's permission, and invited her to go along. "In fact," she wrote in her diary and scrapbook, "this is the first prayer I remember being answered. I am sure there were others but this one was so evident. I had prayed and then I had believed with every fiber of my being that it would happen and it did." This answered prayer was the beginning of her religious awakening, and it was followed by her baptism into the Baptist Church a week later. She wrote:

During the revival, I told the preacher I would like to be baptized. He asked me if I had been saved, and I told him I had. The next night [my sister] Deloris decided she wanted to be baptized too. On Saturday night Mom came to the revival with us. When they had the altar call, she went [with] us and told them she wanted to be baptized too. She said she had been saved many years ago but had never been baptized.

So on July 6th, 1958, Mom, Deloris, and I were all baptized in the Big Piney River along with several other people (York, *Memoir*, 1962).

In her memoir, Maxine recounts many events of her high school experience—roller skating on Saturday nights, her first dates and deciding not to go steady, outings to the caverns in the area, wiener roasts, drive-in movies, formation of a quartet for singing in church, and the senior class trip to Rockaway Beach. Following graduation, she moved to the home of her sister Thelma, which was in Springfield, and got a job as a waitress at Fisher's Hi-Boy, before starting college at Southwest Missouri State, planning a major in elementary education. But college was more of a challenge than she expected. She quit after the first year, and sought employment with the telephone company in nearby Rolla, Missouri. That was when she met her future husband. She recounts the story in her memoir:

On March 28th, 1962, I met the most wonderful man in the world. I had heard a lot about Gerald P. Stone from the girls I worked with. He was a pot and pan salesman, and had obtained a list of all the single working girls at the Telephone Company. He apparently had been given the list alphabetically and since my name was Maxine York I was near the bottom. He said he thought Maxine sounded like an old maid's name anyway. By the time he got to me I had heard about him. In fact, one of my girlfriends kept wanting me to meet him because she thought we would like each other.

The day we met I had just walked home from work and was starting up the outside stairs to my apartment. He said, "Maxine." I turned around and said, "I don't know you!" He said, "You mean you haven't heard of me?" I said, "Oh, you must be that Ol' Pot and Pan Peddler. Well, I don't want to look at your ol' pots and pans. I'm not going to need them for at least five or six years and besides that I HATE SALESMEN!" He said, "Well that's not all I'm selling." I said, "Oh, yeah! Tell me more." Finally, he said, "Well, aren't you going to invite me in?" I didn't know whether to or not, being he wasn't someone I knew, but he seemed nice enough. So I said, "Sure, come on in."

We had a nice little talk. He mentioned my white Bible lying on the table. He said, "You mean to tell me you read this?" I said, "I sure do, and it would do you good to read it too." I didn't know he was a returned missionary for the Mormon Church. He said, "Well, maybe it's because I don't understand it." I said, "It's easy to understand." So he read me a couple of scriptures and asked me what they meant.

I didn't know. I was about to kick him out of the house for a minute or two. [But] we became friendly again.

I liked him even though I did think he was irreverent about the scriptures. I wouldn't ever say anything bad about the scriptures for fear I would have been struck dead. I still think it was very wrong of him to have used that approach toward the Bible (York, *Memoir*, 1962).

In this recounting, Maxine presents herself as an enigma to this returned missionary, even as he questioned her understanding of the Bible and seemed irreverent in failing to recognize its authority for her. Jerry returned the following week and invited her to the Ice Capades in St. Louis, but she backed out when her sister Deloris couldn't also get a date and go along. But he returned again in two or three weeks. Maxine wrote, "I really liked this guy, so much so that I prayed he would come back to see me," and of course he did. She even stayed home from a movie one night rightly anticipating his visit. He suggested a dance at Fort Leonard Wood, but she declined. Then he suggested going to church with him on Sunday, to which she replied, "Sure, I would like that very much." Saturday, she saw him again as he came out of a store, and took hold of his arm while they walked together a short distance. She continues:

Sunday came and I had my first introduction to Mormonism. I thought the Mormons were extinct, but now I found that they were very much alive. I was very impressed with the reverence and sincerity these people displayed. I met people of high caliber. After Church, Jerry took me to St. James to get some gas. On the way back to Rolla, I was sitting on my side of the car. The windows were all down and we were trying to talk to each other. Jerry said, "Come over here, I can't hear you." So I slipped over by him and he put his arm around me. I think I loved him even then.... Before we got to the telephone office he told me he was going to take me back to Utah with him. I said, "Says who?" He said, "Me." I figured he was just joking (York, *Memoir* 1962).

But the romance developed. Maxine reported giving him a first kiss while he was driving, and he nearly drove off the road. They were seeing each other almost every day or night, and she began attending the ward with him every Sunday. She met a local couple, the Proctors, who befriended them.

Their courtship moved swiftly. Jerry first proposed about two weeks after their first date, but Maxine didn't accept until a month later, and then Jerry said he couldn't marry her outside the LDS Church. She told him she didn't expect him to, and that if she couldn't accept his church she wouldn't marry him either. She said, "I always felt it was so important for husband and wife to be of the same faith. Jerry never suggested to me that I meet with the missionaries. I always wondered why he hadn't.... The night he asked me if I would like to meet with [them,] I said I would. So I started taking lessons twice a week with the missionaries."

"Taking the lessons" envisions a clearly defined role for missionaries in the LDS conversion process for which all the training in the MTC prepares them. Ordinary members then call upon them when a nonmember indicates some interest in the church and might be open to learning more. The missionaries are formally attached to a mission, a geographic area in one of the 100 or so countries around the world where missions are established. (All members, technically, are expected to serve informally as missionaries, and may assist in the formal teaching process as well, though under the direction of the formally called missionaries. Local mission leadership is provided by a mission president and his wife who serve for a three-year term at their own expense, bearing any loss of income incident to accepting this leadership calling.)

Jerry and Maxine were engaged on the 13th of June. Maxine's LDS baptism was scheduled for June 24th, but she came down with tonsillitis and a fever. When the elders saw her condition, they explained "that sometimes the Devil would cause sickness to come upon people to delay their baptism." Maxine was not about to let that happen. "I decided if the devil had anything to do with it, I would show him who was the boss of me. So that afternoon I was baptized by my sweetheart and confirmed a member of the Church of Jesus Christ of Latter-day Saints. When I came up out of the water I felt better all over" (York, *Memoir*, 1962). She and Jerry were married one month later on Pioneer Day, July 24, 1962.

If we separate the stories of romance and conversion that are linked in this account, we begin to see the outlines of the conversion process as it is understood among LDS. One of the first elements is that Jerry notices that Maxine has a Bible on her table, and offers a challenge to her about her reading and understanding of it. She returned the challenge. Her comeuppance was that "he read me a couple of scriptures and asked me what they meant. I didn't know." She implies that he interpreted them for her in ways she didn't expect, and that she considered him to be somewhat "irreverent," but was nonetheless impressed. She excuses herself with the disclaimer: "I didn't know he was a returned missionary for the Mormon Church."

Subsequently, Jerry invited her to attend church with him on a Sunday morning. This would be her introduction to sacrament meeting, where she was "very impressed with the reverence and sincerity these people displayed.

I met people of high caliber." Among them were a local couple, the Proctors, who became special friends and models. "Brother and Sister Proctor seemed to be such a happily married couple. They had the kind of marriage and family that I would like to have someday. I became aware of the other married couples and they all seemed to be so happy together. I compared these people with all the people I knew. I came to the conclusion [that] this was what I wanted."

In their discussion of marriage, Jerry made clear that he would only marry within the LDS Church, and Maxine essentially agreed with this stance: that if she couldn't accept his church, then she wouldn't marry him either. But she wanted to accept his church on her terms, and waited until he asked her if she would like to meet the missionaries.

The model of conversion employed by the LDS provides an important mediating role for missionaries. Today this role is developed and performed as an institutional expression of church doctrine, using the five lessons in *Preach My Gospel* (2004) as a basis for recruiting investigators who will declare their commitment to become members through baptism and confirmation. Maxine began taking lessons twice a week with the missionaries to speed the process. She notes, "We met at the home of Brother and Sister Proctor. I felt it best that Jerry didn't attend these lessons, because I wanted my mind to be clear and not affected by Jerry's feelings. I wanted to find out on my own if this Church was the true Church, as they professed it to be."

Becoming a member, and recalling her conversion in composing her memoir, Maxine provides a testimony that emphasizes her own agency, her sense that she was seeking the true church, and asserts that her destiny as a marriage partner and mother was already fore-ordained in the preexistence. In her words:

> I accepted the gospel, and I did it on my own. I am sure that I would have accepted the gospel even if I had not known Jerry, had I had the opportunity. Because as I was growing up, even after I had joined the Baptist church, I knew that someday I would join another church. I didn't know which one. But after I moved away from home and was living in Springfield and Rolla, I had attended many different Churches, but none of them was the one I should join.
>
> I am so grateful things happened as they did. I am sure the Lord had a hand in my meeting Jerry. I believe that he and I knew each other in the preexistence. I believe that we wanted to be husband and wife here upon earth and the Lord granted our wish. I also believe that he and I chose our children while in the preexistence, and they in turn chose us.

We can isolate a number of elements that form the outline of a conversion schema in LDS personal identity narratives. The first element is an affirmation that it is best for marriage partners (and family members) to be members of the same faith, with membership in the LDS Church providing the standard. In anthropological terms, this standard is an affirmation of preferential endogamy (to marry within the church), and Maxine readily agrees with the preference of her husband-to-be.

The second element concerns the role of the missionaries as teaching intermediaries in the conversion process. They represent the church and its priesthood as the authority structure for teaching the church's beliefs and conducting its ordinances. A third element is the set of missionary lessons, which provide the forum within which the belief system is outlined and a commitment invitation is offered and accepted. The structure and content of these lessons or discussions has changed over time, but provide continuity in doctrinal formulations nonetheless.

A fourth element is the role of other church members as a supportive cast who aid in the proselytizing process. The Proctors clearly epitomize this role in Maxine's account. The fifth element is the central one for acquiring an LDS identity in the conversion process. It focuses on making a personal decision regarding the truth of the church's claims. This personal decision itself invokes other schemas for personal agency, the role of the Holy Ghost, the claims of Joseph Smith as a prophet, the role of the Book of Mormon as another testament of Jesus Christ, the authoritative role of the priesthood, the current president of the church as prophet, seer, and revelator, and the church as a divine instrument.

A sixth element involves an expectation that this personal decision regarding Mormon truth claims will be met by opposition—perhaps from friends, family, or others in the world or, perhaps, from Satan (the Devil) himself as an adversary (who may cause inner doubts or use illness or other means of opposition) seeking to prevent the ordinances of baptism and confirmation. The seventh element is this pair of ordinances, each with its schematic implementation. And finally, the eighth and last element involves personal reflection on the meanings of becoming an LDS convert, illustrated by Maxine's interpretation of her marital and family history as fulfilling a destiny from the preexistence. Thus she became a Mormon.

Many, perhaps most, if not all conversion stories involve complications of this basic schema structure, allowing for the tremendous range of episodes that come to characterize individual reports. Certainly, as the church has become worldwide in its reach, these stories take on cross-cultural implications and diversities that continue to expand the variations among the personal accounts.

Entering into Activity:
The Conversion of Claude Welch

In solidifying an LDS identity as a convert, more is required than submitting to the ordinances of baptism and confirmation. A convert must also become an active member of the church. Claude Welch (1994), for instance, was a convert to the church as a young married man in the military with a wife and two children. Claude's wife Vera came from an LDS background in Salt Lake City, though Claude did not. His father, in particular, had little to do with religion, while his mother was a Methodist. Still, Claude said, he was fascinated by some of the Protestant preachers he heard on the radio while he was growing up. Vera, on the other hand, was a descendant of Mormon pioneers, and she and Claude met and began dating during the years of World War II. They were married in a civil ceremony on June 10, 1943. Later, in 1957, with Vera's support, Claude converted to the LDS Church and was baptized. He was then faced directly with the fundamental priesthood divisions within the church and the question of becoming active.

Even as a 33-year-old convert, Claude was first ordained to the Aaronic priesthood (along with 12-year-old boys), but was then moved forward rapidly to become an elder in the Melchizedek priesthood. Claude said:

> I was an adult [in my mid-30s] when I joined the Church, and I started out as a deacon and a teacher and a priest. These are all offices in the Aaronic priesthood. And I was very proud of being a deacon. In the other churches I had gone to a deacon was a pretty important calling. It's a little different [in the LDS Church] in that it's boys who are twelve [who are called as deacons]. But the bishop made sure that I had done every task that a deacon was supposed to do in the Aaronic priesthood of the Mormon Church, and the same as a teacher and as a priest. As you've observed, the deacons pass the sacrament, the teachers prepare the sacrament, and the priests administer the sacrament—all under the authority of the bishop. I've done all of those things, and it was one of the greatest things I've had to do. Any adult needs to have that kind of training.

Clearly, some activity is gender-based, most notably by way of priesthood offices, which are filled only by men beginning in the Aaronic priesthood. Gender partitions the church into men's callings, activities, and assignments and women's activities, callings, and assignments from childhood through the highest echelons of the Melchizedek priesthood. Activity, then, refers to the full range of callings, offices, auxiliary programs, and other undertakings that are part of the church's engagement with members' lives at both personal and social levels. In the most intimate sense, activity includes prayer and scripture reading as well as attendance at weekly sacrament meetings, Sunday school, priesthood meetings for the men, young women, and relief society meetings for the women. "Callings" in one or more of these groups provide institutionally recognized activity. In addition, temple attendance is expected, but that depends upon meeting worthiness standards and usually requires at least a year of activity prior to receiving a temple recommend.

Socially, activity includes family home evenings, fireside gatherings, general conferences (which are broadcast to most parts of the world via church satellite systems), stake conferences, welfare work, and a variety of other gatherings and instructional meetings, and most of these gatherings meet without respect to gender. The LDS Church, in the sense of engagement with activity, is a highly participatory church, and identity as a good (and worthy) LDS member depends upon participation in the round of activities that the church offers, as well as its ordinances. In the Crystal Heights second ward, about one-third of all members held teaching and leadership callings. On the path to becoming a stake president, Claude (and Vera) were engaged in many of these church activities, callings, and assignments. Undoubtedly, the church has provided Claude with his most important reference groups by virtue of priesthood, whose values and norms of participation were beacons of light for him (see Merton 1968:335–355).

During World War II, Claude joined the Navy and after the war decided to make it a career. I asked him to describe how he became an LDS. He said that after the war he was stationed in Morocco and his mother-in-law gave him a Book of Mormon to read with the hope that he wouldn't find this too intrusive. He said he read it "to please my mother-in-law." Stationed in Morocco, he and Vera met a young couple from Utah, the DeHart family, whose nine-year-old daughter was near the age of the Welches' seven-year-old, Claudia. The DeHarts asked if they could share some gospel lessons from a book written by Lowell S. Bennion. Claude said, "Yes, but it won't do you any good."

Anyway, they came back and taught us the gospel, [Claude said,] using a book by Bennion. Excellent book! It was like a primer at school. The DeHarts were very comfortable talking about Jesus and talking about the Lamanites. I had a little difficulty with the Joseph Smith story—not because he wasn't a prophet, but because he had too common a name. I was also reading lots of things besides the Book of Mormon. But in the book of Moroni there's a promise...if you read this book and ask with real intent if this is true, the Lord will make it manifest to you.

But I didn't test it. I prayed about it, but I didn't listen for the answer to my prayers. I also had a good feeling about it. But I was reading other books....And I read it many times, but I was reading it again. And one day, I asked the Lord if it was true. And in the Doctrine and Covenants, it tells you that if you do everything you can and if you ask the Lord, he will give you a...we call it "a warm and fuzzy" feeling [light laughter] or you'll have a confusion of thought. Well, I had a burning in my bosom—oh!—but I didn't know exactly what it was then.

Missionaries would help interpret these various feelings as "feeling the Spirit." But at the same time, Claude described a terrible storm at sea and a downed aircraft. In an attempted rescue, he took his small group of men in a 65-foot crash boat. He had placed the Book of Mormon on top of the cowling, which is where the helm and controls are located, built of mahogany—gorgeous, all waxed and slick, he noted.

We were running what's called "a grid chart search"—out and back and out and back. And we found a stain on the water where the aircraft had made a signal. But we didn't find an aircraft. Neither did any of the aircraft that were up for the search. I mentioned that the Book of Mormon was on this cowling. Well, when we came out of the storm, it was still there on the cowling. And I offered a quick prayer: "Lord, if you'll save my crew and me, I'll know that the Book of Mormon is true, and I'll join the Church. This promise is what the missionaries would see as a commitment. Well, we were out there three or four days and only encountered a little motor ship from Germany. But I believed that the Lord saved the crew, six men and me, and he did save me and I felt good about it, so I wasn't going to go against what I knew to be true. So, the next Sunday I told Brother DeHart that I knew the Church was true and if he was ready to baptize me, I was ready. So that was in July 1957.

My folks disowned me when I wrote and told them I had joined the LDS Church—which was a blow to an only child. But I had Vera and she loved me, and she was happy. And I had two daughters, and being as they were our daughters, they were also my parents' grandchildren. So, we were [in Morocco] for seven or eight months more and come back to the States. We just come back out to Utah and played like there wasn't any difference really, and they let the grandkids in [to the house] and I just followed them. And they accepted us then, but they never said they welcomed me back to the family. I was their only child and when they passed on they left what they had to me—it wasn't much, but it was something. We just made the best of life the best we could.

This story of conversion has a number of classic elements including two social aspects: first, the invitation from Claude's mother-in-law to read the Book of Mormon, on which he acted but without serious intent and a failure to listen for an answer to his prayer; and second, the offer of the DeHarts to teach Claude and Vera some gospel lessons from the Bennion book. This offer to teach meshed with the earlier invitation to raise the question of the truth of the Book of Mormon as further events unfolded, in particular the "terrible storm at sea" and Claude's "quick prayer" that was like a bargain seeking a promise: "Lord, if you'll save my crew and me, I'll know that the Book of Mormon is true and I'll join the Church." Accordingly, Claude was baptized and confirmed. He downplayed his folks disowning him. In essence, his life had changed, and he had found a new church home. Reflecting on this experience, he said:

> I didn't know much about the Mormon Church and there was a lot to learn. I was a deacon, [but] I had to learn about the relief society, young men's and young women's programs, and Primary so [our younger daughter] Holly could go. There was a lot to it. So I found out it was really a way of life. But I had already accepted the Church and my life had changed.

The Conversion Story of Rosa Maria Cromar

Mexico has been a field ripe for the harvest among church missions since the end of World War II (Shepherd and Shepherd 1998:ix–xvi). I met Rosa Maria Cromar (1994) while volunteering at Welfare Square with the Highland stake high priests group. The stake high priest and relief society teams were preparing peaches and pears for canning. Rosa, as she introduced herself, was working across the line from me, separated by a conveyor belt filled with peeled fruit. We had to remove any of the peels missed by the automatic peeling machines. Rosa was a convert from Mexico, one among several in her family who were now members of the LDS Church.

Her grandmother in Mexico, who taught English and French, had sent several of her children to college in the United States. Rosa's own mother, however, had a reputation as the most rebellious among her siblings, and so was sent to the strictest Mexican convent for high school study. At one point, she ran away in a show of independence. She waited to marry until she was 25. Her husband was a farmer and laborer, who often crossed the border to find work in the United States. Rosa Maria was the third of her mother's living children, one of twins (the other was lost during the pregnancy). As the surviving twin, Rosa believed that her mother treated her "as a special child." When Rosa was about 12, the whole family of mother and four children moved from Mexico City to La Paz.

In La Paz, Rosa's mother opened a restaurant as a family business, and it was here that they met Mormon missionaries. From Rosa's perspective, the family was a target of conversion, beginning with her mother, who had been searching "for a church that had a prophet like the times mentioned in the Bible":

A pair of female missionaries came by and gave my mother a Book of Mormon. By then my mother had been visited by [missionaries of] several religions. She was always reading, and she just read it [the Book of Mormon]. I had no idea that she was reading this Book of Mormon and I remember them knocking on the door one time and my mother said, "If somebody comes, say I'm not home." So the missionaries come and ask for my mother and not really knowing them, I say "She's not home." They say they are the Mormon missionaries and we left her a book and my mother yells from the inside, "Let them come in." So they came in and they started talking and they continued teaching her and she became a Mormon. She got baptized. She finally had found a church that had a prophet.

After a few other missionaries came along and kept teaching us...I thought she was going to force us to be Mormons. [Nonetheless,] we learned a little more about the Mormons. We went to Church once and we saw people getting up and bearing their testimonies. We thought that was so weird. So I remember discussing it with my younger brother and sister and saying, "These people are weird." They also required tithing and for me it was more important to pay the bills than to pay tithing....[From our business,] I would give all the money to my mother but I would keep the money that would go towards bills, and never kept any money for myself. So when my mother started separating money for tithing, I would get very angry because we just can't afford tithing. Also the missionaries told me I had to close on Sundays. I said, "No way! Sunday's my best day. There's no way I'm closing on Sunday." So I had to accept paying tithing and the closing of my business on Sundays. Still, I thought there was no way I was going to be

a Mormon and I wished my mother had never met these Mormons
(Cromar, Interview, 1994).

Of particular note, Rosa Maria pointed to two of the church's standards as
instigating some of her resistance—the law of tithing and the general rule
of honoring the Sabbath day by not conducting business. At the same time,
she also recognized the impact of members' testimonies during fast and testimony meetings, even though she calls the practice "weird." It is also clear
in Rosa's account that her mother had learned the lesson of agency well, and
sought to lead her family by example—giving her own testimony, requesting
that the children simply listen to the lessons of the missionaries, helping them
build friendships, and offering contrasts with her own Catholic upbringing.
Rosa Maria notes her mother's approach and its effects:

> "There is only one thing I'm going to ask of you guys. I'm not going to
> force you to be Mormons if you don't want to be, because I feel I was
> forced to be a Catholic and I found things that I never felt comfortable
> with in the Catholic Church. That's why I've been searching for some-
> thing and I think I have finally found what I've been searching for—a
> latter-day prophet. The only thing I'm going to ask of you is to give time
> to the missionaries and listen to their message. That's it. You guys can
> accept it or reject it. I'm not going to force you." Well, with that attitude,
> we decided to listen to the missionaries. If she would have forced us, I
> probably would have resisted. Especially at age [14], you're kind of feel-
> ing rebellious (Cromar, Interview, 1994).

Several additional elements enter into Rosa's account of her conversion experience that are partly a function of the international missionary enterprise of
the church. One is the focus on converting whole families as a way of "building on strength" in accord with the church's family-oriented beliefs. Because
family members may not all be prepared to convert at the same time, repeat
visits by different sets of missionary companions may be a regular experience
of investigators. Because Rosa was not a willing convert at the time of her
mother's baptism, she remained an object of missionary interest. "Anyway,
that's why I went through about seven sets of missionaries," she said. Her
hesitation was amplified by the companionate mission system itself. "Actually
they also changed them often; they moved them around often. It seemed we
had just gone through a lesson by one set of missionaries and we hadn't quite
made up our mind and another set would come, and the first would leave. It
all happened within a year's time."

In addition, cross-cultural differences entered into the conversion process, sometimes in unexpected ways. In some mission settings, the missionaries themselves keep an eye open for better living arrangements than those previously established by the mission authorities. And occasionally, rental income to a convert family may help cement the convert tie itself, while providing a close-up view of cultural differences, and sometimes bridging those differences with friendship. Rosa reported:

> After my mother became a Mormon she offered room and board to the missionaries for a lower fee than what we would [normally] charge, which also made me mad. I would let the missionaries [use the kitchen] sometimes, 'cause they were Americans, and they sometimes liked to make pancakes and they sometimes liked to make their own mashed potatoes because they missed mashed potatoes their way. We would make them different and sometimes they would say, "Can we go in the kitchen and cook for ourselves," and I'd say "Go ahead." So pretty soon they became friends, more at ease (Cromar, Interview, 1994).

In the context of these several sets of missionaries, in April 1971, Rosa Maria's family was introduced to an LDS member from Salt Lake City, Dr. Charles E. Parkin, a dentist who was also looking for a land investment in Mexico, hoping to open a business. The missionaries introduced him to Rosa's mother in La Paz, who offered to show him around. "I tagged along," Rosa said. "We showed him around when we were through with business." Subsequently, this meeting opened a door for Rosa Maria through an invitation from the Parkin family to come to the United States to study. In the meantime, the missionaries' lessons were taking hold as Rosa told of her own conversion.

> The reason I became a Mormon—you know I was so anti-Mormon, I just thought they were so weird—was the fact that I had this dream. In that dream I was walking down the beach and was alone on a beautiful day. I actually saw the heavens open and saw there, what I would consider Christ or someone in white. I was told by this person that the message that those missionaries were giving us was a true message. The plan of salvation was something that I really enjoyed hearing. I never realized that we had life before now. You always wonder how you came to be, so it all kind of made sense to me as to the preexistence— how we were intelligent spirits, the plan for us to come and be tested, and then Christ coming and the atonement. In April 1970 I was baptized (Cromar, Interview, 1994).

The central vision of Christ in this dream experience seems reminiscent of Joseph Smith's vision experience, and it certainly builds upon other affirmations and LDS beliefs, and therefore serves for her as confirmation of them. As Rosa Maria further developed the account of her conversion, she contrasted the Mormon gospel with what she had learned as a Roman Catholic:

> In the Catholic Church I was taught that I was born in sin from Adam and Eve, but the [Mormon] missionaries really made it clear that we weren't [to be] punished for Adam's and Eve's sins but that we would be punished only for our own sins. Because Christ had already taken care of that through the atonement, that if we would accept his sacrifice for us when we've committed a sin, we would be able to be forgiven for our own sins, just as [Adam and Eve] were. That made more sense than going to confession [every week].
>
> I am now 38 years old, and have never been sorry that I joined the Mormon Church. It changed my whole life and the future generations (Cromar, Interview, 1994).

By the time of our meeting, at least three generations of converts were part of Rosa's experience, beginning with her mother, then Rosa herself and her siblings, and then as they married, the third generation was being born and raised in the church. Rosa, in particular, had noted the "weird" testimonies borne by the missionaries and church members, which contrasted with her previous Catholic experience, as well as her experience of being the target of other churches' missionaries.

The Conversion Story of Preethi Bettadapur

One of my students at Penn, Preethi Bettadapur, asked if she could write an "independent study" account of her conversion to the LDS Church, to which I agreed. Preethi was born in the United States of immigrant parents from India who raised her and her sister Priya in the Hindu religious tradition as part of a small Hindu community in Mobile, Alabama. Her earliest family and school memories were associated with this community:

> My family had always attended Indian cultural and religious events such as poojas, dances, and holiday festivals, and I had always actively and enthusiastically taken part in these events. I loved everything about these festivals from elaborate costumes and festive colors to the

wonderful food and rhythmic dance music. My favorite festivals were the ones where I got to perform dances with my friends, [like] Garba (where everyone dances with sticks) and Holi (where everyone poured colored water over everyone else).

I looked forward to family gatherings, with the special food, and many phone calls to and from relatives. I loved when my family would spend those times together, and even more the times when we would go on extended vacations, especially to India. [I came to recognize] almost instinctively many of the religious symbols of Hinduism and knew many of the representative practices from my parents' paintings, photographs, and [the] little worship room in the oversized pantry just off the entrance to the kitchen, even though the full significance had never been explained to me, and I did not know all of the meanings behind the rituals. [However, when I was a child,] the festivities, friendships, food, and excitement never made clear to me the true nature of God.

Thinking back, I believe that it was because of my lack of knowledge of the true meaning of my "religion," if it can so be called (though it was simply my parents' religion being transposed onto me), that I felt the need to search for additional truth (Bettadapur, "Life History," 2003).

Clearly, Preethi's parents were introducing their children to the Hindu ways that they brought with them to the United States. As a family, they could draw upon the cultural practices and other resources of their small, but apparently strong and well-to-do community in Mobile. Preethi notes that her mom and dad were very good parents, who "taught us right from wrong, encouraged us to work diligently, to labor for a good cause, and to always do our best." The only hint that something more lay ahead was signaled by her comment that she "felt the need to search for additional truth." Preethi's parents, of course, were concerned about education, and initially enrolled her in a private Christian (Episcopalian) school in Mobile.

Preethi identifies the first turning point in her life with her entry into fifth grade after a move to a new school closer to home. This school, like her earlier one, was also a private Christian one, but of an evangelical bent rather than Episcopalian. "This new school was different. Here the teachers infused religion into every subject, and there was a daily Bible class that each student was required to attend, just as the other classes. All the subjects were taught from a religious perspective—evolution was discarded in favor of Creationism during science class, geometry was used to demonstrate the order of God's world, and many Biblical historical figures were discussed" (Bettadapur, "Life History," 2003).

In this new school, there were regular readings from the New Testament during Bible class and at the end of the class, the teacher, Mrs. Byrd, said a prayer while the students joined in this practice by also bowing their heads. On one particular day, Preethi followed suit and dutifully lowered her head and closed her eyes as she had become accustomed to doing:

> Yet this time was different. I felt something. I no longer simply sat there listening to the words. Gone was the empty feeling of hearing words being pronounced while I sat immobile at a desk. I felt them, I felt the words, I felt a prompting. It wasn't earth-shattering. But I felt a wonderful, simple feeling of happiness and of peace and of fulfill-ment and...it was joy. I was confused, joyful, excited, nervous. This was something completely alien to me. I didn't understand what was different. I didn't understand how I knew that it was right. I was [only] a ten-year-old girl. I didn't understand religion. I didn't even know any-thing about it. But I recognized the prompting of the Spirit when I felt it, though it was a completely new experience for me (Bettadapur, "Life History," 2003).

Preethi remained at this school for the next three years, from the fifth to the eighth grade (age 10 to age 13). This was a period of increasing Christian religiosity for her, partially hidden from others, but also of tension between Preethi and her parents that was reflected in her inner thoughts and feel-ings. Some of her memories now may have been filtered through her sub-sequent Mormon understandings, though in writing this account, she was making a real effort to keep a sequencing of her religious insights and ten-sions in chronological order, first the evangelical Christian ones, and later the Mormon ones.

In reporting on this period of her life, there seems to be an interpreta-tion placed on her experiences that comes from, or reflects, her subsequent LDS commitments and understandings, as for example, the notion of eternal family relationships, which are not part of evangelicalism. Preethi continued: "My knowledge of the gospel at this time reached to the point of my under-standing that Jesus Christ is the Son of God and truly did live on this earth, and that he loves each of us very much. I tried on multiple occasions to tell my parents about this wonderful new gift I had been given...." But Preethi's parents were not accepting of this gift. They treated her ideas as if she was only joking, that this was a silly schoolgirl phase, and in these ways they discounted her ideas: "They poked fun of the fact that I believed in Jesus, that he could be the Savior of the world." But she also cautioned and sought to protect her parents:

> There came a point when they began to suspect that I wasn't just jok-
> ing, that I wasn't just going through a phase because of the school I
> was going to and because of what all my friends believed. I think they
> were angry and upset and hurt that I would choose to forsake what they
> believed. I think it just tore them apart because if I didn't believe what
> they did, then they thought that meant they had failed in some way. You
> believe what your parents believed and you do what your parents do.

Her initial response to the dilemma posed by the awareness of this disagree-
ment with her parents was a retreat into silence, and to "hidden" encounters
with the members of her evangelical group. But this retreat also resulted in
what William James called the "divided self," the conflicted feeling of being
pulled in two directions at the same time (James 1958 [1902]:143–146):

> So I didn't tell them about it anymore. I kept it to myself. I didn't want
> them to tease me about it, but even more importantly, I didn't want
> to hurt them or have them be upset at all.... It was almost like I was
> leading a double life. I felt that there were two "me's"—one for school
> and another for home. I was terrified that the two would collide and
> that one would recognize the existence of the other. For it wasn't just
> at home that I sometimes felt I was just putting on a façade, I did the
> same with my friends at school. I didn't want anyone to know that my
> parents didn't know or approve of my independent religious decisions.
> I didn't want anyone to know that there was any problem. I wanted
> everything to seem perfect.

Her ideal solution was to be able to talk about her newfound evangelical religion, which her parents and sister would also then embrace and be "saved."
Her parents, however, held to their own belief that her Christian ideas were
only a phase of growing up and that she had returned to their way of thinking.
At school she had her Christian friends. And occasionally she found ways to go
to church with them. She thought about a future when she would be able to go
to church every Sunday, except she didn't know what denomination she would
belong to, and didn't really know enough about any of them to make such a
decision. She therefore claimed to be nondenominational. It was enough for
her to be Christian and to believe in God and Jesus Christ.

When she went to another new school in eighth grade, she seemed drawn to others who believed in Jesus as she did; this continued into high school where she joined a Christian group. She could then attend meetings more freely and had a special group for support. And as a sophomore, she became good friends with two seniors, Ashley and Heather, who were also members of the group. Ashley, in particular, encouraged Preethi's Bible-reading and often sent cards and notes, but this continued to pose the dilemma of hidden secrecy. Preethi said, "I didn't want her to find out that I had to read in secret, that my parents didn't know what I really believed, that I couldn't always go to Church." Then a most fearful and unexpected event happened:

> One night there was a fight [between my parents]. It kept escalating until there were only yells on top of shouts. I frantically tried to calm them both down. I tried to mediate as I had before. I tried to do everything I could. Nothing worked. They wouldn't stop. I didn't know what to do. I just wanted us to be a happy family, for everyone to understand the other. I didn't know if this fight would stop or not.
>
> I couldn't just do nothing. I had to do something, anything to stop the yelling. I couldn't stop myself. I [felt compelled to tell] mom and dad about my [Christian] faith and that it was the only thing that had sustained me through these years [of occasional conflict.] The yelling stopped, replaced by silence. Daddy finally broke [the silence] by saying something that hurt more than the yelling, more than anything had ever [hurt] before. He said if this was so, that he had failed as a father.
>
> Looking back, I realize that it was not the best judgment to spring such an important [commitment] on them while I was [also] in such a panic-stricken state. That made it especially easy for them, when I apologized the next day for being so out of control, to believe that it was simply me trying to say anything to make the argument stop. I never fully revoked my statement [of Christian belief], but I told my dad that I believed he was a wonderful father and that his opinion meant everything to me (Bettadapur, "Life History," 2003).

Before the end of Preethi's sophomore year in high school, her parents told their children that the family would be moving to Salt Lake City, Utah, for dad's new job. This came at a time when relationships at school were "finally falling into place" and she was enjoying school and her friends and she even had a boyfriend. She considered staying behind and living with friends to complete the last two years of high school.

The Bettadapur family went to visit Salt Lake City during spring break to get acquainted with the city, and her father stayed there to start his job. Having considered staying behind in Alabama, Preethi finally "decided" (or so her family allowed her to believe) that she would move with her family to Utah. They arrived just before school began. Preethi was immediately immersed in meeting new people and going to classes. She noted the friendliness of the people in Utah, but had no idea which ones were Mormons and which ones were not.

The second phase of Preethi's shift in religious identity would now begin to unfold—from being an evangelical Christian to becoming an LDS. The process involved her engagement and identification with more new friends and some further tensions and differences with her parents. She continued to affirm her relationship to her family and their mutual love, and saw the eternal family emphasis of the LDS Church as important to its truth for her. But the process was one that unfolded in phases of its own, more or less along the lines suggested by Henri Gooren's process model of a "conversion career" (Gooren 2007). During the first year in this new setting, Preethi had relatively few encounters with the LDS Church, with one exception. One day after a favorite class on "theory of knowledge," she hung around with two friends who had turned to their teacher Dan Campbell for help in understanding their differing religious beliefs. Alyssa was trying to explain to Alex why she was a Mormon, and Dan was trying to help explain her reasons. Preethi reflected on what she saw and overheard and experienced:

> Dan tried to help Alex see why Alyssa believed what she did, and during this time I found out that Dan also was a Mormon. Yet he had a way of explaining [the religious issues] that was not forceful, but was still very clear. Though he didn't go through enough doctrine for me to even really begin to understand [much of anything] about the Church, yet somehow I felt the same Spirit that had testified to me of Jesus Christ. I wasn't entirely sure why [Dan's explanation] had affected me so much, why tears were rapidly filling my eyes and threatening to overflow that day, but I knew that for whatever reason, [his words] had touched me.

In the winter of her senior year, Preethi began to read the Book of Mormon and was discussing it with another one of her friends, also named Dan. She explained to him that she was Christian but that she didn't belong to a specific denomination. So he asked if she would like to learn more about the LDS Church, and she agreed. One day after school they went to Temple Square and entered one of the visitor's centers, where Thorwaldsen's Christus statue stands majestically in the rotunda. While they were there,

Dan explained many things regarding the differences in belief between Mormons and other denominations of Christianity. That was one thing that had always confused me since hearing about them. I wasn't sure whether "Mormonism" was actually a denomination of Christianity or not, and what the differences were, since I had gotten mixed answers from different people. He explained that they were indeed Christians and that they had additional information and revelation.

The main thing that sparked my interest during that conversation was that he explained that Mormons did not believe in a single heaven or hell. They believed that there were different degrees of heaven to which people could ascend at the resurrection, according to their deeds. Though this may have sounded blasphemous to some, to me it made perfect sense, since I had always believed the statement of Paul in the New Testament: "Faith without works is dead" (Bettadapur, "Life History," 2003).

This conversation with Dan resolved Preethi's concern, reassuring her that her parents and sister would not be excluded from the heavens, since she "knew that mom and dad and Priya were truly good and loving people," which prompted her to begin reading the Book of Mormon for a testimony "as instructed by the famous passage from the book of James." In the Book of Mormon, she arrived at the story of Alma the younger and the four sons of King Mosiah (Mosiah 27:1–36), which she said touched her heart. "It felt as though a hand were reaching out and caressing my soul and actually lifting my heart so that it felt as though I were going to spill over with joy. I knew that night that it [the LDS Church] was true." Looking back, all of these steps were part of what Gooren has called "preaffiliation" (Gooren 2007:350). She also then knew that she wanted to be baptized into the church, but was again "terrified" to tell her parents. "I knew how they would react. I knew that they would never let me do such a thing." But Preethi also learned of the church's policy, that she would not be able to be baptized without her parents' consent until after she was 18 years old, requiring her to wait until at least the coming summer.

Nonetheless, in March she began meeting with the missionaries to go through what were then called the six discussions, which "reconfirmed to me that I had actually found the true Church of the Lord and that I needed to be baptized." Her birthday celebration was June 7, 2002, soon after graduation and a happy time. Her baptism was scheduled for June 22, but a crisis intervened:

The night before the baptism, I came home to find mom and dad and Priya all awake and standing in the upstairs hallway with all the lights on. I walked in and looked up to their faces and felt absolutely terrified. They [her parents] were both more upset than I had ever seen them. No one said a word for what felt like an eternity. When I finally spoke to ask what was wrong, it felt as if a voice were speaking from outside my body. Dad began speaking in a quiet, low voice. Dan's sister, one of Priya's friends, had mentioned that I was planning to get baptized the next day. They asked if this was true. I physically could not respond. My heart caught in my throat and I did not know what to tell them. Finally I told them that it was true. They both became almost hysterical. They yelled and asked why I was doing what I was doing, and I tried to explain to them, crying, what I believed. I knew that I had to be calm in explaining it, or it would just be a repeat of what had happened so many years before (Bettadapur, "Life History," 2003).

Preethi tried to explain that she had been a Christian for a long time, and that this was only the next step in finding additional truth, but her parents couldn't accept this. They wanted her to conform to their belief system, even though she did not feel any basis in it whatsoever. She tried to calm herself and explain to them that she still loved them dearly and that she was only trying to do the right thing, but they couldn't understand why what they believed wasn't good enough for her. They were convinced that she was doing it because so many of her friends, especially Dan, were Mormon. Her parents really didn't think that she could decide for herself, that she was not old enough to make such a major decision; they didn't want her to believe what others told her to believe, except for themselves. They said that if she got baptized, they would disown her. She realized later that they probably just said that in the heat of the moment, but at that time, it cut so deeply and hurt so much that she just walked out (Bettadapur, "Life History," 2003):

When I returned, I told them that I wouldn't get baptized the next day. At that point, I was willing to do anything, give up anything to make everything better again. I wanted so much, and needed to continue on the path that was leading to knowledge and righteousness. I had to be baptized. I had been waiting for so long, and had told several friends about it.

The next morning, I talked some with mommy and daddy; everyone was being especially loving, and everyone made a special effort to be nice, as everyone wanted back the peace and happiness that had been there before. Everyone wanted to smooth everything over.

I had to work that afternoon. The only thing I could think to do was to go ahead with [my commitment]. I left from work and went to the stake center where I was being baptized. I had this terrible feeling of anxiousness that they would somehow find out, or that they would see my car, or that someone would tell them. But nothing happened.

I was baptized on June 22, 2002 by Elder Joo. It was amazing. I could not believe that it had finally happened, that everything had worked out for my baptism. Two of my close friends named "Dan" spoke at my baptism to make it an even more special event. I can't even begin to describe the Spirit that was there. Several [people] came up to me afterwards and said that that was the best ceremony they had ever been to (Bettadapur, "Life History," 2003).

For the rest of the summer, Preethi continued learning about Mormonism and reading and trying to grow closer to the Lord. She began to trust again that the Spirit would help her and let her know when it would be the right time to talk to her parents. She also received her patriarchal blessing and went to various temples to baptisms and confirmations for the dead. Several times, her parents asked about her decision and if she was still reading the Book of Mormon, but after leaving for school at the University of Pennsylvania, they mostly dropped the issue. She said:

College was so exciting now, because I was able, for the first time in my life, to go to church every Sunday, as well as family home evening, for which I was the "mom," and I could attend the Institute. I was also appointed as LDS Student Association president and got to work with the missionaries pretty frequently, which I loved. A year later Priya came to visit me during her spring break, affording a time for me to talk about my new beliefs. I waited for a prompting of the Spirit. But by then Priya knew.

She didn't know everything, of course, but even on that fateful night before my baptism, she had known that I truly did believe what I said I did because I knew for myself that it was true, and that I would never change my beliefs simply because someone told me to. She accepted it and still loved me.... I knew that a time would come for me to tell my parents also, but that I must be patient in waiting for that appointed time.

I have become more interested in "India" Indian culture and languages, and recognize the importance of learning and sharing that even more, that I may connect more to those people the truths that I have learned, perhaps by even helping to translate the Book of Mormon into the Indian languages which we speak.

More than anything, however, I have learned the importance of family. I love my parents and my sister. I love them not only because they are my family, but because they are good, loving, fun, and wonderful people. They have been so good to me, even if we have had some differences, and one of the most important things I have learned is to trust that they will come to realize the truth of the gospel, and that we will eventually live together in heaven, as I prayed as a child and continue to do so, that we will [have] eternal life, [and] a truly eternal family (Bettadapur, "Life History," 2003).

P.S.: In July 2008, I received a wedding reception announcement from Dan and Preethi Harbucks. They had solemnized their marriage in the Washington, D.C., temple, followed by a Hindu ceremony at the Mount Vernon Inn. As they said, it may be that two religions are better than one.

Saintmaking

Jan Shipps (1994) introduced the concepts of "consent" and "descent" as a way of thinking about identity acquisition as a Mormon or an LDS and how it is acquired. One process derives from the biophysical aspects of pregnancy and birth and is marked in the church's culture by the creation of a written record referring to the blessing and naming ritual for the infant. The infant's status changes from that of a child of record to that of a primary child until the age of eight and the child's eligibility for baptism and confirmation during that eighth year. This process is one of "descent" in the church's culture.

Once a child has passed eight years of age, he or she has passed the age of accountability and thereafter has the status of a convert and will qualify by consent in subsequently seeking to join the church as a full member. Full membership is acquired by taking the lessons on membership given by full-time missionaries. Maxine York sought out the missionaries so that she would be eligible for membership by baptism and confirmation prior to her marriage to Jerry (even though she had been baptized previously in the Baptist church). Claude Welch had come home from military service in World War II when he agreed to receive the missionary lessons that had been suggested by his mother-in-law. Rosa Marie Cromar was an immigrant from Mexico when she took the missionary lessons preparatory to her baptism and confirmation. And American-born Preethi Bettadapur completed the missionary lessons so that

she would be eligible for baptism and confirmation. For all of these investigators, the first step in their consent decision to seek baptism and confirmation was to take the missionary lessons. In identity terms, membership as a
Mormon or LDS was conditioned on this consent decision. They were now
baptized and confirmed Mormons.

Celestial Marriage: A New and Everlasting Covenant

TODAY, IDENTITY AS a Latter-day Saint (LDS) centers on temple marriage and family relations, creating what are popularly known among Mormons as "for-ever families." Celestial marriages are performed only in LDS temples, which are being built around the world as converts and members born in the covenant spread church membership among all countries open to missionaries in order to reach "every nation, kindred, tongue, and people."

The Civil Marriage and Temple Marriage of Clint and Sally Jensen

Sally Jensen had served in callings in primary for ten years when I arrived in the Crystal Heights second ward; most recently, she had served as primary president. Her husband Clint was scout master to young men in the ward and worked as an attorney downtown. Both were graduates of the University of Utah, and they had four children: Bridger, Anne, Dillon, and Nathan. Bridger was just coming of age to be ordained as a deacon in the Aaronic priesthood.

I asked Sally if she had experienced any "turning points" in her life: "Were there any special people who have affected you? Earlier you mentioned some of your primary teachers." Sally looked at me and said, "It's funny that you should ask, because my mother and father were married in the temple, and they were active until my mother died. Then my whole family quit going [to church], and I continued to go because of that primary teacher. And I continued on through mutual. But when I went to college I wasn't real active. I taught primary one year but other than that I didn't do much." So what was the turning point, I asked? (Jensen, Interview, 1994)

Sally didn't answer directly, but indicated that she met Clint at the university when he was in law school. She said, "Clint and I didn't get married in the temple when we were first married. We were married civilly first. Clint was very inactive and comes from a very inactive family. His parents are not members of the church. The night we got married civilly we just sat up and talked about what our goals would be as a family. We had no children then, but we asked ourselves what we wanted when we had children, what path did we want to follow?"

Sally filled in more background. "There was a short time in Clint's family when his family went to church. Throughout that evening, on our honeymoon night, we both remembered the good feeling that we had when our family prayed together, when our family was at church. It was a bond; there's nothing tangible that I can say to you that would give you the feeling. But there was something more there when our families did this."

Then came the turning point. "We decided that night that that was the road we were going to take. And both of our parents, from what I've told you, you can tell, kind of vacillated back and forth, or totally went away. And we decided if we were going to remain in the church, we were going to do it 100 percent and not be fence walkers and do it when it was convenient."

That was the crucial decision. The immediate result was an increase in extended family tensions. "It was really hard when we were first married because Clint's family is really big into boating. I know we hurt a lot of feelings because in our minds keeping the Sabbath day holy does not include boating any more." The difficulties did not end there, because "a couple of years later we were sealed in the temple and had Bridger by then; he was our only child, and we had him sealed to us."

Essentially, Sally and Clint had two marriage ceremonies, the first a civil marriage under state law, which the church considers to be "for time only." That is, the marital bond lasts only as long as both spouses are alive and is terminated by either the death of one spouse or divorce. On the other hand, the church defines a temple or celestial marriage as a covenant lasting "for time and eternity" when performed under priesthood authority, and as sustained by the fidelity and worthiness of the spouses. This temple marriage was their second marriage, with the sealing of Bridger to them by priesthood authority.

Meeting and maintaining the worthiness standards of the church can drive a wedge among extended family members and sometimes spouses. Sally said, "I can't say it's been easy. We've missed a lot of family parties. We are left out in a lot of ways, and now some people feel uncomfortable around us because we have supposedly risen to these 'great callings' from the church....But when people are looking from the outside, they perceive joining in church activity to be more than it is, or they think you think you're more than you are. I don't know. But it's been hard." That was her assessment of the psychic and social costs of choosing to be an active, temple-worthy member and raising their children in the church. But there have been benefits as well:

> I don't regret it. I feel like we've been a good example for our families, and it's amazing because as much as we're left out, if there's anyone with a problem, Clint and I are the first ones they come to. And I feel like it's because of the gospel. People are always saying when they come to our home, "Your house just feels so homey, you just want to stay." And I firmly believe that it's nothing that we have other than the gospel of Jesus Christ in our home, that there's a feeling of love that is more than just Clint and me and our kids. It's a feeling of love for our Savior and for Heavenly Father.

Sally reflected again on that first wedding night at the beginning of their honeymoon:

> I was much more active than Clint. Clint presented [the choice] to me, saying, "I love you so much I'll do anything to make you happy." And I didn't even initially bring it up; we brought it up together; we both talked about our families, and things that we admired in our families and things that we wanted to do differently in our own family. I'm guessing after two hours of discussion we came to our conclusion.

A temple marriage was the result. Later she said, "I feel like there were forces beyond this earth that led us to that place."

Civil Marriage

Most marriage laws in the United States are state laws, and the marriage contract itself is a secular function of government, whether performed by a state official or a church representative. Every state issues licenses to legalize marriage, allowing state-appointed officials (including those designated by church bodies) to perform the marriage ceremony with required witnesses who sign the license upon completion of the ceremony. The officiator files a certified copy of the marriage license and usually provides the couple with a marriage certificate as a symbolic keepsake. The state then issues an original of both the certified license and the certificate.

Among federal regulations governing marriage are the anti-bigamy act (1862) passed by Congress in the face of the LDS practice of plural marriage. This act of Congress was declared constitutional by the Supreme Court in the 1879 Reynolds decision (Gordon, 2002:137–145), and this decision influenced the LDS to end the practice of plural marriage beginning in 1890. In LDS eyes, the plural wives doctrine was not considered part of secular marriage but rather a religious alternative to it, restricted to worthy men who met the church's standard of righteousness. It was, in that sense, the more "spiritual" form of marriage, though not necessarily the "statistical norm."

Celestial Marriage

Today, temple marriage for time and eternity is the preferred ideal form of marriage for church members as compared to civil marriage. Civil marriage serves as an accommodation to couples who are not ready to make their marriage promises under "the new and everlasting covenant" of temple marriage, or who do not meet the worthiness criteria for entry to the temple. A variety of other factors, such as the public gathering allowed by a civil union may also weigh in this choice, because only those family members and friends with a temple recommend of worthiness may enter the temple to be present at a temple sealing in marriage. This restriction is a source of distress for some parents. If they do not possess a temple recommend, they will be excluded from witnessing their child's nuptials, though they may celebrate at a later date with a separate reception.

Worthiness as a Qualification for Celestial Marriage

Admission to temples is allowed only to those members of the church who are considered worthy of a temple recommend. These are members who meet church standards and principles of righteousness. Bishops are given the responsibility to serve as the primary interviewers of members for a temple recommend, a plastic identification card (like a driver's license) that must be presented for entrance to a temple. The *Encyclopedia of Mormonism* indicates three purposes for which recommends are employed:

(1) for members to receive their own endowment, to be sealed to a spouse, or to be married in the temple for time only; (2) for members who have received their endowment to participate in all temple ordinances for the dead; and (3) for unendowed members to (a) be baptized on behalf of the dead, (b) be sealed to their parents, or (c) witness sealings of living brothers and sisters to their parents.

The same standards of worthiness apply for all recommends (Tucker 1995:413).

Worthiness itself is explored through renewal interviews with the bishop every two years; these cover a standardized set of criteria well known to most Mormons as necessary for endowment: belief in God as the Eternal Father, his Son Jesus Christ, and the Holy Ghost; holding a firm testimony of the gospel restored by the revelations to Joseph Smith; being willing and able to sustain the president of the church as prophet, seer, and revelator, and as the only person on earth authorized to exercise all of the powers (keys) of the priesthood; being willing and able to sustain the other general authorities and local church officials in their callings; conforming to the law of chastity; having nothing in their conduct in family matters that is not in accord with church teachings; whether they affiliate with or sympathize with any group whose teachings and practices run contrary to those of the LDS church; whether they fulfill their duties in sacrament and priesthood meetings, following all rules, laws, and commandments; whether they conduct themselves in honesty; pay a full tithe; keep the word of wisdom; if divorced or separated under a court order, whether they are current in any support payments; whether any unconfessed transgression remains; if already endowed, whether temple covenants are kept and temple garments worn; and whether the members consider themselves worthy in every way to enter a temple.

As is clear from this listing, the interview is not a pro forma undertaking, even though the interviewer is cautioned *not* to "inquire into personal, intimate matters about marital relations between a husband and his wife" or to pursue issues of propriety that may elicit anxiety. The content of the interview is to be kept a private matter between the bishop and member ("Temple Recommend Questions: 1991–1995," http://www.lds-mormon.com/veilworker/recommend.shtml; accessed 10/13/08; Hafen 1992:91–95).

Restrictions on temple access may be due to sexual sins, such as adultery or homosexual activity, or to nonsexual sins such as apostasy, word of wisdom violations, failure to pay a full tithe, or other normative failures. In most of these instances, church discipline is required in the form of a bishop's court for both men and women or, in the case of a holder of the Melchizedek priesthood and if the infraction is serious enough that he may be excommunicated, a disciplinary hearing held before the stake high council. The main effort of these proceedings is directed toward confession, repentance, restitution, and renewal of the penitent's standing after an appropriate amendment of life (as discussed in the following chapter on church discipline).

The Story of Claude and Vera Welch

I met Claude and Vera Welch in the summer of 1994 during my first few weeks attending sacrament meetings in the Crystal Heights second ward, as recounted in a previous chapter. Claude and Vera had been married 51 years, had raised and married off two daughters, and delighted in their numerous grandchildren. Both daughters' families were active LDS members and resided in the area of Pocatello, Idaho, where Claude had earlier served as a stake president. Because it was a substantial drive from Salt Lake City to Pocatello, the Welches saw their grandchildren only on occasional visits. But among those grandchildren, the oldest boy had set out on his mission for the church, which of course delighted the grandparents, who could then foresee the two generations following them as active members of the church (Claude and Vera Welch, Interview, 1994).

But Claude and Vera were not content to see only their living descendants as LDS, they also hoped that their ancestors might become members. So once or twice each week, they also went about doing temple work for their deceased ancestors and others. In LDS beliefs, ordinance work for the dead offers a way by which living members can perform proxy rituals for the dead in the temple, by which the living spirit of the deceased person can accept what was done on his or her behalf. This practice depends on the notion of agency but reverses the idea of causal efficacy from the present to the future and instead directs it to the past. So Claude and Vera were working their way through lists of ancestors to the 17th and even 16th centuries, as best existing records allowed, performing proxy baptisms, ordinations, anointings, endowments, and sealings for them.

Like the Jensens, the Welches initially had a civil marriage, and only later performed a temple marriage. To qualify for a temple marriage, both partners must be temple-worthy and have received their endowments, which meant they had discussed their worthiness with their local bishop and stake president in order to receive a temple recommend.

A young man who had undertaken a mission would have received his endowments as part of becoming a missionary. But a young woman would likely delay receiving her endowments until the time of her marriage, and would then complete both ordinances at the same time, first the endowment and then the ordinance of celestial marriage. Sometimes these ordinances would be done on the same day; in other instances, they might be done on separate days.

Symbolic of the close connection between these two ordinances, the original sealing rooms for celestial marriages for the living and for the dead are immediately adjacent to the celestial room in the Salt Lake Temple (Talmage 1978:161–62). And when a groom has been previously endowed, he may assist his bride in entering the celestial room through the veil as she concludes the endowment, prior to their sealing in marriage in one of the sealing rooms. The Salt Lake Temple now embraces a two-story annex of 14 sealing rooms for both the living and the dead to accommodate the large number of these ordinances that are performed there (Hamilton and Cutrubus 1983:102).

Sometime after their civil marriage, the Welches sought a temple marriage and also had their children sealed to them, so their celestial marriage status and family relations represented the ideal form of marriage and family among LDS married couples entering their retirement years, who were able to enjoy their present life together while looking both forward and backward across the generations with what Erik H. Erikson (1997) has characterized as a sense of generativity and integrity. The Welches' feelings of identity as LDS was full and clear; they knew the path they had traveled, and their sense of personal destiny in the celestial kingdom was assured.

A Blended LDS Family: Terry and Leslie Vernon

During my time in Phoenix, I spoke with Leslie Vernon about her marriage in a civil ceremony to her husband Terry, which occurred when she was in her mid-30s. Terry brought two children with him into this marriage. Leslie explained that "the kids, Wendy and Jason, are both 'special needs' kids. They have educational needs that are not of the norm" (Vernon, Interview, 1995). Their mother had had some major educational problems and was emotionally unstable, so she and Terry divorced. He received custody of the children and remained in his mother's home for a period of time as he cared for them.

At this time, Leslie was having problems maintaining her mortgage payments and feared that she might lose her house. She knew Terry from a clog-dancing group they both belonged to, and offered to rent him the two back bedrooms and a bathroom in her house, while sharing the living room and kitchen. And she also helped him with his two children. She said, "We had a nice platonic relationship; I lived in one half of the house, he lived in the other half, and we crossed paths every once in a while." "I fixed dinner for me and the kids because he usually wasn't home. And we ended up dancing on the same team." Then one night, almost out of the blue, he said in a matter-of-fact way: "Will you marry me?" Leslie felt it was more of a directive than a question, but took the proposal in stride. She agreed, and so they made a simple arrangement:

We met on our lunch hour. He came from work, I came from work. We went down to the Justice of the Peace, got our marriage license, and went across the street to the office of Judge Rudd.... On the back of his desk there's this big sign about five-foot long that says "The Hanging Judge, Be Advised...." And after he performed the two-minute ceremony, he said, "I don't ever want to see you back in my court rooms again, so get out!" And that was nine and a half years ago.

A few years later I adopted the kids with no contest from the mother. The only question she asked is "Can I still see my children?" And I said "that's up to them; they're old enough to make that choice as to whether or not they want to see you. I won't force them to see you, but I won't deny them the privilege either, because I feel it's important that they know you for you." When she calls, sometimes they'll talk to her, sometimes they won't. It just depends on what they're into (Vernon, Interview, 1995).

This civil marriage clearly began as a pragmatic living arrangement in which two adults, one previously married, developed a closeness and attachment that they found growing into love, which they wanted to express more formally. They didn't do it through a church wedding or a temple (celestial) marriage, but simply chose a local justice of the peace who could unite them for as long as they chose, or until "death do us part." The story as Leslie tells it has an impromptu edge to it and a sense of irony, where Terry's children are clearly part of the equation. The full import however is of a legal, secular, and marital companionship subject to death or divorce. An LDS temple marriage is cast as a different matter, structured by church expectations that include the temple setting as a necessary component, which then invokes criteria of worthiness to enter the temple and also offers promises and blessings "for time and eternity."

Terry Vernon had custody of his two children when he married Leslie in 1985. Together, they adopted Karen as a baby, and then Leslie adopted Terry's two older children by his first wife (with her permission). Terry and his two children took the six discussions in preparation for church membership. The children were baptized and confirmed, but Terry wasn't quite ready to be baptized. Leslie said, "I didn't have a problem with that, and I just kept praying and we just kept taking him to church whenever he'd go, and take him to activities; the home teachers would come over and visit with him, and they'd talk computers. That really got his interest. And just one day he decided he was ready, and took the lessons, was baptized, and went off to Ireland [for a job] two days later." Leslie continued:

About a year and a half after Terry joined the church, we went through our temple preparation class, went through all our interviews, prepared ourselves to go to the temple, and on September 17, 1994, went and received our endowments and then were sealed [in celestial marriage] and took the kids and made a wonderful day of it.

It was a very uplifting experience. You can't imagine sitting in a sealing room and having your children brought to you for a sealing, and knowing after that that they're sealed to you and they're yours for eternity. It's an emotional and a spiritual uplifting that you just can't possibly fathom until you're actually there doing it. But people would tell me about these experiences and I'd get all emotional,.... sitting there in that room, and seeing my children enter wearing the white outfits that we had selected, and my four-year-old just totally quiet and at peace and taking it all in. Very reverent, I guess is the word for it, she was three at the time, about three and a half. So it was a neat experience that will live on, that my children will also remember because they were older.

Being that I'll never have children who are born under the covenant [due to medical problems], having them sealed to me is the closest thing and the best thing that could ever happen. I know that for eternity, no matter what happens in our lives, they are mine. And will always be mine. And my three-year-old said it best: she said, "We went to the temple 'cause you love me, right mom?" That's right, I said. And she said, "And I'm yours forever now, aren't I?" She summed it all up, at three years old.

I think that our toddlers are closer to the spirit, to what our Heavenly Father wants of us, than we can possibly fathom. That tie is still a lot closer; as you get older it seems like it drifts, and you have to work for it. And these tiny children don't, they're so honest and truthful and bright and smart, they grasp everything just like that. They're like sponges, and just soak it all in (Vernon, Interview, 1994).

The 19th-Century Plural Marriage Heritage

The LDS are similar to other Americans in their kinship patterns, with one major exception: the role that polygamy has played in the life of the LDS Church. In the 19th century, the Mormons developed and practiced plural marriage, or polygamy (technically polygyny), and early on also polyandry (a woman with multiple husbands), both of which they called "celestial marriage," as part of their patriarchal religious system. This patriarchal bias marks their present kinship relations as part of the legacy of this past practice. Plural marriage was given up toward the end of the 19th century, except among fundamentalist Mormons, so it is practiced in the West among groups that refer to themselves as "fundamentalist Mormons." It has been the subject of an HBO television series, ironically titled *Big Love*. In the plural marriage system, one man might marry several wives where the children of all the wives were considered to be part of the husband/father's progeny and constituted his kingdom, along with his wives.

The special prominence given to the father was a consequence of patriarchal beliefs through which the LDS considered themselves the "new Israel." They believed that they participated in God's covenant with Abraham to raise numerous progeny, which justified the plural marriage system as a God-given command (Cooper 1990; Hardy 1992). The modern LDS Church now excommunicates practitioners of plural marriage.

The Sealing Power of the Melchizedek Priesthood

The *Encyclopedia of Mormonism* traces the church's sealing power to the restoration and bestowal of the Aaronic and Melchizedek priesthoods upon Joseph Smith and Oliver Cowdery. The report is given as an after-the-fact account:

> The Prophet [Joseph Smith] and Oliver Cowdery received the Aaronic Priesthood on May 15, 1829, under the hands of John the Baptist. He informed them that he acted under the direction of Peter, James, and John [the chief disciples of Jesus], who held the keys of the Melchizedek Priesthood, and that that priesthood [also] would be given to them (JS-H 1:72). Although the precise date of this restoration is not known, it is certain that it occurred after May 15, 1829, and before August 1830 (D&C 27:12)....Oliver Cowdery on many occasions bore witness that he "was present with Joseph when an [sic] holy angel from God came down from heaven and conferred, or restored, the Aaronic Priesthood and....was also present with Joseph when the Melchizedek Priesthood was conferred on each other, by the will and commandment of God" (Ballif, 1995 [1992] "Restoration," 189–190).

These accounts of the restoration of priesthood power led to the authority by which the president of the church now grants the right to others in the priesthood to seal (or bind) in heaven an act that is performed on earth. According to Yarn (1995 [1992]:355) in the *Encyclopedia of Mormonism*, LDS believe that "it is this [sealing] authority [that] the Lord Jesus Christ described when he said to Peter, 'I will give unto thee the keys of the kingdom of heaven: and whatsoever thou shalt bind on earth shall be bound in heaven: and whatsoever thou shalt loose on earth shall be loosed in heaven (Matt. 16:19).' " On this basis, the power of the priesthood, under the direction of the prophet-president, can bind in eternal marriage, a husband and wife and any children that are part of their union. This power is the sealing power by which an earthly ordinance may have an eternal effect. Otherwise a marriage is for time only, not for time and eternity. Thus, among Mormons, there are two forms of marriage: one for time only, the other for time and eternity, and the latter is also known as temple or celestial marriage.

Covenants and Dispensations

In LDS understanding, God made a covenant with Adam to "multiply and replenish the earth" and renewed it with Abraham, promising that his descendants would become as numerous as the stars in the heavens or the sands of the sea. In the Old Testament story of Abraham, God gave Hagar to Abraham as a wife because his wife Sarah was barren, along with others, including concubines, and this plurality of wives was included in the renewed covenant with Abraham and therefore in the restoration of the Abrahamic covenant under the prophet Joseph Smith.

Furthermore, the Melchizedek priesthood was restored to Joseph Smith by the blessing of Peter, James, and John, bestowing all of the keys and powers of previous dispensations. Among these powers was the sealing power, so that what was sealed on earth was sealed in heaven not only for time, but also for eternity. Finally, because the ordinances of the gospel were to be performed in mortality, worthy living members of the church could stand as proxies—being baptized, ordained, anointed, endowed, and sealed on behalf of the dead in the temples of the church. Temple ordinances for time and eternity, then, may be performed under priesthood authority for both the living and the dead on condition of worthiness.

Joseph Smith's Revelation on Plural Marriage

The origins of temple marriage are intimately tied to how Joseph Smith conceived his role as a prophet in what he viewed as the dispensation of the fullness of times, when all previous covenants between the Lord and his people would be restored, ushering in the kingdom of God on earth. The central feature of this restoration was Smith's revelation of "a new and everlasting covenant" that would provide the fullness of glory for Heavenly

Father and Jesus Christ. The same glory would come to men and women who rightly understood the conditions of their own exaltation as the continuation of the patriarchal promise of numerous progeny generation upon generation back to Adam, and then forward forever and ever. This revelation was recorded on July 12, 1843, less than a year before Smith's death. It now constitutes section 132 of the D&C and contains within it the doctrine of plural wives.

Section 132 is a complex revelation that provided the basis for celestial marriage as a temple ordinance, first performed in Nauvoo, Illinois. A detailed examination of this revelation shows the ideational basis of the temple marriage ritual and of plural marriage. One important aspect of the revelation is its "voicing" between Joseph Smith as the prophet, seer, and revelator (and holder of the keys of the priesthood), Jesus Christ as the risen Lord of the church on earth, and Emma Smith. The revelation begins with Jesus (as the Lord) recognizing that Joseph was seeking an answer to a specific question: He sought "to know and understand wherein I, the Lord, justified my servants Abraham, Isaac, and Jacob, as also Moses, David and Solomon," concerning "the principle and doctrine of their having many wives and concubines" (132:1). What is at issue in this revelation, then, is the Lord's *justification* for the practice of a man having plural wives.

It is in response to this request that the Lord says, "I reveal unto you a new and everlasting covenant;" that "no one can reject this covenant and be permitted to enter into my glory" (132:4). This covenant, the Lord says, was "instituted from before the foundations of the world" (132:5), and "it was instituted for the fulness [*sic*] of my glory" (132:6). Figure 11.1 depicts Joseph as he contemplates a future that will lead to his demise.

In the revelation the Lord specifies "the conditions of this law" as including only covenants (and other promises) "that are. . . . made and entered into and sealed by the Holy Spirit of promise, of him who is anointed, both as well for time and for all eternity, and that too most holy, by revelation and commandment through the medium of mine anointed, whom I have appointed on the earth to hold this power" (132:7). All other covenants referring to marriage (i.e., civil marriage) "are of no efficacy, virtue, or force in and after the resurrection from the dead." The Lord then indicates that the one through whom this new and everlasting covenant may be made and sealed is Joseph Smith: "[A]nd I have appointed my servant Joseph to hold this power in the last days," adding "there is never but one on the earth at a time on whom this power and the keys of this priesthood are conferred" (132:7). Thus, the Lord addresses the church through Joseph as the prophet, speaking in the Lord's voice.

FIGURE II.I *Monday, 24 June 1844, 4:15 AM: Beyond the Events* (Pino Drago (1947–).

With the realization that his earthly mission is almost over, Joseph Smith looks forward steadily, beyond the viewer, to eternity. The artist has grounded the event in time, choosing 4:15 a.m. three days before the martyrdom as Joseph's moment of truth. That moment is visible in the conflicting emotions of the figure. Joseph's left side is tense—his left hand grasps his knee in a futile attempt to hold onto life, and the left side of his face is cloaked in shadow. In contrast, the right side of Joseph's figure is relaxed and bathed in light, reflecting the peace that allowed him to declare, "I am going like a lamb to the slaughter; but I am calm as a summer's morning." The juxtaposition of Joseph's portrait with that of an Italian humanist thinker invites the viewer to compare the different sources of knowledge available to the two. Twenty-three layers of glaze, which the artist applied over a six-month period, intensify the focus on Joseph's face. Richard G. Oman and Robert O. Davis, *Images of Faith: Art of the Latter-Day Saints* (Salt Lake City, UT: Deseret Book Co., 1995). Reproduced by permission of the Intellectual Property Division of the Church of Jesus Christ of Latter-day Saints.

The Lord's House Is a House of Order

The Lord indicates that his "house is a house of order," and that "no man shall come unto the Father but by me or by my word, which is my law" (132:8, 12). "And everything that is in the world.... that [is] not by me or by my word.... shall not remain after men are dead, neither in nor after the resurrection," but the world "shall be shaken and destroyed" (132:13–14).

The text of the revelation then presents three "cases" that illustrate aspects of the conditions enjoined in the new and everlasting covenant, much like a legal brief, using a hypothetical "if-then" structure. The first case represents what might be deemed "civil marriage." In the Lord's voice, it reads: "[I]f a man marry him a wife in the world, and he marry her not by me nor by my word, and he covenant with her so long as he is in the world and she with him, [then] their covenant and marriage are not of force when they are dead, and.... they are not bound by any law when they are out of the world" (132:15). Essentially, they are bound in marriage by the laws of the land in this world "for time only."

The second case might be termed "false celestial marriage lacking in proper authority." In the Lord's voice, it reads: "[I]f a man marry a wife, and make a covenant with her for time and all eternity, [and] if that covenant is not by me or by my word, which is my law, and is not sealed by the Holy Spirit of promise, through him whom I have anointed and appointed unto this power, then it is not valid neither of force when they are out of the world, because they are not joined by me" (132:18). This case makes clear the authoritative significance of the sealing features of celestial marriage by their failure to be performed in this instance by the anointed and appointed one. What is missing is the authority of the priesthood that would guarantee its validity in the eternal world.

The third case is true celestial marriage. Again, in the Lord's voice:

> [I]f a man marry a wife by my word, which is my law, and by the new and everlasting covenant, and it is sealed unto them by the Holy Spirit of promise, [then] it shall be done unto them in all things whatsoever my servant [Joseph] hath put upon them, in time, and through all eternity; and [it] shall be of full force when they are out of the world (132:19).

Then follows the further promise of endowment: "and they shall pass by the angels, and the gods, which are set there, to their exaltation and glory in all things, as hath been sealed upon their heads." Here, then, is the Lord's glory, "which glory shall be a fulness [sic] and a continuation of the seeds [progeny] forever and ever" (132:19).

The attainment of godhood is their exaltation: "Then shall they be gods, because they have no end; therefore shall they be from everlasting to everlasting, because they continue; then shall they be above all, because all things are subject to them. Then shall they be gods, because they have all power, and the angels are subject unto them" (132:20).

12

Disciplinary Councils

ON SATURDAY AFTERNOON, December 3, 1994, Sam Weller's Zion Bookstore in Salt Lake City held an author's signing for D. Michael Quinn and Richard Van Wagoner, who had each recently published important books in Latter-day Saint (LDS) history. The two authors spoke briefly about their research experiences, fielded questions from the one hundred or so persons who crowded into the store's outer hallway, and then sat at a pair of tables to autograph their volumes for the faithful. I stood in line like the rest, clutching my copy of *The Mormon Hierarchy: Origins of Power* (Quinn 1994), waiting to congratulate Mike.

A young woman in the parallel line moved close to the man behind me and said, "Oh, I'm so sorry that they've called you in. When's the hearing?" "Tomorrow morning," he answered. "It's kind of a relief. But I'll be glad when it's finally over." I couldn't help overhearing this exchange and so introduced myself. The young man said, "I'm Brent Metcalfe," and mentally I put the picture together. A week or maybe ten days earlier, I had read an article in the *Salt Lake Tribune* reporting Metcalfe's call to appear before an impending church disciplinary council. The likely charge was apostasy for contributing to and editing *New Approaches to the Book of Mormon* (Metcalfe 1993). We talked briefly about critical approaches to the Old and New Testaments, and the extension of these scientific methods to questions of the human origins of the Book of Mormon, and then got the autographs for which we had come, and went our separate ways.

A week later in the *Tribune's* "Religion" section, under a headline that read "LDS Church Excommunicates Author, Researcher," the Associated Press reported:

> An author and private researcher has been excommunicated from the Mormon Church after compiling a book of essays that question the historicity of the Book of Mormon.
>
> Brent Metcalfe, 36, was excommunicated Sunday after a disciplinary council before leaders of the church's Brighton Stake (Associated Press 1994).

This exchange and set of newspaper reports was my introduction to the use of disciplinary councils in the LDS Church and prompted my reflections upon them as emotionally potent identity-defining and boundary-maintaining instruments of social control. The charge against Metcalfe was apostasy, a failure to obey priesthood authority within the church. What I soon discovered, of course, was that most disciplinary councils concerned another great set of sins, sexual immorality. The pages of the *Salt Lake Tribune* reported several cases of ward or stake officials who were involved in sexual offenses, and in some instances sought to explore the underlying issues through confidential interviews using pseudonyms (e.g., Jorgensen 1994). Apostasy and sexual immorality are among the more extreme cases (limiting cases) that establish the church's outer boundaries of inclusion, making clear to members and nonmembers alike that crossing those boundaries means risking the loss of membership in the community of LDS (Barth 1969).

Church disciplinary councils have had an important role in what Mauss (1994:196–201) has described as "retrenchment" within the church during the last several decades, clarifying how the church's normative structure differs from the wider society, while the church itself has borrowed modern secular features and many "ideas and practices characteristic of Protestant fundamentalism." But disciplinary councils also deal with issues of group identity in personal, categorical, and evaluative terms—not only what it means to be an LDS, but what it means to be a "good" LDS—where self-appraisal and appraisal by others are made in terms of feared, ideal, and actual actions that are defined in cultural terms (Wallace 1965; see also Hallowell 1967).

Psychologically, disciplinary councils give rise to a variety of emotional responses that are linked to different kinds of cognitive/situational appraisals (Wierzbicka 1999; Beck 1976). Feelings of guilt, for instance, arise in relation to self/situational appraisals involving the violation of internalized normative standards of right and wrong; fear is felt in relation to realistic appraisals of danger to one's personal domain and threats to oneself; anxiety is manifested when personal coping resources seem inadequate to potential threats; and feelings of brotherly and sisterly love arise when a person feels accepted just as they are. Clearly, other feelings, like shame, sorrow, or remorse, are also linked to cognitive/situational appraisals in content-specific ways and may also be manifested in facial displays (Ekman 1994). Discerning the emotional meanings requires a close, personal, and culturally sensitive "reading" of reports about disciplinary councils, usually from the person-in-question's point of view or as inferred from a particular situation defined from the point of view of the church's belief system.

My purpose here is to briefly explore the role of church disciplinary councils from the point of view of the church, and to examine some of their emotional impacts and effects on members' own senses of personal identity. These are topics that have not received much attention, but they are central to some of the current tensions within the church and to the personal identities of individuals as members of the church.

Church Disciplinary Councils

The church's gospel reference manual *True to the Faith* (2004:38) indicates that "[t]he purposes of disciplinary councils are to save the souls of transgressors, protect the innocent, and safeguard the purity, integrity, and good name of the Church." Church discipline may involve informal private counsel, cautionary instruction, or informal probation if the transgression of church norms is relatively minor, the confession is voluntary, and the repentance is clear. Formal disciplinary councils may be necessary in cases of "such extraordinary behavior as murder or other serious crimes, incest, open and harmful apostasy, and flagrant or highly visible transgressions against the law of chastity" (Hafen 1995:93).

Most formal church discipline is administered locally within the wards of the church by the bishopric (a bishop and his two counselors), though the stake presidency has general responsibility among all wards within a stake and specific responsibility if excommunication of a member holding the Melchizedek priesthood appears to be the likely outcome. In the latter case, the stake high council of 12 members, together with the stake president and his two counselors, participate in the disciplinary council. Only members of the priesthood (men) administer church discipline. One former bishop suggested that disciplinary councils serve as "emergency clinics where the most extreme soul-saving measures are taken to help individuals who are in serious jeopardy of losing their spiritual life" (Blandon/pseudonym 1995b). The four possible decisions include (1) no action (the case is to be handled informally); (2) informal probationary restriction (which "restricts or suspends a member's privileges in designated ways until he [or she] shows specified progress or meets prescribed conditions"); (3) disfellowshipment, in which a person remains a church member but may not exercise priesthood callings, partake of the sacrament, or participate in public meetings; and (4) excommunication, which means a person is no longer a member of the church. Excommunicants may not pay tithing and, if previously endowed in a temple, may not wear temple garments. They may attend church meetings. Excommunicants may later qualify for rebaptism after lengthy and full repentance, and still later may apply for a formal restoration of their original priesthood and temple blessings (Hafen 1995: 94).

Obedience to Righteous Authority versus Agency

One area of tension within the church today is between obedience to spiritual authority through the priesthood and agency as the spiritual birthright of
every person descended from Heavenly Father. This tension sometimes leads
to anxiety over what can be advocated in the name of agency, and may result
in fear of actual disciplinary action and excommunication if ideas and actions
do not conform to higher priesthood directives.

I attended a meeting of the B. H. Roberts Society in November 1994 during
which Lavina Fielding Anderson recounted the previous year's series of dis-
fellowshipments, excommunications, discontinuance of status among some
BYU faculty, and resignations from the church. She called these events "the
orthodoxy wars."

> Lynn Whitesides had been disfellowshipped. Avraham Gileadi, Paul
> Toscano, Maxine Hanks, Michael Quinn, and I were excommunicated.
> That was in September [1993]. Also that month, John Beck, who had
> withdrawn in June from BYU's faculty along with his wife, Martha
> Nibley Beck, resigned from the church. In June, David Knowlton and
> Cecilia Konchar Farr had been notified that BYU would not grant them
> continuing status....
>
> In October Steve Benson, the Pulitzer-prize winning cartoonist for
> the *Arizona Republic*, and his wife Mary Ann Benson resigned from the
> church....
>
> David Wright, a scholar of ancient scriptures at Brandeis, was
> excommunicated in April 1994 after a year of increasingly tense meet-
> ings with his bishop and stake president.... Within the week, Michael
> Barrett, counsel for the Central Intelligence Agency, was also excom-
> municated in Washington, D.C., for writing letters to the editor pro-
> viding historical and doctrinal information to correct incomplete or
> inaccurate news stories (Anderson 1994).

In response to the six disciplinary councils in Utah, which received national
media attention (see *Time*, June 13, 1993), the first presidency and the quorum of the twelve issued a statement in November 1993 regarding disciplinary
councils. It read, in part:

> We have the responsibility to preserve the doctrinal purity of the
> church. We are united in this objective. The Prophet Joseph Smith
> taught an eternal principle when he explained: "That man who rises up

to condemn others, finding fault with the church, saying that they are out of the way, while he himself is righteous, then know assuredly, that [that] man is in the high road to apostasy" (Smith 1946:156)....

Faithful members of the church can distinguish between mere differences of opinion and those activities formally defined as apostasy. Apostasy refers to Church members who "(1) repeatedly act in clear, open, and deliberate public opposition to the church or its leaders; or (2) persist in teaching as Church doctrine information that is not Church doctrine after being corrected by their bishops or higher authority; or (3) continue to follow the teachings of apostate cults (such as those that advocate plural marriage) after being corrected by their bishops or higher authority" (Compton, "Apostasy," 1995:12–16).

Most members most of the time are not concerned with the possibility of church discipline over doctrinal issues, and generally there appears to be wide latitude in what individuals may believe, as long as they do not advocate their individual beliefs as having normative application to the church. Still, one evening I arrived at the home of Jim Barker (pseudonym) for an interview about how ideas may be explored in the church, only to discover that the first counselor in the bishopric had just preceded me in response to a father's concern that Jim, in his role as a Sunday school teacher, was teaching from materials written by someone who had recently been excommunicated. The father's son, who was in Jim's class, had brought the matter to the attention of his father, and the father brought it to the bishopric. Needless to say, Jim was somewhat anxious that evening, even though the matter had been amicably resolved (Barker, Interview, 1994).

Anxiety was also reported to have run high in the spring of 1993 as a group of women prepared for a conference called "Counterpoint," intended to discuss the many different voices of LDS women in the church. Many of those who had originally indicated their desire to help plan and participate withdrew, purportedly in response to various official pressures within the church. A reorganized planning committee convened the conference nevertheless, and it drew nearly three times the expected attendance. Lavina Fielding Anderson was one of those who helped plan this conference, and she was called in shortly after by her stake president in relation to an article she had published in *Dialogue* (Anderson 1993a) concerning ecclesiastical or spiritual abuse in the church.

In response to the frequent question, "Aren't you afraid?" she wrote: "What do we have to fear from our Church, the institution into which we were voluntarily baptized, whose meetings we attend, in whose temples we marry and worship, whose classes we teach, of whose divine origin we bear testimony?

How can we say we're afraid of an institution that exists to bring us to Christ? How can we say we fear priesthood leaders who only want what is best for us? All of these goals and purposes are true. I know them. I believe them. But the fear is real, too" (Anderson 1993b).

She then suggested that women are afraid of losing their jobs if they're employed by the church (and so are men), of social stigma and scolding in their wards, of what will happen to their children, of reflecting badly on their spouses, and of losing their temple recommends as a sign of worthiness before God.

In appealing her subsequent excommunication for apostasy to the first presidency, she wrote: "I still love the church and wish to be part of it. I am still attending my meetings, reading the scriptures, holding family prayers, and participating in daily family devotional. I do not feel angry or bitter. My hope is for reconciliation and a healing of this breach" (Anderson 1993c).

These "orthodoxy wars," as Anderson called them, suggest that, despite great leeway, there are some defining beliefs that are not to be questioned within the church, and that among these are the role of the prophet and disobeying priesthood leaders concerning life in the church and the historicity of the Book of Mormon. The first is a question of institutional and spiritual authority, while the second is a question of historical events and the spiritual meaning of a document. As long as the Book of Mormon is believed to ground its spiritual power in certain events that are claimed to have occurred in the historical past, then the occurrence of those events will be subject to historical, archaeological, and cultural scrutiny as a matter of scientific interest, the results of which will be held as true or false as matters of degrees of probability. The evidential status of the Book of Mormon will be treated similarly to the evidential status of any other artifacts that are claimed to be evidence for a cultural past of a certain construction.

The question of institutional spiritual authority is of a different order, and suggests why charges of apostasy, rather than heresy, are brought against members, because it is as much a matter of claims to personal authority and its public meaning in the spiritual realm as of aberrant ideas that is at issue. Clearly, the priesthood under the living prophet, who is the president of the church, is taken to mediate the church's understanding of spiritual relationships against all public individual claims, whether made on the basis of scientific evidence, conscience, new revelation, older practice and tradition, or any other basis. Agency, therefore, has certain limits in relation to the priesthood and the prophet as part of obedience to church authority. When obedience is made the issue in a disciplinary council, the only choice is to obey, leave the church, or be cut off, as in the case of the September six.

Lavina Fielding Anderson's heartfelt appeal to the first presidency confirms how personal identity as an LDS survives even against the institution's severance of membership. Actually, it survives on both sides of this relationship, not only because some of those who have been excommunicated often continue their spirituality in belief and practice, but also because the church will continue to reach out in an effort to reincorporate and restore the apostate to full membership under explicitly defined conditions, gently and eloquently phrased in President Howard W. Hunter's plea to those who have transgressed or been offended to return to the church (Hunter, *Ensign*, November 1994:8). Some might claim that they never left. Still, the voices of other general authorities have not always been so benevolent.

Violations of Church Sexual Standards and the Ideal of Unconditional Love

A second tension within the church today is between the ideal of "unconditional love" as a popular understanding of Christ's atonement and the actual exercise of church discipline, which excludes members from the central blessing of the church in sacrament meetings and temple ordinances. It is a tension that suggests a tough-love model of conditional acceptance as the true operative basis for community acceptance, as indicated by Russell M. Nelson of the quorum of the twelve (Nelson, *Ensign*, 2003:21–25).

With respect to sexuality, the church's normative position today is that sexual relations are acceptable only within a covenant of marriage between persons of opposite genders, either sealed in a civil ceremony for time or in a temple ceremony (the preferred form) for time and eternity. Premarital sex, adultery, fornication, and homosexual sex are all forbidden (first presidency 1991). Yet, one former bishop of a student ward estimated that 90–95 percent of his involvement in church discipline involved responding to sexual sins, and that over the four and a half years of his service as bishop he averaged about one such disciplinary hearing per month (Blandon, Interview, 1995a). As he stated elsewhere, "Sexual immorality in all its varieties seems to be the overwhelming 'sin du jour' in Mormonism, far outweighing in numbers and complexity, the instances of apostasy, crime and other grounds for formal discipline, despite the attention of the media" (Blandon, Interview, 1995b).

Members are told by church authorities that violations of church standards call into jeopardy all of a person's efforts to achieve the highest degree of glory in the celestial kingdom and impede relationships with Heavenly Father, Jesus Christ, the prophets, one's ancestors and descendants, as well as with one's family and members of the church. A violation can provoke a self-consuming spiritual crisis, born of guilt, of considerable magnitude.

Consider the case of Ann White (pseudonym), today a woman in her early 50s who is contemplating remarrying in the church. As an active teenager in young women's mutual, she thought of herself as a "little bit of a rebel" in regard to church standards, because she dated boys outside the church and fell in love with one. In her words,

> I was in love with a non-Mormon fellow—and that's the whole reason for not dating non-Mormon fellows....and I wanted to marry him. Of course, that met with strong opposition from my parents and my friends in the church, and my leaders, and so I broke it off with him, and ended up marrying the good Mormon boy that I was not in love with, thinking that I would settle down and live the Mormon life and be blessed with children, that everything would work out and I would grow to love him. And it kind of backfired on me.
>
> For all of my young married years, I lived an ideal family life with this husband who was very good—a good provider, kindly—but on his career path and me on my path of raising the children and being a very active LDS woman. But deep inside was a feeling I was never quite good enough because I wasn't happy with the plan. I was putting on an act and I knew it (White, Interview, 1995, for this and the following quotations).

Ann was encouraged by her husband to be sealed in the temple, which added to her sense of disenchantment. She had not really wanted to be married to this man for time, let alone for eternity. She was torn inside and felt she was putting on a false front. She said, "I just didn't have integrity. I was not an integrated person because I was feeling different feelings inside than I was expressing outwardly....I was not telling the truth. I was putting up this image that I was a happy little Mormon wife and I wasn't." Vulnerable, she became sexually involved with a younger man. When she could no longer stand the guilt, she turned to her bishop. "It was extremely emotional for me," she said. "I felt really inferior. [My bishop] was very kind, as I remember. He suggested that I tell my husband, which I did. It was a pretty terrible, traumatic time. The bishop asked me to do some reading to see if I couldn't strengthen my own testimony, and suggested that [my husband and I] might have counseling. But we didn't because my husband wasn't interested."

The bishop put her on probation for six months and encouraged her to seek counseling. Five years passed, and she again found herself emotionally involved with another man. This time she spoke both to the bishop and the stake president, who told her that she could not leave her marriage for the sake of the children and that she simply had to adjust to her situation. She was disfellowshipped for a year, which meant that she could not take the sacrament, hold a church position, or pray publicly if called upon. She said,

> People pretty much knew that there was a problem. [My husband] was pretty condescending. It seemed to me that the male authorities and my husband were in cahoots, kind of condescending to the point of [implying]—"this poor, little neurotic, emotional woman who really can't live the way she should—we really have to help her; we really have to give her another chance."
>
> First I talked to the bishop, then I talked to the stake president, and then they sent me a letter requesting that I come to a Bishopric's meeting. I went in and the bishop asked me questions and each member of the Bishopric—the three of them—had a chance to ask me questions. They asked me—not a lot of details, but how this happened. All that I remember is that I cried and that it was very difficult and embarrassing, intimidating—humiliating actually—not pleasant, and certainly I felt that I was probably a woman with a scarlet letter. That's how I felt— [like] an outcast among the good Relief Society sisters.

She became depressed and experienced an emotional breakdown. Then five years later, she again fell in love with another man, but stopped short of sexual involvement. And she said to herself,

> Forget it, I can't do the marriage anymore and I can't do the church anymore. So, I left. I felt that I needed less judgment, and that I just couldn't measure up. I did get divorced against the wishes of my husband....The stake president was the kindest in recognizing my own needs, but still maintained that I not get divorced. So I felt that in order to get a divorce, I had to go against the authorities of the church. And I felt that if I was going to go against their advice, then I didn't want to be there....
>
> I was in counseling at the time, and I felt that if I had not done that, that I would have lost my real self.
>
> When I didn't go to church anymore, I felt very free. Freedom became an obsession with me—freedom to be who I was—and I swore to myself that I would never again be something inside and not be the same outside. That became one of my strongest values....

During the eight years of relative inactivity, the thing that I missed [most] was the friendship, the sense of community, the loving support from other members. When you're used to that on a weekly basis, when your whole life is your neighborhood and your church, and then suddenly you strike out by yourself, you miss it....

I don't believe in church courts....I don't see the need for excommunication unless someone is teaching something or doing something that is really detrimental to the group as a whole, the church as a whole. But for particular failings, I'm not so sure it serves a [useful] purpose. It wasn't a deterrent to me; it only made my problems worse....There's a difference between receiving help in counseling and receiving discipline (White, Interview, 1995).

This is an interesting case for many reasons, foremost of which is Ann's inner sense that she had not followed her own heart in choosing her spouse initially because of pressures about mate selection within the church. But the case also illustrates how guilt over the violation of marriage covenants—made in the temple with God—drove her to confess to her bishop. In the several stake and general conferences I attended, one theme was repeated often: If there has been sexual sin, seek out your bishop immediately, and take those necessary steps for repentance and restitution to restore your standing before Heavenly Father. As Bishop Bradlee Watson of Alderwood ward, Lynnwood stake, Washington, explained to me, "In cases of worthiness, the bishop is the common judge, and he's the only one who can help with those things." In a 1995 article on the role of the bishop in the *Encyclopedia of Mormonism*, Don M. Pearson indicates that he is a "common judge," "conducts worthiness interviews," "counsels ward members," and "administers Church discipline." Bishop Watson went on to say:

The first time I was ever involved with any disciplinary action was when I was serving on the stake high council, and it was a very emotional time—because there's such an outpouring of love and desire to help and to lift, to bless—and yet, [there's] a very real realization that it's the Savior that's going to make the difference. He's the one that's going to be able to heal someone; we're just the instruments, the ones who are there to help. So, there's a real reliance upon the inspiration that comes from prayer. And I've found that to be true [in my role] as a bishop. It's become a real joy to see the change that comes into someone's life as they go through those steps that the Savior has outlined in the scriptures, confessing and repenting, making a change of heart (Watson, Interview, 1995).

In the case of Ann White, she recognized in retrospect that an effort had been made to understand her needs, and that the role of the bishop (or stake president) was one that expressed the community's love, as well as its discipline. This did not, however, prevent her from raising questions about the role of fear as a whip to keep people in line, or about differences between what she experienced in counseling compared to church discipline.

The Smith Family Copes with AIDS

There is no holding back in Tasha Oldham's film *The Smith Family*. It shows a good Mormon family in extreme crisis. When the film opens, the husband, Steve, has symptoms of full-blown AIDS, and his wife, Kim, is HIV-positive. Since their initial diagnosis about five years earlier, Kim and Steve have remained together and informed their two boys, Tony and Parker, of their parents' situation. Some time previously, they had also informed their extended families, the local leaders of the church, and their friends, and decided to allow Tasha Oldham to do a documentary film about how they were coping with AIDS as a family.

Forever Families

The personal narratives provided by Kim and Steve in this film expressed their changing and deepening levels of identity as LDS as they and their family members coped with the threats posed by AIDS. These threats were not only about illness and death, but also about their standing as members of the LDS Church. Their personal and social identities as LDS were centered in relationships that connected the generations through the ordinance of celestial marriage, creating what are popularly known among Mormons as "forever families." Therefore, the film differs from other documentaries because it is framed by beliefs in eternal families whose worthy members may achieve immortality in what the LDS refer to as the celestial kingdom. In Kim's words,

> I was born into a very Mormon LDS family.... I grew up with all of the traditional hopes and dreams that my parents had, and that I was to meet the man of my dreams and to marry him in the temple, where we could be sealed [for time and eternity] and become a "forever family"—because in the Mormon faith we believe that if you are sealed in the temple and that you live according to the covenants and

promises that you have made [there], and you live worthy, [then] you have the promise that you can be together with your family.... beyond this mortal existence (Tasha Oldham, *The Smith Family*, documentary film, 2003).

Images of Self

The family crisis erupted when Steve confessed to Kim that he had been unfaithful to her in their marriage, and that he had been sexually involved with men. Steve said, looking back, that he had two contradictory images of himself and his family relationships. One image was of a husband and father in a good Mormon family: "Here I had a wonderful wife and a wonderful marriage in many ways, and children that I loved. We were a good Mormon family with everything going for [it], and to think [that] that was not the case was just something I could not accept...." At the same time, he held a secret, hidden image of himself as someone whose actions betrayed the most feared identity for an LDS man—that of a homosexual or someone involved in a same-sex relationship. Reflecting later, he said, "I felt so guilty, sorry, unclean. I would pray and fast. And all this was done, of course, in secret. I didn't want to admit this [hidden identity] to anybody. Just the idea of having to go to [Kim] was what.... I think.... drove me to consider suicide.... [Suicide] was always on my mind."

Celestial Marriage

In order to claim identity as a worthy LDS, the church's standards must be met in the context of a biannual worthiness interview with the local ward bishop and stake president. Marriage is the linchpin of the church's ethic, defined as a legally recognized union of a man and a woman. Sexual expression between husband and wife is therefore the only justifiable expression of sexuality, and homosexual expression either within a human partnership or outside of one is strictly forbidden. Of their marriage, Kim said,

Things weren't always perfect; they never are; but in almost every aspect of our relationship we clicked very well together—with the exception of the fireworks department. We just lacked passion. After a long time, I really began to blame myself, feeling that it must be me. I must not be wearing my hair the right way; there must be some deficit on my part. Everything else was just great, until about our ninth.... tenth anniversary.

Disclosure

The conflict between Steve's ideal image of himself as an endowed, married LDS and the secret, hidden, feared image of himself and his homosexual activity created an almost unbearable discrepancy. Telling Kim of this conflict altered their husband-wife relationship. Kim indicated her response to Steve's confession: "It was startling and shocking to me. It was also confirming to me in that it was finally the first time I could go.... 'Well, God, it was not just me.'"

Because of the centrality of fidelity within marriage to their identities as husband and wife, and with covenants that were viewed as binding for time and eternity, Kim felt a sense of injustice and anger toward Steve for his deception:

> By the breaking of those [marital] promises to each other on the normal human level—but then on the Mormon level on top of that—he had put not only our life now but our future life in jeopardy. I was really pissed off! I was really mad, I was really angry, I was really hurt that my husband had betrayed our relationship and that he had been unfaithful, and that he had been unfaithful with men (Oldham, *The Smith Family*, documentary film, 2003).

The Plan of Action

Steve and Kim developed an initial plan of action as parents that involved seeking an explanation for Steve's homosexual actions and getting their two boys tested. Kim provided the narrative:

> We were very honest with the boys. Steve spoke with each of them individually and explained everything to them. He told them about his experience as an adolescent, that as a 13- to 14-year-old he was [sexually] abused [while working as] a groundskeeper for the church....
>
> We took Steve and the boys and had them tested anonymously, and of course the boys are fine. [But] we were scared to death. We didn't want anybody to find out. We were panicked about ramifications for his job, about social implications. We didn't feel like we wanted to tell our families.

Nevertheless, the process was like throwing a pebble into a pond: From the point of impact an ever-widening circle of ripples spreads out, from the marital couple to the children to the extended family to local church authorities.

This more extended impact slowly changed the behavioral environment. Kim said, "Once he told the boys, we spent the next two years without telling anyone, until finally the burden became too heavy to carry alone and we knew we had to reach out to our families."

The responses of family members replicated the shock, anger, frustration, emotional devastation, and slow acceptance of the situation that had characterized Kim's and Steve's and the boys' responses. Don, Kim's father, made his feelings clear: "I would have been very happy to hit Steve by the side of the head with a shovel....to really have gotten his attention, and really mashed him. I really felt extremely angry."

Kim's mother said there was "no happy ending to it....no way there could be a happy ending. I find myself a little bit negative....a lot hurt....spiteful." Kim, of course, was HIV-positive, but she could use her diabetes to "cover" her own physical symptoms. And the wider network of brothers and sisters pulled themselves together, taking the cue for their responses largely from Kim, who sought to keep her family intact.

Encounters with the Church

After their initial two years of silence and then their work within their extended family, Kim and Steve decided to inform their local church leaders. Both Kim and Steve realized that this was a major step, and for Steve in particular, it was a major turning point in his relation to both himself and the church. He was a counselor in the bishopric.

At the time, the church's view was that same-sex behavior can be changed: "In order to change homosexual behavior a person must understand the seriousness of the transgression, feel deeply repentant, and have a firm commitment to change" ("Understanding Homosexual Behavior," p. 2). In particular, church leaders were urged to help members "recognize and overcome common rationalizations such as the following: *'I am not responsible for my behavior because I was born this way.'*" Further, church guidelines suggested that "there is no conclusive evidence that anyone is born with a homosexual orientation" ("Understanding Homosexual Behavior," p. 3).

Steve reflected on the process of confession and repentance in relation to the Lord:

> I went through that process very sincerely. I expected that the Lord would take this away from me....the homosexual desire. I didn't believe that I was homosexual. I believed that I was tempted with this, but I was not identifying myself as a homosexual.

I believed what the church told me about homosexuality. I think I was trying to look back at my life and trying to find the.... you know.... how it happened to me. And so I did look at the abuse as an adolescent as maybe a cause, but I no longer view it that way at all.

After his initial meeting with church authorities, Steve was disfellowshipped. The time and efforts of the next period resulted in his adaptation to and reevaluation of his sexual orientation.

Coming to Self-Recognition

Steve said,

I spent five.... six years still trying to change and believing I could. With the passage of time, I began to gradually realize that this was something that I could not change, that my sexual orientation was a part of me that could not be removed or altered.... It was a liberating experience.... It was a weight that was removed from my shoulders.... to admit that I'm a gay man.

While recognizing and affirming that he was a gay man was a liberating experience for Steve, this new identity was a further threat and test for Kim:

Once he came to this realization, he became so involved with support groups on the Internet and people in the same situation, even people in our circumstances—LDS, Mormon people, gay men who were married and in relationships and had families. He would spend hours on the computer talking to these people;.... and I hated it!.... What he needed to do to work through his stuff came at a very great cost to the rest of us, to me and to the boys, who he basically shut out.

Church authorities appear nowhere in the film; they are committed to maintaining privacy and confidentiality in church disciplinary proceedings and so do not comment on processes of repentance. Steve, however, sought to return to church activity with a personal definition of worthiness rooted in his ability to "stay faithful to Kim for the rest of my life." Nonetheless, as he sought accommodation from the church, Steve moved to another level of denial and dissimulation:

After that we realized that we had a few remaining years in order to face death.... as a worthy person. I felt like I needed to have a church.... I needed the support of activities in the church, and temple attendance. I told my bishop that I was ready....that I was changed....and I knew that I wasn't. I prayed and prayed and hoped that the Lord would forgive me for lying to my bishop and stake president. I felt like....that I would die as a worthy man if I were able to stay faithful to Kim for the rest of my life.

Kim also recognized that she was making a choice about her husband, her family, and her children:

I did make a conscious choice not to leave him. And I did make a conscious choice to try and forgive him. You don't just forgive somebody. It's not something you can just do in a word or in an action....It's a process. And I'm still in the process....of trying to forgive him....for what could have been.

Look, I love this man in spite of his weaknesses, in spite of his dishonesty, in spite of his betrayal, in spite of all those things....And we were invested in each other, and we had a history, and we had a family, and we had all of these things that I was not willing to give up.

I felt very strongly that our children believed what we had taught them, and to excommunicate their dad....now....could be the undoing of all of us.

Resolution before the Lord

Steve finally reached a resolution in his relationship to the church and distinguished his relationship to the church from his relationship to the Lord: "The church felt that I should be excommunicated because they believe that I have transgressed....[In their view,] I needed to be excommunicated in order to receive forgiveness. [But] I no longer look to the church for that reassurance of where I stand before the Lord." In fact, Steve was not excommunicated in deference to the family.

During the last few months of Steve's life, Kim and Steve and other family members participated in a Gay Pride parade, which was their most public affirmation of revalued identity dynamics in the family. The eldest son Tony also received his call to serve a mission for the church, which he very much wanted to do. Steve, and the rest of the family, participated in Tony's farewell and send-off to the MTC. Tony thus served a mission as his father had before him. And in spite of some lingering resentments toward the church, Parker, the younger son, decided that the hope for an eternal family was an important belief: "The lesson I've learned is that we're going to be together again....I'm going for that!" Near the end, Steve reflected on himself: "I would like to be remembered as somebody who tried to live his life honorably. I hope that people will remember me for more than my faults. I don't feel I'm the evil person that many people possibly think that I am. You know, when all's said and done, [I hope they'll say] that he's still a good man." And Kim reported that the church agreed to her wishes to preserve her eternal family and their conditional status for entry to the celestial kingdom. And, "after some heartfelt soul-searching....on the part of our bishop and stake president....some private and personal considerations were made, and they did not excommunicate Steve."

Kim reported Steve's dying:

> Three weeks after Tony left, about 3:45 in the morning, he had another one of those panics....where he woke up....and I snuggled up to him, and we were lying there in silence, and he said: "I hope you know how perfectly I love you." And I told him, "Yes, that I know." And a few minutes later he said, "And I really don't want to leave you." And I said to him, "Do you think you'll be leaving soon?" And....he never answered me.

For Kim, the story does not end there. She still faces the loneliness and frustrations of a single woman who must cope for the rest of her life with the continuing threat of HIV. In doing so, however, she continues to affirm her identity as an LDS:

> I'm still going to try and be true to what I know and believe, and yet I'm going to do it with a little bit more realistic wisdom than I've had up 'til now. I'm still a Mormon because that's who I am. It's who I am in my soul. It's the "me" that's on the inside.

To Live in Hope

HIV and AIDS certainly posed a physical threat to the Smith family, but their implications for the eternal standing of husband and wife, and parents and children were even more threatening to their status as an eternal family seeking the celestial kingdom. Steve sought to affirm his image of himself as both a gay man and a good man in relation to the Lord, while Kim fought to maintain her standing as an LDS wife and mother and the standing of her children in the eyes of church authorities. That Steve was not excommunicated was her (very large) victory.

I spoke with Kim sometime after viewing the documentary film and asked her what effects Steve's death had on their temple covenants. In her view,

> "the whole thought behind the idea of eternal marriage is that, if both parties stay committed to the covenants and promises they have made to each other, [then] those blessings of being able to continue as a couple will remain beyond this time as we know it. We decided that we would hold on to our relationship [as husband and wife], and use this relationship as an even stronger, deeper commitment to each other, to an even deeper love that grew out of that heartache" (Kim Smith, Interview, October 29, 2003).

Conclusion

Church disciplinary councils are boundary-defining instruments for determining who may or may not claim a formal personal identity as a worthy LDS. These councils act in regard to church norms across a range of transgressions, with charges of apostasy and sexual immorality as limiting cases. Both kinds of behavior call into question, from the view point of the church's beliefs, an individual's status within the kingdom of God on earth. And while they complement each other as involving different forms of self-control, and both boundaries can be crossed incrementally, they also contrast with one another in important ways. As one former bishop noted:

> [T]here is less gray area in the realm of sexual sin than in the realm of apostasy. The formal definition of the latter.... allows for, even requires, a formal warning by an ecclesiastical leader before a member can be considered guilty.... No such latitude exists for sexual sin. In short, the line of apostasy seems to be established by ecclesiastical leaders on a case by case basis, with public, persistent, and belligerent opposition to church authority being the defining criterion. Sexual sin is unequivocal and need not be publicly known, formally warned, or even indisputably proven.
>
> The only mitigating circumstance seems to be the moral responsibility and spiritual status of the offender, e.g., single, unendowed teenagers experimenting with newly discovered sexual drives and opportunities are generally dealt with less harshly than are endowed, married adults who should have more knowledge and self-control (Blandon, Interview, 1995b).

The psychological ramifications of disciplinary councils are also important, both in terms of self-appraisal and the evaluations of others, and also in terms of the cognitive/emotional effects they generate. Guilt, fear, anxiety, and love are only a few of these effects. A fuller understanding of the cognitive/emotional dynamics would require a detailed interactional analysis of particular cases, which is beyond the scope of this chapter. This initial incursion, however, suggests something of the rich and multileveled cultural and psychological meanings that LDS disciplinary councils encode.

13

Lives of Service

ROLES AND RESPONSIBILITIES in the church are either by calling or assignment. A call is a request by a presiding authority in the church, under prayerful inspiration, for a member to accept a specific responsibility, such as a priesthood office or a teaching or leadership position in an auxiliary like primary or the women's relief society. The call is explained in a private interview with the member. After the member's own prayerful deliberation, if he or she is willing to accept the call, then the presiding authority presents the member's name to the congregation or other relevant group for a sustaining vote. This vote is not like a political election, but rather an exercise of "common consent," which signifies "that members know of no reason why the individual should be disqualified from service and that they [the members] are willing to offer cooperation and support."

Once sustained, "the call is completed by the laying-on of hands by authorized priesthood holders," either in "ordination" to a priesthood office or by being "set apart" to an office or position. Callings are of variable duration; ordination may extend into eternity; a calling to a presidency or the bishopric may involve a limited time period, such as three to five years, prior to release by the presiding authority. If special training is needed, the church provides it (Pitcher 1992:54–58).

An assignment is a responsibility for a common task, such as overseeing church property or participating in home teaching among the men and visiting teaching among the women. These kinds of common responsibilities and expectations among members derive their authority from the priesthood, but members are not set apart, and participation may be expected of some or all adult members, as indicated in the assignment.

Participation in the church's welfare program is an activity under assignment that also serves as an icon of the church's care for members and non-members alike, giving symbolic warrant to what members do in the way of helping others. Glen L. Rudd (1995) has called the welfare program "pure religion." Begun in 1936 as an alternative (and supplement) to the federal government's efforts to create meaningful work and jobs during the Great Depression, the church embarked on a works project of its own, an undertaking that spawned church farms, home storage, employment missions, and most recently, the church's humanitarian service in the face of global natural disasters (Rudd 1995:203–282).

Canning Pears at Welfare Square

Ennis Anderson was the leader of the Crystal Heights second ward high priests group when I first arrived. The high priests quorum is a stake-level institution comprised of ward-level groups or quorums. The men of the high priests' quorum are holders of the Melchizedek priesthood who have generally held leadership positions in the ward, stake, or church and are held in high esteem by all Latter-day Saints (LDS). One of Ennis's duties as the group leader was to recruit members of the ward to fill a quota of temporary volunteer positions in the stake welfare canning factory; this responsibility was part of the church-wide welfare program. Ennis asked if I wanted to join their small group one night, which I did. On the designated Tuesday evening, I drove to the ward meetinghouse and picked up three other men who also took this assignment at the canning factory for the 8:00 p.m. to midnight shift.

Going to the Factory at Welfare Square

The factory is located on the west side of Salt Lake City, in an area known as Welfare Square, where many of the church's other welfare facilities are also located, including a grain elevator, Deseret Industries (which is a training center and clothing and furniture distribution facility), and LDS Social Services. The bishop's storehouse is also there, a supermarket for distribution of food and basic household goods to persons in need.

We arrived at the canning factory about 15 minutes early, washed and donned aprons, high rubber boots, hats, and gloves, and headed for the factory floor where the process of canning pears was in full swing under the earlier shift that we were coming to relieve. Our group was not alone, but was joined by volunteers from other wards of the stake, perhaps 25 to 30 people total. Throughout the day, teams of volunteers had taken four-hour shifts to keep the factory operating, which is done day after day as the fruit harvest comes in (peaches, pears, and tomatoes are the chief commodities here). The factory manager, who is a salaried employee, tells the stake welfare committee how many teams will be needed over a given span of time, and the stake committee then informs each ward welfare coordinator how many persons from that ward are needed on particular days, and then specific ward organizations—primarily the high priests group, elders, and relief society members—are responsible for making sure that the requisite number of volunteers appears for the designated shift. And this recruitment works, year after year. And those persons who receive church welfare are also expected to work for what they receive, either in the factory or in one of the other church facilities (*Our Heritage*, 1996:109). Welfare is a form of cooperative effort among church members for the temporal and physical benefit of others, both members and nonmembers. An essential aspect is work aimed at achieving self-sufficiency or helping others achieve it (Rudd 1995:238–300).

The food canned in this factory is sent to the bishop's central storehouse (in another part of the city) where commodities from the church's 84 other canneries and 108 production units (like farms, orchards, leather goods factories, and ranches) are also gathered for redistribution to the church's local storehouses in all parts of the country. Thus, when people lose their source of income, they may go to the bishop and ask to draw on the storehouse for the family's basic food and clothing. And members of the family, especially the male head of household, may work in the church's welfare system until they find a job. The family's request is evaluated during a home visit by the president of the relief society, and a grocery list is completed every two weeks (as needed) that can be taken to the storehouse, where the order is filled. No cash is used. Members are taught self-reliance, then reliance on family, and finally reliance on the church so that they can again become self-reliant—and the whole system is supported by the expected voluntary efforts of all church members.

Work on the Line

I was stationed on the belt, a moving conveyor of mostly or partially peeled pears that passed in front of our table. We picked those with bits of peel still adhering and cleaned the remainder by hand, replacing the pears on the belt. The foreman gave me this job so that I could leave the line to shoot pictures of the factory operation. Had I been tied to the peeling machine or the canning machine, I couldn't have done my observing. So I was able to see the whole process. On the docks some of the men unloaded huge crates of pears from semi-trailers to be stored in walk-in coolers; other men moved those pears to the large vats of water where the pears (or peaches or tomatoes) could be rinsed, sorted, and placed on a conveyor belt moving to the peeling machines.

The peeling machines had an array of mechanical "cups" into which workers placed individual pears; these cups then spun the pear into the peeler blades that removed most of the skin and deposited the peeled pears on another conveyor that carried them along the line to a table where a group of us were stationed and the finishing work occurred. After we finished the peeling, the cleaned pears dropped off the end of the conveyor into tubs of water that were moved to the canning machines, or inspectors at the end of the belt picked off still-unfinished pears and sent them back to the beginning of the belt for a second "pass" at the cleaning table.

Other workers collected the pears into tubs at the end of the belt and carried them to the canning machines. These cleaned pears were placed next to a large circular stainless-steel tray that had funnel-like openings about five inches in diameter around the outer rim; empty cans rotated under these openings and workers sorted the pears through these funnel openings into the cans, which were topped off with water and then moved along another conveyor to a machine that fitted and sealed the lids. From there the sealed cans were collected into huge baskets that were submerged in steaming hot baths to cook the pears for about ten or 15 minutes. Then the filled cans were cooled in a cold-water bath, carried to the labeling and boxing machines for packaging, and finally these boxes of canned pears were stacked one box upon another ready for shipping to the bishop's central storehouse. This was a completely church-run, volunteer factory operation.

While I was on the line, I stood next to and talked with Rosa Maria, a young woman of Mexican background who was a convert to the church. Through the course of the evening I heard and was fascinated by her life history, and so asked if I could interview her with a tape recorder as part of my research. Part of her story was included earlier.

Time for Shutdown

At about 11:00 p.m., the call came to shut down the machines and begin cleanup. Out came the brooms, squeegees, and high-powered hoses that shot a stream of water at 180 degrees temperature for cleaning the machines, belts, tables, and floors. Everyone pitched in, and by 11:45 we had the whole place scrubbed for the night. I even received a can of pears to take home for my efforts! Afterward, the other men and I drove to an all-night restaurant for burgers and onion rings, and a chance to reflect on the church's welfare program. It was in those moments of conversation when I began to see how the members themselves come to feel a part of an institution and way of life that is all encompassing and to which they commit large amounts of time and energy, and feel compensated by the good they are doing. In keeping with a church motto, they feel "called to serve."

Use of the Factory for Home Storage

I also learned that on days when the factory may otherwise be idle, groups of members from a ward might sign up to use it for home storage production. Home storage is a church program to guide members in ways to prepare food, clothing, and other necessities for times when unexpected events occur. In using the factory for home storage production, a high priest or relief society member might recruit a team of families who would run the factory and then buy back what they produce, by the case lot, at base cost. In this way a group could put up a portion of a year's worth of canned goods for those who wish to participate. This is one way that the church system also aids members in meeting the suggested goal of storing a year's worth of basic necessities in each home against the possibility of natural disaster or calamity of any kind, including unemployment. These men told me of their own or a neighbor's experiences of injury or unemployment where that year's backup supply of home storage helped tide a family over. It is a very practical approach to possible future calamity, fulfilling the boy-scout oath to be prepared!

A Further Tour of Welfare Square

I returned to Welfare Square two days later for a guided tour. Two retired couples held volunteer assignments as guides. The men drove a van to Temple Square to pick up any tourists or visitors who wished to see the welfare operation. Their wives remained at Welfare Square to meet other visitors who arrived on their own, as I did. I had taken this tour once before, in the early 1970s, when I had my young family with me. This time, when I explained my research, one of the women took me on a personal guided tour.

We began in the bishop's storehouse, which was organized like any supermarket and was filled with goods displayed on shelves (but without the commercial flyers and advertisements). These goods carried the "Deseret" brand of church factory production—including cans of pears like those we had produced two nights before. But instead of boxes of canned pears, there were shelves of freshly baked breads, other varieties of canned fruits and vegetables, pasta, chili, bins of fresh vegetables, counters of cut and packaged meats—all the basic necessities. And people were there filling grocery carts with food according to a shopping list prepared in consultation with the relief society president for two weeks' need.

For transients to the city (perhaps homeless) who sought welfare, a bishop's office was on the premises where the person could be interviewed, their ability to work assessed, a shopping list prepared, and work assignments agreed upon. Immediately adjacent to the storehouse is a cafeteria where breakfast and lunch are available for workers, welfare recipients, and staff alike, so that no one need be turned away hungry. In the same complex of buildings were facilities for processing milk, cheese, powdered milk, and powdered eggs, so I had a chance to see those processes in operation as well. And we concluded our tour by entering Deseret Industries (also known as "DI") from the loading dock area, where used goods are brought from contributing wards and individuals to be sorted, cleaned, repaired, and bundled for further redistribution, including overseas shipment. A full large-scale commercial laundry handled the clothes. Men and women worked at shop tables repairing clocks, radios, microwaves, computers, and other mechanical and electronic devices. These workstations were also used for skills training so that unemployed people could upgrade their skills or acquire new ones.

And there was a furniture repair area that complemented the church's own furniture and mattress production factory, which was another job training site. From this cleaning and repair area, we went out front where used goods (and new low-cost furniture) were displayed for sale. Like Goodwill Industries, Deseret Industries helps to recycle things that would otherwise be discarded but still has a useful life for those that need them. Wards also establish regular collection schedules and drives in addition to individual drop-offs. The card table I was using as my own kitchen table came from a local DI store, and it was one of the places I was checking for a used slide projector and even ski equipment.

Fast Offerings and Church Membership

Support for the sick and those in need in the local areas of the church is provided by members who fast one Sunday each month. To fast is to go without food and drink for a brief period of time as a form of personal discipline. The practice of the fast receives full support and expression among the LDS, who treat the first Sunday of each month as "fast and testimony Sunday." In the words of *True to the Faith* (2004:67–68):

> The Church designates one Sunday each month, usually the first Sunday, as a day of fasting. Proper observance of fast Sunday includes going without food and drink for two consecutive meals, attending fast and testimony meeting, and giving a fast offering to help care for those in need.
>
> Your fast offering should be at least the value of the two meals you do not eat. When possible, be generous and give much more than this amount.

In addition to observing the fast days set aside by Church leaders, you can fast on any other day, according to your needs and the needs of others. However, you should not fast too frequently or for excessive periods of time.

In the Crystal Heights second ward, the young deacons made the rounds of homes among church members after fast and testimony meeting to secure fast offerings from those who hadn't brought them to church. These fast offerings, the equivalent of the cost of two meals foregone on the first Sunday of the month, are contributions to the church beyond tithing and are used at the bishop's discretion to help meet local welfare needs. This fast offering is given in addition to regular tithing.

Church Callings as Social Identities

Among other attributes, LDS acquire social identities that are specific to church callings, such as a primary teacher or a ward bishop. A calling is both an opportunity for personal spiritual development and a responsibility within the church's social organization. And these callings form a table of organization for the ward. In the Crystal Heights second ward, the number of members over age 12 was approximately 560. In the published ward directory, the table of organization that specified the publicly recognized callings showed 206 positions as distinctive callings (including primary teachers and leaders within young women classes and young men Aaronic priesthood offices), a very high participation rate. At any one time, more than one-third of the members (in this instance about 37 percent) actively served in specific roles in relation to persons holding other roles in the ward.

The core institutional groupings that constitute explicit callings within the context of the Crystal Heights second ward begin with the stake presidency and the ward bishopric as the presiding groups in the ward, then the quorums of elders and high priests, the Aaronic priesthood quorums (deacons, teachers, and priests), the young men and young women, the relief society, the primary, Sunday school, and ward mission leaders. Each of these institutional groupings is ordered by a similar structural organization with a presidency (usually with a president, and a first and second counselor). Therefore, no person presides alone. As leaders, the presiding authorities are responsible for helping identify other persons to fill other support positions, plus a further variety of positions by assignment to help carry out the ward and stake programs. And these institutional callings are differentiated in general terms by age (and experience), gender, and functions—to carry out purposes in church activity.

In noting this high active participation rate, I am excluding the most extensive set of callings in the ward—men on assignment as home teachers and women as visiting teachers. These assignments are distributed and rotated among Melchizedek priesthood holders (often paired with teachers in the Aaronic priesthood) on the one hand, and the relief society sisters on the other, such that pairs of visitors, either two men or two women (and occasionally couples), are assigned to visit three or four families once each month, using enough pairs to cover all households in the ward. That means that each family household may expect to receive two different sets of visitors on a monthly basis, in addition to the regular group gatherings during the three-hour Sunday block of meetings.

The purpose of these monthly visits is to support, nurture, and guide the members in their homes, using brief lessons (suggested in *Ensign* magazine), blessings, and prayers. These visitors may ask whether family needs are being met or if there is any message that should be conveyed to the bishop. This practice of home visits expresses the wards and stakes as relatively small, intensive, face-to-face communities of activity in which personal knowledge and sentiment are interwoven with the privileges, duties, and responsibilities of membership. No one easily avoids friendly observation or the obligations of mutual support. And as these callings are rotated within the relief society and the priesthood quorums, social and personal identity relationships are established and reinforced (Caughey 2006:53; 1980). Therefore, what it means to be a "good" LDS becomes directly observable within the community of members.

Ward leadership and oversight are the responsibility of the bishopric, lodged in the roles and social identities of the bishop, and his first and second counselors, with supporting staff positions of secretaries and clerks—all of whom are men (holders of the Melchizedek priesthood). And though the social identities are clearly named and labeled as a structure of positions in the wards of the church, the personalities and individual styles of leadership vary dramatically, giving rise to personal identity features as well (Caughey 1980).

The Formal Role of Bishop

Justin Bell had been bishop of the Crystal Heights second ward for almost five years when I joined in ward activities. His full-time occupation was as manager of a computer company operation in Salt Lake City, and serving as bishop of the ward was at least an equivalent work responsibility in terms of time, energy, and focus. Essentially, he had two full-time jobs. When I asked him to describe his calling as bishop, he replied readily in terms of the church's formal priesthood authority structure and mission:

> I believe that the Savior restored his priesthood authority and power here upon the earth to operate and officiate in his kingdom. We believe that we have a three-fold mission in the church to redeem the dead, perfect the Saints, and preach the gospel. And if we keep those things in mind, ... then I see my calling in this ward is to ... inspire, train and motivate the folks—lead, educate, and train—us as a group to meet those goals. ... That in a nutshell is the calling.

Then he continued:

> That's done through weekly sacrament meetings, weekly meetings with the leaders of the teaching programs, where we reach out to the members of the ward through callings of people in order to fill ward structure and organization that have assignments: we have missionary folks, we have family history folks, and we have quorums of the priesthood that are assigned tasks to do.

Bishop Bell's description of his role or social identity places an emphasis on mission, social organization, and leadership. He is fully aware of the church programs that underlie callings and of the need for meetings to keep programs "on task." His programmatic awareness and the commitments entailed by his role as bishop are equally clear in his response to my question about his activities as bishop during a normal week. He began his description with Sunday morning at about 7:00 a.m., when he arrives at the ward bishopric office:

> I start early and prepare first with just myself and plan for the day starting with the bishopric meeting. Then we have an hour's bishopric meeting, my counselors and I, where we counsel on callings and staffing and ward issues, budgeting, funding, assignments from the stake presidency, and assignments from welfare square and the temple, and how we're going to administer those. Then we go into an expanded meeting that's called the PEC, the priesthood executive council, where brethren who have leadership callings join in and we make assignments and counsel together about how we can meet those missions of the church. And then I have individual meetings and appointments with members of the ward, counseling situations, marriage counseling, recommend interviews and then the block program consisting of

Sunday School, Relief Society, Primary, Young Women, Young Men, and sacrament meeting, and then I finish up with some further interviews as necessary—and that's Sunday, usually from about 7:00 a.m. to 6:00 p.m. at night.

Then I spend time with the family on Sunday night. Monday night is family home evening. Tuesday night is again a bishopric meeting with many of those same issues that we discussed earlier, and other matters—visiting hospitals, families with newborn babies, and that's usually from 7:00 p.m. I usually have an appointment at 6:30 p.m., with someone who needs counseling, help, or a welfare situation. The bishopric meeting starts about 7:00 p.m. and is done about 10:30 p.m. or 11:00 p.m. Wednesday night is youth night. I attend those with the youth. It's usually scouting on the boy's side and young women's achievement recognition on the girl's side. That's usually from about 7:00 p.m. to 9:00 p.m.

Thursday nights I usually do my own home teaching, my own temple attendance and have my own time. Friday nights are open for my wife and I to have a "date" night. And then there are always activities on Saturday—father and son's time, funerals, baptisms or some things like that. So that's really the week. On a good week, if I'm doing what I should be doing I feel good about it, when I spend 25 or 30 hours in my calling.

I probed further about the meetings of the bishopric and priesthood executive committee (PEC). The first involves both the first and second counselor and the clerk and executive secretary, and serves as "an opportunity to receive their counsel." The PEC then includes other leaders whose callings are to preside, such as the relief society president, the elders' quorum president, and the high priest group leader. Bishop Bell said he had "a great testimony of that system, where everybody [who presides as a priesthood leader] gets a 'say' but one person then makes a decision." I asked him at what point the relief society gets involved, and pieced together his response:

The Relief Society is involved on a monthly basis in the ward council. We have a council meeting the last Sunday of each month, and that expands one more step. It involves the presidents of Young Women, Primary, Sunday School, and Relief Society, and leaders of the music committee, activities committee, [and] the editor of the ward newspaper. And we [the bishopric] meet with all those sisters on a monthly basis and individually to review their stewardships and their callings, budgeting, staffing and everything else that makes sure we're in step together. We try to meet with the Relief Society presidency bi-monthly or tri-monthly—the president and her counselors.

So, in ward council, we [the bishopric] meet with the Relief Society at a set time of the month. The Relief Society president and her counselors will come in to talk about the threefold mission of the church, their assignments of stewardship, their feedback from visiting the sisters, and their problems temporal or spiritual: "Sister so-and-so is ill or broke her hip and is in the hospital or is struggling in her calling, or in her marriage, or something." It isn't spying, but a system of love and concern, and we try to maintain confidentiality.

The relief society president receives reports from the visiting teachers, among others. The high priests' group leader also receives the reports of the home teachers, either of elders or high priests. Bishop Bell noted that "a brother who holds the priesthood belongs to one of two quorums, the elders' quorum or the high priests' quorum. If they're a high priest it's usually because ... they've held a position of leadership or sometimes because of their age, where most of the brothers are the same age and their spirit has advanced to a level of maturity where it's right to recognize their wisdom" (Bell, Interview, 1994). In general, elders will be home-taught by the elder's quorum members, and high priests families will be home-taught by high priests. Though this appears to be an age-graded system, the bishop argued that the distinguishing factors were leadership and wisdom rather than age, and that scriptural directives indicate that the elders' quorum ought to be, in his words, "the backbone" to members in need.

A *View of the Role of Bishop as*
"the Best Job in the Church"

My experience with Bishop Kent Barnes of the Country Club ward in Phoenix East stake was much different than the organizational formality I felt with Bishop Bell. This is somewhat odd since Bishop Barnes was a military man who trained helicopter pilots. When I met him, I said that I thought a bishop's calling was the hardest job in the church. And then in response he told me a story about funerals and endowments:

One sister had an older daughter who had strayed and had gotten in with some drug people, and she came to me the day I was to be set apart as bishop, before it was even announced, and she said, "I don't know why but I feel so impressed to tell you my daughter is missing and feared dead and I need some help." And that's how I started my tenure as bishop. The girl was found mutilated and dismembered. And that was my first funeral.

But at that service I also felt the presence of a young woman that I had never met. And I felt her put her arms around me and comfort me and say the words that needed to be given that day. And to receive those thoughts has been wonderful.

This will sound odd, but I think the two most spiritual meetings in the church outside of the temple are baptisms and funerals. And with the funerals there are so many people there to greet, so many unseen spirits, and the veil is very thin, and the Spirit directs everything.

The workings of the Spirit are wonderful. We have six people lined up right now that are going through the temple. They are going for their own endowments, and their sealings. [One sister] in her 60s finally made it through the temple [and] was sealed to her parents, who had been dead for some time. The Spirit was strong and healthy that day....I used to say to my counselors, "don't you see that?" and they were quiet, so I don't say it anymore. I've learned. They just don't get to see as much of the Spirit as I do. That's why this is the best job in the church.

Kent Barnes believed he was an unlikely choice as bishop. Pointedly, he said, "I never in my wildest dreams ever thought that an obnoxious, recalcitrant guy like myself would be a bishop. And I'm sure there are quite a few others that felt the same way. Stake president Lynn Hatch called me into his office when Jack Russell was still bishop, and he said the Lord has work for you to do, you need to prepare yourself. And you need to study your scriptures more." Barnes was then called to a military tour of duty in El Paso but received a phone call from this stake president on his return to Phoenix. "I wondered what in the world could he want to talk to me about? And that was the first time ever that I have not known what my calling was going to be before it happened."

I was called to be a varsity coach, I was called to be a scout master, I was called to work in the Young Men's program, I knew the minute I looked in their face they were coming to call me to a position, and what it was. And this time it didn't happen. I just didn't know. I must really be out of it. Then when he said we're here to call you, as he sat in my front room with my children gathered around and my wife there, "We're here to call you to be the bishop of the Country Club Ward." And I never heard him say anything beyond the word "bishop." My ears closed up, my eyes shut down, and I went back in the chair and almost tipped over. And then I caught myself.

It was a shock. It was like getting hit with a lightning bolt. But the spirit bore witness to me the next day. I immediately went to my knees after the president left. I went to my room, I wanted to be alone. I needed to have time, I needed to know that this was correct. I was in charge, I was the senior trainer for an Apache battalion that was going to spend 30 days at Fort Hood, Texas, and there was going to be three years of extremely intensive training, and going to require a lot of time. And you don't sleep a lot when you get these calls. I drove down to Miranda where I was working, that's an hour and a half south of here, and my boss finally said, "You're in a daze, go home, get yourself together, take a day or two, something's wrong with you." So I was driving home and I was saying "Father, whatever did you mean? You know what I'm going through, yet you call me to be a bishop." And he said, "Bishop, you take care of my ward, and I'll take care of your work." And it was as clear as you just heard. And I felt comfort from that time on.

The central thrust of Barnes's story was to suggest how unlikely his call to serve as bishop was. It also seemed to me to tell a great deal about how the church works, hierarchically and in terms of using a diversity of talents. Barnes's appointment as bishop was a result of his stake president's assessment of both the Country Club ward and Kent Barnes as a military leader who knew how to motivate and lead his men. He was training Apache helicopter pilots.

The church, like the military, moves its noncommissioned officers up through the ranks. They learn the values of their organization by on-the-job experience and are rewarded by upward mobility (and more responsibility). And sometimes those appointments from above simply fulfill expectations, while other times they come to their recipients as a complete surprise and reveal hidden talents.

Bishop Bradlee Watson and the Mantle of Leadership

When I arrived in Lynnwood stake, Washington, Bradlee Watson was serving as the bishop of Alderwood ward. He understood that he wore the mantle of authority and held considerable responsibility because of the training and guidance he had received growing into adulthood. He and his wife, Suzanne, were raising three children, a clear mark of adult identity as an LDS.

Growing up and being baptized in the church at age eight, Bradlee then entered the Aaronic priesthood at age 12 and progressed through the offices of deacon, teacher, and priest, and then entered the Melchizedek priesthood at age 18 as an elder. He said,

> For me, the latter part of high school, when I served as Seminary Council president, was an important period of growth. I really started to learn a lot of the administrative type of skills—working with commit-tees and working with other groups of people, and organizing and get-ting things done. And that carried over to the mission field where I had many great opportunities and experiences. (Watson, Interview, 1995)

He served a mission in Sacramento, California, covering most of northern California. In the mission field, he served as a district leader and zone leader, which put him in close touch with the mission president, where he "learned about working with others and interacting with them to resolve conflict." LDS say that someone has "magnified" their calling when they have been set apart and fulfill it with a certain amount of zeal and attention to its opportunities, and this Bradlee did.

And after coming home from an 18-month call, he went to work as a teacher at the MTC while completing four years at Brigham Young University. For two of those years, he also served as a counselor in the branch presidency, which reinforced many of his earlier lessons. "I worked with a couple of great branch presidents and got to see much of the counseling side of [administration] and how to help missionaries going into the mission field, when for the first time they couldn't rely on mom and dad, but were more on their own." While teach-ing at the MTC was a paid position for him and about 300 other teachers, serv-ing in the MTC branch presidency was an ecclesiastical [volunteer] calling.

After graduating from BYU, Watson moved to the Alderwood ward, Lynnwood stake, Washington area, and was called to serve as elders' quorum secretary, and then as executive secretary to Bishop Marcus Bell Nash.

> That was a great experience to work so closely with the bishop, obviously a great leader, then a stake president, and now a General Authority. And that was an interesting calling because I'd schedule and plan a lot of what he does. As an executive secretary, to a large degree, you're the first line of [contact for] anybody that wants to see the bishop or needs to see the bishop, whether it's for a temple recommend or problems and struggles. So that is an important calling in that somebody that's coming to the bishop in need of help is often very wary, maybe weighed

down by things that they've done, or just problems, and so how they're met and how they're greeted and the kind of response they get at that level sets them at ease. So that was an enjoyable calling. I probably knew the ward better as an executive secretary, than in any other calling except for my current calling as a bishop, because I saw so many people and talked to them.

I invited Bishop Watson to join me in a role-play as a way of demonstrating the kind of interaction that was part of these role relationships. The role-play with Bishop Watson, taking his earlier role as executive secretary, went like this:

MEL (ACTING AS A WARD MEMBER): Brad, I would like to see Bishop Nash. Can I make an appointment with him through you?
BRADLEE WATSON (ACTING AS EXECUTIVE SECRETARY): Yes, of course. That would be fine. Is there a time-frame for when you'd like to see the bishop?
M: Well, I really want to set up an appointment for a temple recommend interview. This is something my wife and I have talked about, because I don't have a recommend now and I think I'm ready to go to the temple.
B: Is this your first recommend?
M: Yes, it is.
B: Okay. We'll schedule a little more time so that Bishop Nash can have more time for talking with you about the meaning of the temple and make sure he answers any questions you may have. What's better for your schedule, a week night or a Sunday?
M: Either one would be fine with me, whatever is convenient for him.
B: Okay. Why don't we set a meeting for Sunday afternoon about 3:30 p.m. or whatever time you have open.
M: That's fine. Thanks. How long do you think we'll spend?
B: Probably 45 minutes to an hour.
M: Okay. 3:30 p.m. to 4:30 p.m. I'll schedule it in my appointment book.

Clearly, this interview was scheduled as a routine meeting for a temple recommend, and it demonstrates the interaction of roles within the ward. We then continued to scheduling a meeting for something less routine:

M (ON THE PHONE): Brad, I'd like to schedule an interview with Bishop Nash, and it's fairly urgent.
B: Okay. How much time do you think you'll need with the bishop?
M: My guess is maybe an hour or so. I really have some personal problems, and my wife and I are having some problems, and we'd like to spend a little time.

B: Would you and your wife like to come in together, or would you just like to see him on your own?

M: I think I'd like to see him by myself first.

B: Well, why don't we go with 9:00 p.m. on Wednesday night. Would that work for you?

M: Yes, that works fine.

B: Okay. I'll put you down as the last appointment that night.

M: All right. Thanks.

The role-play makes clear how these interactions are structured as part of the top-down ordering of the church, and indicates that members are comfortable (though not without some anxiety) in coming to the executive secretary when they wish to see the bishop. In the parlance of the church, a ward bishop is viewed as a "common judge" (Pearson, "Bishop," 1992:35). I asked Bradlee Watson as the bishop, "Do some people call you directly?" He said, "Yeah, a lot of them do."

> And it takes some time, too, depending on how a member works with the bishop and how many times during the week they may need to talk. Sometimes people will call me as bishop and want to schedule an appointment and I'll direct them to Brother Hendrickson in my case [since he's now the executive secretary], just because I don't know for sure how many appointments he's already put on the calendar; so, we talk frequently. If they go to him first, he can make the schedule.
>
> Once in a while I'll do an interview at home or go to somebody's home. But as a practice, I won't interview a female by myself; I always have the executive secretary there. But if I'm going over and talking to a member of the Melchizedek priesthood, I might meet at their home. It was very time consuming when I had the executive secretary's job because when the bishop was at the ward or stake center, then I was there with him. But not in everything; I have since learned that he did a lot of things that I never knew about. As bishop, you have lots of late nights and long hours. But often times it was Bishop Nash's practice that when you came in you were the only one there. And he didn't work off the clock and say, "Well, an hour's up, sorry, come back next week." He was very conscious of what was going on the whole evening, but at the same time was never hurried or rushed. And consequently, people would sometimes wait for him, and there again the executive secretary has a real key role in waiting, being with a member and talking to him or her. We'd discuss gospel principles or just talk about a basketball

game. That was always a fun role for me just to get a chance to talk to people. But it also puts people at ease, especially if they're going in with something that's really heavy on their mind and they can just talk for a while and feel comfortable and get in that mode of expressing themselves, even if it's just about the weather.

On occasion, we would try and direct people to their priesthood leaders. Certainly, the bishop is not the only one that can help and assist. In cases of worthiness, the bishop is the common judge, of course, and he's the only one who can help them with those things. We also try to get the priesthood leaders, the Elder's Quorum president, the high priest group leader, the home teachers involved as much as we can in helping transition them to their priesthood leaders.

Not every bishop followed the well-marked path of increasing responsibilities keyed to life stages that was true for Bishop Watson, but many followed variants similar to this pattern. In that sense, the very large numbers and range of roles and identities that members can experience provide an important background for mobility within the identity structure of church callings. These callings are alternative ways in which the value orientations of the church are realized in the lived experience of members. Bradlee Watson said:

I found that the real joy and the real success come when we do less administrative and more "ministrative" work. Getting out and into the homes of the members, and talking to them there, and meeting them and being with them, is when we really reach and touch lives, and help people overcome [their challenges] with a little more hope and faith.

Relief Society and the Diversity of Needs

In the course of her 21 adult years in the church, Virginia Beach, relief society president in the Country Club ward, Phoenix East stake, has held many callings—as a teacher and secretary in primary, as the ward activity chairperson responsible for coordinating and assisting in the calendar of repeated and special events, and in the relief society as secretary, homemaking counselor, and coordinator of compassionate service—before accepting the call as relief society president. In her 40s, she now has a bad back and various aches and pains. She said,

I don't walk well, and I don't carry things. But if I can lay down and then get up again and stretch, I'm fine. And the ideal of service was why I couldn't turn down this calling. I thought, "Why not me?" And then my husband gave me a blessing, and so did the bishop, that I might have the strength to do it, and I've done things that I haven't done in quite a while. But it's usually in the capacity of helping someone else.... And my children are grown and this is just a good way for me to serve because I have the time.

As president of the relief society, Virginia and her two counselors participate in the monthly welfare meeting with the bishopric, the elders' quorum presidency, the high priests' group leader and assistants, and the employment people. The meeting is intended to address welfare needs in the ward, but is done without "real specifics." Virginia said, "I may say something like 'the sister that had the knee surgery needs someone to help with her yard,' or that 'she needs help with medical appointments' (and the relief society usually cares for her appointments), or that 'she needs some kind of help' at home. But we don't talk about personal problems that we're aware of; these are passed on to the bishop on a more confidential basis." Virginia said, "I always have an interview with him or talk with him afterwards. And I'm always in contact with him about food needs because, as the need is made known to him, he then calls me and says, 'give them [the household] a food order for one or two weeks,' as the case may be."

Helping Members Solve Their Own Problems

If anyone knows of a family or household where there is a serious marital problem or something else considered equally difficult, that problem is put in the bishop's hands, and others step back from it. Virginia said,

> You help where you can, but one thing that I'm learning...is that you can't take that person's problems on yourself, and you can't solve it for them. So what I'm trying to do is, when they come and talk to me about something, instead of saying, "Oh, you know what you should do about that," I now usually say, "Well, what is your feeling? How do you feel you're going to handle this?" And I don't take it on. Or assist them in any way. It's the same way with some of the younger sisters; we have many who have a real hard time managing their family or managing their homes. And you can go in there and do it for them, but it'll be the same way a couple days later. So we try to keep from enabling someone; we just try to help them by making suggestions.

For example, there was one young sister who was having a terrible time, and I went to her home and her laundry was just piling up. So I told her "Well, you know what we'd like to do, we'd like to help you with this laundry and I'd like to make a couple of suggestions." She had a little fenced-in backyard; she's in an apartment; so I said, "Why don't you just get a bucket—it was summertime, the children are just wearing little underpants and little shorts—and put those clothes into the bucket and leave them overnight to let them soak, then you wouldn't have to scrub them." She was pregnant and was really in a bad way. "And then just hang them out there in back, and they'd be dry by the time the children would get up in the morning. Put the same things back on them. And then they wouldn't be piling up like this." You can't believe that she couldn't have thought of that. So those are the kinds of things that I would like to say, just easy little stuff. Young people don't seem to have learned that today. They think they have to have the washing machine and the dryer in the house!

Connecting Problems to Homemaking Lessons

This story stirred my curiosity. So I asked Virginia: How would you connect a problem like this one to a homemaking lesson in the relief society?

That's a hard thing to do, [she said] because some people's way of living is that they have been messy all their life. But we would talk about it in the context of trying to get organized. You're telling your sisters to read the scriptures, and that has to be kind of a comparison...it's just like you wash your dishes after you eat your meal, and how much easier it is than to let things stack up. Why wait until you have a spiritual problem to open up your Bible. Have that in your head, so you can call on it. So it's the whole organizational thing.

We have lessons, we do little skits to get a point across, we have a lot of lessons on orderliness....We usually always have a cooking lesson, something that would be fairly easy, something fairly fast, but yet nourishing and so that's how we just kind of keep tying things together. Like last time we had a lesson on gardening. We had a man come in from one of the nurseries here and he had a class on gardening and we invited the men.

Then there was another class, which sounds sort of silly, but the young sisters that had little children loved it. They made these little hair ribbons. I didn't see exactly what they were made of, but they looked very professional. So then this one girl while she's making hers, said, "I'm going to make these for all my little nieces for Christmas and for their birthdays." So that was very helpful to them and they maybe had a quarter put into it, or maybe a dollar. So we try to help in that sort of a way, make it something that they can use but maybe a little nicer than what they could afford to buy if they were going out and buying it.

Sometimes the distance between the diversity of "real world" problems and the spiritual lessons of the relief society is like a yawning gap, but there the rationale is less important than the fact of providing helpful activity.

Relief Society Problems with the Elderly and Single Sisters

I also asked Virginia about the kinds of problems that arise over and over again in the context of the ward. And she replied that problems with the elderly don't go away and in a church dedicated to the eternal family, single sisters are also a special concern. Virginia said that one time she talked to the bishop about developing a list of elderly concerns, "a small questionnaire that we could make out on each of the elderly. Many of their children are living away from their home of origin, and communication often is not so frequent or deep." So Virginia called a mortuary and asked: "What's the first thing you need to know when you get a call that someone has passed away? And they said, 'The main thing is what is to be done with the body? That's very crucial to know right off, even if it's going to be shipped somewhere else.' So we made this brief little questionnaire, and now is the time to ask these people. So we have this brief questionnaire that gives their preferences about their body, and we got relatives' names and telephone numbers, and some of their other preferences." Other elderly women need hospice care with attention to their routines of daily living:

> We have a sister now that I just got a call for...she saves everything, they've lived through the Depression, and their appetite's gone but they still have this food and...it's got mold on it but they won't throw it out, and their taste goes away and so they're starting to eat bad food. So I'm going to have a woman that she really likes go in and go through the refrigerator with her and me, and trust me, I can tell you whether this should be saved or if it should be thrown out.
>
> We had [another] instance where we were going to have to break in and I called my husband when he was over at the employment office

and said, "It looks like we're going to have to break in; she's not answering her phone." So we went over there with tools and I just told Rex that however you break in, you're going to have to secure it again, because if the police come they'll just knock things down. It'd be a lot better to break out one pane than to have [them] break down the whole door! Those are real concerns (Beach, Interview, 1995).

The church is widely viewed as a family church because of the doctrine of eternal families and sealing ordinances in the temple. Some older statistics suggest that up to 30 percent of North American LDS adults are currently widowed, divorced, separated, or have never married. One response in the church has been the development of singles' wards (Young, "Single Adults," 1992:375–378). Virginia noted:

We have a lot of single mothers that aren't in homes. That is another concern, and the thing that I find the most disturbing is when women are living in situations where they've had bad marriages, where there's been abuse to her or the children; I think that what happens with the women is that they almost make a friend out of their child, and the child just grows up so fast. Then when it comes time to parent [with some authority], then this child resents it because the mother has come to them so many times with all of her problems; so the child is [frustrated and resentful]…and the mother tells them that they can't stay out or the mother tries to choose their friends for them, and it's like "Why are you coming down on me?" So we have that in our ward. The mothers are out of the home. The children are there. That is probably the biggest heartache that I feel personally.

We used to always go to the home and we would make an appointment with that sister and see her. Well, now so many of the sisters work, and they all have different work schedules, so that it's very, very hard to make contact.

So we don't always have one-on-one, face-to-face contact but we either have to make a phone call, or we have to send a letter, or we have little visiting messages that we send out (Beach, Interview, 1995).

Relief Society and the Ideal of Compassionate Service

Dorothy Saley was serving as the relief society president in the Crystal Heights second ward and described the real duty of this organization of

adult women as providing "compassionate service ... to help the needy and
do whatever we can to make people's lives better. It doesn't matter whether
they're LDS" (Saley, Interview, 1994). She pointed to a variety of efforts,
both local and international, that characterized the efforts of the relief society women:

> In 1992 we celebrated 150 years of Relief Society. The General Board
> indicated that it would be a year of service not just for Latter-day Saints,
> but for everyone in need. So each ward had special service projects for
> a whole year for people around the world, for unwed mothers, for the
> homeless. In our ward we did many things. We collected books to give
> to schools with limited means so that children could have books to take
> home. We collected over 600 books for children in districts where oth-
> erwise books were not available (Saley, Interview, 1994).

In addition, each sister in the ward was assigned another sister for a year, to
call her by telephone periodically, remember her birthday, and watch over her;
these "partners" were known as "sisters of charity." The purpose was to instill
the idea of service. Dorothy reported another effort in which "every month we
passed a sheet around and had people sign up to have frozen rolls available in
their home freezers, so that at a moment's notice we could send several to any
sister in need." There would always be five women with rolls in their freezers
who could be called on, and this practice was rotated among the women so
that there were always rolls in reserve, which when not needed could then be
used for their own families.

The church's ongoing program of family visitation coordinates relief society visiting teachers with Melchizedek priesthood home teachers. In this program, as described earlier, pairs of sisters are assigned three or four homes
that they are to visit each month to provide "a brief spiritual message." Dorothy
indicated that some of the older members don't want a message, "so we just
go there to make sure everything's okay, and to see if we can be of help."

As members of the priesthood, the men provide a parallel program of
home teachers, so that ideally, each home would receive two pairs of visitors
each month. In Dorothy's words,

> We should know what's going on in our ward. And that's one purpose,
> to keep contact with whoever needs help, and to see what we can do.
> Maybe some members will tell the home teachers something they
> wouldn't tell the visiting teachers [and vice versa]. And [besides] the
> visiting teachers have a big job to keep track of all the people moving in

and moving out [of the neighborhood], and this way they have someone who makes contact with them (Saley, Interview, 1994).

Sometimes older couples work as visitation teams, providing one visit for both the priesthood and relief society because there may not be enough high priests to visit in pairs. And some of the older high priests are also paired with the young Aaronic teachers, which is a good experience for both because "it pairs the generations."

The relief society meets every Sunday as part of the ward block system of weekly meetings, and in addition meets monthly for a Tuesday night home-making meeting. "We have a little ten-minute lesson that we can take out to the sisters [at home], and then we have a 20-minute lesson, a homemaking lesson, and then either a craft project or a service project: Recently we made 65 pairs of booties to send to foreign countries." The church also has a pro-gram where the wards are making receiving blankets for newborns and other things for overseas distribution to young children. In addition, family history (genealogy) is undertaken as a program essential to the doctrines of salvation, agency, and exaltation:

> It is the plan of God that all persons shall have the opportunity to hear the gospel of Jesus Christ and receive the saving ordinances, regardless of when they lived on earth. If they do not hear the gospel preached through the Lord's authorized servants in this life, they will hear it in the spirit world after death. Latter-day Saints identify their ancestors and arrange for baptism and other ordinances to be performed by proxy—that is, with a living persons standing in for the deceased person—in a temple (Pratt, "Family History, Genealogy," 1995).

Similarly, in the home ward, when a young mother has a baby, the relief society women generally prepare four or five meals for the mother when she comes home from the hospital so she doesn't have to worry about meals for herself or her family. And if she has other children, the relief society is there to help with those children until the mother gets on her feet again.

If a death has occurred in the ward, the relief society generally plans a lun-cheon following the funeral for those attending. Dorothy said,

> I know of one of the sisters, and she and her husband never came to church. Her husband died. And as soon as we learned of this death, the bishop and I went over to see what we could do to help, and asked if we could prepare a meal. And she said, "Oh, no, we don't come to church.

We don't want anything like that." And I said that coming to church "doesn't make any difference, we want to do this regardless." With this woman's permission, the Relief Society prepared the luncheon. And afterwards, this woman said she really appreciated this gesture. And that's what compassionate service is about. It's a wonderful experience [to help somebody in need].

Dorothy also reported on the following situation:

We have a young man in our ward with three children, and he has Lou Gerig's [sic] disease, which just breaks your heart. The visiting teachers for this family are just marvelous. This family is very independent. They don't want [to be a burden to anyone else]. They moved here from [out of state] and did not want any special attention. So I chose visiting teachers who I believed could [touch] their hearts. The wonderful thing about the church is that the young boys, the young girls, the elders, and the high priests all work together. They knew the time would come when this young husband and father could not walk down steps, and so the elders got together and built a ramp for his wheelchair; and they knew that over time he would have difficulty speaking, so they fixed a computer for text messaging. So the whole program, the whole plan, is that we work together to help one another (Saley, Interview, 1994).

These organizational responses of the relief society require forethought and planning under the direction of the bishopric, coordinated through a monthly welfare meeting and a monthly ward council meeting. The ward welfare meeting includes the presidencies of each of the ward organizations, who help compile and review the lists of people who may have needs in the ward—the ill, those who have lost their mate, and any others having other kinds of problems. And then the bishop assigns one of the organizations to meet the needs of those people. Dorothy noted, "In the summer, when some of the sisters who are widowed or ill and can't do yard work, we have a monthly welfare meeting [with the bishopric] where we get all of the information from each organization and we find out who are the brothers and sisters who may need help. And if it's a widow the bishop will assign the elders to find a young man to go over and help [with the household chores]."

The result of this meeting is that the bishop knows of the situations in the ward that need his attention, where he can delegate and assign other members to carry out the ministerial services. He is responsible, with the aid of the relief society president, for allocating local resources from fast offerings or the welfare system to meet individual and family needs. And both he and the relief society president sign-off on the appropriate church forms. Dorothy notes:

> At the moment we have a young sister who has four children and doesn't have a husband and is trying to make the best of what she has. She may need blankets or sheets or clothing. We fill out an order form and the bishop has to sign it and I have to sign it, and she can take her order to the Bishop's Storehouse at Welfare Square and fill her cart just like everyone at the grocery store (Saley, Interview, 1994).

Dorothy also wanted me to know that the welfare system was not restricted to LDS church members, but served all persons in the community:

> I'd like to tell you the story of a Catholic girl in our ward. She's just a darling girl. Her husband recently left her while she was pregnant. I went to visit with her to see if there was anything I could do to help her cope. She was just heart-sick. She had delivered a baby; she didn't have a job; and she needed to catch up on her bills. I discussed [this situation] with the bishop and he went over and visited with her. He helped her pay some of her bills. So it's not like [the church] is a closed group of people. The [welfare plan] is for whomever we can help. That's its purpose. It's all over the world, not just in Utah (Saley, Interview, 1994).

Beyond the Ward and Church Boundaries

Two large-scale programs now consolidate much of the church's efforts to impact global needs in terms of the church's gospel message: One is a program of humanitarian service that provides human and material aid in the face of overwhelming disasters anywhere in the world; the other establishes the Perpetual Education Fund (PEF), a revolving loan program within the church to underwrite the costs for educational advancement and career development in the third-world countries of returning missionaries and other young adults. Both programs allow members to contribute money and time in ways that extend their own lives of service.

Isaac C. Ferguson (1995) described the aim of the church's humanitarian service as providing Christian service "among the world's peoples without regard to race, nationality, or religion," and therefore to provide material aid to the people of the world in the face of poverty, famine, sickness, and natural disasters. From their earliest lives, members are taught the obligation to help others from the story of Alma in the Book of Mormon:

> They did not send away any who were naked, or...hungry, or that were athirst, or that were sick, or that had not been nourished; and they did not set their hearts upon riches; therefore they were liberal to all, both old and young, both bond and free, both male and female, whether out of the church or in the church, having no respect to persons as to those who stood in need (Alma 1:30).

The church has always felt obliged "to care for its own" members through special fast offerings and donations. But over the course of the 20th century, the church has expanded this norm of caring for those in need beyond the boundaries of the church, as far as resources were available. As early as 1851, church President Brigham Young initiated a program to meet the needs of Native Americans in the valleys of Utah territory using an aphorism that "It's better to feed than fight them." The church also sought to teach Euro-American farming techniques and fair trade practices, yet kept personal and social differences as marks of group separation (Arrington 1985:214–215).In the course of the 20th century, the church's humanitarian service became less self-serving and more responsive to global needs. World War I brought agricultural devastation to Europe, and the LDS church (along with others) aided the U.S. government by providing contributions of wheat for allied soldiers, sailors, and civilians. Then, in the midst of the Great Depression, in 1936, the church developed a welfare services plan of its own complementary to that of the federal government, emphasizing "frugality and provident living and encouraging donations for the needy." The welfare plan included a work initiative as the basis of church aid in order to teach self-reliance. During and after World War II, the church also sought to assist members and nonmembers in need, and in 1946, sent Apostle Ezra Taft Benson to Europe to supervise the distribution of food, clothing, and medical supplies, including aid for local childcare and family household needs.

Utah churches also developed a cooperative effort of relief for Greece in 1953 in response to the devastation caused by earthquakes. This was an interdenominational effort for which the Greek consul in San Francisco publicly acknowledged "that the contribution of the Mormon Church was the greatest single contribution to the relief fund" (Ferguson 1995:244). Two decades later, the church included welfare service missionaries in a mission program in which health professionals and agricultural experts were added to the missionary ranks. Ferguson notes: "By 1980, some 768 welfare missionaries (volunteers to give humanitarian aid) were serving in more than 40 Church mission areas throughout the world" (Ferguson 1995:245). In the period from 1985 to 2008, the church's humanitarian cash donations reached more than $282 million, with total humanitarian material aid reaching $834 million. Humanitarian services are now a well-established component of the church's philanthropic donations for meeting world needs through five specific projects: neonatal resuscitation training, clean water projects, wheelchair distribution, vision treatment, and measles vaccinations (//newsroom.lds.org/ldsnewsroom1/eng/background-information/ html, accessed 11/2009).

The Perpetual Education Fund

The announcement on March 31, 2001, to establish the Perpetual Education Fund (PEF) struck many members of the church like a lightning bolt illuminating a dark terrain. President Gordon B. Hinckley said that the church must do all it can to help its own people lift themselves in the face of widespread poverty, to establish their lives on a foundation of self-reliance. Education is the foundation for new opportunities (Hinckley 2001:51). President Hinckley's new proposal was clearly aimed at solving an ongoing problem. The church has moved into a situation of many missionaries, both young men and young women, who are called locally and who serve with honor in Mexico, Central America, South America, the Philippines, and other places. They have very little money, but they make a big contribution with what they have.

They become excellent missionaries working side by side with elders and sisters sent from the United States and Canada. While in this service, they come to know how the church operates. They develop a broadened understanding of the gospel, and they learn to speak some English. They work with faith and devotion until the day of their release. When they return to their homes, their hopes are high. But many of them have great difficulty finding employment because they have no skills. They sink right back into the pit of poverty from which they came (Hinckley 2001:51–52). President Hinckley's announcement follows:

> In an effort to remedy this situation, we propose a plan—a plan which we believe is inspired by the Lord. The Church is establishing a fund largely from the contributions of faithful Latter-day Saints who have and will contribute for this purpose.... Based on similar principles to those underlying the Perpetual Emigration Fund, we shall call it the Perpetual Education Fund.

From the earnings of this fund, loans will be made to ambitious young men and women, for the most part returned missionaries, so that they may borrow money to attend school. Then when they qualify for employment, it is anticipated that they will return that which they have borrowed together with a small amount of interest designed as an incentive to repay the loan.

It is expected that they will attend school in their own communities. They can live at home. We have an excellent institute program established in these countries where they can be kept close to the Church. The directors of these institutes are familiar with the educational opportunities in their own cities. Initially, most of these students will attend technical schools where they will learn such things as computer science, refrigeration engineering, and other skills which are in demand and for which they can become qualified. The plan may later be extended to training for the professions.

Those desiring to participate in the program will make application to the institute director. He will clear them through their local bishops and stake presidents to determine that they are worthy and in need of help. Their names and the prescribed amount of their loans will then be sent to Salt Lake City, where funds will be issued, payable not to the individual but to the institution where they will receive their schooling.

We shall have a strong oversight board here in Salt Lake and a director...who will be an emeritus General Authority, a man with demonstrated business and technical skills and who has agreed to accept this responsibility as a volunteer.

We shall begin modestly, commencing this fall. We can envision the time when this program will benefit a very substantial number. With good employment skills, these young men and women can rise out of the poverty they and generations before them have known. They will better provide for their families. They will serve in the Church and grow in leadership and responsibility. They will repay their loans to make it possible for others to be blessed as they have been blessed. It will become a revolving fund. As faithful members of the Church, they will pay their tithes and offerings, and the Church will be much the stronger for their presence in the areas where they live.

Now this is a bold initiative, but we believe in the need for it and in the success that it will enjoy. It will be carried forward as an official program of the Church with all that this implies. It is affordable. We have enough money, already contributed, to fund the initial operation. It will work because it will follow priesthood lines and because it will function on a local basis. It will deal with down-to-earth skills and needed fields of expertise.... It will not be a welfare effort... but rather an education opportunity.

The beneficiaries will repay the money, and when they do so, they will enjoy a wonderful sense of freedom because they have improved their lives not through a grant or gift, but through borrowing and then repaying. They can hold their heads high in a spirit of independence. The likelihood of their remaining faithful and active throughout their lives will be very high (Hinckley 2001:52–53).

A high-profile team of experienced administrators was assigned the task of creating a functioning PEF organization, led by John K. Carmack, who was called to the first quorum of the seventy in 1984 and was now concluding his service as a general authority. He was joined by Chad L. Evans, a man in his 40s who had been involved with the church's initiatives in establishing employment resource centers; Rex J. Allen, who was released a year prior from his assignment presiding over the Geneva, Switzerland, mission and was engaged with his brother in developing a company training upper-level employees of large corporations; and Richard E. Cook, who was serving in the Asia area presidency, located in Hong Kong, and had known John Carmack from Asia area experiences. A number of other volunteer positions were also filled in the six months leading up to the first group of loan recipients.

The results have been dramatic. "In the first year of this initiative, about 60 percent were men and 40 percent were women. Of the men, about 85 percent have been returned missionaries and about 30 percent of the women have also filled missions" (Carmack 2004:163). As three years drew to a close, Carmack estimated that about 10,000 loans had been initiated with projections running to about 65,000 loans in the course of the next six to seven years, justifying John Carmack's first fund report in a book titled *A Bright Ray of Hope* (2004).

The LDS Church places a theological and social emphasis on lives of service. In practical terms, this emphasis means that members are drawn into an extensive array of activities, roles, and responsibilities. Some of these organizational roles, or identities, are replicated in the triadic form of presidencies comprised of a president, first counselor, and second counselor, with additional roles attached in the form of a secretary, clerk, or further support personnel, such as teachers and musicians. This kind of triadic social structure applies to primary, young women and young men, the relief society, the bishopric, and the stake presidency (which is supplemented by a ten-member high counsel). It also applies to elders' quorums and the stake high priests' quorum and ward level groups (using the terms group leader and first and second assistants). Each of these is a replication of administrative structures as described by Anthony Wallace (1971), reinforcing the overall hierarchical structure of the church as a whole.

This hierarchical replication begins at the top with the president of the church as the presiding high priest, whose responsibilities have to do with guiding the whole church under the authority of Jesus Christ; he has available to him the counsel of the first and second counselors in the first presidency. At the next somewhat lower level are members of the quorum of the twelve, who are also prophets, seers, and revelators in joint authority with the first presidency. At the next lower level are the seven presidents of the seventy and the first and second quorums of the seventy, whose responsibilities comprise area authority presidencies (including a president and two counselors for each of the 29 areas of the world into which the church has been divided by the actions of the first presidency and quorum of the twelve). These men are also known as general authorities, and they, in turn, are supported by six additional seventy quorums, who serve for terms of office in programmatic aspects of church service.

Statistically, as of October 1, 2007, the church was divided into 2,776 stakes, plus 348 missions, and was further subdivided into 27,475 wards and branches (at the most local level). At these levels, the Aaronic and Melchizedek priesthoods express the church's priesthood authority structure as distributed among all of the family units of the church, comprised of a population now numbering in excess of 14 million members. More than half of this population now resides outside the United States. Thus, every household is subject to priesthood authority, and that authority stands behind and supports the activities of all members—men, women, and children—in their lives of service. By virtue of "telephone trees," which are networks of people connected by telephone numbers at each level and from one level to the next, information can be transmitted among groups and subgroups in the church's social organization in a matter of hours, not days or weeks. This transmission process is most telling in the way in which the church members can respond to earthquakes, tsunamis, and other disasters as they occur around the world. Help is almost always available on relatively short notice. These lives of service keep members active and engaged on a daily basis.

14

'Til We Meet Again

THE PAIN, SUFFERING, and sorrow were nearly unspeakable. On Friday night, February 9, 2007, a car crash killed three members of Bishop Christopher Williams's family from the Crystal Heights second ward, and left the bishop, 42, and his six-year-old son Sam in critical condition. As reported in the Saturday morning edition of the *Deseret News*, dead at the scene were "Williams's wife, 41-year-old Michelle Williams, who was about five months pregnant; 11-year-old son Ben; and 9-year-old daughter Anna. The Williams's 14-year-old son Michael was not with the family at the time." The newspaper report continued:

> Authorities said the family was going under the I-80 overpass at 2000 East when a Jeep Cherokee hit their Volkswagen Jetta.
>
> "The victim tried to swerve out of the way and it was T-boned," Salt Lake City Police Lt. Mike Tuttle said Saturday.
>
> Police said the 17-year-old driver of the Jeep was captured several blocks away. Shortly after flipping his SUV, witnesses said the boy climbed out of the car and, in a daze, took off running. He was found by police officers near 2700 South and 1700 East. Police said they found alcohol in the Jeep.
>
> Meanwhile, residents of the Sugar House neighborhood where Christopher Williams is the bishop are trying to cope with the horrible tragedy.
>
> "They were beautiful people trying to follow the Savior," said family friend Justin Bell, who was the former bishop over Williams' ward.
>
> At the scene of the crash near 2000 East and Stratford Avenue, people stopped to pay their respects. Amid the shattered glass, orange accident-scene paint and cat litter used to sop up the oil, someone placed a small pot of flowers. A card attached read "You will be missed."

At the top of the underpass is the LDS chapel where Christopher
Williams is bishop. The ward is planning to fast and pray on Sunday
for the family.

(Winslow, *Deseret News*, Feb. 10, 2007)

Sorrow, Grief, and Forgiveness

Both the *Salt Lake Tribune*[1] and the *Deseret News* continued to report on this
tragedy over the next several days, weeks, and months. Slowly, the details of
the tragedy came to light. The *Salt Lake Tribune* reported that Christopher
Williams, from his hospital bed late Saturday afternoon, "asked for a prayer—
not for him[self], but for the teenage driver of the car that smashed into his
family sedan, killing his wife and two children." Further, Williams requested
that "the 17-year-old's name [be] added to the prayer roll of an LDS temple,
hoping to give some comfort to a teen now jailed on suspicion of automobile homicide." "I don't know of anyone who believes in redemption more
than Chris Williams," said his lifelong friend, Paul Winterton, who also said
that the father readily forgave the juvenile driver from his hospital room on
Saturday. "[Chris] is a beautiful, sweet man."

The *Salt Lake Tribune* also reported that a steady procession of tear-stained
children visited the Williams crash site on Saturday. Teachers from Highland
Park Elementary School met with some students on Saturday to talk about the
crash, including Amy Jessee, an 11-year-old Highland student who knew Ben personally. "He was like a brother to me," she said. "I've known him all my life. I'm
going to miss him." Grief counselors were expected at the school on Monday.

A vigil for the family and congregation was held at the Crystal Heights
second ward meetinghouse Saturday evening, with a fast and prayer meeting on Sunday. Christopher Williams has been the Crystal Heights second
ward bishop for about 18 months, and his wife also held ward callings, having
served in primary and in the young women presidency. The *Salt Lake Tribune*
reported that "neighbors tied dozens of ribbons to a tree outside the Williams'
home, remembering a family who they describe as 'well-loved' by the entire
neighborhood" (Stettler and Rizzo, Feb. 11, 2007).

The *Deseret News* added some further information from Stake President
James Wood, who served as a family spokesman. "Williams is asking peo-
ple to pray for the person who hit his car, killing half his family," President
Wood said. Late Saturday, he reported that Bishop Williams had improved

---

1. All quotations from the *Salt Lake Tribune* are reproduced with permission.

considerably, suffering a broken rib, but that six-year-old son Sam remained in intensive care at Primary Children's Medical Center with bleeding and swelling of the brain.

On Monday, Chris Williams described the accident as "a test by God and his late wife," saying, "This is truly a bitter cup my family was asked to partake in." He also indicated that when he was 16, he accidentally struck and killed a four-year-old boy. According to the *Salt Lake Tribune*'s files, on July 18, 1981, when he was driving to work as an orderly at the LDS Hospital, two young boys ran from between parked cars and onto 8th Avenue. Williams's car struck both boys, who were brothers. James B. Forster, four, of Salt Lake City, died three days later at Primary Children's Medical Center. His three-year-old brother survived. Police said Williams was traveling at about 20 miles per hour.

> "He had absolutely no chance to react," said Williams' father, Paul Williams, in an interview on Monday. As a result of that accident, said Paul Winterton...Williams "knows exactly what this young man [in Friday's accident] is going through." Following the 1981 accident, "People showered [Williams] with forgiveness and kindness," said Winterton.

Police Actions and Reports

The teen driver was booked into the Salt Lake County juvenile detention center, having performed poorly on a sobriety test. Initially, the driver's name was not released because he was a juvenile. A Salt Lake police traffic investigator said he "had trouble walking, turning and keeping his balance. He was pretty distraught over the whole thing and pretty upset. He knew he'd been in a pretty serious accident, but I don't know if he knew how serious," the investigator said (Stettler and Rizzo, *Salt Lake Tribune*, Feb. 10, 2007).

A witness, Michael Lee, who came across the accident while dust was still in the air, said, "It looked like a war zone." The father was "still belted in the front seat with his wife lying face-down beside him. The man was conscious but said nothing. Three children were covered with blankets, coats and a dislodged car seat in the back of the sedan" (Stettler and Rizzo, *Salt Lake Tribune*, Feb. 11, 2007).

> As firefighters were extricating Williams from the car and placing him on a backboard, he said he knew his wife and two children "were gone." "And I had a decision to make because I knew it was going to be a lot of healing that I needed in my life," Williams said. "I did not want that

healing to be hampered by another step in the [grieving] process, and
that was getting over anger. And so perhaps it was the easy way out.
I decided to forgive then and there. And interestingly enough, that's
when I heard the voice of my youngest son, six-year-old Sam, cry out
from the back" (Carlisle and Rizzo, Feb. 13, 2007).

Williams said that "he was drawing strength from the example
Michelle Williams set during their 18 ½ year marriage. Williams called
her a forgiving person. "I look at this as kind of an exam to see if I was
listening," Williams said. Williams described Ben and Anna as "sweet,
wonderful souls; very outgoing, very gregarious." The father asked the
public to "extend a single act of kindness, a token of mercy or an expression of forgiveness" by Valentine's Day. He asked the public 'to write
down those acts and send them to him in an e-mail so he can share
them with his two surviving sons. I can think of no greater valentine
that you can present to someone or that my sons and I can present to
my sweetheart than that," Williams said.

The Funeral

Funeral services were held Saturday, February 17, 2007, at 12:00 noon at the
Salt Lake Highland stake center. Nearly 1,000 people gathered for the triple
funeral service at the local LDS chapel. No one disparaged the teen driver, but
instead prayed for forgiveness—as Christopher Williams had done earlier—
and asked the congregation to pray for the driver's family as well (who were
also neighbors to Michelle's parents).

In a somber service broken by occasional smiles, friends and family
remembered little Anna as a "nurturer from birth" who swaddled dolls, flow-
ers, and even rocks. They described Ben as an ever-smiling comedian who
loved athletics, never shied away from a camera, and stayed up late to polish
school projects.

Of Michelle, speakers mused about her frequent ironing of everything
from shirts to sheets, and they smiled as they recounted her habit of lingering
outside parties well after the festivities had ended. Her brother, C. J. Dorney,
described her as an exemplary mother whose home was the "noisiest, most
peaceful, place on earth."

At the Larkin Sunset Gardens cemetery in Sandy, family and friends carried the caskets one by one to the burial plot—first Anna, then Ben, and finally
Michelle. All three were laid to rest with Christopher Williams's dedicatory
prayer. Sam remained hospitalized at Primary Children's Medical Center, but
was expected to be released soon.

Arraignment and Charges

The *Salt Lake Tribune* reported that on Thursday, February 15, the Salt Lake County District Attorney's Office filed a motion in 3rd District Juvenile Court asking that Cameron Howard White, of Salt Lake City, be certified as an adult. He would turn 18 in the coming May. He was "charged with four counts of second-degree felony automobile homicide, one count of third-degree felony driving under the influence and causing serious bodily injury, one count of class A misdemeanor failure to stop at the scene of an injury accident" (Hunt, Feb. 16, 2007a).

The auto homicides were committed in an aggressive, violent, and willful manner, according to the motion. Convictions of auto homicide in adult court carry potential prison terms of one to 15 years. In juvenile court, White could be held only until his 21st birthday if found guilty.

When police tried to administer field sobriety tests, White told them he was "too drunk" to take them. A blood test measured White's blood-alcohol content at 0.15, which is nearly twice Utah's legal limit (Hunt, *Salt Lake Tribune*, Feb. 16, 2007a).

Resolution: One Year Later

Judge Andrew Valdez decided that Cameron Howard White would not be tried as an adult. The decision on May 10 followed a day-long hearing in which defense witnesses testified that the juvenile system offers the 17-year old a better chance for rehabilitation and treatment for his apparent alcohol problem (*Salt Lake Tribune*, May 10, 2007).

Valdez said he also took into account the testimony of Christopher Williams, the father and husband of the victims, who said he wanted "what's best for Cameron." Williams added that he feels "love" and "a genuine concern" for White. Upon hearing the judge's ruling, White's mother and other family members began sobbing. The other side of the gallery broke into tears when Valdez offered White a chance to speak. "I'm sorry for what I've done to your family," White told Williams and his two surviving sons in an emotion-choked voice. "If I could take back anything I've done, I'd give your family back to you."

Noting that White turns 18 in less than three weeks, prosecutor Katherine Bernards-Goodman argued that White met the majority of the criteria for sending a juvenile to adult court (*Salt Lake Tribune*, May 11, 2007).

After pleading guilty to four counts of second-degree felony automobile homicide, Cameron Howard White, who had just turned 18, was sentenced to remain in juvenile detention until he is 21.

How long White actually stays incarcerated will be determined by the Youth Parole Authority, the juvenile equivalent of the state parole board.

Christopher Williams told the court he wanted "peace and healing rather than retribution," adding that he hopes White will "make something of himself."

The judge said that could be accomplished, in part, if White chooses to speak to other teens about the dangers of drinking and driving.

"You still decide who you are and what you will become," Valdez told White. "I believe you can do it. It's one reason I kept you in the juvenile system. It's on you now" (Hunt, *Salt Lake Tribune*, June 5, 2007b).

Dean May's Obituary

Dean Lowe May was a good friend. We met at a conference of the Mormon History Association, if I remember correctly, about the time that he was completing his Ph.D. at Brown University and was then anticipating joining the history division of the LDS Church under Church Historian Leonard J. Arrington. Dean and I almost always had breakfast, lunch, or dinner together during my forays to Salt Lake City from the early 1970s on. And we were age mates, born in the same depression year. His death due to a heart attack on May 6, 2003, came very much as a shock to me because it was so unexpected for a man in his mid-60s who regularly played racket ball without any physical symptoms and just two years earlier had returned from an adventure as "ship president" on the three-masted sailing vessel, the *Christian Radich*, which completed without steam power a Sea Trek reenactment in 2001 of a Mormon pioneer voyage from Europe to America. That was just the kind of participatory history that Dean thoroughly enjoyed.

He had a wondrous career, outlined in fascinating detail in his obituary (*Salt Lake Tribune*, May 9, 2003), from work on the family farm near Middleton, Idaho, to graduating at the head of his class from BYU in 1964. He served a mission for the LDS Church in Northern California, studied French and German in Paris and Berlin, and in 1977, joined the department of history at the University of Utah, which became his academic home.

He loved the people of the Mormon Church and the state of Utah, and had a special place in his heart for nonmembers like me who sipped an occasional beer. In 1985, he wrote and directed a television series called *A People's History of Utah*, plus many other public history projects that earned him special recognition. He was awarded two Fulbright lectureships, one in 1991 to Germany and another in 1998 to Egypt, served as president of the Mormon History

Association in 2001–2002, and was honored by the Days of '47 awards committee as a pioneer of progress in historic and creative arts in 2002. And he enjoyed the 2002 Olympics in good humor.

Through all of this, he honored the priesthood, serving as a bishop and as a member of the university fifth stake high council. He made friends of everyone willing to reciprocate, and so accepted my wife Hong (from China), with an all-embracing bear-hug that she remembers to this day. She urged me to attend his funeral, which I did. It was held on Saturday, May 10, 2003, at the Sugarhouse stake center in Salt Lake City. I listened to the speakers with tears in my eyes and deep respect in my heart, and to a choir comprised of members of the Utah Symphony Chorus in which Dean was a tenor. It was directed by Craig Jessop, with Dean's chair left empty while the choir sang the Brahms requiem "How Lovely Is Thy Dwelling Place" as a fitting memorial.

Dean May's obituary closes by indicating that "few people could count as many friends who considered him a soul mate. [But] his family was always his chief joy and delight. He indulged them shamelessly, and they all bloomed in the light of his love. Survivors include his wife Cheryll, his sons Timothy and Thaddeus, and daughter Caroline, his daughters-in-law Kirse and Lisa, his grandchildren Ethan and Karina, and his brothers Joseph, Reid, and Daniel."

An obituary, even of a stalwart person like Dean May, is an outward manifestation that fails to fully capture the inward meanings that motivated and sustained his life. Dean had a testimony of the gospel, which meant that he affirmed certain beliefs as fundamental to the ways in which he understood himself and the world about him, from which he drew the considerable energy and joy with which he lived his life. The obituary only hints at what stands behind the curtain that stretches across the stage of his life and that he shares with other LDS. Onstage, an observer can see only outward actions as signs of inward states. To understand both motivation and meaning requires access to the interpretative framework of the actor. One must go backstage. And so it was with Dean. He invited us to know him better.

Joseph Smith's Sermon at the Funeral of Elder King Follett

Behind the curtain stands the worldview of the gospel first offered up by the Prophet Joseph Smith, portions of which he revealed in his most famous funeral sermon, known as the King Follett discourse. On April 7, 1844, during general conference in Nauvoo, Illinois, the Prophet Joseph Smith Jr. delivered a funeral sermon for Elder King Follett before about 20,000 gathered LDS. Elder Follett had died several days earlier after being "crushed to death in a well, by the falling of a tub of rocks on him." Smith's address was recorded by scribes Willard Richards, Wilford Woodruff, Thomas Bullock, and William Clayton, who collated their notes into a version published in the "Times and Seasons" of August 15, 1844, about six weeks after the prophet himself was murdered by a mob set on destroying his church. (This discourse is reprinted as "The King Follett Discourse: A Newly Amalgamated Text," *Brigham Young University Studies* 18 [Winter 1978], Stan Larson, ed., 193–208.)[2]

This sermon was Joseph Smith's valedictory. It condensed and expressed the beliefs that he had introduced to his 19th-century followers and that continue to inform the beliefs of members of the LDS Church today. These beliefs were grounded in Smith's experience, and they have come to guide the experience of his followers into the 21st century, in spite of opposition, conflict, and martyrdom. To friend and foe alike, Smith said:

> You don't know me—you never will. You never knew my heart. No man knows my history. I cannot do it: I shall never undertake it. I don't blame you for not believing my history. If I had not experienced what I have, I could not believe it myself....
>
> I cannot lie down until my work is finished.... When I am called at the trump and weighed in the balance, you will know me then. I add no more. God bless you. Amen. (208)

Smith began his sermon with a challenge:

> If men do not comprehend the character of God, they do not comprehend their own character. They cannot comprehend anything that is past or that which is to come; they do not know—they do not understand their own relationship to God.... If a man knows nothing more than to eat, drink, sleep, arise, and not any more, and does not comprehend what any of the designs of Jehovah are, what better is he than

---

2. The amalgamated text edited by Stan Larson is reproduced as "I Now Call the Attention of this Congregation," a sermon delivered on April 7, 1844, in *The Essential Joseph Smith*, foreword by Marvin S. Hill (Salt Lake City, UT: Signature Books, 1995), 232–245. An incomplete version of "Joseph Smith's King Follett Discourse" appears as appendix A in Richard N. Ostling and Joan K. Ostling, *Mormon America: The Power and the Promise* (San Francisco: HarperSanFrancisco, 1999), 387–394. The conference report for April 1844 includes the King Follett sermon as chapter XIV in *History of the Church*, period I, volume VI, with an introduction and notes by B. H. Roberts (Salt Lake City, UT: Deseret Book, 1978), 302–317, including subheadings; it was reprinted as a pamphlet in 1963 and again in 1994.

the beast, for it comprehends the same things—it eats, drinks, sleeps, comprehends the present and knows nothing more about God or His existence.

He went on to pose several pointed questions: "What kind of a being is God? Does any man or woman know? Have any of you seen Him? Or heard Him? Or communed with Him? Here is a question that will, peradventure, from this time henceforth occupy your attention while you live" (Joseph Smith, April 1844 [199]).

Smith asked these questions in a context in which he had been accused of being a false prophet. In response, he argued for tolerance: "[No] man is authorized to take away life in consequence of religion. All laws and government ought to tolerate and permit every man to enjoy his religion, whether right or wrong.... Every man has a right to be a false prophet, as well as a true prophet" (200).

He proceeded further: "I am going to inquire after God because I want you all to know God and to be familiar with Him. If I can get you to know Him, I can bring you to Him. And if so, all persecution against me will cease. This will let you know that I am his servant; for I speak as one having authority and not as a scribe" (200).

From the back of his mind, Joseph held out the concept of an exalted human being as one who was Godlike, a design for the members of the human family that would transcend death:

> I am going to tell you the designs of God for the human race, the relation the human family sustains with God, and why He interferes with the affairs of man. First, God himself who sits enthroned in yonder heavens is a Man like unto one of yourselves—that is the great secret! If the veil were rent today and the great God that holds this world in its sphere and the planets in their orbit and who upholds all things by His power—if you were to see Him today, you would see Him in all the person, image, fashion, and very form of a man, like yourselves. For Adam was a man formed in His likeness and created in the very fashion and image of God. Adam received instruction, walked, talked, and conversed with Him as one man talks and communicates with another (200).

Joseph then brought forward the subject of those who had died and the consolation of those who mourned. In order to understand the subject of exaltation among the dead and to speak for the consolation of those who mourned for the loss of their friends, it was necessary to understand the character and being of God, how God came to be God. "The first principle of truth and of the Gospel is to know for a certainty the character of God [as an exalted being], and that we may converse with Him the same as one man with another, and that He once was a man like one of us and that God Himself, the Father of us all, once dwelled on an earth the same as Jesus Christ himself did in the flesh and like us" (201).

To know these first principles of the gospel is to pierce the fabric of eternal life. The authority to which Joseph appeals, then, is the scriptural authority of the Bible accepted by Christians, but with transformed meanings. What did Jesus say? "As the Father has power in Himself, even so has the Son power in himself." To do what? Why, what the Father did. That answer is obvious; even in a manner to lay down His body and take it up again. Jesus, what are you going to do? "To lay down my life as my Father laid down His body that I might take it up again." Do you believe it? Smith proceeded to argue that God the Father has power in himself, and similarly the Son also has such power. This is the pattern: As God has laid down His body that he might take it up again, so Jesus will lay down his body: These successive transformations of one exalted being after another is what comes to be known as eternal progression. It is the Mormon quest for glory:

> Here then is eternal life—to know the only wise and true God [as an exalted being]. You have got to learn how to make yourselves Gods in order to save yourselves and be kings and priests to God, the same as all Gods have done—by going from a small capacity to a great capacity, from a small degree to another, from grace to grace, until the resurrection of the dead, from exaltation to exaltation—till you are able to sit in everlasting burnings and everlasting power and glory as those who have gone before, sit enthroned. I want you to know that God in the last days, while certain individuals are proclaiming His name, is not trifling with you nor me.... (201).

Again, turning to those who mourn, Joseph said:

> I want you to know the first principles of consolation. How consoling to the mourners when they are called to part with a husband, father, wife, mother, child, dear relative, or friend, to know, though they lay down this body and all earthly tabernacles shall be dissolved, that their very being shall rise in immortal glory to dwell in everlasting burnings and to sorrow, die, and suffer no more. And not only that, but to

contemplate the saying that they will be heirs of God and joint-heirs with Jesus Christ.

What is [this first principle]? To inherit and enjoy the same glory, powers, and exaltation until you ascend a throne of eternal power and arrive at the station of a God, the same as those who have gone before. What did Jesus Christ do? "Why I do the same things that I saw my Father do when worlds came rolling into existence." Saw the Father do what? "I saw the Father work out His kingdom with fear and trembling and I am doing the same, too. When I get my kingdom, I will give it to the Father and it will add to and exalt His glory. He will take a higher exaltation and I will take His place and am also exalted, so that He obtains kingdom rolling upon kingdom." So that Jesus treads in His tracks as He had gone before and then inherits what God did before. God is glorified in the salvation and exaltation of His creatures (201).

When you climb a ladder, you must begin at the bottom rung. You have got to find the beginning of the history and go on until you have learned the last principle of the Gospel. It will be a great thing to learn salvation beyond the grave and it is not all to be comprehended in this world.

Post-mortal Existence

A funeral marks the completion of the mortal phase of existence for the spirit, to be reunited with the body as the complete immortal person. The body is dressed in temple garments if the deceased person was the holder of a temple recommend at the time of death. Female relatives and/or relief society sisters often assist with dressing a deceased woman, while male relatives and/or Melchizedek priesthood holders assist for deceased men.

A local funeral director, Gary Russon, in Salt Lake City indicated with a certain amount of pride that he and his colleagues are all temple-worthy and therefore bring their priesthood knowledge and practices to bear in their conduct of the funeral of a church member:

Speaking for myself, he said, we think of ourselves as a kind of dual being—there's the spirit and the body, and at death there's a separation of the spirit and the body, so the body is then laid in the grave and the spirit continues to live in the spirit world. The spirit still lives and is vibrant and living and conscious in a different place, in the spirit world, awaiting the time when the resurrection will take place, so the body will be reunited with the spirit.

A funeral is sad and difficult at times because of the separation now, but knowing that the person isn't annihilated, or gone forever, but is still alive, and so continues to live, and is like going through a door. They've gone somewhere else for now, and at some point we're going to be going through that door, and we're going to be reunited, and then comes the resurrection, and then you live as families forever.

The resurrection is a reuniting of the physical body with the spirit, so at that point a person enters an eternal state—of immortality—no more death or anything like that, but you become a glorified being of both spirit and body.

A service is usually held in the ward chapel, followed by burial attended by family members and close friends. (Cremation is allowed but discouraged except in countries where it is legally mandated. In LDS belief, the post-mortal spirit initially enters a state of existence called either "Paradise" (if the person lived a righteous life) or "Spirit Prison" (if their life was unrighteous).

Not all persons will have completed their ordinance work or met the conditions of righteous obedience necessary for progression to the highest degree of glory in the celestial kingdom, and some may have actively opposed the plan of salvation. However, those who have met conditions of obedience may serve as missionaries to those in spirit prison, and all individual spirits may progress along the path toward perfection by repenting and accepting the vicarious temple work done on earth on their behalf, until all the ordinances are completed. In this way, members of the church recognize and honor the agency of the spirit in a person's post-mortal existence. Then, members believe, that with the First Resurrection all spirits will be clothed with immortal bodies of flesh and bones, and Christ will reign with the Saints for a thousand years (Underwood 1993).

The Second Resurrection will inaugurate the final destiny of all spirits. The highest hope and glory of the plan of salvation, as foretold in the endowment ordinance, is that these re-embodied spirit persons who have fulfilled their covenants will return to Heavenly Father and Mother as married persons in their own extended family. They will meet the Lord face to face in the highest realm of the celestial kingdom. There, with their spouses and children, they will become gods among the gods on the earth transformed into the full kingdom of God. This hope is the hope of happiness, joy, and perfection. It is what LDS conceive as the ultimate goal of life, the achievement of exaltation, the culmination of their quest for glory in building the kingdom of God on earth.

Exalted Immortal Eternal Families

Since the 1960s, anthropologists Clifford Geertz (1973) and Victor Turner (1969) have emphasized ritual as a cultural performance that employs symbolic actions and images to dramatize a certain worldview. Such a ritual performance took place after the death of Gordon B. Hinckley, the president of the LDS Church, who died on January 27, 2008, at age 97. His passing initiated a series of symbolic actions that resulted in a transition to new church leadership through a divinely appointed prophet.

In cultural terms, LDS members view the church as a "house of order" under the Melchizedek priesthood, with the president as their prophet, seer, and revelator, and the family as the basic social unit of the church. Both aspects—the priesthood hierarchy and the multigenerational family—were fully evident during this ritual transition.

The first presidency is the highest leadership quorum in the church and includes the president and his two counselors, Thomas S. Monson and Henry B. Eyring. Upon the death of President Hinckley, this first presidency automatically dissolved and the interregnum began. The two counselors reverted to their places of seniority in the second highest leadership quorum, the quorum of the twelve apostles, as determined by the date of their ordination as quorum members. Now numbering 14 members, the quorum of the twelve assumed temporary church leadership, led by Senior Apostle Thomas S. Monson. This reflected the church as a house of order.

On Saturday, February 2, 2008, President Hinckley's funeral service took place in a manner similar to any family ceremony within the church, albeit with two exceptions—it was held in the 21,000-seat LDS Conference Center rather than a local ward meetinghouse, and the Mormon Tabernacle Choir provided the music. Family members and friends took the primary roles, though they asked Senior Apostle Monson to preside. One daughter opened the service with a family prayer. Hinckley's youngest son then offered the invocation. Next, another daughter was the first speaker, followed by two friends who were senior church officials, and then three members of the quorum of the twelve. The choir then sang a hymn written by President Hinckley, the opening line of which is "What is this thing called death" and the last verse of which begins "There is no death, but only change." This was a direct reflection of the worldview of the LDS in which the spirit of a person lives on even as the body is buried. Hinckley's third daughter then gave the benediction, and his eldest son dedicated the grave at the Salt Lake City cemetery. President Hinckley had five children, 25 grandchildren, and 62 great-grandchildren, emphasizing the family as a cross-generational social unit of the church.

During the interregnum, the quorum of the twelve apostles assembled to consider whether the first presidency should be reorganized, or whether the church should proceed under the presiding authority of the quorum. On February 4, the quorum passed a motion to reorganize the first presidency, unanimously selecting Thomas S. Monson as the new president and prophet. He then chose Henry B. Eyring and Dieter F. Uchtdorf as his two counselors, thereby establishing the three of them as the new first presidency. This followed the tradition that the senior apostle is named and sustained by his fellow apostles as president of the church. Boyd K. Packer is now next in line as the senior member and president of the twelve, who, in turn, chose D. Todd Christofferson to fill the vacancy in that quorum.

The final step in this ritual of transition to new leadership occurred in early April 2008 when a solemn assembly formed part of the LDS general conference proceedings. There, all of the quorums and members of the church sustained the new first presidency by raising their hands in a collective gesture of affirmation. Through this orderly cultural script and social drama, Thomas S. Monson became the 16th president since the Prophet Joseph Smith organized the church in 1830. He now leads a church of international dimensions, numbering more than 14 million members.

The rituals marking and confirming the transition in leadership among the LDS gave symbolic expression to the hierarchical authority of the church's Melchizedek priesthood and to the church's multigenerational family culture. Victor Turner would certainly note the liminal quality of this transition, and Clifford Geertz would see it as one important feature of the church's public culture. For the LDS, the renewal of the first presidency and its prophetic leadership again brings order to both the church and the world.

References

Affirmation: Gay & lesbian Mormons [website]. (2006). The proclamation on the family: A ten-year assessment (www.affirmation.org, accessed 5/25/2006).

Agar, Michael H. (1996). *The professional stranger: An informal introduction to ethnography*, 2nd ed. San Diego, CA: Academic Press.

Allen, James B. (1966). The significance of Joseph Smith's "first vision" in Mormon thought. *Dialogue: A journal of Mormon thought 1* (Autumn):29–45.

Allen, James B. & Glen M. Leonard. (1992). *The story of the Latter-day Saints*, 2nd ed. Salt Lake City, UT: Deseret Book.

Allen, James B., Ronald W. Walker, & David J. Whittaker. (2000). *Studies in Mormon history, 1830–1997: An indexed bibliography*, with a topical guide to published social science literature on the Mormons, compiled by Armand L. Mauss & Dynette Ivie Reynolds. Urbana, IL: University of Illinois Press.

Anderson, Lavina Fielding. (1994). The year of the axe. Paper presented at November meeting of the B. H. Roberts society. Salt Lake City, UT.

———, ed. (2001). *Lucy's book: A critical edition of Lucy Mack Smith's family memoir*. Salt Lake City, UT: Signature Books.

———. (2006). True to the faith: A snapshot of the church in 2004. *Dialogue 39*:4 (Winter), 68–81.

Anderson, Robert D. (1999). *Inside the mind of Joseph Smith: Psychobiography and the Book of Mormon*. Salt Lake City, UT: Signature Books.

Arrington, Leonard J. (1958). *Great basin kingdom: Economic history of the Latter-day Saints, 1830–1900*. Lincoln, NE: University of Nebraska Press, by arrangement with the president of Harvard College.

———. (1998). *Adventures of a church historian*. Urbana, IL: University of Illinois Press.

Arrington, Leonard J., Feramore Y. Fox, & Dean L. May. (1976). *Building the city of God: Community and cooperation among the Mormons*. Salt Lake City, UT: Deseret Book.

Associated Press. (1994). LDS Church excommunicates author, researcher, Dec. 3.

Associated Press. (2007). Hearing postponed for teen in triple fatal DUI crash, April 6.

Ballard, M. Russell. (2002). The greatest generation of missionaries. *Ensign* 32(11):46–48.

Ballif, Jae R. (1995). Melchizedek priesthood. In *Priesthood and church organization, selections from the Encyclopedia of Mormonism*, Daniel H. Ludlow, ed., 182–190. Salt Lake City, UT: Deseret Book.

Bancroft, Herbert Howe. (1890). *History of Utah*. San Francisco: History Company.

Barber, Allan H. (1989). *Celestial symbols: Symbolism in doctrine, religious traditions and temple architecture*. Bountiful, UT: Horizon Publishers.

Barth, Friedrick.(1969). *Ethnic groups and boundaries*. Boston: Little, Brown.

Beck, Aaron T. (1976). *Cognitive therapy and the emotional disorders*. New York: New American Library.

Benson, Ezra T. (1986). To the youth of the noble birthright. *Ensign* 5:43.

———. (1990). *Missionaries to match our message*. Salt Lake City, UT: Bookcraft.

Bernard, H. Russell (2002). *Research methods in anthropology: Qualitative and quantitative approaches*, 3rd ed. Walnut Creek, CA: Alta Mira Press.

Bigler, David L. (1998). *Forgotten kingdom: The Mormon theocracy in the American west, 1847–1896*. Spokane, WA: Arthur H. Clark Company.

Bohannan, Paul, & Dirk van der Elst. (1998). *Asking and listening: Ethnography as personal adaptation*. Prospect Heights, IL: Waveland Press, Inc.

Borg, Marcus. (1997). *Jesus and Buddha: The parallel sayings*. Berkeley, CA: Seastone.

Breakwell, Glynis M. (1986). *Coping with threatened identities*. London: Methuen.

———. (1990). *Interviewing*. Leicester, UK: The British Psychological Society.

Brodie, Fawn M. (1971). *No man knows my history: The life of Joseph Smith, the Mormon prophet*, 2nd ed., revised and enlarged. New York: Alfred A Knopf.

Buerger, David John. (1994). *The mysteries of Godliness*. San Francisco: Smith Research Associates.

Burns, David D. (1980). *Feeling good: The new mood therapy*. New York: William Morrow and Company.

Bushman, Claudia L. (2006). *Contemporary Mormonism: Latter-day Saints in the modern world*. Westport, CT: Praeger.

Bushman, Richard Lyman. (2005) *Joseph Smith: Rough stone rolling*. New York: Alfred A. Knopf.

Carlisle, Nate, & Russ Rizzo (2007). Man who lost wife, 2 kids: crash is a "bitter cup." *Salt Lake Tribune*, Feb. 13.

Carmack, John K. (2004). *A bright ray of hope: The perpetual education fund*. Salt Lake City, UK: Deseret Book.

Caughey, John L. (1980). Personal identity and social organization. *Ethos* 8(3):173–203.

———. (1984). *Imaginary social worlds: A cultural approach*. Lincoln, NE: University of Nebraska Press.

———. (2006). *Negotiating cultures and identities: Life history issues, methods, and readings*. Lincoln, NE: University of Nebraska Press.

Chapple, Eliot D., & Carleton S. Coons. (1942). Rites of intensification. In *Principles of anthropology*, 507–528. New York: Henry Holt and Company.

Charles, John D. (2004). *Endowed from on high: Understanding the symbols of the endowment*. Springfield, UT: Horizon Publishers.

Children's songbook. (1989). Salt Lake City, UT: Corporation of the Church of Jesus Christ of Latter-day Saints.

Church handbook of instructions, book 2, section 1: *Melchizedek priesthood*. (1998). Salt Lake City, UT: Intellectual Reserve.

Church handbook of instructions, book 2, section 2: *Aaronic priesthood*. (1998). Salt Lake City, UT: Intellectual Reserve.

Church handbook of instructions, book 2, section 3: *Relief society*. (1998). Salt Lake City, UT: Intellectual Reserve.

Church handbook of instructions, book 2, section 4. (1998). *Young women*. Salt Lake City, UT: Intellectual Reserve.

Church handbook of instructions, book 2, section 5: *Primary*. (1998). Salt Lake City, UT: Intellectual Reserve.

Compton, Todd. (1995). *Apostasy. In Priesthood and church organization*, 12–16. Salt Lake City, UT: Deseret Book.

Conze, Edward. (1959) [1951]. *Buddhism: Its essence and development*. New York: Harper & Brothers.

Cooper, Rex Eugene. (1990). *Promises made to the fathers: Mormon covenant organization*. Salt Lake City, UT: University of Utah Press.

Corcoran, Brent, ed. (1994). *Multiply and replenish: Mormon essays on sex and family*. Salt Lake City, UT: Signature Books.

Cornwall, Marie, Tim B. Heaton, & Lawrence A. Young, eds. (1994). *Contemporary Mormonism: Social science perspectives*. Urbana, IL: University of Illinois Press.

Cottle, Thomas L., & Stephen L. Klineberg. (1974). *The present of things future: Explorations of time in human experience*. New York: The Free Press.

Crane, Julia G., & Michael V. Angrosino. (1992) [1984]. *Field projects in anthropology: A student handbook*, 3rd ed. Prospect Heights, IL: Waveland Press.

Csordas, Thomas J., ed. (1994). Introduction: The body as representation and being-in-the-world. In *Embodiment and experience: The existential ground of culture and self*, 1–24. Cambridge, UK: Cambridge University Press.

D'Andrade, Roy G. (1992) Afterword. In *Human motives and cultural models*. Roy G. D'Andrade & Claudia Strauss, eds., 225–232. New York: Cambridge University Press.

———. (1995). *The development of cognitive anthropology*. New York: Cambridge University Press.

Davies, Douglas J. (2003). *An introduction to Mormonism*. Cambridge, UK: Cambridge University Press.

Deseret News. (2005). *2006 church almanac*. Salt Lake City, UT: Church News.

———. (2009). *2010 church almanac*. Salt Lake City, UT: Church News.

Dew, Sheri L. (1996). *Go forward with faith: The biography of Gordon B. Hinckley.* Salt Lake City, UT: Deseret Book.

Dollahite, D. C., ed. (2000). *Strengthening our families: An in-depth look at the proclamation on the family.* Provo, UT: Brigham Young University, School of Family Life.

Douglas, Mary. (1996) [1966]. *Purity and danger: An analysis of the concepts of pollution and taboo.* London: Routledge.

Durkheim, Emile. (1965) [1915]. *The elementary forms of the religious life.* New York: The Free Press.

Duties and blessings of the priesthood. 2000. Salt Lake City, UT: Intellectual Reserve, Church of Jesus Christ of Latter-day Saints.

Ekman, Paul. (1994). Facial expression of emotion. *American psychologist* 48:384–392.

Eliade, Mircea. (1987) [1957]. *The sacred and the profane: The nature of religion.* San Diego, CA: Harcourt Brace.

Eller, Jack David. (2007). *Introducing anthropology of religion.* New York: Routledge.

Embry, Jessie L. 1987. *Mormon polygamous families: Life in the principle.* Salt Lake City, UT: University of Utah Press.

———. (1994). *Black Saints in a white church: Contemporary African American Mormons.* Salt Lake City, UT: Signature Books.

Endowed from on high: Temple preparation seminar, teacher's manual. 1995. Salt Lake City, UT: Church of Jesus Christ of Latter-day Saints.

Erikson, Erik H. (1968). *Identity, youth and crisis.* New York: W. W. Norton.

———. (1980) [1959]. *Identity and the life cycle.* New York: W. W. Norton.

Erikson, Erik H., & Joan M. Erikson. (1997). *The life cycle completed.* New York: W. W. Norton.

Eternal marriage, student manual. 2001. Salt Lake City, UT: Intellectual Reserve, prepared by the Church Educational System.

Evans, John Henry (1966) [1933]. *Joseph Smith: An American prophet.* Salt Lake City, UT: Deseret Book.

Faerber, Ryan Michael. (2006). From the land of Sinim: Examining the history and future prospects for the LDS church in China. M.A. thesis in international studies, Lauder Institute and School of Arts and Sciences, University of Pennsylvania.

Ferguson, Isaac C. (1995) [1992]. Humanitarian service. In *The church and society,* selections from the *Encyclopedia of Mormonism,* Daniel H. Ludlow, ed., 242–246. Salt Lake City, UT: Deseret Book.

First presidency and council of the twelve apostles. (1995). The family—A proclamation to the world. *Ensign* 25(11):102 [originally read at the general meeting of the relief society on Sept. 23, 1995].

First presidency and quorum of the twelve apostles. (1995). The family—A proclamation to the world. *Ensign* 24(11):102.

Flake, Chad J., & Larry W. Draper, eds. (2004). *A Mormon bibliography, 1830–1930,* 2nd ed., 2 vols. Provo, UT: Brigham Young University, Religious Studies Center.

Francoeur, Robert T. (1991). *Becoming a sexual person*, 2nd ed. New York: Macmillan Publishing.

Frazer, James G. (1958) [1922]. *The golden bough: A study in magic and religion*. New York: Macmillan.

Geertz, Clifford. (1973). *The interpretation of cultures*. New York: Basic Books.

Gilkey, Caroline F. (1994). Verbal performance in Mormon worship services. Ph.D. dissertation on folklore, University of Pennsylvania.

Goffman, Erving. (1959). *The presentation of self in everyday life*. New York: Doubleday.

Goldstein, Melvyn C., & Matthew Kapstein, eds. (1998). *Buddhism in contemporary Tibet*. Berkeley, CA: University of California Press.

Goodenough, Ward H. (1965). *Cooperation in change: An anthropological approach to community development*. New York: Russell Sage.

———. (1967). Right and wrong in human evolution. *Zygon* 2(1):59–76.

———. (1969). Rethinking "status" and "role": Toward a general model of the cultural organization of social relationships. In *Cognitive anthropology*, ed., Stephen A. Tyler, 311–330. New York: Holt, Rinehart and Winston.

———. (1981). *Culture, language, and society*, 2nd ed. Menlo Park, CA: Benjamin/ Cummings.

Gordon, Sarah Barringer. (2002). *The Mormon question: Polygamy and constitutional conflict in nineteenth century America*. Chapel Hill, NC: University of North Carolina Press.

Hafen, Bruce C. (1995). Disciplinary procedures. In *Priesthood and church organization*, selections from the *Encyclopedia of Mormonism*, Daniel H. Ludlow, ed., 91–95.

Hallowell, A. Irving, ed. (1967) [1955]. *Culture and experience*. New York: Schocken Books.

———. (1967). The self and its behavioral environment. In *Culture and experience*, 75–110. New York: Schocken Books.

Hamilton, C. Mark, with C. Nina Cutrubus. (1983). *The Salt Lake temple: A monument to a people*, 5th ed. Salt Lake City, UT: University Services Corporation.

Hammarberg, Melvyn (1977). *The Indiana voter: Historical dynamics of party allegiance during the 1870s*. Chicago: University of Chicago Press.

———. (1992). Penn inventory for post-traumatic stress disorder: Psychometric properties. *Psychological assessment: A journal of consulting and clinical psychology* 4(1):67–76.

———. (1996). Guilt, fear, anxiety and love in identity dynamics among the Latter-day Saints today. *Mormon identities in transition*, ed. Douglas Davies, 102–112. London: Cassel Press.

———. (2002a). The world of the Latter-day Saints: A life plan model. *Expedition* 44(1):7–15.

———. (2002b). Research note: The Olympic face of the LDS Church. *Expedition* 44(2):6–7.

———. (2008a). The current crisis in the formation and regulation of Latter-day Saints' sexual identity. In *Revisiting Thomas F. O'Dea's, the Mormons: Contemporary perspectives*, eds. Cardell K. Jacobson, John P. Hoffmann, & Tim B. Heaton, 184–235. Salt Lake City, UT: University of Utah Press.

———. (2008b). Ritual drama of leadership transition among the Latter-day Saints. *Expedition* 50(2):42–43.

Hammarberg, Melvyn, & Steven M. Silver. (1994). Outcome of treatment for post-traumatic stress disorder in a primary care unit serving Vietnam veterans. *Journal of Traumatic Stress* 7(2):1–22.

Hardy, B. Carmon. (1992). *Solemn covenant: The Mormon polygamous passage*. Urbana, IL: University of Illinois Press.

Harkin, Michael, ed. (2007). *Reassessing revitalization movements: Perspectives from North America and the Pacific Islands*. Lincoln, NE: University of Nebraska Press.

Harkness, Sara, & Charles M. Super, eds. (1996). *Parents' cultural belief systems: Their origins, expressions, and consequences*. New York: Guilford Press.

Hawkins, Alan J., et al. (2000). Equal partnership and the sacred responsibilities of mothers and fathers. In *Strengthening our families: An in-depth look at the proclamation on the family*, 63–82. ed. David C. Dollahite. Provo, UT: School of Family Life, Brigham Young University.

Heaton, Tim B., Stephen J. Bahr, & Cardell K. Jacobson, eds. (2004). *A statistical profile of Mormons: Health, wealth, and social life*. Lewiston, NY: Edwin Mellen Press.

Hinckley, Gordon B. (1986). To the youth of noble birth. *Ensign* 16(1):43.

———. (1995). This is the work of the master. Report of the 165th annual general conference of the Church of Jesus Christ of Latter-day Saints. *Ensign* 25(5):69–71.

———. (2001). The perpetual education fund. *Ensign* 31(5):51–53.

———. (2002). To men of the priesthood. *Ensign* 32(11):56–59.

———. (2008). What is this thing that men call death. In memoriam (1910–2008), supplement to *Ensign*.

Hunt, Stephen. (2007a). Teen charged in family car deaths. *Salt Lake Tribune*, Feb. 16.

———. (2007b). Utah DUI story of forgiveness. *Salt Lake Tribune*, June 5.

Hunter, Howard W. (1994). Exceeding great and precious promises. Report of the 164th semiannual general conference of the Church of Jesus Christ of Latter-day Saints. *Ensign* 24(11):7–9.

Hyde, Kenneth E. (1990). *Religion in childhood and adolescence: A comprehensive review of research*. Birmingham, AL: Religious Education Press.

Hymns of the Church of Jesus Christ of Latter-day Saints. 1985. Salt Lake City, UT: Church of Jesus Christ of Latter-day Saints.

Jacobson, Cardell K., John P. Hoffmann, & Tim B. Heaton, eds. (2008). *Revisiting Thomas F. O'Dea's, the Mormons: Contemporary perspectives*. Salt Lake City, UT: University of Utah Press.

James, William. (1890). *The principles of psychology*, 2 vols. New York: Henry Holt.

———. (1958) [1902]. *The varieties of religious experience: A study in human nature*. New York: Mentor Books.

Jensen, Andrew. (2004). *Exporting the faith: The LDS Church in Mexico*. M.A. thesis in international studies, Wharton School and the School of Arts and Sciences, University of Pennsylvania.

Jensen, Richard L., & Richard G. Oman. (1984). *C. C. A. Christensen, 1831–1912: Mormon immigrant artist* (catalogue: An exhibition at the Museum of Church History and Art). Salt Lake City, UT: Church of Jesus Christ of Latter-day Saints.

Jensen, Sally. (1994). *Interview*, Aug. 2nd. Notes in possession of the author.

Jessee, Dean C. (1969). The early accounts of Joseph Smith's first vision. *BYU Studies* 9(3):275–294.

———. (1971). The writing of Joseph Smith's history. *BYU Studies* 11(4):439–473 [incorrectly bound signature].

Kearney, Michael. (1984). *World view*. San Francisco: Chandler and Sharp.

Kefalopoulos, Gus. (1996). The contemporary Mormon missionary experience: Life before, during, and after a mission. Research paper (Anthropology 594), University of Pennsylvania.

Kimball, Spencer W. (1969). *The miracle of forgiveness*. Salt Lake City, UT: Bookcraft.

Kincaid, Janet M. (2000). Tell Eve about the serpent!: A qualitative study of the effects of temple participation in the lives of young adult Mormons. M.A. thesis. Berkeley, CA: Graduate Theological Union.

Knott, Kim. (1998). *Hinduism: A very short introduction*. Oxford, UK: Oxford University Press.

Kuhn, Thomas S. (1970) [1962]. *The structure of scientific revolutions*, 2nd ed. Chicago: University of Chicago Press.

Kutsche, Paul. (1998). *Field ethnography: A manual for doing cultural anthropology*. Upper Saddle River, NJ: Prentice Hall.

Laake, Deborah. (1993). *Secret ceremonies: A Mormon woman's diary of marriage and beyond*. New York: William Morrow.

LDS public affairs, news release. (2000). (Aug. 18). Re: Elder Dallin H. Oaks.

———. (2006). (April 6). Re: Elder Russell M. Nelson.

Letter of the first presidency, Dec. 11, 2002. Church of Jesus Christ of Latter-day Saints. *The Latter-day Saints for civil same-sex marriage* [website] (2006). Latter-day Saint doctrine: www.lds4gaymarriage.net/ [accessed 8/2/2006].

Linde, Charlotte. (1993). *Life stories: The creation of coherence*. New York: Oxford University Press.

Luschin, Immo. (1995). Ordinances. In *Priesthood and church organization*, selections from the *Encyclopedia of Mormonism*, Daniel H. Ludlow, ed., 221–223. Salt Lake City, UT: Deseret Book.

Lyman, Edward Leo. (1986). *Political deliverance: The Mormon quest for Utah statehood*. Urbana, IL: University of Illinois Press.

Mauss, Armand L. (1987). Culture, charisma, and change: Reflections on Mormon temple worship. *Dialogue* 20(4):77–83.

———. (1994). *The angel and the beehive: The Mormon struggle with assimilation.* Urbana, IL: University of Illinois Press.

———. (2003). *All Abraham's children: Changing Mormon conceptions of race and lineage.* Urbana, IL: University of Illinois Press.

May, Dean L. (1988). Body and soul: The record of Mormon religious philanthropy. *Church history 57.*

———. (1997). *Interview,* June 6. Notes in possession of the author.

———. (2003). Obituary, *Salt Lake Tribune,* May 9.

May, Tad. (1997). Field notes collected by M. Hammarberg, June 15. Salt Lake City, UT: Emerson ward.

Mayne, McKenzie. (1997). Interview, May 26. Notes in possession of the author.

McDannell, Colleen. (1995). Mormon garments: Sacred clothing and the body. In *Material Christianity,* ed. Colleen McDannell, 198–221. New Haven, CT: Yale University Press.

Melchizedek priesthood leadership handbook. 1990. Salt Lake City, UT: Corporation of the President of the Church of Jesus Christ of Latter-day Saints.

Merton, Robert K. (1968). *Social theory and social structure,* enlarged ed. New York: The Free Press.

Metcalfe, B. L., ed. (1993). *New approaches to the book of Mormon: Explorations in critical methodology.* Salt Lake City, UT: Signature Books.

Miller, George A., Eugene Galanter, & Karl H. Pribram. (1986) [1960]. *Plans and the structure of behavior.* New York: Adams-Bannister-Cox.

Miracle, Tina S., Andrew W. Miracle, & Roy F. Baumeister. (2003). *Human sexuality: Meeting your basic needs.* Upper Saddle River, NJ: Prentice Hall (Pearson Education).

Missionary guide: Training for missionaries. 1988. Salt Lake City, UT: Corporation of the President of the Church of Jesus Christ of Latter-day Saints.

Moen, P., Glen H. Elder, & J. Lusher, eds. (1995). *Examining lives in context: Perspectives on the ecology of human development.* Washington, DC: American Psychological Association.

Money, John. (1988). *Gay, straight, and in-between: The sexology of erotic orientation.* New York: Oxford University Press.

Mortimer, William James (1995). Patriarchal blessings. In *Priesthood and church organization,* selections from the *Encyclopedia of Mormonism,* Daniel H. Ludlow, ed., 255–257. Salt Lake City, UT: Deseret Book.

Murphey, Murray G. (1967). American civilization as a discipline. *Emory University Quarterly* 23:48–61.

———. (1970). American civilization at Pennsylvania. *American Quarterly* 22:489–502.

———. (1979). American civilization in retrospect. *American Quarterly* 31:402–406.

———. (1982). *American character and culture in the 1980's: Pluralistic perspectives*, ed. Gene Wise, 23–27. Boston: University of Massachusetts.

———. (1987). Signs, acts, and objects. *Social Science History* 11(2):211–232.

———. (1992). *Anthony Garvan: Culture, history, and artifacts: A memorial tribute*, presented at a special meeting of the Library Company of Philadelphia (Mar. 25).

———. (1994). *Philosophical foundations of historical knowledge*. Albany, NY: State University of New York Press.

———. (1999). American civilization as a discipline? *American Studies* 40:5–21.

Nadel, S. F. (1957). *The theory of social structure*. London: Cohen and West.

Nelson, Russell M. (2003). Divine love. *Ensign* 33(2):20–25.

Oaks, Dallin H., & Lance B. Wickman. (2006). Same-gender attraction (http://www. lds.org/newsroom/issues/answer).

Oaks, Dallin H. (1995). Same-gender attraction. *Ensign* 10:7–14.

———. (2006). Dating versus hanging out. *Ensign* 6:10–16.

O'Dea, Thomas F. (1957). *The Mormons*. Chicago: University of Chicago Press.

Oldham, Tasha. (2003). *The Smith family* (documentary film), available from New Day Films, P.O. Box 1084, Harriman, NY 10926.

Olsen, Steven L. (1996). The meaning of the Joseph Smith story: A structural analysis. Unpublished paper dated July 16.

Ostling, Richard N., & Joan K. Ostling. (1999). *Mormon America: The power and the promise*. San Francisco: HarperSanFrancisco.

Oswalt, Wendell H. (1986). *Life cycles and lifeways: An introduction to cultural anthropology*. Palo Alto, CA: Mayfield.

Our heritage: A brief history of the Church of Jesus Christ of Latter-day Saints. (1996). Salt Lake City, UT: Intellectual Reserve.

Packer, Boyd K. (1980). *The holy temple*. Salt Lake City, UT: Bookcraft.

A parent's guide. (1985). Salt Lake City, UT: Corporation of the President of the Church of Jesus Christ of Latter-day Saints.

Parry, Rich. (1995). *Field notes collected by M. Hammarberg*, Mar. 19. Salt Lake City, UT: Crystal Heights second ward.

Pearson, Don M. (1995). Bishop. In *Priesthood and church organization*, selections from the *Encyclopedia of Mormonism*, Daniel H. Ludlow, ed., 33–36. Salt Lake City, UT: Deseret Book.

Persuitte, David. (2000). *Joseph Smith and the origins of the Book of Mormon*, 2nd ed. Jefferson, NC: McFarland.

Petersen, Mark E. (1954). *For time and eternity*. Salt Lake City, UT: Bookcraft.

Pike, Kenneth (1954). *Language in relation to a unified theory of the structure of human behavior*, part I, prelim. ed. Glendale, CA: Summer Institute of Linguistics.

Pitcher, Brian L. (1995). Callings. In *Priesthood and church organization*, selections from the *Encyclopedia of Mormonism*, Daniel H. Ludlow, ed., 54–58. Salt Lake City, UT: Deseret Book.

Pratt, David H. (1996) [1992]. Family history, genealogy. In *The church and society, selections from the Encyclopedia of Mormonism*, Daniel H. Ludlow, ed., 204–208. Salt Lake City, UT: Deseret Book.

Preach my gospel: A guide to missionary service. (2004). Salt Lake City, UT: Intellectual Reserve.

Preparing for exaltation. (1998). Salt Lake City, UT: Intellectual Reserve, Church of Jesus Christ of Latter-day Saints.

Primary handbook. (1985). Salt Lake City, UT: Church of Jesus Christ of Latter-day Saints.

Primary 1: I am a child of God. (1994). Salt Lake City, UT: Church of Jesus Christ of Latter-day Saints.

Primary 3: Choose the right B, ages 4–7. (1994). Salt Lake City, UT: Church of Jesus Christ of Latter-day Saints.

Primary 7: New Testament, ages 8–11. (1994). Salt Lake City, UT: Church of Jesus Christ of Latter-day Saints.

Primary 2: Choose the right A, ages 4–7. (1995). Salt Lake City, UT: Church of Jesus Christ of Latter-day Saints.

Primary 4: Book of Mormon, ages 8–11. (1995). Salt Lake City, UT: Church of Jesus Christ of Latter-day Saints.

Primary 5: Doctrine and covenants; church history, ages 8–11. (1996). Salt Lake City, UT: Church of Jesus Christ of Latter-day Saints.

Primary 6: Old Testament, ages 8–11. (1996). Salt Lake City, UT: Church of Jesus Christ of Latter-day Saints.

Quinn, D. Michael. (1978). The prayer circle. *BYU Studies* 18(1):79–105.

———. (1985). LDS church authority and new plural marriages, 1890–1904. *Dialogue* 18:9–105.

———. (1994). *The Mormon hierarchy: Origins of power.* Salt Lake City, UT: Signature Books.

———. (1998). *Early Mormonism and the magic world view*, rev. ed. Salt Lake City, UT: Signature Books.

Redfield, Robert. (1960). *The Little community.* Chicago: University of Chicago Press.

Report of the 164th semiannual general conference. (1994). *Ensign* 24(11).

Rozsa, Allen Claire. (1992). Temple ordinances. In *Priesthood and church organization, selections from the Encyclopedia of Mormonism*, Daniel H. Ludlow, ed., 407–410. Salt Lake City, UT: Deseret Book.

Rudd, Glen L. (1995). *Pure religion: The story of church welfare since 1930.* Salt Lake City, UT: Church of Jesus Christ of Latter-day Saints.

Ruthven, Malise. (2006). *Islam in the world.* Oxford, UK: Oxford University Press.

Salisbury, David C. (2000). Cultural conflict and Christianity in Japan: A case study of the LDS Church. M.A. thesis in international studies, Lauder Institute and the School of Arts and Sciences, University of Pennsylvania.

Scouting handbook. (1985). Salt Lake City, UT: Church of Jesus Christ of Latter-day Saints.

Shepherd, Gary, & Gordon Shepherd. (1998). *Mormon passage: A missionary chronicle*. Urbana, IL: University of Illinois Press.

Shipps, Jan. (1985). *Mormonism: The story of a new religious tradition*. Urbana, IL: University of Illinois Press.

———. (1994). Making saints: In the early days and the latter days. In *Contemporary Mormonism: Social science perspectives*, eds. Marie Cornwall, Tim B. Heaton, & Lawrence A. Young, 64–83. Urbana, IL: University of Illinois Press.

———. (1996). The genesis of Mormonism: The story of a new religious tradition. In *Religion and American culture: A reader*, 169–184. New York: Routledge.

Shipps, Jan, Cheryll L. May, & Dean L. May (1994). Sugar house ward: A Latter-day Saint congregation. In *American congregations, volume 1: Portraits of twelve religious communities*, James P. Wind & James W. Lewis, eds., 293–348. Chicago: University of Chicago Press.

Smith, Christian (with Melinda Lundquist Denton). (2005). *Soul searching: The religious and spiritual lives of American teenagers*. New York: Oxford University Press.

Smith, George D., ed. (1995) [1991]. *An intimate chronicle: The journals of William Clayton*. Salt Lake City, UT: Signature Books.

Smith, Joseph. (1978). *History of the Church of Jesus Christ of Latter-day Saints*, period I, 2nd rev. ed., 7 vols. Salt Lake City, UT: Deseret Book.

Smith, Joseph Fielding, comp. (1946). *Teachings of the prophet Joseph Smith*. Salt Lake City, UT: Deseret Book.

———. (1958). *Answers to gospel questions: The classic collection in one volume*, 5 vols. Salt Lake City, UT: Deseret Book.

Smith, Lucy Mack. (1979) [1853]. *History of Joseph Smith by his mother*. Salt Lake City, UT: Bookcraft.

Spradley, James P. (1979). *The ethnographic interview*. New York: Holt, Rinehart and Winston.

———. (1975). *Anthropology: The cultural perspective, second edition*. New York: John Wiley and Sons.

Spradley, James P., & David W. McCurdy, eds. (1972). *Culture and cognition: Rules, maps, and plans*. San Francisco: Chandler.

Stettler, Jeremiah. (2007). Father who lost wife, kids in crash requests prayers for other driver. *Salt Lake Tribune*, Feb. 10.

Stettler, Jeremiah, & Russ Rizzo. (2007). Teen driver in Friday's crash facing at least three counts of vehicular homicide. *Salt Lake Tribune*, Feb. 10.

Stettler, Jeremiah & Russ Rizzo. Out of tragedy, forgiveness. *Salt Lake Tribune*, Feb. 11.

———. (2007). Crash victims memorialized. *Salt Lake Tribune*, Feb. 18.

Stewart, David G., Jr. (2007). *Law of the harvest: Practical principles of effective missionary work*. Henderson, NV: Cumorah Foundation.

Strauss, Claudia, & Naomi Quinn. (1997). *A cognitive theory of cultural meaning.* Cambridge, UK: Cambridge University Press.

Suggs, David N., & Andrew W. Miracle, eds. (1993). *Culture and human sexuality: A reader.* Pacific Grove, CA: Brooks/Cole Publishing.

Taber, Susan B. (1993). *Mormon lives: A year in the Elkton ward.* Urbana, IL: University of Illinois Press.

Talmage, James E. (1978) [1912]. *The house of the lord.* Salt Lake City, UT: Deseret Book.

Tanner, Jerald, & Sandra Tanner. (1990). *Evolution of the Mormon temple ceremony, 1842–1990,* appendix A. Salt Lake City, UT: Utah Lighthouse Ministry.

True to the faith: A gospel reference. 2004. Salt Lake City, UT: Intellectual Reserve.

Tucker, Robert A. (1995). Temple recommend. In *Priesthood and church organization,* selections from the *Encyclopedia of Mormonism,* Daniel H. Ludlow, ed., 412. Salt Lake City, UT: Deseret Book.

Turner, Victor. (1969). Liminality and communitas. In *The ritual process: Structure and anti-structure,* 94–130. Chicago: Aldine.

Tylor, Sir Edward B. (1958) [1871]. *Primitive culture,* 2 vols., New York: Harper Torchbooks.

Underwood, Grant. (1999) [1993]. *The millenarian world of early Mormonism.* Urbana, IL: University of Illinois Press.

van der Elst, Dirk. (2003). *Culture as given, culture as choice,* 2nd ed., Prospect Heights, IL: Waveland Press.

van Gennep, Arnold. (1960) [1908]. *Rites of passage.* Chicago: University of Chicago Press.

Vernon, Leslie. (1995). *Interview,* Feb. 22. Notes in possession of author.

Vogel, Dan. (2004). *Joseph Smith: The making of a prophet.* Salt Lake City, UT: Signature Books.

Wallace, Anthony F. C. (2003). Revitalization movements. In *Revitalizations and mazeways: Essays on culture change,* vol. 1, 9–29. ed. Robert S. Grumet. Lincoln, NE: University of Nebraska Press. First published in *American Anthropologist* 58(2):264–281.

———. (1966). *Religion: An anthropological view.* New York: Random House.

———. (1967). Identity processes in personality and in culture. In *Cognition, personality, and clinical psychology,* eds. Richard Jessor & Seymour Feshbach. San Francisco: Jossey-Bass.

———. (2003). Mazeway resynthesis: A biocultural theory of religious inspiration. In *Essays on culture change,* vol. 1, 164–177. ed. Robert S. Grumet. Lincoln, NE: University of Nebraska Press. First published by the NY Academy of Sciences (April 23, 1956).

———. (1971). Administrative structures. In *Addison-Wesley modules in anthropology.* New York: Addison-Wesley.

Weber, Max. (1968). The nature of charismatic authority and its routinization. In *On charisma and institution building: Selected papers*, ed. S. N. Eisenstadt, 57–61. Chicago: University of Chicago Press.

Whittaker, David J. (1995). *Mormon Americana: A guide to sources and collections in the United States*. Provo, UT: BYU Studies.

Widtsoe, John A., selected and arranged. (1977). *Discourses of Brigham Young*. Salt Lake City, UT: Deseret Book.

Wierzbicka, Anna. (1999). *Emotions across languages and cultures: Diversity and universals*. Cambridge, UK: Cambridge University Press.

Wilcox, S. Michael. (1995). *House of glory: Finding personal meaning in the temple*. Salt Lake City, UT: Deseret Book.

Wilson, William A. (1981). *On being human: The folklore of Mormon missionaries*. Logan, UT: Utah State University Press.

Winslow, Ben. (2007). Prayers, tears for S. L. family. *Deseret News*, Feb. 10 morning edition.

———. (2007). Neighborhood reacting to tragic crash. *Deseret News*, Feb. 10.

Wortham, Stanton (2001). *Narratives in action: A strategy for research and analysis*. New York: Teacher's College, Columbia University.

Scriptural References

Bible	Book of Mormon	D&C		Pearl of Great Price	
				Moses	Abraham
ACT 2:38	2 Nephi 2:11–13	1:8–9	20:48	1:39	JS_H 1:72
ACT 7:55–56	2 Nephi 2:27	107:14	20:57	1:4,6	JS_H 1:71
AMOS 3:7	2 Nephi 31:4–7	107:18	20:59	4:13–27	JS_H 1:68–72
EPH 2:20	2 Nephi 9:23–24	107:68	20:68–74	4:1–4	JS_H 1:65
James 1:5	3 Nephi 11	107:8	20:70	4:2	JS_H 1:62
JN 15:16	3 Nephi 11–18	124:123	27:12	6:62	JS_H 1:56
JOB 27:5	3 Nephi 12:16	128:5	28:2–7		JS_H 1:53
John 1:32–34	Alma 24:14	132	29:36–40		JS_H 1:42, 46
JOSHUS 24:15	Alma 42:15	132:1	33:15		JS_H 1:33–35
LK 9:1–2	Alma 42:30	132:12–14	38:23		JS_H 1:28
Mark 1:9–11	Alma 42:8	132:18	42:30		3:25–28
MT 16:17	Celma 1:30	132:19–27	43:1–4		3:22–26
MT 16:17–19	Helamon 10:7	132:28–34	65:2		
MT 16:19	Mormon 7–9	132:34–38	68:2,12		
MT 2:16	Moroni 10:32	132:39–42	76		
Exodus 2;1–10	Moroni 10:3–5	132:44–49	78:7		

Bible	Book of Mormon	D&C		Pearl of Great Price	
				Moses	Abraham
		132:50–57	81:2		
		132:59–61	84:111		
		132:63–65	84:20–22		
		132:7	84:26–27		
		132:7,8,12	88:118		
		14:7	93:33–34		
		18:10	93:36		
		20:38–43			
		20:46			
		20:46–47			

Index

Page numbers in bold indicate illustrations.

Aaron, 135
Aaronic priesthood
  age grades, 12, 119, 143
  baptism ordinance, 38, 59
  as calling, 293
  conversions, 143
  Cowdery as first, 131
  duties of, 146–47
  home teachers, 25, 38
  lesser priesthood, 142–43
  missionary work, 208
  ordination to, 38–39, 143–45, 147, 235
  scouting program, 150, 169–70
  sealing, 262
  senior primary, 133
  solemn assembly, 15
  teachers, 38, 143
  temple ordinances, 194
  ward bishop, 145–46
  worthiness interviews, 141
  See also Melchizedek priesthood;
    young men organization
Abrahamic descent, 226–27, 262
accountability, 36, 59, 76, 96–97. See also
    baptism ordinance
achievement day, 38, 296
Achieving a Celestial Marriage: Student
    Manual, 42
Adam, 83, 189

Adam and Eve, 104, 184, 188–92, 223,
    263–64
adolescence, 33, 138–39, 285
adultery, 257, 274
adulthood, 39–43, 45, 49, 51
Africans, 23
age grades
  Aaronic priesthood, 12, 119, 143
  callings, 293
  children's characteristics, 99–100
  Crystal Heights second ward, **32**
  curriculum materials, 12
  descent model, 251
  junior primary, 76–77
  Melchizedek priesthood, 12
  missionary work, 197n
  nursery, 77, 85
  primary, 12, 76, 85, **86**, 87
  relief society sisters, 12, 41–42
  senior primary, 76–77
  singles' wards, 200–201
  spiritual awareness, 110–11, 114–16
  Sunday school, 12
  teaching programs for, 76–84
  worship attendance in Crystal
    Heights, **108**
  young women organization, 151
agency
  accountability, 36, 59

agency (*Cont.*)
  baptism and confirmation
    ordinances, 62
  baptism of the dead, 175–77, 258
  consequences, 107–8
  conversions, 233–34, 240
  CTR (Choose the Right), 96, 104
  For the Strength of Youth, 161,
    163–65
  genealogy, 309
  junior primary, 105
  Mormon values, **140**
  normative standards for youth, 141
  and obedience, 108, 271–74
  ordinances of the gospel, 59
  ordination of the dead, 177
  plan of salvation, 32–35, 97
  post-mortal life, 328
  pre-mortal life (preexistence), 53
  primary, 107–8
  spirit children, 107
  spirit self, 51, 96–97
  worthiness, 102–4, 107–8
age of accountability, 36–37, 96, 104–7,
    251. *See also* baptism ordinance
aggression, 116–17
AIDS, 278–85
Alderwood second ward, 11, 71–72
All Abraham's Children, 10
Allen, James B., 8, 72, 122
Allen, Rex J., 315
American Philosophical Society, 7, 8
Anderson, Ennis, 55, 66–67, 185,
    288–89
Anderson, Lavina Fielding, 4, 37,
    271–74
Anderson, Robert D., 4
Anderson family, 25–27
angel Moroni, 121, 124–27, 129, 133
anointings, 49
anthropology of religion, 3, 18–21
anti-bigamy act, 255–56

Anton, Charles, 127–28
anxiety, 269, 272, 286
apostasy, 49–50, 131, 133–36, 257,
    268–69, 272, 285–86
apostles, 45, 143
Apostles of Jesus, 190–93, 262–63
Arrington, Leonard J., 7–8, 322
Articles of Faith, 55, 84
aspersion, 59
assignments, 209–10, 287,
    291, 294–95
assimilation, 225, 227
atonement of Christ, 30–31, 35, 49,
    182, 186, 190, 274
authority, 16, 23, 134–35
autobiography, 120
auxiliaries, 48–49, 77, 287

Ballard, M. Russell, 204
Bancroft, Herbert Howe, 181
baptism of the dead, 27, 39–40, 43,
    175–77, 250, 258, 309
baptism ordinance
  Aaronic priesthood, 38, 59
  age of accountability, 36–37,
    53, 56, 104–6
  conversions, 58, 60
  CTR (Choose the Right), 96
  culture as choice, 77
  as gateway to immortality
    in Heaven, 90
  identity construction, 225
  immersion, 57–60, **61**, 62
  Mayne family, 53–58
  Melchizedek priesthood, 55, 59
  missionary work, 222–23
  plan of salvation, 55–56, 58, 106
  as rite of passage, 53, 58–59,
    75, 103, 176
  rites of intensification, 182
  schema analysis, 59–60, **61**
  Smith baptizes Cowdery, 131

See also baptism of the dead;
      confirmation ordinance
Barnes, Kent, 297–99
Beach, Virginia, 303–7
Beehives, 38, 150–51
Bell, Justin, 57, 63, 65–67, 294–97, 317
Bennion, Dean, 137–38
Bennion, Lowell S., 236–38
Benson, Ezra Taft, 8, 13, 15,
      17–18, 208, 312
Bernard, H. Russell, 11
B. H. Roberts Society, 271
Bible, 130
Bigler, David L., 10
Big Love, 262
birth, 35, 43, 79, 109–10, 309
birthright Saints, 226
bishops
   as best job in the world, 297–99
   bishop's storehouse, 288–89,
      291–92, 311
   as calling, 63, 66, 293–95
   church discipline, 257
   church organizational structure, 25,
      46, 63
   common judge, 277, 302–3
   disciplinary councils, 270, 277–78
   fast and testimony Sunday, 293
   hold a calling, 45
   marriage counseling, 304
   ordination, 63
   Perpetual Education
      Fund (PEF), 314
   priesthood executive council (PEC),
      295–96
   recommends, 295
   relief society sisters, 310–11
   role of, 294–97
   sacrament meetings, 295
   social identities, 294–95
   temple marriage, 256–57
   as village elders, 64

   as volunteers, 48
   ward bishop, 143, 145–46, 254
   welfare work, 304
   worthiness interviews, 202–4,
      258, 277
   young adult leadership, **149**
Bitton, Davis, 8
Blazers, 38
blended families, 259–61
blessing of children, 35
Book of Abraham, 101–2, 119, 130
Book of Mormon
   angel Moroni, 126
   commentaries on, 12
   curriculum materials, **86**
   distribution, 229
   *New Approaches to the Book of
      Mormon*, 268–69
   orthodoxy wars, 273
   publication of, 131–33
   sealing, 174
   senior primary, 119–20
   testimonies, 131
   translation of gold tablets, 129–30
   translation to other languages, 212
Book of Moses, 101–2, 119, 130
born in the covenant, 26, 36, 43
boundary-defining instruments,
      285–86
Bountiful, Utah, 65, 171
branches, 63, 65
Breakwell, Glynis M., 28–29, 156
brethren, 47, 143
Brigham Young University, 271, 300
A Bright Ray of Hope, 315
Brodie, Fawn M., 4
Buerger, David John, 174–75, 187
Building a Relationship of Trust (BRT),
      217–19
building blocks, 20
Bullock, Thomas, 324
burning testimony, 41

Bushman, Claudia, 11
Bushman, Richard Lyman, 4,
  123–24, 130

callings
  age grades, 293
  assignments, 294
  auxiliaries, 287
  bishops, 63, 66, 293–95
  church leadership, 66
  church organizational structure, 293
  counselors, 146
  definitions of, 287
  gender roles, 235–36, 293
  high priests, 45, 293
  hold a calling, 45, 48–49
  identity construction, 303
  laying-on-of-hands, 287
  magnified, 300
  mobility, 303
  priesthood authority, 287
  primary teacher, 85, 97–98
  relief society sisters, 296–97
  seventies, 45, 293
  social identities, 293–94
  Sunday school, 66, 293
  temple marriage, 254
  worthiness interviews, 141, 236
  See also missionary work
canneries, 238, 288–90, 291
Carmack, John K., 315
Caughey, John L., 4, 28–29, 156
celestial glory, **31**, 50
celestial kingdom, 274, 278–79
celestial marriage. *See* temple marriage
celestial room, 185, 194–96, 259
celibacy, 42
Charles, John D., 187
chastity ethic
  disciplinary councils, 270
  endowments, 192
  For the Strength of Youth, 160–65

gays and lesbians, 166–67
Mormon values, 139, 170
New Era magazine, 160
same-sex relationship, 44
worthiness, 39, 202–3, 257
children
  age grade characteristics of, 99–100
  age of accountability, 36–37
  baptism ordinance, 53, 58, 60, **61**
  born in the covenant, 36
  children of record, 76, 226, 251
  confirmation ordinance, 57–58
  early childhood, 36
  family home evenings, 74
  Joseph Smith as, 106
  later childhood, 37–38
  naming and blessing ordinance, 76
  and prayer, 111–13
  pre-mortal life (preexistence), 78–80
  primary exercises, 82
  sealing, 259, 261
  as sign of adult identity, 299
  spiritual awareness, 108–18
  tithing, 100
  young adulthood, 38–39
  See also primary; spirit children
Children's Songbook, 56, 81–82
choir director, 66
Choose the Right (CTR). *See* CTR
  (Choose the Right)
Christianity, 23–24
Christiansen, C. C. A., 41
Christofferson, D. Todd, 330
church discipline, 49–50, 257. *See also*
  disciplinary councils
Church Educational System (CES),
  159–60
Church News, 12
church organizational structure
  bishops, 25, **46**, 63–64
  callings, 293
  priesthood authority, 66–67, 143

primary, 77
senior primary, 131–33, 136
top-down structure, 302
triadic social structure, 315–16
See also first presidency; quorum
   of the twelve Apostles; seventies;
   stakes; wards
City of Zion, 64
civil law, 107
civil marriage
   as government function, 255–56
   investigators, 43
   Jensen marriage, 253–57
   life plan, 51
   revelation, 266
   and sexual activity, 166, 274
   for time only, 254, 264
   Vernon marriage, 260
   Welch family, 258–59
   and worthiness, 42
Clayton, William, 52, 324
clean water projects, 313
cognitive development, 118
cognitive/emotional dynamics, 286
Colesville, New York, 131
commercial laundry, 292
commitment pattern. *See* conversions
common consent, 287
common judge, 277, 302–3
companion rule, 212–14
compassionate service, 307–11
conceptual core, 186–87, 219, 222–23
confession, 202, 257
confirmation ordinance
   age of accountability, 37, 104–6
   children, 57–58
   CTR (Choose the Right), 96
   culture as choice, 77
   fast and testimony Sunday, 35, 58
   identity construction, 58–59, 75, 225
   laying-on-of-hands, 58, 60, **61**, 62
   ordinances of the gospel, 35, 37

plan of salvation, 106
   as rite of passage, 58–59, 75,
      103, 176
   schema analysis, 60, **61**
   See also baptism ordinance;
      Holy Ghost
congregations, 171, 173
consent decision, 225–29, 251–52
consequences, 107–8
continuing revelation, 22, 24, 134
conversions
   Aaronic priesthood, 143
   agency, 233–34, 240
   assimilation, 225
   baptism ordinance, 58, 60
   Bettadapur conversion, 242–51
   commitment pattern, 215, 223, 234,
      237–38
   consent decision, 225–29, 251–52
   conversion career, 247
   Cromar conversion, 238–42
   descent model, 251–52
   drop outs, 156–57
   gathering, 227
   under Hinckley presidency, 22
   identity construction, 225–26,
      234–35
   nuclear family, 221, 240
   preaffiliation, 248
   primary teacher, 85
   resolve concern, 215
   Saintmaking, 225–29, 251–52
   schemas (scripts), 234
   seekers, 225
   six discussions, 248, 260
   social identities, 226
   tithing, 240
   Welch conversion, 235–38
   York conversion, 229–34
   See also investigators; missionary
      work
Cook, Eugene R., 137–38

Cook, Joseph V., 209
Cook, Richard E., 315
cooking lessons, 305
Cooper, Rex, 227
council in heaven, 32, 103–5, 107
council of the twelve apostles, 47–48
counselors, 25, 46, 63–64, 76–77,
    145–46, 270
Counterpoint conference, 272–74
Country Club ward, 11, 71–72, 84, 98
covenants of fealty, 263, 266
Cowdery, Oliver, 129–31, 134–35, 262
Creation, 30
creation room, 185, 188–89
cremation, 50, 328
Crystal Heights second ward
    age and gender by religious
        affiliation, 32
    auxiliaries, 48–49
    baptism ordinance, 53–54
    church attendance, 228
    church organizational structure,
        63–65
    demographic profile of, 70–71
    primary, 77
    religious groups in, 26
    research in, 11
    seminary, 159
    street map of, 68, 69
    Williams family, 317–22
    worship attendance in by age, 108
Csordas, Thomas, 62
CTR (Choose the Right)
    accountability, 96–97
    agency, 96, 104
    age of accountability, 104–7
    confirmation ordinance, 96
    curriculum materials, 85, 104–5
    feeling the Spirit, 83, 118
    For the Strength of Youth, 161
    heavenly council, 103–5, 107
    identity construction, 96

junior primary, 77, 96
    normative standards for youth,
        140, 141
    primary, 101–4
    revelation, 107
    senior primary, 123
    spirit children, 104–5
culture, 2–3, 18–21
culture as choice, 30, 77, 169
culture as given, 30, 77, 169
Cumorah hill, 126
curriculum materials, 12, 85–95,
    86, 97, 104–6, 119–21, 208
custodian, 66

dances, 158, 162, 164, 167
D'Andrade, Roy, 30, 59–60
dating pressure, 161–62, 164
Davies, Douglas J., 174, 180
Days of '47, 323
deacons, 38, 143–44, 293
death, 52. See also baptism of the dead
defense of marriage acts (DOMA),
    44–45
descent model, 226–29, 251–52
Deseret Industries (DI), 288, 291–92
Deseret News, 12
Dew, Sheri, 17
Dewsnup, Ralph, 63, 66–67, 183–84
Dialogue, 272
dietary rules, 23
disabilities, 100
discernment, 140, 141
disciplinary councils
    apostasy, 268–69
    bishop's role, 270, 277–78
    boundary-defining instruments,
        285–86
    chastity ethic, 270
    cognitive/emotional dynamics, 286
    disfellowshipment, 270
    endowments, 285

fear, 269, 278, 286

first presidency, 271, 274

group identity, 269

guilt, 269, 286

homosexuality, 281–82

infidelity, 275–78

obedience and, 273

punishment from, 270

quorum of the twelve Apostles, 271

repentance, 270, 281

retrenchment, 269

sexual immorality, 269, 274–78

social control, 269

See also excommunication

discipline, 49–50, 111

disfellowshipment, 50, 270–71, 276, 282

dispensations, 83–84

divided self, 244

divorce, 43–44, 201, 203, 254, 257, 276, 307

Doctrine and Covenants, 12, 86, 119–20, 174, 237, 264

Dollahite, David C., 45

Douglas, Mary, 181

drunk driving, 319–22

Durkheim, Emile, 19, 121

Dutcher, Richard, 199

duty to God, 41

early childhood, 36

elderly, 306–7

elders

bishops as, 64

home teachers, 297

Melchizedek priesthood, 143, 201

missionaries, 143, 197

priesthood executive council (PEC), 296

relief society sisters, 304, 306–7

volunteers, 289

Eller, Jack David, 3, 19–20

Elohim (Heavenly Father). *See* Heavenly Father

Embodiment and Experience, 62

emergency preparedness coordinator, 66

emic/etic models of culture, 2

empowerment, 98

enculturation, 27–35, 225

Encyclopedia of Mormonism, 173, 184–86, 256, 262–63, 277

endowments

Adam and Eve, 184

celestial room, 194–96

chastity ethic, 192

conceptual core, 187

creation room, 188–89

disciplinary councils, 285

females, 42, 258

gender roles, 180

immortality, 195

law of consecration, 193

life plan, 51

marriage, 258

Masonic rites, 175

missionary work, 40, 179–81

new name ceremony, 179, 188, 191

passwords, 186–87

plan of salvation, 40, 50, 184

prayer circle, 193

recommends, 256

rites of anticipation, 183–96

rites of passage, 180, 195

rituals for, 184–86

sealing, 180

telestial room, 190–92

temple garments, 194, 257

temple marriage, 40, 180–81, 257–58, 261, 266–67

temple ordinances, 173

temple work, 49

terrestrial room, 192–93

three-part structure of, 180–81

endowments (*Cont.*)
   washings and anointings, 40, 178–80
   witness couple, 190, 192
   worthiness, 141, 195, 202–4
Ensign magazine, 12, 46n, 120, 294
Erikson, Erik H., 33, **34**, 51,
      138–39, 259
eternal progression, 326–27
ethnicity, 226, 227
ethnography, 2–3, 11–13
Evans, Chad L., 315
Evans, John Henry, 4
exaltation, 51, 309, 325–28
excommunication, 16, 165, 257, 262,
      268–71, 283
executive secretary, 300–302
Expedition magazine, 3
Eyring, Henry B., 47, 329–30

Fairbanks, Bob, 66
Fairbanks, Kathy, 108–9
fallacy of confirming the consequent,
      218
Fall from Grace, 30
"The Family: A Proclamation to the
      World," 43, 221
family home evenings, 72–75, 90–91,
      114, 120, 207
farewell gatherings, 197–200, 204–8,
      283
fast and testimony Sunday, 35, 58, 76,
      292–93, 310–12
fasting, 35
father/child relationship, 87
Faust, Drew Gilpin, 4
Fayette, New York, 132, 134–35
fear, 269, 278, 286
feared identity, 29
feeling the Spirit
   Bettadapur conversion, 247, 248
   CTR (Choose the Right), 83, 118
   Doctrine and Covenants, 237

family home evenings, 73
immersion, 62
inner voice, 94
investigators, 214–15, 217, 224
Jensen marriage, 254
Missionary Training Center (MTC),
      213
missionary work, 237
mortal life, 89–90
posture for prayer, 82–83
prayer circle, 193
spiritual awareness, 114–15, 117–18
testimonies, 37
translation of gold tablets, 130
See also Holy Ghost
fellowshipping, 217
females
   achievement day, 38
   auxiliaries, 48–49
   Beehives, 38
   Counterpoint conference, 272–74
   divorce, 43–44
   endowments, 42, 258
   Laurels, 38
   mate selection, 277
   Merrie Misses, 38
   MIA Maids, 38
   missionary work, 197n
   motherhood as primary role, 38
   polyandry, 261
   single adults, 306–7
   singles' wards, 42
   See also gender roles; relief society
      sisters; young women organization
Ferguson, Isaac C., 311–13
fidelity in marriage, 139, 254, 280
finding, 225
firesides, 137, 158, 199
first counselor, **46**, 316
first presidency
   church organizational structure,
      46, 63

continuing revelation, 134–36
disciplinary councils, 271, 274
For the Strength of Youth, 160
fullness of time, 47
general authorities, 47–48
high priests, 316
homosexuality, 166–67
missionary work, 222
Monson as president, 330
Preach My Gospel, 220
First Resurrection, 328
first vision, 121–24
fitting in, 227
five lessons, 219, 222–23, 233
focus groups, 67
Follett, King, 323–27
forever families, 253, 274, 278–79,
    284–85, 307, 328
forgiveness, 168–69, 318–22
Forgotten Kingdom, 10
For the Strength of Youth, 139,
    160–65, 169
Franklin County, Idaho, 65
Frazer, James, 19
Freud, Sigmund, 33
The Friend magazine, 12, 120
fullness of time, 47, 84
fundamentalist Mormons, 262
funerals, 50–51, 309–10, 320, 323–30

garden room, 185, 189–90
Garvan, Anthony N. B., 4
gathering, 227
Gay Pride parade, 283
Geertz, Clifford, 20, 329–30
gender identity, 44–45
gender roles
    assignments, 287
    callings, 235–36, 293
    Crystal Heights second ward, **32**
    demographic profile Crystal
        Heights, **70**

endowments, 180
funerals, 327
heavenly mother, 105–6
life plan, 30, 51
Melchizedek priesthood, 270, 294
missionaries, 197
missionary work, 12, 41–42, 199, 207
ordination, 169
priesthood authority, 144, 235
primary, 38, 85
religious groups for the Crystal
    Heights Second Neighborhood, **26**
rites of passage, 147
singles' wards, 200–201
washings and anointings, 178–80
Wednesday night activities, 38
welfare work, 289
youth, 154–55
genealogy, 26, 43, 309
general authorities, 46–48
General Authority, 314, 316
General Board, 308
generativity, 259
Gilkey, Carolyn Flatley, 10, 37
goal schema, 81
God. *See* Heavenly Father
godhead, 267
God's Army, 199
Goffman, Irving, 28
gold plates, 121, 125–30, 132
Goodenough, Ward, 2, 28, 97
Goodman, Kristen L., 43, 99–100
Goodwill Industries, 292
Gooren, Henri, 247–48
Grandin, Egbert B., 132
Grant, Jedediah M., **9**
Great Depression, 288, 312
great plan of happiness. *See* plan of
    salvation
Greece, 312
group activity, 84–85
group identity, 62, 269

group membership, 226–29
guilt, 269, 275, 277, 286
Hale, Isaac, 127
Hallowell, A. Irving, 3, 20, **21**
Hammarberg, Melvyn
  background of ethnographic study,
    4–10
  Building a Relationship of Trust
    (BRT), 217–19
  canneries, 288–90
  Expedition magazine, 3
  girls camp field notes, 153–54
  house-to-house survey, 67–68, **69**,
    70–71, 72
  The Indiana Voter, 10
  May obituary, 322–23
  research background, 13, 65
  role-play, 300–302
Harmony, Pennsylvania, 127, 134
Harris, Martin, 127–28, 131
Heavenly Father
  council in heaven, 32
  covenants of fealty, 263
  endowments, 188
  father/child relationship, 87
  and the first presidency, 47
  first vision, 122
  God's name, 3
  Jesus Christ as son, 88, 91–92
  and the living prophet, 22
  prayers to, 74, 89–91, 94
  pre-mortal life (preexistence), 89
  priesthood authority, 145
  Second Resurrection, 328
  Smith visitation, 92–93
  See also plan of salvation
Heavenly Mother, 3, 105–6, 328
hierarchy, 63–64, 77, 145–46, 188,
    293, 297, 299. *See also* church
    organizational structure
high council, 63
Highland High School, 159
Highland stake, 11, 63–65, 68

high priests
  callings, 45, 293
  definitions of, 288
  duties of, 25
  first presidency, 316
  home storage production, 291
  home teachers, 297
  Melchizedek priesthood, 288
  priesthood executive council (PEC),
    296
  relief society sisters, 304
  volunteers, 289
Hinckley, Gordon B., 11, 13–15, 17, 22,
    47, 207–8, 313–16, 329–30
Hinduism, 242–51
History of Utah, 181
HIV, 281
hold a calling, 45, 48–49
Holy Ghost, 37, 56–58, 60, 62, 83,
    92–95, 115, 129
homeless, 291–92, 308
homemaking lessons, 305–6
homemaking meeting, 309
home storage production, 291
home teachers, 25, 38, 66, 287,
    294, 297, 308
home visits, 289
homosexuality, 165–66, 257, 279–82
Hopewell Baptist Church, 229
Horton, Robin, 20
house of order, 329–30
house-to-house survey, 67–68, **69**,
    70–71, 72
humanitarian services, 22, 52, 311–13
Hunter, Howard W., 13–18, 274
Hyde, Kenneth E., 100
Hyde, Orson, **8**

I Am a Child of God, 80–81
ideal identity, 29
identification card, 256
Identity and the Life Cycle, **34**, 51
identity construction

adolescence, 33, 138–39

baptism and confirmation ordinances, 58–59, 75, 225

callings, 303

consent decision, 252

conversions, 225–26, 234–35

CTR (Choose the Right), 96

enculturation and, 27–35

marriage and, 42

missionaries, 217

missionary work, 223–24

Mormons, 51–52, 138

Mormon youth, 156, 169–70

pre-mortal life (preexistence), 33

primary, 87

Saintmaking, 228

schemas (scripts), 60

sexual orientation, 165–70

temple marriage, 253, 259

threatened identity, 28–29, 156

worthiness, 236

immersion. *See* baptism ordinance

immortality, 33, 188, 195. *See also* post-mortal life

immortals, 131

incest, 270

The Indiana Voter, 10

indifferent identity, 29

infancy, 76

infidelity, 275–80

initiatory ordinances, 178–80

inner voice, 94

institutionalization of charisma, 18

interregnum, 329–30

Introducing Anthropology of Religion: Culture to the Ultimate, 19

Introduction to Mormonism, 174

intuition, 79

investigators, 43, 60, **61**, 214–15, 217–20, 222, 224, 229. *See also* conversions; missionary work

Ipsen, Cathy, 78–80

Jagger, Mick, 137

James, William, 19, 21, 226, 244

Jensen, Sally, 73, 76–77

Jensen marriage, 253–57

Jessee, Barbara, 76

Jessee, Dean C., 8, 122

Jessop, Craig, 323

Jesus Christ

Apostles of, 131

as creator of earth, 89–90, 101

endowments, 188

as exemplar, 101–4

First Resurrection, 328

first vision, 122

and John the Baptist, 92

keys of the priesthood, 145–46

and the living prophet, 22

meridian of time, 83

Mormon relationship to, 3

New Testament, 119

parent/child relationship, 88, 91–92

posture for prayer, 83, 91

pre-mortal life (preexistence), 81

priesthood authority, 295

as redeemer, 32, 49, 56

temple marriage, 264

See also atonement of Christ

John the Baptist, 56, 59, 92, 131, 262

Joseph (protector of Mary and Jesus), 92

Joseph Smith: Rough Stone Rolling, 4

journal records, 12, 220

junior companion, 216

junior primary

age grades, 76–77

agency and, 105

age of accountability, 36–37, 96, 106–7

CTR (Choose the Right), 77, 96

curriculum materials, **86**, 97

exercises for, 81–82

heavenly mother, 105–6

Jesus Christ as exemplar, 101–4

prophetic dispensations, 84

Kearney, Michael, 3
Kelly, Gordon, 4
keys, 145–46
keys of the kingdom of heaven, 184, 263
Kimball, Heber C., **8**, **9**
Kimball, Spencer W., 18, 33–36
Kincaid, Janet M., 173
King Follett discourse, 323–27
kin networks, 26
Kuhn, Thomas S., 23

languages, 113–14, 118, 212
later childhood, 37–38
Laurels, 38, 151
law of consecration, 193
law of sacrifice, 190
laying-on-of-hands, 58, 60, **61**, 62, 287
LDS (Latter-day Saints). *See* Mormons
Lee, Harold B., 18, 93–94
Lefevre, Don, 14
Leonard, Glen M., 8, 72
letter of acceptance, 210
Levi-Strauss, Claude, 121
Liahona magazine, 12, 120
lifecycle, 33, **34**
life plan
    age-adjusted, **39**
    civil marriage, 51
    as cultural model, 3, 30
    death and, 52
    ethnographic study of, 2–3
    gender roles and, 30, 51
    humanitarian services, 52
    as model of human development, 20
    obedience, 51
    plan of salvation, 30–31
    schemas (scripts), 30, 51
    temple ordinances, 51–52
    worldview orientations, 20
life worlds, **31**, 32–33
liminal purity, 178, 181, 330
liminal rites, 59

limiting cases, 269, 285
living prophet, 24
Long, John V., **9**
Long, Sarah Ann Burbage, **9**
Lucifer (Satan)
    conversion opposition, 234
    endowment ceremonies, 189–92
    vs. Jesus, 96
    plan of salvation, **31**, 94
    as redeemer, 32–33
    sin, 49
    war in heaven, 33, 96, 102–4
Luschin, Immo, 58
Luther, Martin, 133
Lynnwood Washington stake, 11,
    71–72
Lyon, John, **9**

magic underwear. *See* temple garments
Major, William W., **8**
males, 38, 43–44, 48. *See also* gender
    roles; priesthood authority;
    scouting program; young men
    organization
Malone, Patrick, 4
marriage
    blended families, 259–61
    children as sign of adult
        identity, 299
    counseling, 304
    endowments, 258
    identity construction, 42
    and infidelity, 275–77
    post-mortal life, 50
    preferential endogamy, 234
    and sexual activity, 274, 279
    as temple ordinance, 42
    See also civil marriage; temple
        marriage
Mary, mother of Jesus, 91
Masonic rites, 174–75, 194
mate selection, 277

Maudsley, Sutcliffe, **6**
Mauss, Armand L., 10, 174, 180, 269
May, Cheryll, 63–64
May, Dean Lowe, 63–64, 227, 322–23
McDannel, Colleen, 180
McKay, David O., 17–18, 173
measles vaccinations, 313
meetinghouses, 35, 64
Melchizedek priesthood
  age grades, 12
  baptism ordinance, 55, 59
  callings, 294
  church discipline, 257
  elders, 143, 201
  excommunication, 270
  funerals, 50
  higher priesthood, 142–43
  high priests quorum, 288
  home teachers, 25, 308–9
  house of order, 329–30
  *Melchizedek Priesthood Leadership
    Handbook*, 1
  missionaries, 221
  naming and blessing ordinance,
    35–36
  obedience to spiritual authority, 24
  ordinances of the gospel, 35
  ordination of the dead, 177
  ordination to, 40
  restoration, 263
  rites of passage, 177
  sealing, 262–67
  senior primary, 133
  Smith as first, 131
  solemn assembly, 15
  temple ordinances, 194
  terrestrial room, 192–93
  See also Aaronic priesthood
mentors, 34
meridian of time, 83
Merrie Misses, 38
Merton, Robert K., 2–3

Metcalfe, Brent, 268
Methodists, 226
Mexico, 238
MIA Maids, 38, 151
Michael (Adam), 189
The Miracle of Forgiveness, 33
missionaries, 22–23, 143, 197, 217,
    220–21. *See also* missionary work
Missionary Guide, 197, 214–16
Missionary Training Center (MTC), 41,
    210–14, 216–17, 224, 300
missionary work
  Aaronic priesthood, 208
  age grades, 197n
  assignments, 209–10
  burning testimony, 41
  and church growth, 225
  commitment pattern, 215, 223, 234
  conceptual core, 219, 222–23
  curriculum materials, 208
  endowments, 40, 179–81
  farewell gatherings, 197–200, 204–8
  feeling the Spirit, 237
  finding, 225
  firesides, 199
  first presidency, 222
  five lessons, 219, 222–23
  gender roles, 12, 41–42, 199, 207
  God's Army, 199
  identity construction, 223–24
  junior companion, 216
  letter of acceptance, 210
  Missionary Guide, 214
  Missionary Training Center (MTC),
    201
  *Mormon Passage: A Missionary
    Chronicle*, 12
  opportunities and effects, 199–200
  Perpetual Education Fund (PEF), 52,
    311, 313–16
  Preach My Gospel, 197, 219–24
  primary, 77, 199, 208

proselytizing, 215, 234
putting in papers, 201–2
raising the bar, 204–5, 221
recommends, 202–4
recruitment, 200–201, 204–5
restoration, 221–24
role of in conversions, 232–34
scouting program, 208
six discussions, 248
taking the lessons, 232
teachers, 216–17
teaching by the Spirit, 220–22
temple marriage, 179
voluntary nature of, 199–200
worthiness, 201–8, 221
See also conversions; investigators;
    missionaries
missions, 65
mission statement, 1
mobility, 299, 303
modular, 20–21
Monson, Thomas S., 13–14, 47, 52,
    197n, 329–30
moral agency, 30
Mormon History Association, 322–23
*Mormon Passage: A Missionary
    Chronicle*, 12
Mormons
  birthright Saints, 226
  and Christianity, 23–24
  church discipline, 49–50
  conceptual core, 186
  cultural change and stability, 22–24
  divorce, 307
  fundamentalist Mormons, 262
  Hinckley ordained as president, 17
  house of order, 329–30
  humanitarian services, 311–13
  leadership of, 13–18
  life plan, 51–52
  marriage statistics, 307
  The Mormons, 7

Mormon Tabernacle Choir, 329
Mormon Youth Chorus, 15
multigenerational family, 329–30
National Study of Youth and Religion
    (NSYR), 160
new Israel, 262
normative standards for youth, **140**
participation in, 236
Pearl of Great Price, 121
pioneer phase, 10
priesthood authority, 144
revitalization movements, 183
same-sex relationship, 44–45
sexual immorality, 274
spiritual awareness, 114
standard works, 136
temple work, 49
testimonies, 10
theocracy, 24
worldview orientations, 3, 89, 92
worldwide numbers, 316, 330
See also church organizational
    structure; missionary work; Smith,
    Joseph, Jr.
mortal life
  age-adjusted, **39**
  celibacy, 42
  feeling the Spirit, 89–90
  life plan, 51
  passing through the veil, 35, 109–10
  plan of salvation, **31**, 101–2
  as testing, 33, 117, 168–69
Moses, 87–88, 135
motherhood, 38, 42, 154, 170
multigenerational family, 329–30
murder, 270
Murphey, Murray G., 4
music, 162, 164
mutual, 157–58
Mutual Improvement
    Association, 119
The Mysteries of Godliness, 174

naming and blessing ordinance, 35–36, 76, 206–7

Nash, Marcus Bell, 300–301

National Study of Youth and Religion (NSYR), 160

Native Americans, 312

natural disaster, 291, 312–13, 316

Nauvoo, 5, 175, 227, 264, 323–27

Nelson, Russell M., 274

neonatal resuscitation training, 313

Nephite prophets, 126

New Era magazine, 12, 120, 160

new Israel, 262

new name ceremony, 179, 188, 191

New Testament, **86**, 119–20

No Man Knows My History: The Life of Joseph Smith, 4

normative orientations, 21

nuclear family

  as basic social unit, 26, 329

  blended families, 259–61

  conversions, 221, 240, 244, 248

  "The Family: A Proclamation to the World," 221

  family home evenings, 72–75

  fast and testimony Sunday, 76

  forever families, 253

  homosexuality, 280–81

  law of obedience, 190

  parents responsible for welfare of children, 78

  plan of salvation, 31

  and prayer, 112–13

  spiritual knowledge, 95

  Strengthening Our Families: An In-Depth Look at the Proclamation on the Family, 45

  temple marriage, 259

  Welch family, 258–59

nursery, 77, 80, 85

obedience

  and agency, 108, 271–74

  CTR (Choose the Right), 107

  disciplinary councils, 273

  hierarchy of three, 189–90

  life plan, 51

  normative standards for youth, 141

  plan of salvation, 33, 102–3

  post-mortal life, 328

  to spiritual authority, 24

  worthiness, 39, 104–5, 202

obituary, 322–23

object orientation, 21

O'Dea, Thomas F., 7

Old Testament, **86**, 88, 119–20, 263

Olsen, Steven L., 121

Olympics, 11, 13

orderliness, 305

ordinance of endowment. *See* endowments

ordinances of exaltation, 183–84

ordinances of salvation, 183

ordinances of the gospel, 1, 16, 35, 39, 49, 183. See also *individual ordinances*

ordination

  Aaronic priesthood, 38–39, 143–45, 147, 235

  bishops, 63

  deacons, 144

  of the dead, 177

  gender roles, 169

  hold a calling, 45

  priesthood authority, 287

organizational structure. *See* church organizational structure

orthodoxy wars, 271, 273

Ortner, Sherry, 20

Oswalt, Wendell H., 51

outer darkness, **31**

Packer, Boyd K., 330

Page, Hiram, 134–35

Palmyra, New York, 122, 132
Paradise, 50, 328
parent/child relationship, 88, 91–92
passing through the veil, 35, 79–80,
    109–10
passwords, 186–87
patriarchs, 45, 143, 261–62, 264
P-Day, 214
Pearl of Great Price, 12, 88, 119–26
Pearson, Don M., 277
Pennsylvania Philadelphia Mission, 11
A People's History of Utah, 322
Perpetual Education Fund (PEF), 22, 52,
    311, 313–16
personal authority, 273
personal identity, 29, 156–57, 270, 274
personhood, 51
Persuitte, David, 4
Petersen, Mark E., 7–8
Philadelphia mission, 72, 208–9
Phoenix East stake, 72
Pioneer Day, 232
pioneer phase, 10, 227
plan of mercy. *See* plan of salvation
plan of redemption. *See* plan of
    salvation
plan of salvation
    agency, 32–35, 97
    atonement of Christ, 30–31, 186
    baptism ordinance, 55–56, 58, 106
    celestial glory, **31**
    conceptual core, 186–87
    confirmation ordinance, 106
    council in heaven, 103–4
    Cromar conversion, 241
    endowments, 40, 50, 184
    five lessons, 223
    genealogy, 309
    heavenly council, 103–4
    life plan, 30–31
    life worlds, **31**
    Lucifer (Satan), 94

nuclear family, 31
obedience, 33, 102–3
post-mortal life, **31**, 50, 328
pre-mortal life (preexistence), **31**,
    32–33, 89
primary exercises, 82
scriptural basis of, 101–2
Second Resurrection, 328
Smith revelation, 263–64
plural marriages
    Abrahamic descent, 227
    anti-bigamy act, 255–56
    apostasy, 272
    and divorce, 43–44
    Doctrine and Covenants, 264
    end of, 10, 227
    excommunication, 262
    history of, 261–62
    revelation about, 23
    worthiness interviews, 203n, 256
polyandry, 261
polygamy, 261
polysemy, 59, 182–83
popular culture, 138–44, 155–65
post-mortal life
    age-adjusted, **39**
    agency, 328
    funerals, 50–51
    immortality, 33
    life plan, 51
    marriage, 42
    paradise, 50
    plan of salvation, **31**, 50, 328
    primary curriculum, 95
    quest for glory, 35
    spirit prison, 50, 328
    spirit world life, 327–28
    worthiness, 35
poverty, 313
Pratt, Orson, **8**
Pratt, Parley P., **8**
prayer

Adam and Eve, 191
callings and, 287
family home evenings, 74, 114
feeling the Spirit, 118
as means of communicating with
    Heavenly Father, 74, 89–91, 94
posture for prayer, 82–83, 91, 111–13,
    213
prayer circle, 193
pre-mortal life (preexistence), 112
primary, 82
Preach My Gospel, 197, 219–24, 233
preaffiliation, 248
preexistence. *See* pre-mortal life
    (preexistence)
preferential endogamy, 234
premarital sex, 274
pre-mortal life (preexistence)
age-adjusted, **39**
agency, 53
Cromar conversion, 241
identity construction, 33
life plan, 51
plan of salvation, **31**, 32–33, 89
and prayer, 112
spirit children, 78–81, 89, 107
True to the Faith, 32–33
York conversion, 233–34
presentation of self, 28
priesthood authority
Abrahamic descent, 227
apostasy, 269
assignments, 287
baptism of the dead, 176–77
baptism ordinance, **61**
bishop's role, 295
callings and, 287
church organizational structure, 143
confirmation ordinance, 59, 226
gender roles, 144, 235
hierarchy, 145–46, 297
from Jesus Christ, 295

John the Baptist, 56, 262
keys for, 145–46
missionaries, 234
ordinances of the gospel, 287
orthodoxy wars, 273
Pearl of Great Price, 121
*Priesthood and Church
    Government*, 58
priesthood executive council (PEC),
    295–97
restoration, 262
sealing, 174–75
senior primary, 133
Smith visitation, 131, 134–35
standard works, 136
temple marriage, 254, 266
temple ordinances, 263
worthiness, 202
See also Aaronic priesthood;
    first presidency; Melchizedek
    priesthood
priests, 38, 48, 143. *See also* priesthood
    authority
primary
age grades, 12, 76, 85, **86**, 87
agency and, 107–8
auxiliaries, 77
as calling, 66, 293
church organizational structure, 77
CTR (Choose the Right), 101–4
culture as given, 77
curriculum materials, 80–81, 85–95,
    105–6
early childhood, 36
goal schema, 81
group activity, 84–85
identity construction, 87
missionary work, 77, 199, 208
organization and content, 76–84
Primary Handbook, 38, 80–81
Proclamation on the Family, 100
relief society sisters, 48–49

primary(*Cont.*)
  sharing time, 82–83
  spirit children, 87–89
  spiritual awareness, 114
  Sunbeams, 80–81
  teachers, 84–85, 97–98
  testimonies, 10, 95
  worldview orientations, 85, 90
  See also junior primary; senior
    primary
privacy, 282
probation, 50, 270, 275
Proclamation on the Family, 44, 100
prophets, 13–18, 22, 83–84, 126, 273.
    See also Smith, Joseph, Jr.
proselytizing, 215, 234
Protestant fundamentalism, 269
Provo, Utah, 65, 201, 210
proxies, 173, 176–78, 180, 188, 258, 263,
    309
purification, 59
purity, 139, 162, 164
putting in papers, 201–2, 209

Quakers, 226
quest for glory
  divorce, 44
  eternal progression, 326–27
  exaltation, 51, 328
  kingdoms of glory, 24
  post-mortal life, 35
  Second Resurrection, 328
  temple work, 49
  this great work, 1–2
  See also plan of salvation
Quinn, Michael, 23, 268
quorum of the twelve Apostles
  church organizational structure, 46,
    63, 143, 316
  disciplinary councils, 271
  interregnum, 329–30
  leadership of, 18
  marriage, 44

pictured, **8**
Preach My Gospel, 220
selecting a new senior living apostle,
  13–18
tough-love model, 274

Radin, Paul, 19
raising the bar, 204–5, 221
real identity, 29
rebaptism, 270
recommends
  appointment for, 301
  bishops, 295
  endowments, 256
  funerals, 327
  missionary work, 202–4
  temple marriage, 256, 258
  temple ordinances, 40, 256
  three purpose for, 256–57
  worthiness interviews, 40, 141–42,
    202–4, 236
recruitment, 204–5
redemption, 49
Redfield, Robert, 3
relief society sisters
  age grades, 12, 41–42
  auxiliaries, 48–49
  bishops, 310–11
  as calling, 293–94, 303
  compassionate service, 307–11
  elders, 306–7
  fast and testimony Sunday, 310–11
  females' organization, 38
  funerals, 50, 309–10
  genealogy, 309
  high priests, 304
  homemaking lessons, 305–6
  home storage production, 291
  priesthood executive council (PEC),
    296–97
  primary, 48–49
  solemn assembly, 14
  Sunday meetings, 157

visiting teachers, 297, 308–10

volunteers, 289

religion, definitions of, 19–20

Religion in Childhood and Adolescence, 100

religious education, 158–60

renewal interviews, 257

repentance, 49–50, 142, 168–69, 202, 257, 270, 281–82

Research Information Division (RID), 67, 99–100

Research Methods in Anthropology, 11

resolve concern, 215

restitution, 49, 202, 257

restoration, 133–36, 221–24, 262, 270

resurrection, 35, 50, 248, 326–28

retrenchment, 269

revelation

access to, 18, 135–36

civil marriage, 266

continuing revelation, 22, 24, 134

CTR (Choose the Right), 107

and the living prophet, 22–23

plan of salvation, 263–64

Smith as first prophet, 132

translation of gold tablets, 130

washings and anointings, 23

worthiness interviews, 257

revelator, 47

reverence, 82

revitalization movements, 23–24, 52, 182–83

revivals, 229–30

Richards, Willard, **8, 9**, 324

righteousness, 256

rites of anticipation, 183–96

rites of incorporation, 59

rites of intensification, 182–83, 184

rites of passage, 60, 144–45, 147, 176–84, 195. *See also* baptism ordinance; confirmation ordinance

rites of separation, 59

rites of transition, 59

rituals, 175–76, 329

Romney, Mitt, 13

Rudd, Glen L., 287–88

Sabbath, 240, 254, 309

sacrament meetings, 295–96

Saintmaking, 225–29, 251–52

Saley, Dorothy, 307–11

Salt Lake City, 14, 64–65, **172**, 259, 288

Salt Lake City Tribune, 268–69

Salt Lake Highland stake center, 320

same-sex relationship, 44–45, 51, 71, 274, 279

Satan *See* Lucifer (Satan)

schemas (scripts)

agency-obedience-worthiness schema, 103–4, 107–8

conversions, 234

definitions of, 60

family home evenings, 74

goal schema, 81

identity construction, 60

life plan, 30, 51

prophetic dispensations, 83–84

schema analysis, 59–60, **61**

translation of gold tablets, 130

scouting program

Aaronic priesthood, 150, 169–70

auxiliaries, 48

bishop's role, 296

as calling, 66

duty to God, 41

gender roles, 38

missionary work, 208

Wednesday night activities, 157–58

young men organization, 148, **149**, 150

scriptures, 12, 37–39, 166

sealing

Aaronic priesthood, 262

baptism of the dead, 176–77

sealing (*Cont.*)
  children, 259, 261
  endowments, 180
  Melchizedek priesthood, 262–67
  priesthood authority, 174–75
  proxies, 263
  recommends, 256
  temple marriage, 258–59, 266
  washings and anointings, 180
Sea Trek, 322
second counselor, **46**
Second Resurrection, 328
seekers, 225
seer stone, 130, 134
self-appraisal, 269
self-control, 111, 116–17, 285
self-esteem, 158
self-recognition, 282–83
self-reliance, 289, 312–13
self-sufficiency, 289
self-talk, 94
seminary, 39, 41, 48, 147,
    158–60, 208–9
senior primary
  age grades, 76–77
  church organizational structure,
    131–33, 136
  CTR (Choose the Right), 123
  curriculum materials, 85, **86**, 119–21
  exercises for, 81–82
  foundational stories, 131–34
  priesthood authority, 133
  sharing time, 84
  standard works, 136
  testimonies, 37–38
  translation of gold tablets, 128–30,
    133
  Valiant, 77, 119
  visions of Joseph Smith, 121–26
September six, 273
seventies
  callings, 45, 293

church organizational structure, **46**,
    63, 143, 316
  general authorities, 48
  Perpetual Education
    Fund (PEF), 315
  solemn assembly, 14–15
seventy, 14–15
sexual abuse, 280
sexual immorality, 269, 274–78, 285
sexuality, 44–45, 139, 155, 165–70, 279
sexual orientation, 165–70
sexual sins, 49–50
sharing time, 82–83
Sharon, Vermont, 122
Shepherd, Gordon and Gary, 12, 24
Shipps, Jan, 63–64, 225–29, 251–52
single adults, 199, 284, 306–7
single-parent families, 100
singles' wards, 42, 200, 307
sins, 49–50, 165, 168–69, 204, 257, 285
sisters (missionaries), 197
sisters of charity, 308
six discussions, 215–16, 248, 260
Smith, Alvin, 127
Smith, Christian, 160
Smith, Emma Hale, **6**, 127, 129, 264
Smith, George A., **9**
Smith, Hyrum, **8, 9**
Smith, Joseph Fielding, 18
Smith, Joseph, Jr.
  Abrahamic descent, 226–27, 263
  Articles of Faith, 84
  autobiography, 120
  baptism of the dead, 177
  biography of, 4
  childhood of, 106
  City of Zion, 64
  establishes his church, 13
  as false prophet, 325
  as first prophet, 132
  first vision, 121–24
  King Follett discourse, 323–27

marriage to Emma, 127
as Mason, 174–75
Melchizedek priesthood, 131
murder of, 7, 324
nature of God, 325–26
Pearl of Great Price, 12, 88, 119–26
pictured, 5, **8, 9, 265**
plural marriages, 263–64
priesthood authority, 131, 134–35
primary curriculum, 92–93
prophetic dispensations, 83–84
restoration, 133–36, 262
translation of gold tablets, 125–30,
 133
See also Pearl of Great Price
Smith, Lucy Mack, 4, 126, 128
The Smith Family, 278–85
Smoot, Reed, 23
Snow, Lorenzo, **9**
social control, 269
social identities, 28–29, 156–57, 226,
 278–79, 293–95, 315–16
social relations, 113–14
Social Services, 288
social stigma, 273
solemn assembly, 13–18
Soul-Searching, 160
spatial-temporal orientation, 21
spirit children, 78–81, 87–89, 103–5,
 107, 112. *See also* passing through
 the veil
spirit prison, 50, 328
spirit self, 43, 51, 96–97
spiritual awareness, 108–18
spiritual knowledge, 95
spirit world life, **31**, 35, 49, 327–28
sports, 157–58
stake president, 203–4, 270,
 293, 298–99
stakes
 baptism ordinance, 177
 canneries, 289

church organizational structure,
 63–64
definition of, 11, 63
firesides, 158
high priests quorum, 288
Melchizedek priesthood, 25, 143
patriarchs, 143
temple marriage, 254
worldwide numbers, 65
standardized curriculum, 86–87
standards day, 137–38, 167
standard works, 136, 158–59
stimulants, 139
Stoal, Josiah, 127
*Strengthening Our Families: An In-Depth
 Look at the Proclamation on the
 Family*, 45
suicide, 279
Sunbeams, 77, 80–81, 85
Sunday meetings, 157
Sunday school, 12, 38, 48, 66, 120,
 199, 293
support payments, 257
Supreme Court, 256
Susquehanna River, 131

Taber, Susan Buhler, 35, 38
taking the lessons, 232
*Talking with the Children of God:
 Prophecy and Transformation in a
 Radical Religious Group*, 24
Talmage, James E., 177
Tarbill, Squire, 127
teachers, 38, 84–85, 97–98, 143, 216–17,
 293–94, 297, 308–10. *See also*
 home teachers
teaching by the Spirit, 220–22
telecenter, 212
telephone trees, 316
telestial glory, **31**
telestial room, 185, 190–92
temple clothing, 23

temple garments, 50, 178–80, 190, 194, 257, 270, 327

temple marriage

Achieving a Celestial Marriage: Student Manual, 42

born in the covenant, 26, 36, 43

callings, 254

endowments, 40, 180–81, 257–58, 261, 266–67

"The Family: A Proclamation to the World," 43

fidelity in marriage, 254, 280

godhead, 267

as highest form of marriage, 167, 263

identity construction, 253, 259

and infidelity, 275–78

Jensen marriage, 254

life plan, 51

missionary work, 179

naming and blessing ordinance, 206–7

nuclear family, 259

and plural marriage, 263–64

priesthood authority, 254, 266

recommends, 256, 258

sealing, 258–59, 266

social identities, 278–79

temple ordinances, 42

for time and eternity, 254, 256

Veil of the Temple, 259

worthiness, 254, 256–57, 280

See also forever families

temple ordinances

endowments, 173

genealogy and, 26–27

life plan, 51–52

meaning and purpose, 171–76

ordinances of exaltation, 183–84

priesthood authority, 194, 263

proxies, 173

recommends, 40, 256

as rite of passage, 176–83

temple ordinances, 264

washings and anointings, 178–81

worthiness, 173, 263

See also baptism of the dead; temple marriage

Temple Square, 14, 25, 64

terrestrial glory, **31**

terrestrial room, 185, 192–93

testimonies, 10, 37–38, 95, 131, 182, 198–99, 239–42

testing, 33, 168–69, 189

theocracy, 24

this great work, 1–2

threatened identity, 28–29

"Times and Seasons," 324

Tingey, Steven, 65, 77, 82

tithing

children, 100

church discipline, 257

conversions, 240

fast and testimony Sunday, 293

For the Strength of Youth, 164

normative standards for youth, 141

worthiness, 39, 155, 202–3, 257

tough-love model, 274

trainers, 216–17

transgressors, 270

translation of gold tablets, 125–30, 133

triadic social structure, 315–16

true messengers, 190–93

True to the Faith, 30–33, 37, 270, 292

Turner, Victor, 181, 329–30

Uchtdorf, Dieter F., 47

unconditional love, 274

"Understanding Homosexual Behavior," 281

Uniform System for Teaching the Gospel, 215

United States Information Agency, 10

University of Pennsylvania, 4, 13, 67

University of Utah, 322

unwed mothers, 308
Urim and Thummim, 125, 127,
   129–30
Utah Symphony Chorus, 323

Valdez, Andrew, 321–22
Valiant, 77, **86**
van der Elst, Dirk, 18, 30
van Gennep, Arnold, 53, 58–59,
   180–81
Van Wagoner, Richard, 268
The Varieties of Religious Experience, 226
Veil of the Temple, 192–94, 259
Vernon marriage, 259–61
village-life model, 64
vision treatment, 313
Vogel, Dan, 4
volunteers, 288, 300, 314–15

Wade, Susan, 97–99
Wagstaff, Frank E., 209
Wallace, Anthony F. C., 20, 23–24,
   27–29, 175, 182–83, 316
ward bishop. *See* bishops
ward mission programs, 48
wards, 11, 63–64, 68, 296, 328
ward sacrament meeting, 182
war in heaven, 33, 96, 102–4
washings and anointings, 23, 40,
   178–80, 188
Watson, Bradlee, 277, 299–303
Weber, Max, 18
Wednesday night activities, 38, 157–58
Welch family, 258–59
welfare meeting, 304
Welfare Square, 288–92
welfare work, 48, 287–90, 292–93, 310,
   312
Wells, Daniel, **9**
Wentworth, John, 84
wheelchair distribution, 313
White, Cameron Howard, 321–22

Whitmer, David, 131
Whitmer, Peter, Sr., 132
Whitmer family, 134
widows, 310
Williams, Roger, 133
Williams family, 317–22
Winter Olympics 2002, 72
witness couple, 190, 192
Wood, James, 318–19
Woodruff, Wilford, 23, 324
Woolley, Edwin, **9**
word of wisdom, 39
work for the dead, 49, 188
world room. *See* telestial room
worldview orientations
   conceptual core, 186
   curriculum materials, 120
   life plan, 20
   Mormon religion, 3, 89, 92
   pictured, **21**
   primary, 85, 90
   spiritual knowledge, 95
worldwide numbers, 65
worthiness
   agency, 102–4, 107–8
   bishops interviews, 202–4, 258, 277
   callings, 141, 236
   chastity ethic, 39, 202–3, 257
   civil marriage, 42
   criteria for, 257
   endowments, 141, 195, 202–4
   For the Strength of Youth, 163–65
   homosexuality, 282–83
   identity construction, 236
   life plan, 51
   marriage, 42
   missionary work, 201–8, 221
   Mormon values, **140**, 170
   obedience, 39, 104–5, 202
   Perpetual Education
      Fund (PEF), 314
   plural marriages, 203n, 256

worthiness (*Cont.*)
post-mortal life, 35
priesthood authority, 202
role of, 277
schemas (scripts), 103–4, 107–8
standards for, 202
standards for youth, 138–44
temple marriage, 254, 256–57, 280
temple ordinances, 173, 263
tithing, 39, 155, 202–3, 257
washings and anointings, 178
young adulthood, 39
young women organization, 141,
150, 152–53
See also recommends
Wycliffe, John, 133

Young, Brigham
ascends to leadership, 7
consent decision, 227
endowments, 175, 186, 188
as leader, 17
Native Americans, 312
pictured, **8, 9**
revitalization movements, 52
Young, John, **9**
young adulthood, 38–39
young men organization

Aaronic priesthood, 145, 147–48,
169–70
formerly Mutual Improvement
Association, 119
identity construction, 169–70
leadership of, **149**
scouting program, 148, **149**, 150
Sunday meetings, 157
young women organization
age grades, 151
as calling, 293
formerly Mutual Improvement
Association, 119
girls camp, 153–54
identity construction, 169–70
leadership of, **149**
missionary work, 208
motherhood, 154, 170
personal progress program, 151
purpose of, 150–51
Sunday meetings, 157
values of, 152–54
ward bishop and, 145
worthiness, 141, 150, 152–53
Young Womanhood Recognition
certificate and medallion, 151

Zion, 134, 193